"This book is a must for those considering publishing as a business, for writers who want to investigate self-publishing, and is eminently useful for its new and old ideas to those who have already begun to do it. A fine and handy guide by a fine and successful publisher." - *Small Press Review*.

"Never before has this reviewer seen such accurate, concise information covering all the aspects of self- publishing as will be found in this helpful book." - Naples, Florida, *Daily News*.

"Poynter is at his best when discussing such specifics as starting one's own publishing house; dealing with printers; establishing discount, credit and return policies; promoting, advertising and selling a book; and order fulfillment." - *Publishers Weekly*.

"Self-publishers: This how-to book and encyclopedia will be your most important investment. The subject matter is succinctly stated, well-organized with excellent illustrations, and particularly notable are the sections on how to gather and refine material for any nonfiction book, no matter who publishes it." - *Teacher-Writer*.

"A handy, concise and informative sourcebook . . . Expertly organized and chock full of hard facts, helpful hints, and pertinent illustrations . . . Recommended for all libraries . . . ." - *The Southeastern Librarian*.

"The most comprehensive, readable, and informative book about self-publishing on the market today. None better. **If you can afford to buy only one book on self-publishing, buy this book.** It is indispensable." - John Kremer, *Self-Publishing Book Review*.

"*The Self-Publishing Manual* is by far the best on the market, and a fabulous addition to my library. More than that, it is a handbook, an encyclopedia, a friend, a companion, and a labor of love." - Paul E. Harris, Jr., Soccer For Americans, Inc.

The Self-Publishing Manual
The guide that has launched thousands of books

The Self-Publishing Manual

How to Write, Print and Sell Your Own Book

By Dan Poynter

Seventh edition, completely revised

Para Publishing, Santa Barbara, California

The Self-Publishing Manual

How to Write, Print and Sell Your Own Book

By Dan Poynter

Published by:

 Para Publishing
Post Office Box 4232
Santa Barbara, CA 93140-4232 U.S.A.

Copyright © 1979, 1984, 1986, 1989, 1991 and 1993 by Daniel F. Poynter
First Printing 1979
Second Printing 1980, revised
Third Printing 1984, completely revised
Fourth Printing 1986, revised
Fifth Printing 1989, completely revised
Sixth Printing 1991, revised
Seventh Printing 1993, revised
Printed in the United States of America

Library of Congress Cataloging in Publication Data
Poynter, Daniel F.
The Self-Publishing Manual: How to Write, Print and Sell Your Own Book / by Dan Poynter. — 7th ed., completely rev.
  p. cm.
Bibliography: p.
Includes index.
1. Self-Publishing—Handbooks, manuals, etc. I. Title.
2. Desktop Publishing—Computer publishing, etc.
3. Publishers and Publishing—Handbooks, manuals, etc.
4. Printing, Practical—Handbooks, manuals, etc.
5. Authorship—Handbooks, manuals, etc.
Z285.5.P69   1989   070.5'93—dc20   CIP 89-8599
ISBN 0-915516-90-X: $19.95 Softcover

Table of Contents

Chapter One   **9**
Your Publishing Options. Why Self-Publishing Makes Sense.

Chapter Two   **29**
Writing Your Book. How to Generate Material.

Chapter Three   **67**
Starting Your Own Publishing Company.

Chapter Four   **87**
Printing Your Book: Materials-Design-Printing.

Chapter Five   **117**
Announcing Your Book. Getting Listed.

Chapter Six   **135**
Prices, Discounts, Terms, Collections & Returns.

Chapter Seven   **159**
Promoting Your Book Without Spending For Advertising.

Chapter Eight   **215**
Who Will Buy Your Book? Distribution Channels.

Chapter Nine   **263**
Advertising your Book. Direct Mail to Space Advertising.

Chapter Ten   **309**
Fulfillment: Order Entry, Picking, Packing and Shipping.

Chapter Eleven   **347**
Computers for Book Publishing.

Chapter Twelve   **357**
Coping With Being a Published Author or *What Do I Do Now?*

Appendix   **363**
Your Book's Calendar.   363
Resources.   369
Index.   411

About The Author

Dan Poynter fell into publishing. He spent eight years researching a labor of love. Realizing no publisher would be interested in a technical treatise on the parachute, he went directly to a printer and "self- publish-ed." The book sold, the orders poured in and he suddenly found he was a publisher himself.

In 1973, he became interested in a new aviation sport, couldn't find a book on the subject so he sat down and wrote one. After four months of writing and intense research which took him from coast to coast, he delivered the manuscript to the printer. So far, *Hang Gliding* has sold over 130,000 cop-ies—a "best seller!"

Continuing to write, Dan produced 60 books and revisions, of which some have been translated into Spanish, Japanese, Russian and German. Over the years, Dan has developed a system of writing which makes it all so easy and fun. His books are loaded with facts and figures and contain detailed inside information. They are always up-to-date, as he prints small quantities so they may be periodically revised. Dan has sold over a million of his books, including several best sellers, for millions of dollars in sales. Many of his books sell at the rate of a steady 10,000 copies per year, every year.

Dan has become one of the most successful author/publish-ers. For many years, he was billed as the world's largest one-person publishing company. As a one-man show, an author/publisher who handles all the writing, publishing and promotion himself, Dan is in the best position to advise a first time self-publishing author who is on a limited budget.

Dan was prompted to write this book because so many of his friends, noting his success, approached him to publish their manuscripts. Now he is revealing to you the secrets of writing, printing and selling your book—the good life of self-publishing.

Acknowledgment

I have not attempted to cite in the text all the authorities and sources consulted in the preparation of this manual. To do so would require more space than is available. The list would include departments of the Federal Government, libraries, industrial institutions, periodicals and many individuals.

Scores of people contributed to the earlier editions of this manual. Information and illustrations have been contributed to this seventh edition by Judy Appelbaum, Walter Becker, James Scott Bell Mindy Bingham, Jerry Buchanan, Gordon Burgett, Robbie Fanning, Peggy Glenn, Don Hausrath, Bradford Lyttle, John Kremer, John McHugh, Jan Nathan, Ed Wright, Jr., Dr. Fred Decker, Becky Quas, and Jan Venolia. Special thanks to Kathy Peters for her copy editing.

I sincerely thank all these fine people. I know they are as proud of the part they have played in the development of **"entrepreneurial publishing,"** as they are of their contribution to this work.

Cover by Robert Howard

Warning—Disclaimer

This book is designed to provide information in regard to the subject matter covered. It is sold with the understanding that the publisher and author are not engaged in rendering legal, accounting or other professional services. If legal or other expert assistance is required, the services of a competent professional should be sought.

It is not the purpose of this manual to reprint all the information that is otherwise available to the author and/or publisher, but to complement, amplify and supplement other texts. You are urged to read all the available material, learn as much as possible about self-publishing and to tailor the information to your individual needs. For more information, see the many references in the Appendix.

Self-publishing is not a get-rich scheme. Anyone who decides to write and publish a book must expect to invest a lot of time and effort. For many people, self-publishing is more lucrative than selling manuscripts to another publisher, and many have built solid, growing, rewarding businesses.

Every effort has been made to make this manual as complete and as accurate as possible. However, there **may be mistakes** both typographical and in content. Therefore, this text should be used only as a general guide and not as the ultimate source of writing/publishing information. Furthermore, this manual contains information on writing/publishing only up to the printing date.

The purpose of this manual is to educate and entertain. The author and Para Publishing shall have neither liability nor responsibility to any person or entity with respect to any loss or damage caused, or alleged to be caused, directly or indirectly by the information contained in this book.

If you do not wish to be bound by the above, you may return this book to the publisher for a full refund.

Chapter One

Your Publishing Options

Why you should consider self-publishing

Everyone wants to "write a book." Most people have the ability, some have the drive, but few have the organization. Therefore, the greatest need is for a simple system, a "road map." The basic organizational plan in this book will not only provide you with direction, it will promote drive and expose ability no one thought existed.

Magazines devoted to men, business and sales are littered with full page advertisements featuring people with fabulous opportunity offers. Usually these people discovered a successful system of business in sales, real estate or mail order, and, for a price, they are willing to let the reader in on their secret. To distribute this information, they have written a book. Upon close inspection, one often finds that the author is making more money from the book than from the revealed original enterprise. The irony is that purchasers get the wrong information; what the reader needs is a book on how to write a book.

Writing a book is easy! If you can voice an opinion and think logically, you can write a book. If you can *say* it, you can *write* it. The trick is to break a mammoth project down into little, bite-sized chunks. Most people have to work for a living and, therefore, can spend only a few minutes of each day on their book. Consequently, they can't keep the whole manuscript in their head. When overwhelmed and confused, it is easy to quit the project. The solution is to break up the manuscript into many small easy-to-attack sections (and never start at page one where the hill looks steepest). Then concentrate on one section at a time and do a thorough job on each one.

Since poetry and fiction are very difficult to sell and, even when sold, have a short sales life, we will concern ourselves with nonfiction. Writing nonfiction doesn't require any great literary style; it is simply a matter of producing well-researched, reorganized, up-dated and, most important, repackaged information. Some of the recommendations here may be applied to fiction, just as the chapters on publishing, promotion and the mail order business may be taken separately and used elsewhere. However, all the recommendations are written toward, and for, the reader who wishes to become an author or an author/publisher of useful information.

People want to know "how-to" and "where-to," and they will pay well to find it. The information industry, the production and distribution of ideas and information as opposed to goods and services, now amounts to over one-half of the gross national product. There is money in information. To see how this market is being tapped by books, check the best seller lists in the back of *Publishers Weekly*; noting especially the "Trade Paperback" section.

Your best sources for this saleable information are from your own experience, plus research. Write what you know. Whether you already have a completed manuscript, have a great idea for one, or need help in locating a suitable subject, this book will point the way.

The number one reason any professional writes is to pay the bills. This isn't the Lawn Tennis Association, where you play for the thrill of it. - Jimmy Breslin

The prestige enjoyed by the published author is unparalleled in our society. A book can bring recognition, wealth and an acceleration in one's career. People have always held books in high regard, possibly because in past centuries they were very expensive and were, therefore, purchased only by the rich. Even one hundred years ago, many people could not read or write. To be an author then was to be an "educated" person.

Many enterprising people are using books to establish themselves in "the ultimate business." Usually starting with a series of non-paying magazine articles, they develop a name and make themselves visible. Then they expand the series of articles into a book. Now with their credibility established, they operate seminars in their field of expertise, command high speaking fees and issue a high-priced business advice newsletter. From there, they teach a course in the local junior college and become a consultant, advising large corporations and commenting on legal briefs for lawyers. They find they are in great demand. People want their information or simply want them around. Clubs and corporations fly them in to consult, because it is cheaper than sending all their people to the expert.

This "dream product" is the packaging and marketing of information. Starting with a field you know, then researching it further and putting it on paper will establish you as an expert. Then your expert standing can be pyramided with interviews, articles, TV appearances, talks at local clubs, etc. Of course most of this activity will promote your book sales.

In turn, all this publicity not only sells books, but opens more doors and produces more invitations leading to more opportunities to prove your expert status and make even more money for yourself. People seek experts whose opinions, advice and ideas are quoted in the media. Becoming an expert does not require a great education or a college degree. You can become an expert in one small particular area if you are willing to go to the library, read up on it and write down the important elements.

People can be divided into three groups: those who make things happen, those who watch things happen and those who wonder what happened. - John W. Newbern

A book is like a new product design, similar to an invention but usually much, much better. A patent on a device or process runs only 17 years whereas, since the 1978 change in the law, a copyright runs for the author's life plus 50 years. Patents cost hundreds, often thousands, of dollars to secure and normally require a lot of legal help. By contrast, a copyright may be filed by the author with a simple form and $20; there is no waiting period. Once you write a book, it is yours. You have a monopoly and there is no direct competition.

Many people work hard at a job for 40 years and have nothing to show for it but memories and pay stubs. Some take their knowledge and write a book, the result is a tangible product for all to see. A book lasts forever like a painting or a sculpture, but there are many copies of the book, not just one. Whereas a sculpture can only be admired by a limited number of persons at any one time in the place where it is displayed, books come in multiple copies for all the world to use and admire simultaneously.

The next secret is to cut out the middlemen by by-passing the commercial publishers to produce and sell the book yourself. You can take the author's royalty, the publisher's profit, the distributor's markup, the retailer's piece of the action. You get all the rewards because you *are* all of them. Now, in addition to achieving the wealth and prestige of a published author, you have propelled yourself into your own lucrative business: a publishing house. This shortcut not only makes more money (why share it?), it saves you the frustration, trouble and time required to sell your manuscript to a publisher. You know the subject and market better than some distant corporation anyway.

Publishing doesn't mean purchasing a printing press to actually put the ink on the paper yourself. Some people feel this is the best part and enjoy the actual printing process, but most would prefer to write and publish leaving the production to an experienced printer.

You cannot avoid making decisions. Every time you fail to act on a question, you have, in effect, made a decision to do nothing.

In addition to the writing and publishing of your book, you will want to investigate its distribution. Today, more books are sold through the mail than through book stores. In fact, books are the leading mail order product. One-third of all these books are in the "how-to" category. Mail order is considered one of the best ways for the beginner with no previous business experience to start a venture of his or her own. Selling books by mail is a good, solid day-to-day business opportunity.

Mail order is not only the simplest way to distribute books, it is an ideal way to build a second income or a new life. You don't have to give up your job, there is little overhead, there are tax breaks, you work for yourself and the business can be operated anywhere: you need only be near a Post Office. No one knows about your age, education, race or sex; your opportunities are indeed equal.

Direct mail marketing is like fishing. You throw out a line by promoting your products and you find out almost immediately if you have made a sale. Everyday is like Christmas; opening envelopes and finding checks is great fun.

Initially, you will warehouse your books in a closet or your garage, and will slip them into padded bags for mailing. It is quite easy and starting out is not expensive or time-consuming.

Your writing/publishing/mail order company is actually combining three profitable fields and concentrating on only the best parts of each. A business of your own is the great American dream and it is still an attainable possibility. In your own business, you make the decisions to meet only those challenges you find interesting. This is not "goofing off," it is making more effective use of your time; "working smarter, not harder." After all, there are only 24 hours in a day and only one day at a time for each of us. You have to concentrate on the good areas if you are to prosper.

I guess every normal writer has a desire to give birth to a book someday—to become, in fact, an author. Books are . . . a chance at immortality. - Margaret Bennett in *Publishers Weekly*

Running your own enterprise will provide you with many satisfying advantages. You should earn more money because you are working for yourself rather than splitting your efforts with someone else. You have job security and never have to worry about a surprise pink slip. If you keep your regular job and "moonlight" your own enterprise as recreation, it will always be there as a fall back position should you need it. You start at the top, not the bottom, in your own company and you work at your own pace and schedule. You will meet interesting people because, as an author and publishing executive, you will be sought out by them.

In your own small business, you may work when and where you wish; you do not have to go to where the job is. You can work 'til dawn, sleep 'til noon, rush off to Hawaii without asking permission: This is flexibility not available to the clock punchers.

Being an author-publisher sounds like a good life, and it can be. Working for yourself requires organization and discipline, but work doesn't seem so hard when you are counting your own money. To help you understand what is ahead, here are some definitions and some background on the book publishing industry.

"Publish" means to prepare and issue material for public distribution or sale or "to place before the public." The book doesn't have to be beautiful, it doesn't even have to sell, it needs only to be issued. Saleability will depend upon the content and the packaging.

A "Publisher" is the one who puts up the money, the one who takes the risk. He or she has the book printed and then distributes it hoping to make back more money than has been gambled. The publisher may be a big New York firm or a first-time author but he or she is always the investor.

> . . . *writing. It was a private thing that I could do. I could just send it out and see what it did. If someone laughed, I could stand up and say, "I did that." -* Erma Bombeck in *The Writer*

A "**Book**" by international standards is a publication with at least 49 pages, not counting the covers. The U.S. Postal Service will accept publications with eight or more pages for "book rate" postage. Books should not be confused with pamphlets, which have less than 49 pages, or periodicals. Magazines and newspapers are examples of periodicals. They are published regularly and usually carry advertising.

The book publishing industry in the U.S. consists of nearly 35,000 firms by R. R. Bowker's count, but there are many thousands more publishers who do not bother to apply for a listing. About 100 publishers are considered to be the big firms and most of them are located in New York City. Altogether, more than 60,000 people are employed in book publishing in the U.S. Sales amount to $14.7-billion per year for the over 850,000 active titles listed in *Books in Print*. Even though most of the titles are reprints of older books, the volume of brand new titles still amounts to about 35,000 per year, or almost 100 new books every day. For more information, statistics and trends, see the *Gallup Report on Book Buying* ($95.00). The Gallup Organization, P.O. Box 310, Princeton, NJ 08542. (609) 924-9600.

How books get from writer to reader

Your choices. An author who wishes to get into print has many choices. You may approach a large New York general publisher or a smaller specialized "alternative" publisher. You may work with an agent or deal with a "vanity" press. If you decide to self-publish, you may go to a book printer, to a regular printer who can manufacture books or you may get your own printing press. As you expand your list of titles and take in other authors, you may graduate to the ranks of the alternative or small publisher. You could, one day, even become a major conventional publisher. Here are the choices.

—The big publishing firms are like department stores; they have something for everyone. They publish in many different fields and concentrate on books that anticipate audiences in the millions. Recently these large publishers have grown even bigger by acquiring other publishing companies. A look at the numbers in big publishing will help us to better understand their problems.

It has been estimated that some 350,000 book-length manuscripts are written each year, but that only 35,000 new titles and 5,000$^+$ reprints go into print. Many of the larger publishers receive 10,000 unsolicited manuscripts each year. Reading manuscripts takes an enormous amount of editorial time, and a very high percentage of the submissions are poorly written or do not fit the publisher's line; they are a waste of editorial time.

The 12,000 bookstores in the United States don't have the space to display all the 40,000 titles published each year, so they concentrate on the books that move the best. Consequently, most publishers figure than even after selecting the best manuscripts and pouring in the promotion money, only three books of ten will sell well, four will break even and three will be losers.

Ever wonder why all the books in the store have very recent copyright dates? They are seldom more than a year old because the store turns them over so fast. Shelf space is expensive and in short supply. The books either sell or they go back. If one title doesn't move, it is replaced by another.

> *I hope you get as much pleasure reading my book as I got spending the money you paid me for it.*

Most initial print runs are for 5,000 books. Then the title remains "in print" (available for sale) for maybe a year. If the book sells out quickly, it is reprinted and the publisher dumps in more promotion money. If the book does not catch on, it is pulled off the market and "remaindered" (sold off very cheap) to make room for new titles. The publisher has a business to run; there is overhead to consider and bills must be paid.

The financial demands cause the publisher to be terribly objective about the line. To many publishers, in fact, a book is just a book. If they already cover a subject, they won't be interested in a new manuscript on the same topic. They already serve that interest and do not care that your version might be better. Many big publishers are not interested in whether it is a good book; all they want to know is whether it will sell. Therefore, they concentrate on authors with good track records, or Hollywood and political personalities who can move a book with their name. Only occasionally will they accept a well-written manuscript by an unknown, and then it must be on a topic with a ready and massive audience. A published writer has a much better chance of selling than an unpublished one, regardless of the quality of the work. Large publishers usually must sell close to 10,000 copies in hardcover to break even. They hope to make their money on subsidiary rights for the paperback edition, book club, and movies. They spend several thousand dollars on promoting most titles, and often more than $50,000 on a projected blockbuster. This makes it tough on the small publisher with less volume who must compete for shelf space based on sales, and can't afford large scale promotion.

Publishers, like most business people, seem to follow the "80-20 principle." That is, they spend 80% of their effort on the top 20% of their books. The remaining 20% of their time goes to the bottom 80% of their line. Most books have to sell themselves to induce the publisher to allocate more promotion money.

There is a story about one author who sent her relatives around to bookstores to buy up every copy of her new book. The sudden spurt in sales excited the publisher, who increased the ad budget. The increase in promotion produced greater sales and her book became a success.

One person in the sales department has to love your book, or it's gone. - Charles Oviatt, McGraw-Hill.

The author will get a royalty from the large publisher of 6% to 10%, usually on a sliding scale, and the economics here are not encouraging. For example, a print run of 5,000 copies of a book selling for $15 will earn $75,000, and 10% royalty on this is $7,500. That isn't enough money to pay for all the time spent at the typewriter. The chances of selling more than 5,000 copies is highly remote because, after a year or two, the publisher takes the book out of print. In fact, the publisher will probably sell less than the amount printed because some books will be used for promotion while others will be returned by the bookstores, unsold.

If your manuscript is a blockbuster with potential sales in the millions, you may need a big publisher; and they certainly want you. They will take care of all the printing and distributing and you can have your royalty checks sent to you in Bimini. If yours is a nonfiction book, they will ask you to furnish sales leads and, in any case, you will be expected to go on tour. You will wind up doing most of the promotion yourself while losing control over the program. When sales drop off, you will probably ask to buy back the book and the remaining stock from the publisher so you can pursue the marketing yourself. At this time you may also discover to your dismay that your contract provides that you must submit your next two manuscripts to this same publisher.

The big publishing houses provide a needed service, but for many first-time authors they are unapproachable. Once in, the author doesn't get the best deal and getting out may be very difficult. To begin with, the publisher may sit on the manuscript for many months before rejecting it. Then once accepted, they often chop it up editorially and change the title; you lose artistic control of your book. The publisher will change everything in the name of enhancing commercial appeal.

All these changes might be acceptable if the big commercial publishers were great financial successes. They aren't, or at least they haven't been so far. One publishing house even admits it would have made more money last year if it had vacated its New York office and rented out the floor space.

A little publishing house may surface with one or two books—how-to, self-help, pop psychology—and start a trend. - Patricia Holt, Book Editor, San Francisco Chronicle

The publishing industry attracts lovely, creative people who find their rewards in its non-material aspects. They often come from tax-supported academic or library communities; they have never been marketing-oriented. In fact, the editorial function in most publishing houses jealously guards its independence so it won't be "corrupted" by the marketing department. This leads editors into the greatest trap in publishing: producing titles which "should be published" but do not sell. When a book fails to earn back its investment, the publishing house calls it a "prestige" book and justifies its production as a public service.

Many of the people working in the big firms know the editing-marketing approach is wrong (or that losing money is not what business is all about) and they are frustrated by it. But no matter how many seminars they attend or books they read, they can't move their companies out of their rut.

In the big firms, salaries are too low to attract highly motivated marketing people. Without better marketing, the companies can't afford to pay more. It is a vicious circle and there has been little effort to reverse it.

The answer is for the marketing department to select the manuscripts they feel they can sell and to confine the editors' work to editing.

But there is a brighter side for the small publisher who understands what the public wants to read. Since the old-line big *department store-like* publishers do not pursue marketing and the new big ones concentrate on the top selling books only, there is a lot of room left for the smaller *boutique-like* publishing house and self-publisher.

Be careful if you hang around with people from the book industry. Learn, but don't let their ways rub off. Study the big New York publishing firms, but don't copy them. You can do a lot better.

I'll be damned if I'll do my publishers' job for them. If I had wanted to become a hustler, I would have hit the streets long ago. I am a creative artist—I know it sounds pretentious, but that's what I am. I am no businessman or salesman. From an article by Rebekah Jordan in *Publishers Weekly*.)

—**The small presses** or "specialty publishers" are the smaller and newer firms which specialize in serving certain specific interests, such as specialized technical fields, particular geographic regions or their own personal interests. One definition of a small press is a publisher with no more than 12 full-time staff members, issuing fewer than 25 titles per year for receipts under $1-million. Many small presses emerged from the anti-establishment movement of the sixties and their entry into publishing was made possible by the coincidental introduction of newer, simpler, cheaper (offset) printing methods and then computers. Some of these publishers are very small, while others are fairly large, but most concentrate on a single subject area. Many people in the publishing industry are attracted to the flexibility offered by small publishing. When their firm grows too large, they break off to form a new small firm. There are thousands of small presses and, because of lower overhead, they can produce books at much lower cost than the big publishers.

> Two of the more successful new presses are Bruce Lansky's Meadowbrook Press in Minnesota and Fisher Books in Tucson. Both combine their instincts about the marketplace with the best research they can buy to direct quality products at the right buyer. The key to their success is that these publishers came from the world of marketing, not from the academic or library communities.

However, while the smaller publishers may be closer to their market, their royalty rates are the same, and some do not promote a title any harder than a big publisher. Most authors will agree that small publishers are usually nice to deal with and provide good personal attention, but they are faced with many of the same economic problems as the rest of the industry and don't always have the resources to combat them. To find a small press, consult Dustbook's *International Directory of Little Magazines and Small Presses* and *Literary Market Place*. In *LMP*, check the subsections in section one for classifications by fields of activity and by subject matter. Look for a publisher who specializes in your type of book. Do not take an aviation book to a cook book publisher. They would not take it and would not know where to sell it if they did. You want a publishing house who knows its own market, one who can plug your book into its promotion/distribution system.

> *Small publishing is exhibiting robust health, while the traditional industry is ailing.* - Paul D. Doebler.

—**The tiny press** has been defined as those publishers who normally make press runs of 500 books or less. Often these firms concentrate on fiction, poetry or very specialized material. Many do their own printing and some do quite beautiful work.

—**Co-op publishing** houses have been formed in many areas. Usually three to ten people join to share the work of editing, design, layout, typesetting, compilation and financing. Often these people contribute more labor than money to the publishing venture. A good article on this subject appeared in the August, 1978, edition of *Writer's Digest* magazine.

Another variation on co-op publishing is one publisher producing a book to be carried by both it and another publisher who will market it to another field. Co-publishing reduces financial committment and risk while increasing marketing clout.

—**Vanity or subsidy publishers** produce around 6,000 titles each year; some twenty firms produce about 70 percent of all the subsidized books. Many of these businesses advertise in the *Yellow Pages* under "Publishers." Subsidy publishers offer regular publishing services, but the author invests the money. Under this arrangement, the author pays the full publishing (more than just printing bill) costs, receives 40% of the retail price of the books sold and 80% of the subsidiary rights, if sold. According to *The Wall Street Journal*, the cost is between $2,000 and $15,000 to get into print, depending upon the size of the book. Others say you can figure roughly on $25 per page. The vanity publisher claims he will furnish all the regular publishing services including promotion and distribution. All this might not be so bad if they had a good track record for delivery. But according to *Writer's Digest*, vanity publishers usually do not deliver the promotion they promise and the books rarely return one-quarter of the author's investment. In fact, some of the larger vanity publishers are the worst offenders and have given the entire industry a bad name.

Legitimate publishers don't have to look for business. - L.M. Hasselstrom

The ads reading "To the author . . ." or "Manuscripts wanted by . . ." easily catch the eye of the writer with a book length manuscript. Vanity presses almost always accept a manuscript for publication and usually do so with a glowing review letter. They don't make any promises regarding sales and usually the book sells fewer than 100 copies. The vanity publisher doesn't have to sell any books because the author has already paid him for his work. Therefore, subsidy publishers are interested in manufacturing the book, not in editing, promotion, sales or distribution.

Since binding is expensive, the subsidy publisher often binds a few hundred copies; the rest of the sheets remain unbound unless needed. The "advertising" promised in the contract normally turns out to be only a "tombstone" ad listing many titles in the *New York Times*. Sales from this feeble promotion are very rare.

The review copies sent to columnists by a subsidy publisher usually go straight into the circular file. The reviewer's time is valuable, and they do not like vanity presses because they know that so little attention was paid to the editing of the book. Further, they realize there will be little promotional effort and that the book will not be available to readers in the stores. The name of the publisher on the spine of the book is a kiss of death.

Only a local bookstore might be persuaded to carry an author's vanity press book. The rest know there won't be any public demand for it.

The vanity publishers can get your book into print if this is all you want, and they will not cut the manuscript all to pieces. But, even then, they are not the least expensive way to go. It would make more sense to contact a book printer or book packager (see listings in *Literary Market Place*). Publishing yourself should save 25% to 45% over vanity publishing.

Subsidy publishing is closer to trade publishing than it is to self-Publishing. - Freda Morris

---

Vanity publishing is to legitimate publishing as loansharking is to banking. - Martin J. Baron

Before considering a subsidy or vanity publisher, send for *Should You Pay to Have it Published* (Writer's Digest, 1507 Dana Avenue, Cincinnati, OH 45207.) From everything you read, it appears that no one likes vanity publishers. Some have been in trouble with the Federal Trade Commission (FTC) and at least one has been sued by a client author. But then, many beginning authors don't like any publishers at all. Reasoning that they must do most of the work anyway, they opt for self-publishing.

Other publishing choices. *Textbook* publishers offer the author a royalty based on the net amount received by the publisher. *Contract books* are those written for a company on a subject of their choice. For example, a mail order house might need a book on a particular subject to round out its line. *Sponsored books* are commissioned by a company. They are usually about the company and, in addition to their regular sale, may be used as a promotional tool.

—Literary agents provide publishers with a valuable service by screening out the bad manuscripts, and most new material comes to big publishers through them. The agent has to serve the publisher well, for if he or she submits a poor manuscript, the publisher will never offer another appointment. Therefore, agents like sure bets too, and are reluctant to even consider an unpublished writer. When they do risk their time on a new author, their fee is often higher than their normal commission of 10-15%.

For the author, the agent will make manuscript suggestions, negotiate the contract and try to sell the book to one of his or her many contacts; the agent will exploit all possible avenues. If your manuscript is a winner, it is wise to have professional management. Some authors feel it is best to contract with an agent based in New York; he or she will have closer contacts and can deal in person.

I was thrilled at the cooperation of agents, but was a little alarmed when I found, more than once, a rejection letter from the first recipient in the manuscript. - Ruth Nodkins Nathan in *Publishers Weekly*

According to *Literary Agent's Marketplace* about 40% of the book agents will not read manuscripts by unpublished authors and a good 15% will not even answer query letters from them. Of those agents who will read the manuscript of an unpublished author, 80% will charge for the service. Eighty percent of the agents will not represent professional books; 93% will not touch reference works; 99% will not handle technical books; 98% will not represent regional books, satire, musicals and other specialized manuscripts. While most agents will handle novel-length fiction, only 20% are willing to take on either novelettes or short stories, and only 2% have a special interest in literature or quality fiction.

On the fringe, there are several "agents" who charge a "reading fee" and then pay students to read and critique the manuscript. They make their money on these fees, not from placing the manuscripts. For a list of literary agents, see *Fiction Writer's Market, Literary Agents Marketplace* and *Literary Market Place*.

—**Self-publishing** is where the author by-passes all the middlemen, deals directly with the printer and then handles the marketing and distribution. You maintain complete control over your product. You have to invest your time as well as your money but the reward is greater; you get it all.

Self-publishing is not new. In fact, it has solid early American roots; it is almost a tradition. Many authors have elected to go their own ways after being turned down by regular publishers and many others have decided to go their own ways from the beginning. Well-known self-publishers include Mark Twain, Zane Grey, Upton Sinclair, Carl Sandburg, James Joyce, D.H. Lawrence, Ezra Pound, Edgar Rice Burroughs, Stephen Crane, Mary Baker Eddy, George Bernard Shaw, Edgar Allen Poe, Rudyard Kipling, Henry David Thoreau, Walt Whitman, Robert Ringer, Spencer Johnson, Richard Bolles, Richard Nixon and many, many more. These people were self-publishers, though today the vanity presses claim their books were "subsidy" published. Today's success stories are usually in the nonfiction how-to books.

> *I can't understand why a person will take a year or two to write a novel when he can easily buy one for a few dollars.* - Fred Allen

There are thousands of these very small author/publisher firms, many of them in California. Some are growing and some are withering, but practically all are hanging on. They are proving that a self-published book is not inferior to one marketed by a big New York firm. Many self-publishers are very successful and some are making a lot of money.

Self-publishing is not difficult. In fact, it may even be easier than dealing with a publisher. The job of the publishing manager is not to perform every task, but to see that every task gets done. The self-publisher deals directly with the printer and handles as many of the editing, proofing, promotion and distribution jobs as he or she can. What they can't do, they farm out. Therefore, self-publishing may take on many forms depending on the author's interests, assets and abilities. It allows you to concentrate on those areas you find most challenging.

Properly planned, there is little monetary risk in self-publishing. If you follow the plan, the only variable is the subject of the book. Unlike poetry and fiction, most nonfiction topics sell easily. In fact, many authors publish themselves because this method provides the best return on their labor in the long run. Because the big publisher only tries a book for a year or two and then lets sales dictate its fate (reprint or remainder), the first year is most important. The self-publisher, on the other hand, uses the first year to build a solid market for a future of sustained sales. While a big publisher may sell only 5,000 copies total, the self-publisher can often count on 5,000 or more each year, year after year.

Here are eight good reasons to self-publish:
1. To make more money. Why accept 6% to 10% in royalties when you can have 40%? You know your subject and you know the people in the field. Certainly you know better than some distant publisher who might buy your book. While the trade publisher may have some good contacts, he doesn't know the market as well as you, and he isn't going to expend as much promotional effort. Ask yourself this question: Will the trade publisher be able to sell four times as many books as I can?

2. Speed. Most publishers work on an 18 month production cycle. Can you wait that long to get into print? Will you

miss your market? The 1 1/2 years doesn't even begin until *after* the contract negotiations and contract signing. Publication could be three years away! Why waste valuable time shipping your manuscript around to see if there is a publisher out there who likes it? Richard Nixon self-published *Real Peace* in 1983 because he felt his message was urgent; he couldn't wait for a publisher's machinery to grind out the book.

Typically, bookstores buy the first book on a popular subject. Later books may be better, but the buyer will pass on them since the store already has the subject "covered."

3. To keep control of your book. According to *Writer's Digest*, 60% of the big publishers do not give the author final approval on copy editing. Twenty-three percent never give the author the right to select the title, 20% do not consult the author on the jacket design and 36% rarely involve the author in the book's promotion.

The big New York trade publishers may have more promotional connections than you, but with a stable of books to push, your effort may get lost in the shuffle. The big publishers are good at getting books into bookstores but they fail miserably at approaching other outlets. Give the book to someone who has a personal interest in it—the author.

4. No one will read your manuscript. Many publishers receive more than 100 unsolicited manuscripts for consideration each day. They do not have time to unwrap, review, rewrap and ship all these submissions so they return them unopened. Unless you are a movie star, noted politician or have a recognizable name, it is nearly impossible to attract a publisher. Many publishers work with their existing stable of authors and accept new authors only through agents.

5. Self-publishing is good business. There are more tax advantages for an author/publisher than there are for just authors.

If you would be thrilled by watching the galloping advance of a major glacier, you'd be ecstatic watching changes in publishing. - John D. MacDonald in *InfoWorld*

6. Self-publishing will help you to think like a publisher. You will learn the industry and will have a better understanding of the big picture. A book is a product of one's self. An analogy may be drawn with giving birth. The author naturally feels that his book is terrific and that it would sell better if only his publisher would dump in more promotion money. He is very protective about his book (ever try to tell a mother her child is ugly?). The publisher answers that he is not anxious to dump more money into a book that isn't selling. So, if the author self-publishes, he gains a better understanding for the arguments on both sides. It is his money and his choice.

7. You will gain self-confidence. You will be proud to be the author of a book. Compare this with pleading with people to read your manuscript.

8. Finally—you may have no other choice. There are more manuscripts than can be read. Most publishers don't have time to even look at your manuscript.

Should you self-publish? Would-be author/publishers should be cautioned that self-publishing is not for everyone. Writing is an *art,* while publishing is a *business,* and many people are unable to do both well. If you are a lovely, creative flower who is repelled by the "crass commercialism" of selling one's own product, you should stick to the creative side and let someone else handle the business end. On the other hand, some people are terribly independent. They will not be happy with the performance of any publisher, no matter how much time and effort are spent creating and promoting the book. These people should save the publisher from all this grief by making their own decisions. What is important is that writers understand all the alternatives so that they may make an intelligent, educated choice.

Selling out. Many self-publishers find that once they have proven their books with good sales, they are approached by the big publishing houses with offers to print a new edition. Some use self-publishing to break into the big time. Others keep on self-publishing, keeping the work and the money to themselves.

Book printers are those print shops which specialize in the manufacture of books. They are not regular publishers or vanity presses, they are simply specialty printers with book machinery. The major book printers are listed in the Appendix. Many of them advertise in magazines like *Small Press* and *PMA News,* and every self-publisher should compare their quote with that of the local printers.

The future. Packaged information is becoming increasingly specialized. More and more books are being printed in smaller quantities. The information in books is going out of date faster. Books are being produced more rapidly. Computerized equipment is being used to write, edit, layout and print books. The customer wants more condensed information fast.

The chapters which follow describe in detail an alternative route to traditional publishing. They will enable you to get your book into print at minimum cost. There is no reason you shouldn't gain great fame and considerable financial reward.

This book could be your "second chance." It will show you the way to the wealth and prestige you never thought possible. Even if you just want the satisfaction of being published and are not interested in, or do not require, the extra income, this book will lead the way.

Obviously your success cannot be guaranteed but many people are doing very well in the writing/publishing business. This isn't a pipe dream, there is work involved. While you are working for yourself, at your own pace, it is still work. You won't get rich overnight. Building a sound business venture takes several years.

The secret is to invest your labor. Your time is precious, like gold. There is a finite quantity; you have only 24 hours of it each day. You may use your time in several ways: You may throw it away, sell it or invest it. You can waste your valuable time in front of the television set; time is easy to "lose." Most people punch in at the clock, go to work and get a check. They trade their labor for money on a one-for-one basis. If you don't punch in, you don't get paid. How much better it is to invest your time in a book which will sell and generate income while you are away doing something else. Your labor becomes an investment which pays dividends for years while you are playing, or working on another investment.

Chapter Two

Writing Your Book

How To Generate Saleable Material

Where are your talents and what do you want to do? Do you enjoy writing or do you want to be a published author without the "pain" of writing? Analyze yourself. Do you want to write, publish or sell books, any combination of these activities, or even all three? Here we will cover all three to help you make an educated choice. First we will cover how to get your thoughts on paper. Then we will discuss both sides of publishing: as seen by the author and as seen by the publisher.

Picking a subject is the first step. Sitting there waiting for inspiration is called "writer's block." You cannot write about a subject until you select it. So, do not waste time thinking about what to write; think about what to write about. Consider the four elements necessary for producing good non-fiction.

To avoid writer's block, do not sit waiting for inspiration, get out and search for a subject.

---

1. The subject is interesting to you.

2. You have the necessary expertise and the information is available.

3. The subject is of interest to others and is, therefore, saleable.

4. The subject matter is tightly focused.

The book should be on a subject in which you are interested and one in which you are an expert or would like to become an expert. You have spent years working at, specializing in, and learning something and there are thousands of people out there willing to pay good money to get the inside information on it. Write what you know! If you select your hobby, there are a number of advantages: You know what has been written in the past, you have the contacts for gathering more information and your further participation in that hobby will become tax deductible.

Poetry is very difficult to sell, which is one reason this book concentrates on non-fiction. For more information on publishing poetry, contact Poets & Writers, 72 Spring Street, New York, NY 10012 and The American Poetry Association, P.O. Box 1803, Santa Cruz, CA 95061-1803.

Fiction. It is possible to sell fiction, or at least some people are doing it, but it isn't easy. Dorothy Bryant, a novelist in Berkeley, California, publishes and promotes what she writes. She calls her publishing company Ata Books. You might be able to sell your fiction if you consider the market first. Stories tailored to a specific geographic area might sell well locally.

In Santa Rosa, John Martin's Black Sparrow Press is well-known for successfully publishing quality fiction and poetry. Martin has a publishing formula and an established following. He knows just how many books to publish in softcover, hardcover, signed editions, etc. and many buyers take everything he produces, sight unseen. He is so sought after by writers that he operates Black Sparrow from a Post Office box and maintains an unlisted telephone.

There are three rules to successful writing: 1. Have something to say, 2. Know how to say it, and 3. Be able to sell it. - David Hellyer

Very generally speaking, a large New York publisher will do a better job on fiction, while you will do a better job yourself with non-fiction.

For more information on selling unpublished novels, see the January, 1983, edition of *Writer's Digest*. For a list of fiction publishers, see *Fiction Writer's Market*. Both should be available at your public library. Also see *Sell Your Short Stories and Poetry to the Right Markets!* by Jaye L. Montgomery from Multi Media Arts, P.O. Box 14486, Austin, TX 78761.

Non-fiction. The subject of a book, not the name of the publisher or the comments of a reviewer, is what sells it. Every new national craze requires how-to books. According to *Newsweek* there are over 1,300 books on fitness and health currently in print. Do not be discouraged if your subject has already been covered. That just proves someone else thought it was important. Using your own experience and the latest information, you can do it better. The subjects with the best sales potential are how-to's, money, health, self-improvement, hobbies, sex and psychological well-being. Find a need and fill it.

Women provide a growing market for nonfiction books. Many women have entered the world of business management with a lack of necessary education or experience. Once out of the kitchen and into the office, they are faced with a shortage of time. They need information and their employment provides them with the money to pay for it. Business and other informational books aimed at women have great sales potential.

One specialized book that has been selling for years is *Hang Gliding*, by this author, which has been through the press ten times for 130,000 copies in print.

Anticipate reader interest and pick a subject which will sell on its own, even if the buyer has never heard of the book.

The how-to article is to writing as McDonald's is to restaurants; it enjoys no epicurean status. Nevertheless, McDonalds advertises "billions and billions sold," a point the writer might keep in mind. - Leonard S. Bernstein

Regional guide books are easier to write and market since both the information and the distribution are local. Tourists' guides, restaurant guides and historical books are a good way to get started in publishing.

You do not have to be an expert—yet. If you are new to a subject, you could produce a better book than an old hand because you are better able to understand and relate to the reader-novice. You know what his reactions and needs are, as well as what he is thinking. Once you are finished researching and writing, you too will be an expert.

There may be more money publishing your information in short monographs than in longer books. Timely monographs usually command a higher price, can be published in shorter runs and they take less time to produce. Do not overlook well-researched, short reports.

Now, to obtain a manuscript, you have the choice of buying it from others or writing it yourself (are you an author or a writer?). In this chapter, we will discuss the many possibilities—only one has to be right for you. If one possibility "clicks," you are on your way. First we will cover how to write material yourself, and then we will show you how to obtain some or all the material from others.

Write it yourself. Creating your own material is easy if you have a system; all it takes is organization and discipline. Following the system outlined below, creating copy becomes challenging fun and allows you to see the progress you are making which is encouraging. While this method may be of some help in writing fiction, it has been developed specifically for non-fiction.

While writing a book is not difficult, it is not for the lazy. Like AA or a diet, you will have to change your life-style. This means waking up one morning and making a decision: to do it now. To get into the system and develop good habits will provide you with a sense of purpose and a feeling of accomplishment. Once you have selected a topic, only the decision to go stands between you and the finished book.

> *The writer does the most who gives his reader the most knowledge and takes from him the least time.* - Sydney Smith

Time or lack of it is the most frequently heard excuse. But somehow we always find the time for those things most important to us. We just put them first. Often we can fit in an hour of writing time each day by completing our other chores faster. One way is to get up one hour earlier each day. This is perfect scheduling as the house is quiet, the telephone does not ring and most writers find the early morning to be their most creative and productive time. But you must put this hour first and not let anything interfere with it. Once you gather momentum in your project, you will find arising early will be easy; you won't even miss that hour of sleep.

Set up a writing area in a spare room or a corner of the living room. Keep all your writing materials and research tools there. Your creative writing time is precious, do not waste it trying to get started.

Write your back cover copy before you write your book in order to set your sights on your objective. The back cover of a book is important sales space. Using the back cover of this book as a guide, draft a paragraph on each of the following:

1. First you need an arresting headline addressed to potential buyers, so they can relate to the book and find themselves in it. For example: The back cover copy of *Choices, A Teen Woman's Journal for Self-Awareness and Personal Planning*, starts off *A book that every mother, grandmother, aunt, and mentor will want to give to the teenage women in their lives*. The buyer of this book is not the teenager but the adult so the headline is directed toward the adult.

2. Sales copy. Concisely state what the book is about. What will the reader gain by reading this book? The back cover of *The Self-Publishing Manual* recommends that all authors read the book even if they do not plan to self-publish. Your sales copy should promise health, wealth, entertainment or a better life. Stress benefits. Promise to make readers better at what they do.

3. Make the author look like the ultimate authority on the subject.

4. Testimonials and endorsements. Dream up three different endorsements from people you would like to quote. If *"This book changed my life.*—Colin Powell," would look good, try it. Use *names* or *titles* recognizable in your field—sources that might impress potential buyers.

5. End with a sales closer in bold type. Ask the browser to buy the book.

6. Price. Bookstores like a price on the back cover. Pick a price for your book and be realistic. Do not go too low.

7. Bar code with International Standard Book Number. The bar code on a book identifies the ISBN, which in turn identifies the publisher, title, author and edition (hardcover, etc.). Make room for, but do not worry about, the bar code and ISBN just now.

The back cover copy will help you to focus on who your audience is and what they want, so you will be able to slant the book to their needs. Now all you have to do is to deliver on all your promises.

Unfortunately, most nonfiction books are written without a specific market in mind, and since the book does not provide what the potential buyers want, it does not sell. Do not ignore other markets, though. If you have an instruction book aimed at students of flying schools and the book stores pick it up, so much the better. But the bookstore sales are the frosting, not the cake. The more areas the book may be fitted into, the better its chances of success.

Research is simply reading, making notes, condensing and rearranging the gathered pertinent information. The importance of the library cannot be over-emphasized. All research must begin there and most of the required information will be found within its walls. The first library visit will be to determine whether the subject has already been beaten to death. If not, then on to the book.

Faulty research is like a faulty septic tank. Sooner or later the evidence will surface and become embarrassing. - Rex Alan Smith

Ask the reference librarian for Bowker's *Books in Print* which lists all books currently available by subject, title and author. Make a list of those books you would like to read. Research the library's card file to see which books may be obtained there. The others you may purchase at your local bookstore or by writing direct to the publisher; addresses are listed in the back of *Books in Print*. You will find that some of the books listed in *BIP* never went to press. And remember that this is probably not the only library in town. Try the local college, too; it will have different types of books. Research the *Reader's Guide to Periodical Literature* which lists magazine articles on every subject. Also see the Business Periodicals Index. The telephone books will help you find firms offering materials and services. Look for newspaper indexes such as *The Wall Street Journal* Index. There are at least three directories listing thousands of associations. The associations are sources of information and many have their own special interest magazine. Ask the librarian to see the periodical directories and the newsletter directories. Then look for periodicals in the field you are researching.

The flow of the manuscript

The ideal best-seller would be about a quiche-eating cat with thin thighs.

Be a detective. When you run out of leads, ask the librarian. Libraries carry hundreds of indexes, listings and source books. Gather everything ever written on your subject. Load yourself up with so much material you will have to decide what to leave out. Overdo it, and you will be proud of the result, secure in the knowledge that you have covered the subject completely.

Every conceivable piece of information imaginable is available somewhere in your local public library. There are indexes and references on everything. Ask the Reference Librarian for help. Check out those books and magazines you can. With those restricted to the reference room, make notes of small bits of information, and use the photocopy machine to record longer pieces. Where you wish to use photos and drawings of material with expired copyrights, use a plain paper photocopier for the drawings and use a camera to reshoot the photos (more on this later). But even where the copyright has not expired, make a photocopy of valuable illustrations to guide you in your research. Photocopy checked-out books and magazines at the local copy center.

After exhausting the library of its information, there are many other sources. Write for *U.S. Government Books* to the Superintendent of Documents, USGPO, Washington, DC 20402. This is a monthly catalog of government publications. Many of these pamphlets are also available at U.S. Government bookstores in the larger cities. Check the white pages. The Bureau of the Census can provide you with sales and revenue data and much other information on virtually any industry. For ordering information on the *Census Catalog & Guide*, write Public Information Office, Bureau of the Census, Department of Commerce, Washington, DC 20233. The National Technical Information Service maintains abstracts and data bases in 28 technical areas. Write for a copy of their *Published Search Master Catalog* to: NTIS, Department of Commerce, 5285 Port Royal Road, Springfield, VA 22161.

Professionals sell, then write, while amateurs write, then try to sell. - Gordon Burgett

For more information on your field of study, there are interviews with the experts you uncover in your research. You may write or call them. If you have a computer, get a modem to search distant data bases for information. For example, there is a way to dial up the California University library system to search for books in all the university libraries throughout the state by title, author or subject. This is a lot faster than visiting the nearest college library.

Now that you are researching, you are a member of the print media and will be able to attend a lot of related events free. Use your new business card to get a press pass, media packet and preferential treatment.

Copyright is the subject which most interests potential authors. They want to know how to protect their precious material from others and to know how much they, themselves, may steal.

A copyright covers exact printed words, not ideas or thoughts, so you are safe if you just do not copy word-for-word. The copyright law was completely overhauled in 1978 and it will be many years before every aspect of it has been interpreted by the courts. The courts seem to deal with each case individually, when determining infringement. One test has been whether the original work is any less saleable once it has competition from an alleged infringer.

Copying ideas is research, copying words is plagiarism. Make it a personal rule never to copy any three words in a row. If your book is not recognizable as being a copy, you should be safe. Since 1978, copyright runs for the life of the author plus 50 years.

If you find material that you wish to use as is, contact the author for permission. Your letter might go like this:

<u>**Permission to reprint material**</u>

Dear _____:

I am writing a book tentatively titled *Parachuting, The Skydiver's Handbook.* I would like your permission to include the excerpts as outlined below in any and all editions of the book, as well as in advertisements and promotion, non-exclusively, throughout the world.

In exchange for your permission, you will be listed in the Acknowledgements and will be sent a copy of the book. I hope you will agree to our giving your book greater exposure.

For your convenience, here is a self-addressed, stamped envelope and a duplicate copy of this letter for your records.

Sincerely,

Material to be reprinted

Title and author:

Copyright date and holder:_____

Page:_____, Line_____ To Page:_____, Line_____.

Permission granted by:_____

Permission letter

Many documents are not copyrighted. If you want to find out whether some material is protected under either the current or pre-1978 law, the Copyright Office will conduct a search for you. Send them as much information as possible, such as the author, title, publisher and publication date. The easiest way is to photocopy the title page and copyright page of the book. They charge for the time, and they should be able to make two searches per hour. Government and military publications are in the public domain. Even if they weren't, they would probably be covered by the Freedom of Information Act. If you really need a piece of material, military or civilian, ask for permission. It is safer and cheaper than hiring a lawyer later to prove you have a right to it.

Your copyrighted material is valuable property, or it may be so one day. File copyright forms on all those magazine articles you don't get paid for. You may need an article for inclusion in a book someday and the expenditure on fees will justify to the IRS that you really are in the word business.

If you are asked for permission to reprint some of your work, you might consider a limit of a section or two and stipulate that an editor's note indicate that it was used with your permission and came from your book. This will show once again that you are an expert and is good publicity for the original work. A copyright on your book is not only for protection. It is prestigious; it shows you are a professional. Copyright is discussed in several places in this book. See the Index. For more information on copyrights, see the discussion in *Writer's Market* and read *A Business Guide to Copyright Law* by Stuart and Young, and the other copyright references listed in the Appendix.

Organize your material with the "pilot system." Start by drawing up a preliminary table of contents; just divide your message into 10 or 12 chapters. Then sort all your research material and "pile it" as required. Decide on your chapter titles and, using scissors, tape and staples, sort all this photocopied material into the applicable chapter piles. During your library research, you must have written down a number of interesting observations and many of your own experiences. Add your own notes to the piles.

Now spread out the individual chapters. They will probably completely fill the living room. Pick an interesting pile, any one, not necessarily the first, and go through it, underlining important points and writing in your additional comments. Write out longer thoughts on a tablet and file them in order in the pile.

Writing is one of mankind's most important endeavors, the primary vehicle by which man leaves his mark. - James Warren in *Writer's Yearbook*

This floor spread will enable you to see the whole interrelated project, lending excitement and encouragement—a great incentive. Move the piles around to insure a good, logical flow of thought and to avoid duplication of copy. Condense the material by discarding unnecessary and duplicate material.

This use of other information from other sources is not plagiarizing, it is research. Your notes insure that you will not leave out any important points. However, you will be entertained as you compare what other authors say about the same item. The similarities are often remarkably coincidental, sometimes to the point of including the same words and phraseology. This experience also emphasizes the importance of being accurate. Your work will be researched by others in the future.

As you read what others say on a particular point, your memory will be jogged. You will have additional points, a clearer explanation or an illustrative story. Where you disagree with another author, you can always say "some people believe . . ." and then tell it your way. You have the advantage of the most recent information since you came last.

Carry paper and pen with you at all times, especially when driving, running or engaging in any solo activity. This is a time to think, create, compose; this is when there is no one around to break your train of thought. Some authors keep a pad in their car and compose while commuting. When you are confined, captive, isolated, you have nothing else to do but create. Make use of any available time. A lot of good material develops while attending dull meetings.

Some people like to work with a small pocket tape recorder, but remember that someone must transcribe this noise onto paper. It all depends on what you are used to, how you perform best. If you often dictate letters and have a secretary to transcribe your tapes, this may be the most comfortable and most efficient method for you.

When a particularly original thought or creative approach hits you, write it down or you will lose it. Keep on thinking and keep on note-taking. Add your thoughts and major pieces to the piles. As you go along, draw up a list of questions as they come to mind, so that you will remember to follow them up for an answer.

Strip your notes by cutting, sorting and taping. Paste the strips together with Magic transparent tape. If your photocopies were made on a plain paper copier, you will be able to write on the tape and the paper when adding notes.

Writing from the pasted strips may be done, as above, with a tape recorder, typewriter or word processing computer. With practice you will learn to think, create and compose at the machine. Keyboard or dictate a rough manuscript the first time. Write as you speak; relax and be clear. Make notes where you are considering illustrations. Do not worry about grammar, punctuation or style—you will edit later. Right now, all you want to do is to get your thoughts and research material into the machine.

A computer allows you to layout your pages as you go along. Use a format 4" wide by 7" deep so you can get a good feel for the look of the book and its length.

Do not start your writing with chapter one—to do so makes book writing look like an impossible mountain climb. Select the chapter pile that looks the easiest. It may be the smallest or the most interesting, but it is sure to go the fastest. Once you have drafted it, take the next most interesting chapter and so on. Soon you will be past the half-way mark and the going will be down-hill. You will be encouraged and will gather momentum. Using this approach, you will probably find you are writing the first chapter last. This is as it should be as the first chapter is usually introductory in nature, and you cannot know what the first chapter should say until the rest of the work is drafted. Many authors wind up rewriting and re-slanting the first chapter because they wrote it first.

Do not be concerned with what goes down on paper the first time around. The important thing is to get it down. Often these first impressions are the best; they are complete, natural and believable. Later you will go through the draft, making corrections, additions and deletions.

Writing from notes is not plagiarism but solid, thorough research and an efficient system made possible by Xerox. There is nothing new in the universe. Practically every non-fiction book is simply a re-packaging of existing and new material.

Read the whole pasted-together section to grasp the overall theme. Then boil it down and use your own words. Think about the section and how you might explain the basic message better. Can't you say it more clearly with fewer words? Do not just write from the paper strips sentence-by-sentence; that method approaches plagiarism. For organization, list the main points and rearrange the pieces. If you are having trouble with a section, arrange it as best you can and then sleep on it. If you still cannot bring it all together with a few well-chosen sentences, you may have to call another expert for his or her explanation of the subject matter.

As you keyboard the rough first draft, and later as you review it, you will decide whole paragraphs are misplaced and belong elsewhere. Using a computer, it is an easy matter to move material.

If you lack a certain piece of information, a number or fact, leave a blank space, put a note in the text to remind you and go on. Do not lose momentum. Some authors use "***" as asterisks are easy to find visually or with a computer search. Similarly, if you find yourself repeating material, make a note with three asterisks so you may compare it with the other material later.

Keyboard one complete section at a time if possible. One chapter at a time is better, and the whole book straight through is the best way to go. Most beginning authors must work at other jobs and are able to devote only a short period each day to their writing. But the more time you can put into each piece of the book, the better, as there will be greater continuity, less duplication and clearer organization. If you can only do a small section at a time, try arranging the pieces in the evening, reviewing them in the early morning, thinking about them while commuting, etc. and then come home to type it all up.

On the other hand, if you can, take two weeks off from work, shut out all distractions and become totally involved in the manuscript. Do not pick up the mail or answer the telephone. Eat when hungry, sleep when tired and forget the clock except as a gauge of your pace. Keep up the pressure and keep on keyboarding. Pace yourself at, say, one chapter per day. You should not have to force yourself to write, but you will need organization and discipline. After a couple of books, you will find yourself making very few major changes in your original draft. In fact, using a computer, you will alter type styles for body type, bold face, italics and captions as you go along.

Writing from notes is much easier than composing from thin air. Thin air produces writer's block. Incidentally, many writers say the hum of a computer—knowing the electricity is on—prompts them to work.

Do not throw out your materials once your draft is typed. Put them in a cardboard carton. Someone may ask where you found a particular piece of information and you may wish to trace it. Traceability is especially important with photographs and artwork.

Writing style. Before writing a magazine article, always read one or more editions of the magazine thoroughly to absorb the style. Reading the magazine will help you to subconsciously adapt to that magazine's way of writing. The same technique may be used in writing a book by reading a couple of chapters of a book by a writer you admire.

Writing is a communication art. You should not try to impress. Write as you speak, avoiding big words where small ones will do. Most people regularly use only 800-1,000 of the some 26,000 English words available to them. Use simple sentences and be precise in your selection of words. Vary sentence and paragraph length and favor the shorter ones. Try to leave yourself out of the copy: Avoid the word "I."

Use action nouns and verbs. Help the reader draw a mental picture by introducing sight, sound, smell, touch and taste to your copy. Be precise by avoiding superlatives and overuse of adverbs and adjectives. Study newspaper writing and place the words you wish to emphasize at the beginning of the sentence. The important sentence should start the paragraph and the main paragraph should head the chapter.

There's nothing to writing. All you have to do is sit down at the computer and open up a vein. - Red Smith

Relax, talk on paper, be yourself. Explain each section in your own words, as you would help a friend who is new to the subject. Do not use contractions in your writing as you do in your speech as they're (there is one now) more difficult to read. "Which" and "that" can usually be left out to the benefit of the sentence. Keep your writing short. You are paying for the words so edit out the junk.

Writing is hard work; it is an intellectual and emotional workout. Some authors enjoy the discipline it requires, but more have a greater appreciation for the reward of the results.

Like a speech, every paragraph of your book should have a beginning, a middle and an end. Each paragraph should tie together with both the preceding and following paragraphs (good transitions). The first sentence of the paragraph is called the "topic sentence"—stay with one subject per paragraph.

Be a professional and give the readers their money's worth. Your material will be used by others in coming years and you will be quoted. If you are accurate and correct now, you won't be embarrassed later by the written legend you have created. As a published author you have the responsibility of being a recognized expert. Use proper terms; don't start a new language. Steer away from highly technical expressions; you will only turn off your reader.

In the early 1970s, hang gliding was a hot new subject. It was the rebirth of aviation, using a wing made in the sail industry and whose participants were kids off the streets. The terms for flying and parts of the glider could have come from the aviation community, the sail industry or popular (new) jargon could have been used. Obviously aviation terms were in order. This was impressed upon the early book and magazine writers; aviation terms were used almost exclusively, and this usage aided the introduction of hang gliding into the community of sport aviation.

One technique for educating your readers to the correct terms is to use the proper term and then follow it with the more popular word or explanation in parentheses. Educating the reader as you progress through the book is preferable to making readers wade through a glossary in the Appendix.

Surely you don't believe Lee Iacocca wrote those two bestsellers without help.

Anticipate trends to keep your work up to date. Use non-sexist terms.

Help is available to those who still cannot write even after learning the tricks mentioned above. If you can talk, you can write, so get a tape recorder. Do the transcription yourself or hire someone else to do it. Type the manuscript as you dictated it. Then either edit the language or leave it as it is. Sometimes a basic speaking style adds to the book.

If you still cannot get your thoughts on paper, try the team approach. There are a lot of writers out there without an original idea—people who love to put good thoughts into words. Look for a moon-lighting newspaper reporter. They are trained to listen and put your thoughts down accurately. Once they have your material written out, you may edit the work for rewriting. The reporter may even wind up doing a feature story on you and his or her media contacts are invaluable.

Joe Karbo sold millions of dollars worth of *Lazy Man's Way to Riches* and while he "authored" the book, he did not write it. He gathered his original thoughts and material and hired a writer to put it all on paper.

Perhaps you can get your thoughts down on paper but all that good information does not read very well. What you need is an *editor*, someone who can take your information and put energy into it.

Doctor Hartbrodt wrote a medical book about a common disease. The manuscript contained a lot of solid, helpful information but was hard to read. He contacted writers' groups, editorial services and secretarial services through the *Yellow Pages* and located four people who were willing to help. He gave each a copy of the first chapter and asked them to edit a couple of sample pages and to quote their fee. Some editors only want to dot "i's" and cross "t's" while other want to do complete rewrites. Using this method, he was able to compare their work and select the one he liked most at the best per-page price.

Many big name authors cannot type or spell so they hire people who can. To contact people in the "word game," go to libraries, PR firms, advertising agencies, or college English departments Check the *Yellow Pages* under "Writing" and see the *Writer's Digest Yearbook*. There are a lot of people out there who will be happy to work for you at a reasonable rate. You have the knowledge of the subject and a writer knows how to put your thoughts on paper. The big winner is the reader/bookbuyer who receives good information expressed well.

Whenever you use the team approach to book writing, you should have a contract stating clearly whose name will be on the book and who is working for hire. For a sample contract and a thorough explanation, see *Is There A Book Inside You?*, listed in the Appendix. Many people who are not professional writers get into print. If they cannot pick up the skills, they ask for help. You can too.

—Commissioned writing. Many of the more successful book houses approach publishing from a hard-nosed marketing position. They know what they have been able to sell in the past and they often stay in their field of expertise by assigning writers to produce more of these "commissioned books." Once you decide on an area of concentration, you too may approach others to write for you by paying cash outright, or using modest royalty advances as an inducement. The accounting is easier and the arrangement is often more cost effective when you pay outright for material rather than paying royalties. Flat fees for shorter books are often around $3,500, half on assignment and half on acceptance. These books may be wrapped up in less than sixty days by moonlighting advertising copywriters.

—Author submissions. Another source of material is the traditional one of unsolicited author submissions. If you are concentrating on a certain interest area and are selling books to a select market, you are also in contact with those people best qualified to generate new material for you. And once you publish something they like, they will come to you. Many people have always cherished the dream of becoming an author, and they will seek you out once they recognize your success.

Of course, you can always wait for manuscripts in your interest area to come to you, but you will save time and a lot of useless manuscript reading by issuing one-paragraph outlines of books you need to round out your list. Send them to writing magazines such as *Writer's Digest*. Also fill out a form for a listing in *Writer's Market*. Make it easy for qualified writers to find you.

—Co-authorship. If you have a book you want to do yourself, but recognize that you lack the required technical expertise, consider co-authorship. Find an expert in the field to write part of it while you write the other part, and then each of you can edit the other's material. This approach has many advantages, including the endorsement of an expert, more credibility for the book and another body to send on the promotional tour. The disadvantages are smaller royalties, extra accounting and author hand-holding.

> This author shared the responsibilities for the *Frisbee Players' Handbook* with disc expert Mark Danna. Danna wrote the throwing and catching chapters while Poynter wrote on history, record attempts, competition and assembled the appendix. Poynter came up with the unique package and marketing idea but did not have enough expertise or credibility as a Frisbee player. Mark Danna rounded out the team well.

Spouses without experience outside the home may choose to co-author a book with their partner on their area of expertise. A project like this gets both of them published, provides them with a common project (which may do great things for the marriage) and elevates their job stature.

—Republishing articles. Many author-publishers have gone the easy route by simply editing the material of others. Deeply interested in an area, they have thoroughly researched a subject only to find that many fine experts have already written good material on several aspects of it. The collection of these articles, one per chapter, formed a book. To pursue this course, contact each author for permission to use his material, and ask him to go over a photocopy to update it with any new information or changed views. This makes your chapter better than the original article. If the chapter must be shortened, ask the author to do it. This is faster and easier than doing it yourself and then negotiating your changes with him.

If, for example, you are deeply involved in the sport of parachuting, you might contact the national association and their magazine about gathering like articles which have appeared over the years and re-publishing them in a series of booklets. Booklet Number One might consist of all the best articles on student training. Your primary market would be the members of the association: You would sell them through the organization's "store" and via mail order by advertising in their magazine. Thus, the association is providing both the material and the customers. As an editor, you simply re-package the information.

—Out of print books. Sometimes you can find good books which large publishers have let go out of print. Normally, the copyright has reverted to the author. These authors are usually thrilled to have a new publisher put their book back into print. Often the original page negatives can be purchased from the publisher for a few hundred dollars so the book does not even have to be typeset. See the Bowker directory *Books Out Of Print*, available at your library.

> Bill Kaysing discovered an out-of-copyright book called *Thermal Springs of the World*. He abstracted just the data on hot springs in the western U.S., added some original comments and reprinted it as *Great Hot Springs of the West*. Review copies sent to several major magazines resulted in an entire column of flattering coverage in *Sunset*. Some 3,000 copies were sold in a little over a year.

—Translations offer another source of material and are a royalty consideration. A good translator is a highly skilled artist who issues a product which does not read like a word-for-word translation. He or she will spend hours searching for the single right word or phrase to convey the original meaning. Translators must not only be bilingual, they must be good writers, too. There may be some 1200 literary translators in the U.S., but few are very good. To find a translator, write the American Translators Association, 109 Croton Avenue, Ossining, NY 10562. The going rate is $30 or less per 1,000 words, so few can make a living at translating. Citing their creative input, some translators are now requesting royalties, but few have been successful so far. The English language rights to foreign language books are rarely expensive so this is another interesting source of material.

Negotiating and contracting with authors. The object of an author-publisher contract is to clarify thinking and positions by laying out all the details on the table and arriving at a mutually beneficial agreement. There will never be a second book if one side takes unfair advantage of the other; it pays to keep the future in mind. Small publishers should not offer less than the industry norm unless they will be satisfied with just one book per author, and there is no need to offer more. Most likely, if the author had a chance with a big publishing concern, he would not even be talking to you. Then again, he may be working on one of your ideas. Each contract will be a little different but you can start with a standard one. For sample contracts with explanations, see *Publishing Agreements* by Charles Clark. For sample contracts, ready to load into your computer, see *Publishing Contracts on Disk*. See the Appendix. It is easier to edit than it is to create.

First-time authors will be eager to become published and may not be terribly concerned about the contract initially. Many creative people are not business or commercially oriented. It is imperative that contract negotiation and signing be taken care of first. Rough draft the contract and ask the author whether it is generally acceptable. If he or she has made any other commitments, such as for some subsidiary rights, this information must be added into the contract. Include a work schedule and a clause allowing you to cancel if he or she fails to meet deadlines; always keep the pressure on writers to perform. See *Is There a Book Inside You?*

Unless you have a narrow field of interest or the writer has very strong feelings about a particular area, you will want a contract which includes all possible rights. Once you have published the basic book, you will want to entertain the possibilities of translations to other languages or co-publishing in other English-speaking markets (however, unless the market is quite large, it will be more economical to ship your own print run in "direct sacks of prints"). Then there are book club adoptions, film rights, magazine excerpts, newspaper serializations and the mass market paperback rights. Your promotion will rub off on all areas so take advantage of it by taking complete control of the manuscript. Remember that people who write contracts slant them their way. Take control. Use *Publishing Contracts on Disk* to provide your own contract.

Advances against royalties depend on the proposed selling price, projected print run and the sales potential of the book. The advance seals the deal, which is an important legal consideration while it puts pressure on the author and the publisher to perform. The advance makes the author feel accepted and has great psychological value; it does not have to be large to work as an incentive.

I just sat down and started all by myself. It never occurred to me that I couldn't do it as well as anyone. - Barbara Tuchman

Advances generally range from $100 to $5,000, and small publishers often keep them low. A good rule of thumb is to offer an advance equal to the projected first year royalties. One way to create an incentive, or at least make the author feel morally obligated, is to make progress payments. One-third may be paid on signing the contract, one-third when the writer submits the first draft and one-third when he or she completes the proofreading. Advances are paid against royalties; they are not in addition to this percentage. Ordinarily, advances are non-refundable; the author keeps them even if he or she fails to deliver the manuscript. This is another good reason to protect your investment with progress payments.

Advances work both ways. Authors demand high advances from publishers in order to commit the publisher to the book. The publisher, with a lot invested in a book, has to bring it to market quickly and market it well. The advance is the publisher's gamble. The author keeps it even if the book fails to sell and generate enough royalties to cover the advance. Some authors with little faith in their manuscript or the publisher will, therefore, request larger advances.

Flat fees or royalties. Should contributors get a percentage of the book or be paid a flat fee? Obviously flat fees are simpler and they are occasionally cheaper. An illustrator creating a major portion of the book should get royalties, while someone doing basic research, typing or contributing a drawing should be paid a set fee. Everyone must understand clearly what is in it for him. If you require a few drawings, go to a graphic artist and have them drawn to order. Then pay the bill and be done with it. The artist deserves a piece of the action no more than the person does who painted your car before you sold it. One exception is a book for children where the illustrations are usually as important as the text.

The royalty formula, traditionally, has been to pay the author 10% of the list (cover) price for each hard cover book sold through regular channels, such as book wholesalers, book stores and libraries. Remember that after discounting the book to dealers, this amounts to 15-20% of the publisher's budget. Or graduated royalties for the hardcover edition might be 10% of the list price on the first 5,000 books sold, 12.5% on the next 5,000 and 15% on sales over 10,000. Often softcover authors command 7% for the first 12,000 sold and 9% above that number.

Recently some publishers have changed their terms by offering authors a flat 10% of the **net** on books. Percentages of the net rarely work out to the author's advantage as it is too easy for the publisher to pad the expenses. Even if the publisher is referring to "net sales" (both wholesale and retail), the author's royalties for a given percentage will be much less. Further, the accounting required is a heavy burden, and this is another expense to be considered. A percentage of the **list price** is preferable, as it is easy to calculate and difficult to pad.

Royalties for college texts range from 10% to 18% while those for heavily illustrated elementary and secondary schools run from 4% to 10%. Royalties for juvenile books range between 10% and 15%, to be split between the author and illustrator. Mass market paperback publishers usually pay 4% to 7.5%, but they print in much greater quantities.

Most contracts call for the author and publisher to split the subsidiary rights (films, book clubs, etc.) 50-50. Many of the big publishers barely break even on the book itself and hope to make their money on the subsidiary rights.

Layout the binder. Now that you are generating copy, you need a place to store it. Find a large 3", three-ring binder and add divider cards corresponding to the chapters you have selected. Insert the rough-typed pages as you complete them. As the piles come off the floor, cross the desk and flow through the computer into the binder, you will gain a great feeling of accomplishment.

You will be further encouraged by setting up the front matter of the book. Soon you will have a partial manuscript, the book will be taking shape and you will have something tangible to carry around. This makes you feel proud and gives you the flexibility to proof and improve your manuscript away from home. Carry the binder around and work on it whenever you can. If the book is a short one, you may even use the binder to collect your material, and this will allow you to avoid the piles of notes. Write your name and address in the front of the binder with a note that it is a valuable manuscript. You do not want to misplace and lose your future book.

It is wise to photocopy your manuscript periodically so that a copy may be stored in another location. You may lose a lot of important things in a fire, but to have the fruit of your creativity destroyed would be a financial and emotional disaster.

Parts of a book. Most books are divided into three main parts: preliminary pages or *front matter*, the *text* and the *back matter*. We will discuss each of them in order so you can add a sheet for each to the binder with as much information as you have so far. It is not necessary to have all the pages mentioned or even to place them in any given order, but it is recommended that convention be followed unless you have a good, specific reason to stray. Set up these sections as best you can so the book will begin to take shape. You will make additions and revisions to the binder later.

There are two pages to each sheet or leaf of paper. The *verso* pages are on the left-hand side and are even numbered while the *recto* pages are opposite.

The front matter is that material placed at the beginning of the book. It includes everything up to the beginning of Chapter One.

—**End papers** may be plain or printed, usually of heavier paper, and are glued to the inside front and back covers of a hardbound (casebound) book. End papers dress up the book and hold it together.

—**Testimonials**, endorsements and excerpts from reviews are being seen more and more on the first page of softcover books. This is important sales space.

—**The bastard title** or half title is usually the first printed page of a book and is more often found in hardbound books than in paperbacks. It contains only the title and it is a right-hand page. Until the later 1800s, books were usually sold without covers—so the buyer could have all his books bound in the same style for a matching library. The bastard title page was just a wrapper for the text. It was often removed before binding.

No man but a blockhead ever wrote except for money. - Samuel Johnson

—**The frontispiece** is a photograph or *plate* usually found on a left-hand page facing the title page. Before modern printing machinery, illustrations were expensive and the frontispiece had the only picture in the book. Often the frontispiece was an engraving of the author. Today this page is left blank or it is used to list other books by the same author.

—**The title page** is on the right-hand side and lists the full title and subtitle of the book. This page may also include the name of the author or editor, the publisher, whether this is an original or revised edition, location of the publisher and the date.

Choosing a title. Spend some time on your title. Title testing has shown a good one will sell some 15% more books. In some cases, the title made the book go.

Start with a short, catchy and descriptive title, and a lengthy explanatory subtitle. The first word of the title should be the same as the subject to make the book easy to find. The book will be listed in Bowker's *Books In Print* by title, author and subject. If the title and subject are the same, you have doubled your exposure. Most other directories list only titles in alphabetic order; position your book where it can be found.

Book listings in *BIP* include only the title, not a description of the contents so get more mileage with a sub-title to tell what the book is about. For example, *COMPUTER SELECTION GUIDE, Choosing the Right Hardware & Software: Business-Professional-Personal* is listed under the most common heading "computers" while the rest of the title and subtitle tell what the book is about.

Many self-published books are sold by mail order, and to be marketed they must be advertised. Here the title must grab the attention of the reader and make him a promise such as: "Buy this book and make a million dollars." Test proposed titles out on your friends and acquaintances.

Good book titles are your best teaser copy, whether they are selling the book from a magazine advertisement or the book shelf. Brainstorm the title and come up with a good "one-liner" which tells a complete and compelling story. The title is perhaps the single most important piece of promotional copy you will draft for the book.

—The copyright page or *title page verso* is on the reverse of the title page and is the most important page in the book. Proofread it a dozen times! Here you print the copyright notice, show the printing history (number of printings and revisions), list the Library of Congress Catalog number, the ISBN, the Library of Congress Cataloging in Publication Data, name and address of the publisher (you) and *printed in the United States of America* (to avoid export complications).

Those who know the book trade will turn to the copyright page first when picking up a book. Next to the cover, this page is the most important in selling a book to the trade, so make it look professional. You want to look like a big time publisher, not a kitchen-based word shop.

Each time you revise the book, it is worthwhile to re-strip and re-shoot the copyright page in order to add, for example, *Second Printing, revised, 1993*, as this lets the potential purchaser know the book is up-to-date. Most big publishers do not make any changes to the copyright page and print a string of numbers on it instead. You will note: "10 9 8 7 6 5 4 3 2 1," which indicates to the trained eye that this is the first edition. On reprinting it, they will opaque out the "1" on the photographic negative. Actually, many big publishers will print the full number of books they think they can sell. They never expect to go back to press.

—The dedication page usually contains a short statement, if one is made at all, but some authors like to praise their parents—presumably without whose help, *the author would not have been possible*. It is not likely that anyone other than the person mentioned will care about the dedication. This right-hand page was used historically by writers to acknowledge their patrons: the person or institution that supported them during the writing.

—The epigraph page contains a pertinent quotation which sets the tone of the book. Using a separate page for an epigraph is sometimes a nice touch but often is a waste of space.

Publishing is an active life while writing is a quiet life. - Linda Meyer.

—**The table of contents** should start on the right-hand side. This page will include the chapter numbers, chapter titles and beginning page numbers. You can leave these page numbers blank for now. They will be filled in when the book is laid out. Remember, when buying technical, professional or how-to books, most people turn immediately to the Table of Contents to check the coverage. Use some imagination when drafting your chapter titles—make them descriptive.

—**A list of illustrations** is in order if the book is heavily illustrated, has many important tables or if it is a picture-type book. Most books do not need this list.

—**The foreword** is positioned on the right-hand side and is a pitch for the book by someone other than the author. It is doubtful that many people read them; most turn directly to the action. The name of the contributor appears at the end of the foreword. If you include a foreword, note the correct spelling, it is not "forward."

—**The preface** is written by the author and tells why and how he or she wrote the book. It gets about as much attention from the reader as a foreword and appears on the right-hand side. If you have an important message and want to be sure the reader receives it, put it in Chapter One, not in the preface or introduction.

—**Acknowledgements** are a great sales tool. List everyone who helped you in preparation of your manuscript. People love to see their name in print, and each one will become a disciple spreading the word on your great contribution to literature. On this blank sheet in your binder, add names of contributors as you encounter them so that you do not forget anyone.

—**The introduction** was covered above in the discussion of the preface.

—**The list of abbreviations** is only required in some very technical books.

—**The repeated bastard title** is next, is optional and is a waste of space in most books.

I love being a writer. What I can't stand is the paperwork. - Peter De Vries

—**Disclaimers** are showing up in more and more books today. Law suits are an unfortunate fact of life in the United States and, while disclaimers are not absolute protection against them, the warning can't hurt.

Obviously, if all the front matter pages listed above were included in your book, you would have a large number of pages already. You do not need all these pages and it is recommended that you do away with most, except the title page, copyright page, table of contents, acknowledgements, about the author and disclaimer. Check over several other books for layout, especially old hardbound books which followed convention.

The text of the book is the meaty part on which the front matter and back matter hang. This is the second or main section.

Start your book off with an *action chapter*. Like the introductory part of a speech, Chapter One should arouse the reader and whet his or her appetite. Too many authors want to start from the *beginning* and put a history chapter first. The reader wants to know where-to and how-to. Do not lose the reader in the first chapter.—Divisions are sometimes made in long books with distinct but related sections. Their title pages contain the name and number of the section and their reverse sides are usually blank.

—**Chapter titles** should reveal the subject of the chapter to aid the reader in finding what he or she wants. The reader may be skimming the book in a store, pending possible purchase, or may be referring back to something he or she read. In either case, you want the description to be as clear as possible.

—**The subhead** is a secondary heading or title, usually set in less prominent type than the main heading, to divide the entries under a subject. Subheads can contribute a logical progression, aid in finding needed material and help to break up long chapters.

> *The publisher is financing the author on the one end and the bookstore's inventory at the other.* - Sol Stein, President of Stein and Day

—**Footnotes** are not needed except in technical publications. If your book will be used as a research tool, the readers may want the footnotes so they can follow up on the material. Where footnotes must be used, some people recommend they be placed at the end of the chapter or in the appendix. Placing extensive footnotes at the bottom of the page can make for some short pages, and the increasingly complicated typesetting becomes more expensive.

—**The afterword** is sometimes seen in manuals. Often it is a personal message from the author to the reader, wishing the best of luck and/or requesting suggestions for improvement.

The back matter is reference material such as the glossary, resources and index placed at the back of the book. It is less expensive to revise lists at the end of the book when reprinting; avoid printing lists subject to change in the text.

—**The appendix** contains important charts, graphs, lists, etc. and it may be composed of several sections. Books with a large appendix often become valuable references. It is permissible to set this reference material in smaller type.

—**The glossary** is an alphabetically-arranged dictionary of terms peculiar to the subject of the book. Some authors like to save space and simplify use by combining the glossary and the index.

—**The bibliography** lists the books used in writing the book.

—**The addendum** has brief, late additional data. It is printed as part of the book or on a loose sheet.

—**Errata** are errors discovered after printing. The list is printed on a separate sheet and may be pasted-in or loose.

—**Author's notes** come next and include additional information in chapter order.

—**Colophon** is Greek for *finishing touch* and details the production facts by listing the type style, designer, typesetter, printer, kind of paper, plate maker, binder, etc. The colophon is not as common as it once was, but is still found today in special *labor of love*-type publications.

—**The index** aids the reader in locating specific information in the pages and is particularly important in reference works. Many librarians will not purchase books without indexes. Assembling the index is very time consuming unless you use a word processor. The index must be revised every time the book is updated because the page numbers change.

—**Order blank.** The last page of the book should contain an offer for more books and an order blank; place it on a left-hand page—facing out. Some readers will want to purchase a copy for a friend, while others may want a copy for themselves after seeing your book at a friend's home or in the library. Make ordering easy for them by listing the full price including sales tax (if applicable) and shipping. This order blank system works. Several orders on the coupon are received for *The Self-Publishing Manual* each week.

Make a page for each of the sections listed above that you wish to include, and fill in as much information as you now have. Keep adding with a pencil to your manuscript in the binder as you progress. The collected information does not have to be neat or in order; the important thing is that now you have a place to store your material. As you add pages, as the book fills up, you will have more work to carry as you venture away from home. When you find a few idle moments, open the book, draft and revise a section, bit by bit.

Editing your manuscript is where you cut, rearrange and add material. Go through the manuscript section by section and clean it up. Tighten your writing, change words, cut out those which fail to add to your message. Revise and improve.

Photos and drawings are easily indicated in the manuscript with page and position numbers. The second photo on page 40 would be marked "40-B," for example. Mark the location both in the manuscript and on the back of the photo or drawing. Mark the photo near its edge and do not press too hard; you may push through to damage the photo. Incidentally, it is sometimes necessary to indicate which end of the photo goes up, if it is not obvious to someone not familiar with the subject. Type the captions into the manuscript under the photo position number. Make photocopies or contact prints of the photos and paste them into the manuscript (set the copy machine on "light"). This will make the draft clearer to both you, your peer reviewers, copy editor and the typesetter or printer. Never paste in the photos themselves; they are hard to get off and could be damaged.

Typesetting. Most books today are being typeset with computer-driven laser printers. Ordinarily, the money saved on traditional typesetting will pay for the equipment. See *Publishing Short-Run Books*, listed in the Appendix.

Proofreading has to be done again and again. You will proof your manuscript for content and style, and then you will proof the book as it makes its way through the various stages of production.

Ask friends to proofread your manuscript for grammar, punctuation and content. Do they find it easy to read? Do they understand what you are saying? If no one has time to read the whole book, ask them to go over an interesting chapter.

For technical proofing, send chapters off to various experts for "peer review." Just make a photocopy of your draft and ask them to make notes right on the copy. Enclose a self-addressed, stamped envelope and remember to give them credit in the acknowledgments. You will not only produce the best book, you will gain their support for it and this is very important to its marketing. Incidentally, it is not necessary to pay for peer reviews. Most people are happy to be the first to see a manuscript, have their name in the acknowledgments and three copies of the finished book.

There will be a lot of proofing. The manuscript must be proofed and marked before final typing, the final draft has to be proofed for the typesetter, the set type or "boards" have to be proofed and the blueline prints of the book signatures have to be proofed. You will have some errors anyway, but without careful proofreading, you will have more. Being familiar with your own writing style, you will find it difficult to catch all your own errors. Now is the time to hire a professional wordsmith to proof your copy.

There are books of which the backs and covers are by far the best parts. - Charles Dickens.

There is an interesting story about a professor who wanted to publish
an errorless book. He brought it out in loose computer printout form
and offered his students 10 cents for each error they could find during
the term. They found quite a few. Then he corrected the copy and ran
off another set. This time he offered the new class 25 cents per error.
They searched harder and found fewer. By the fourth time around at $1
per error, only a very few errors turned up and the professor was satisfied. Incidentally, this game also proved to be an effective way to encourage the class to read the required text thoroughly.

Proof well. Get it right the first time. "What you (don't) see
is what you get." There is no practical way to take ink off
paper.

The printer will take your typeset pages, photograph them,
make negatives and paste the negatives into "flats." Then he
will shoot a blueline proof for your review. Bluelines are large
folded blueprints which are assembled into signatures just like
the proposed book. They enable the printer to make sure the
pages are in order and that everything is in place. This is your
last chance to proofread. Check especially the page numbering,
sentence continuation from one page to the next, the chapter
page numbers in the table of contents, chapters beginning on a
right-hand page, proper insertion of the illustrations (right-
side-up?) and captions, the numbers on the copyright page, the
ISBN and bar code on the cover, etc. Most important, hold the
pages up to the light to check registration. The blocks of text
and page numbers should be superimposed. Do not proof
bluelines outdoors; the sun will turn them solid blue—fast.

Compare the bluelines with your typeset pages. Use "PE"
(printer's error) next to your correction in the manuscript
where the printer made the mistake, so you will not be charged
for the change. If the change is your fault, it is called an
"author's alteration" and they cost. Use a red pen to mark the
proofs so your notes cannot be missed. Write in small corrections but type out and paste in large ones. To change even a
punctuation at this point, it is necessary to reset the entire
line, paste it on the board, reshoot the negative, strip it into
the flat and reshoot the blueline. Expensive! If you delete or
add words, entire pages may have to be reset, and this may
affect more than one page. It may be necessary to reset the
rest of the chapter.

> *Don't use "I", the perpendicular pronoun.*

No matter how carefully you proofread, some errors will always show up in the final printed book. Do not be too concerned; resign yourself to this event and make the corrections in the next printing.

Many publishers like to make a small press run (perhaps 3,000) the first time to help them catch the errors. Keep a "correction copy" of the book near your desk and pencil in changes as they come to your attention. Then when you are ready to reprint, you will be ready to go.

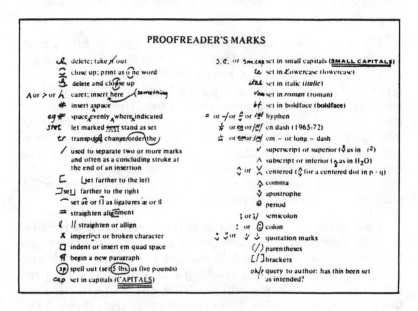

A complete set of proofreader's marks can be found in your dictionary under *proofreader's marks*.

Proofreader's marks are standardized to enable you to communicate clearly with your typesetter and printer. A complete set of marks can be found in your dictionary under "proofreader's marks." Stick to the standard marks. If you make up your own, you will only confuse those who must understand them. Use these marks throughout the editing/proofreading process.

Artwork consists of *line work* and *halftones*. Line work is a clean black on white drawing without any shading. Line drawings may be pasted directly on the boards unless their size must be enlarged or reduced. Camera work costs extra. Halftones are made from photographs, or drawings with shading, by taking a photograph of them through a screen. You will notice the result, using a magnifying glass to look closely at a printed photograph. A screened photograph is composed of many tiny dots of various sizes (shading). This takes camera work and you will be charged for each shot. Camera charges are a start-up cost; the cost of an individual photo, when spread over the entire print run, is very small. It is foolish to be cheap at this point.

If you need line work and cannot draw, you can hire a commercial artist. Most typesetters have illustrators on their staff, or know some, and they usually work inexpensively. Your typesetter or printer may also have a large file of "clip art" and you may find something there you can use. These are commercially-provided drawings on a large variety of subjects that may be used without permission. Many people lift art from reprints of old Sears catalogs and other publications where the copyright has expired. Depending on your subject, you may be able to clip drawings from certain military and government publications which are in the public domain.

Photographs, rarely seen in fiction, are almost a requirement in nonfiction, especially how-to books. The most successful how-to books are those that manage to integrate words and pictures into an attractive teaching tool. Unless you are writing an art-type book, you will use black and white rather than the more expensive color. Color requires four trips through the press, plus pre-press "color separations." The best photos are large (they become sharper when reduced), glossy, black and whites with a lot of contrast. Color photos and slides may be reproduced in black and white but will not be as clear. Photographs which have already been printed once may be pasted-in directly or reduced and rescreened, but the results are not as good as with an original glossy photo. When in doubt about the suitability of a photo, ask your printer. Occasionally the screening improves the photo.

Life is too short for reading inferior books. - James Bryce

Cameras. You will want to get a good camera with attachments, and buy a book on how to use it. There are many types of cameras but the most popular and versatile is the single lens reflex. Many used models and accessories are available at your discount photo shop and they have good resale value. If you are shooting fast-moving people or objects, you may need a camera with automatic features and/or motor drive. (Aircraft mounts may dictate motor drives and a remote firing device too.) And do not overlook the new zoom lenses which make framing faster and easier. Olympus has a five shots per second motor drive, and that still is not fast enough to get a series of photos to show the windup and throw of a Frisbee disc. But it is fast enough for most subjects, and the motor drive allows you to keep your eye on the subject rather than pulling away to advance the film.

Using the camera. As you compile your manuscript, make a photo list so you will know what pictures you need. Then set out with your gear to take them. Try to frame your shots on the object, person or activity you are trying to show; avoid distracting clutter. For good black and white contrast, avoid tonal shades. Put people in your photos. If you are showing a number of pieces of equipment which are better modeled, such as parachutes, invite as many different people as possible to wear them. You can bet that each model will buy a copy of the book. When taking still-shots of people, make them smile. Get their teeth in the picture. Most people do not know how to pose for a photo and complain that they do not photograph well. Catch them smiling and they will love you for it. Try to capture action in your photos, make them move. Seek the unusual, tell a story, look for human interest, shoot from a different angle. Then have your film processed by a custom photo lab. Do not send it out through your supermarket. Slide processing is easy, but in black and white processing the enlarger must be focused.

Handle negatives and photos carefully, you have a lot invested in them. Keep them clean and mail them flat between cardboard sheets. When you wish the typesetter or printer to crop a print, do not take out the scissors; draw crop marks on the edges. If a photo needs retouching, such as to remove an extraneous object like your camera bag, let the graphic artist do it. Do not use paper clips. When writing on the back, use a fine point felt tip pen, concentrate on the edge and do not push down too hard. Make sure the ink is dry before restacking the photos and to be safe, put a piece of plain paper between them. For more information on cameras and photography, see the discussion in *Writer's Market* and get a copy of *Publishing Short-Run Books*. See the Appendix. .

Photo release forms are advisable, particularly for pictures of minors. Permission might cost $20 to 500 but normally your subjects are just tickled to be in the book. A news photo does not require a release unless it is used in an advertisement. Permission fees are normally paid to the subject by the author upon publication. For an example of a photo release form, see *Publishing Contracts on Disk*. See the Appendix.

Often you will overlook getting permission and occasionally a subject will ask about his rights. The best way to handle this is to tell him that you are about to go back to press with a revised printing and, while it will cost you to replace the photo, you can take him out. I have yet to hear of a subject who wanted to be deleted from a book.

Other photo sources. Freelancers with a stock of photos will sell them for a few dollars each. Or you can have them custom shot for $5 to $20 per photo. Photo syndicates are in the business of selling stock photos. The chamber of commerce, private firms, trade associations and some governmental departments have public relations departments who provide photos as part of their function. Libraries and museums sometimes have photo files. Photos from old books with expired copyrights are easily copied with your camera. Just carry the book over to the light, lay it out flat and snap a photo. These photos of photos come out very nicely. When covering an event, make contact with the other photographers and get their cards. They may have just what you need. Picture sources are listed in *World Photography Sources, Writer's Market* and *Literary Market Place*. Ask for them at your library.

When to finish. If the book is 100% accurate and 99% complete, go to press. That one last photo and that one extra item can wait for the reprint. If you delay the printing, you are tying up your money longer and you may miss the market.

In this work, when it shall be found that much is omitted, let it not be forgotten that much likewise is performed. - Dr. Samuel Johnson upon completion of his dictionary, 1755.

Mailing the manuscript or boards. If you are not dealing with a nearby typesetter and/or printer, you will have to ship the manuscript or typeset boards. Stack the photos and drawings and enclose them in cardboard to avoid folding. Enclose both manuscript or boards and illustrations in plastic bags and pack them in a sturdy cardboard carton. The Post Office does offer a special manuscript rate (same as book rate), but most authors prefer United Parcel Service because the service is good and the parcel must be signed for on the receiving end. Another alternative, if you are not near a UPS office, is certified, priority (air) mail through the Post Office. A couple of extra dollars now is well worth the expense. Be sure the carton contains your complete return address.

Always keep a copy of the manuscript. This is to protect you if the original is lost in the mail or by the printer, and it is your ready reference when the printer calls with questions. Take the manuscript to a copy shop. They usually give reduced rates for overnight service and are reasonably inexpensive.

Writing a book can be easy if you have a system. With the organization outlined here, a decision to go and some discipline, you will start a whole new rewarding life. See the list of books on how to write on specialized subjects listed in the Appendix.

Dan's first book took eight years to produce. He worked on this labor of love without guidance or direction. The huge, steady-selling manual on parachutes became the foundation upon which he built his publishing company. His second book was a study guide for an obscure parachuting rating; it sold better than expected.

In 1973, he became interested in the new sport of hang gliding. Unable to find any information at the library, he wrote the first book on the subject. He foresaw a trend and cashed in on it; the book has sold 130,000 copies and is still going strong. Total writing time: two months.

By this time, he had developed a writing formula. His fourth book took less than 30 days from idea and decision, until he delivered the boards to the printer. And most of this time was used in waiting for answers to his many letters requesting information. The first draft took only five days.

> *Today, as always, if a talented author remains unpublished and unnoticed, the fault is the author's.* - Bill Henderson

From there he concentrated on several high-priced, low-cost course pamphlets, turning out most within a week. His ninth book took all of two weeks to first-draft and it was typed "clean." Very few editing changes had to be made to the original copy, and he even used different type styles in his IBM Selectric typewriter to indicate those he wanted in the book.

Using a word processor, Dan took 31 days to write, edit and typeset a book on computers. The actual time spent working on the book was just 18 3/4 days. Lately, his books have been longer and have required more time, but Dan still produces manuscripts efficiently. Writing a book is easy if you know the formula.

Before going on to Chapter Three, turn to "Your Book's Calendar" at the beginning of the Appendix. You might also like to skim Chapter Twelve. Before you start, it is nice to know where you are going. For more information on publishing choices and self-evaluated quizzes to help you make a decision, see *Is There a Book Inside You?* It is listed in the order blank at the end of this book.

> The last thing one discovers in writing a book is what to put first. - Blaise Pascal

Chapter Three

Starting Your Own Publishing Company

Forming your own publishing company is not difficult and many of the requirements may be postponed until you are ready to send your manuscript off to the printer. But you do need a system and must get into the habit of using it. This is, after all, a business.

Having a business is just good business. Tax laws favor business. Businesses get to deduct goods and services which the wage earner must pay for with after-tax dollars. If you don't have a business, you do not get to deduct very much.

Gross ⟶ Taxes ⟶ Net
Job

Gross ⟶ Expenditures ⟶ Net ⟶ Taxes
Business

My take home pay won't take me home anymore.

If you own a business, a lot of what you are already buying becomes deductible (car, dues, subscriptions, travel, etc.) A wage earner would pay for these items with what is left after taxes.

There are three forms of business: sole proprietorship, partnership and corporation, and each choice has advantages and disadvantages which you will have to weigh. You do not have to make the choice right now. If you do not file for corporation status, you will be operating as a sole proprietorship anyway. All you have to do is say "I am a business" and file a Schedule C with your tax return. Here are a few things to keep in mind while you are concentrating on your most important project: your manuscript.

—In a **sole proprietorship** you have the choice of keeping your financial records on a modified *cash basis* or an *accrual basis*. The cash system is easier to understand, allows you to defer more income and requires less bookkeeping, which makes more sense for a small business. You may always switch to accrual when you grow larger. Once you use the accrual system, however, you cannot switch back to cash and you must get IRS permission to make any switch.

—Many business consultants discourage the formation of **partnerships**, as their success rate is not much better than marriages—for a lot of the same reasons. It is a rare pair who complement each other well enough to divide the work so that both are happy. If two or more people want to form a company, they should consider a corporation.

In a *corporation*, you are an employee, not the company itself. This means more accounting, payroll taxes, paperwork, annual meetings with published minutes, more taxes and annual registration fees.

—**Corporations** are separate legal "beings" and can be sued, but their stockholders cannot normally be touched. A sole proprietor does not have the protection of this "limited liability" and could lose his home and other possessions if he lost in a legal action. There is more to consider in publishing than just the debts of the business. Someday, a reader may sue, claiming your book mislead him to his great damage. In fact, this has already happened with a cook book and a diet book. The plaintiff will, of course, sue both the author and publisher, trying to collect from both you and your incorporated company. Therefore, if you are the author, incorporation will not protect you from suits. Today, many books contain disclaimers warning readers not to rely on the text.

Libel might be another reason to sue, but again, the plaintiff would seek damages from both author and publisher. Keeping some of these problems in mind and considering your book's subject, talk to other people around you in small businesses and to your accountant and attorney.

Publications. When your manuscript is near completion and you have a "product," you will want to concentrate on the business end of publishing to get it printed and off to market. The Small Business Administration has many free publications, and some sold at a slight charge, which should help you. Write SBA, Washington, DC 20416 and request a *Directory of Business Development Publications*. The SBA also provides a toll free answer desk to provide information on free counseling, prebusiness workshops and other SBA services. Call (800) 827-5722.

It is strongly recommended that you subscribe to *Publishers Weekly* and *Writer's Digest* magazines. They will teach you about the writing/publishing trade, provide many stimulating ideas and generate enthusiasm. Purchase a copy of *Literary Market Place*; it is *the* resource of the book industry. I used to recommend referring to it in the library whenever it was needed, but it has become too important for just occasional use. Check accounting and business books such as Bernard Kamoroff's *Small Time Operator*. Purchase a copy of *The Business Planning Guide* by David H. Bangs. See the Appendix. Your writing references such as dictionaries, thesauri and style manuals can be purchased inexpensively in used book stores.

SCORE is the Small Business Administration's volunteer network, the letters of which stand for "Service Corps of Retired Executives." These are retired men and women who will call on you to help with your problems. There is no charge for this service except for occasional out-of-pocket traveling expenses. There are several hundred SCORE chapters around the country. Call the SBA office nearest you to see if there is a nearby SCORE chapter. Look in the *White Pages* under "U.S.

Small Business Administration." Tell them what you need and they will find someone tailored to you and your business. Naturally, it is always best to get this advice before you get into trouble; do it sooner, not later.

Your company name will have to be selected before you go to press so keep thinking about it. You could name it after yourself, say *Mindy Bingham Enterprises* or *Alan Gadney Publishing Co.*, but these choices do not make you look as big as a separate name. The use of "enterprises" is the sign of a rank beginner; as though you don't know yet what your company is going to do. If the business succeeds and one day you decide to sell out, the name will be sold with it. A good name will have more value. After all, what is the value of *Scott Hamilton Publishing* without Scott Hamilton? Looking big may be important when applying for credit from your vendors, or asking a paper mill for samples. A company name will create the impression that you have a going business.

Starting the name with an "A" will place your company high in alphabetic listings. Peggy Glenn changed her *PiGi Publishing* to *Aames-Allen* to assure top billing in directories.

Foreign names can pose cataloging problems. Would you list "La Cumbre Publishing" under "L" or "C"? If people do not know where to catalog you or where to look for you, you may not be found, and you could lose business.

Geographical names can be limiting. Which sounds larger, East Weedpatch Press or North American Publishing? Which would you rather run, and what happens if you move to West Weedpatch?

To find a new name, one that isn't being used in the publishing industry, go to the library and look through *Writer's Market, International Directory of Little Magazines and Small Presses, Books in Print, Literary Market Place* and your local telephone directory. This search is fun and you will note that the newer publishing companies have some pretty interesting names. As a new, little outfit, it does not hurt to have a handle that attracts attention. Pick a name that isn't being used by anyone else.

An entrepreneur spends 16 hours a day to avoid having to work for someone else for eight hours. - James Healey.

After you select a name for your new publishing company, you will probably be required to file it as a "fictitious business name" with your city or county and run a notice in a local newspaper. This notice is your way of letting the public know that you and the publishing company are the same person.

Your logo is a graphic image, an easily recognizable symbol; it may consist of a drawing or just the company name in a distinctive style of type. If you can dream up something clever and easily recognizable, start putting it on all your letterheads, labels, business cards and brochures.

Your place of business will be your residence for a while. You will not need a lot of space to write, store or ship books initially. When you have several titles and need more space and employees, you may have to move out. But for now home has many advantages. Working out of your home (house, mobile home, camper, wherever you live) will save additional rent, utilities and the headaches of a second property. And, as we will discuss later in this chapter, you can write off part of the household expenses on your tax return. Working at home requires some organization and discipline, but for many it is very comfortable working in this lower-stress atmosphere.

Before you begin sorting, shipping and selling books in your front room, quietly check the zoning ordinances. Local regulations may allow some types of business to be run from your home. Your business will be small at first and as long as you don't have employees, and large trucks aren't pulling into the drive every few minutes, no one is likely to complain. Avoid walk-in traffic and refer to yourself as an "author" rather than a "publisher," and you shouldn't encounter any difficulty. Sometimes when local regulations prohibit operating a business in a residential neighborhood, author/publishers post their business licenses at a friend's store and continue to quietly work out of their home.

Working from your home should not be confused with "office in the home." The IRS has cracked down on the offices which are in addition to one's place of business. If you use one-half of your home for your business activities, and do not have another office, you may deduct 50% of most of the house expenses. Some of those deductions are for mortgage or rent, electricity, heat, insurance and water.

If you are worried that a visiting vendor or client might not be favorably impressed with your home setup, make a lunch appointment in a restaurant. Actually, the visitor will probably envy you. In the U.S., two percent of the work force enjoys the "short commute." Working out of your home is more comfortable, more efficient and cheaper.

P.O. box or street address. There are many good arguments for each one. Some people feel quite strongly that a street address is more effective in a mail order ad because the location reflects more substance and stability. But today, even the big firms are using boxes. This is probably the result of the high incidence of urban crime. There was a time when the mail was sacred and no crook would dare to touch it, but not anymore. Depending on your address ("1234 Northwest Whispering Valley Parkway, Suite 1701" or "Box 3") a long street address could cost you more in classified ads where they charge by the word.

You will have to go to the Post Office regularly to ship books, so you might as well pick up your mail there; and with a box, you will be able to pick up your mail a few hours earlier. Another advantage of a box is that you can maintain the same address even though you move (the Post Office forwards mail for one year). Perhaps the most important reason to maintain a box is to keep your excited, loyal readers from dropping in at all hours to meet their author who *must be interested in them and their project.*

Apply for a box now and consider a big one. In some areas boxes are in short supply and there is quite a waiting list. It may take you months to get one. Write your name, your company name and the title of your book on the box registration card so you will get your mail no matter how it is addressed. Remember, all your stationery and business references need an address, so get a box now.

Your stationery is you. It should look nice but you do not want to tie up a lot of money here. Windowed envelopes save time as you only type the name and address once. Also order business cards and a rubber stamp with your company name and address.

Profit is not a dirty word.

Your telephone may be listed under your name or the company name, and if you request a commercial listing or a *Yellow Page* ad, you will get hit with the higher commercial rate. When business picks up, install a second line for outgoing calls. This way you won't be tying up your order line. The power company may also wish to charge you commercial rates if they find out you are running a business from your home.

Keep costs down when doing your research by dialing direct during the early morning, evenings and on weekends. For exact hours on the lower rates, consult the initial pages of your telephone directory.

Your computer (see Chapter Eleven) is your most important piece of machinery; spend the money and get a good one. You are a "wordsmith" now and require the best word processing machine you can afford.

It is hard to beat the combination of the Apple Macintosh or IBM Personal Computer (or workalike) with word processing software and a laser printer. Not only will this system speed up your writing, it may be used for correspondence, mailing list maintenance, typesetting, order entry and bookkeeping. See the computer chapter for the machinery used in writing and typesetting this book. When you figure the money saved in typesetting, and the mechanization computers provide your business, they are quite inexpensive. For specific details see the Special Report *Computers for Publishers* by the author. See the Appendix.

No one takes better care of your money than you do. - Cliff Leonard in *License to Steal*

If you are already in a high tax bracket, you should consider leasing all your office equipment. The costs are tax deductible and you tie up less money. Ask your accountant.

Better Business Bureau membership may offer some credibility to a mail order business operating out of a Post Office box with a name like "Joe Smith Enterprises," and many people recommend joining. Look up the BBB in your telephone directory and call to request literature on what they have to offer. Membership fees vary from one locality to the next and often run $100 per year for the small business.

The legal requirements of operating a business are covered in many parts of this book just as you will encounter them in every facet of your daily publishing life. The following is what you need to run your business, but remember that most of this may be postponed until you are ready to go to press, move out of the house or hire employees. These tips, of course, are food for thought, not a substitute for legal counsel.

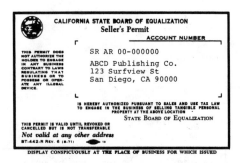

Licenses

Interview a friend or acquaintance who has recently set up a small business in your community. They will be happy to tell you what happened to them, where to get various licenses, recommend an accountant, etc. In some areas you must register your business with local authorities, but not in all. Ask this same friend where to find the office. As a sole proprietorship, your business won't need a separate bank account, and until you hire employees, you will avoid tax numbers and special accounts.

FIRM NAME _____

I HEREBY CERTIFY,

That I hold valid seller's permit No. _____

issued pursuant to the Sales and Use Tax Law: that I am engaged in the business of selling

that the tangible personal property described herein which I shall purchase from:

will be resold by me in the form of tangible personal property; PROVIDED, however, that in the event any of such property is used for any purpose other than retention, demonstration, or display while holding it for sale in the regular course of business, it is understood that I am required by the Sales and Use Tax Law to report and pay the tax, measured by the purchase price of such property.

Description of property to be purchased: _____

_____

Dated: _____ 19 _____   Signature _____

at _____   By and Title _____

Phone _____   Address _____

Example of a California resale number request card

Sales taxes. Most states have a sales tax. If your state does, you will be required to collect it ONLY on those sales shipped to destinations within the state which are NOT for resale by another dealer. The sales tax is collected only once at the retail level from the ultimate purchaser. As a commercial firm, you must either collect the sales tax, show by the shipping address on the invoice that the goods are going out of state, or claim to be selling the books to another dealer, such as a bookstore, "for resale." Many states will require you to maintain a file of customer resale numbers. Some dealers will list their resale number on purchase orders, but usually you have to send a standard resale number request card, available from your stationer, with the invoice. Type "for resale" on the invoice and record the resale number there if you have it.

In some states, shipping supplies, such as cartons and tape, are not subject to the sales tax. Other states exempt certain non-profit or public institutions such as libraries and schools.

Before you go to press, obtain your resale permit. Then if you are printing locally, you won't have to pay sales taxes on your books when you pick them up from the printer. Find the office in the telephone directory. In California it is called the *State Board of Equalization*, in Massachusetts it is the *Sales and Use Tax Bureau* of the *Department of Corporations and Taxation*. Check the posted resale permit at a nearby store; the name of the controlling agency will be on it.

When you apply for your resale license or seller's permit, say you are just starting out as an author and hope to sell a few of your books. Tell them that most sales will be wholesale to bookstores or shipped out of state. This way you may be able to avoid giving them a deposit and you may be allowed to report annually instead of quarterly, thus saving both money and paperwork. For example, in California, if you say your taxable sales (retail and within the state) might amount to more than $300 per month, you must place at least $100 on deposit with the Board of Equalization before you start. If you say you might be collecting over $12.50 per month in sales taxes, they will want you to fill out the forms and remit the taxes quarterly instead of annually. When you apply, the tax office will supply you with an explanatory sheet detailing your responsibilities for the sales tax in your state.

The law you must know as an author/publisher concerns copyright, defamation (libel), right of privacy and illegal reproduction. Briefly, copyrights work both ways: They protect your work from others, and their work from you. Take pride, do your own original work and make it better. For a detailed explanation of the copyright, see Chapters Two and Five.

Defamation is libel in the printed word, and slander when spoken. *Black's Law Dictionary* defines defamation as: "The offense of injuring a person's character, fame or reputation by false and malicious statements." Libel may take the form of either words or pictures. The offense is in the "publication" of the matter so you are not "covered" just because you read it somewhere else first. You are safe if the statement is true; this is the perfect defense, but check the source. The best advice is never to say anything nasty about anyone. You will need all the support you can get to sell your book. If you disagree with another authority, leave his or her name out and write "some people will argue . . ." or "many authorities believe . . ." and then tear up their position with your view. If you don't like someone, the worst thing you can do to them is to leave them out of your book altogether. Cover yourself and stay out of court; the legal game is expensive.

Right of privacy is another area of law you may face. Unless part of a news event, a person has a right to keep his photo out of publications. Most people love to see their photo in a book and, in fact, they are prime customers for the finished product. But if you suspect there may be a problem, have them sign a written release.

Illegal reproduction covers the promoting of lotteries, financial schemes, fraudulent activities, printing of securities, stamps, etc. In other words, don't print money. If you are writing about these subjects, you probably already know about the problems, and the Postal and other laws relating to them. If not, seek legal advice.

Taxes are one place an author/publisher gets a big break. Not only are the costs of printing your book deductible, so are all the direct expenses incurred while writing and promoting it. If you are writing about your favorite hobby, you can deduct the expenses in pursuing it, too. For example, if you are writing on aviation, you can probably deduct flying lessons and trips to the national convention. There are sales and publicity tours, and you can even write off a portion of your home, its rent or mortgage, utilities, etc. Assuming you are already employed and Uncle Sam is withholding 30% or more from your weekly check, that amounts to thousands of dollars a year. The game is to see how much you can get back. How much did you pay to the IRS last year? Would you like to get a full refund? Getting money back is fun and rewarding. Of course, if your book is a great success, you will make more money and have to pay taxes on it. For complete details, get a copy of the *Small Business Tax Guide* from your nearest IRS office. Under "record keeping," below, we will list possible deductions.

We don't *charge* sales tax here, we just *collect* it.

Record keeping must be done from the beginning of your writing, because you cannot deduct what you do not have written down. Many small business people get themselves into a jam by coming up with a great business idea and then charging off pursuing it. At the end of the year they suddenly realize that they have forgotten to fill out forms or record expenses. At that point their only choice is to hire an accountant to straighten out the mess. Accountants charge much more for this sort of work, and they are rarely able to reconstruct the records completely or take all the deductions the business is entitled to take. The IRS is plugged into your bank, and when they notice that $25,000 went through your bank account when you reported only $15,000, they will be by with questions. And you can't avoid the bank, as you have to cash all those checks which come in the mail for your book.

Dun & Bradstreet claims that 80% of all business failures are due to poor records. A University of Pittsburgh survey found that 40% of the retailers surveyed did not keep proper records. It is silly—no, tragic—because record keeping is easy with a simple system. As the business grows, you will also need financial information on your past in order to project the future properly.

Start right now. Pick up a few sheets of ledger paper from your office supply store; get paper with at least 20 columns. Label the columns in the expense ledger as follows: meals, lodging, gas/lube/wash, office supplies, shipping & postage, advertising, entertainment, transporation fares, travel expenses, cost of supplies (book printing), dues & licenses, subscriptions, telephone, electricity, water, mortgage/rent, parking & tolls, car repairs, car tires & supplies, refunds and miscellaneous. The income ledger sheet will probably only reflect sales from your wholesale invoices and retail labels (see Chapter 10). For a detailed explanation of the items that fit into these columns, see the IRS publication *Small Business Tax Guide* mentioned above. The best way to get into the habit and to learn what is deductible is to list EVERY cent you spend the first year. Get receipts whenever possible, at the Post Office, for parking, tolls, meals, motels, etc. Your accountant will decide what is deductible when doing your taxes.

You can't deduct it if you don't record it.

You have already decided to carry pen and paper at all times to record your thoughts for your manuscript, so carry one more sheet for recording expenditures. Any money spent in the pursuit of income is deductible, so write down every cent. As you learn what is deductible, you will find that you become generous where an expenditure can be written off and stingy where it can't. This is good discipline and good business. Keep an envelope in the car. Each day as you get in and start the car, let the engine warm up a moment as you record the date, odometer reading and places you intend to go. Use the envelope to hold the receipts you acquire during the day. Start a new envelope every month.

At the end of each month, sit down at the ledger and post the expenses from your pocket notes, car envelope and check book. If you are not sure what column an expenditure might go in, place it in miscellaneous. At the end of the year, total up the columns and take the ledger and totaled figures to your accountant. The accountant will do the rest and the charge will be reasonable. You will be amazed at the size of your refund, and the accountant will compliment you on your work. Record keeping is so easy, and yet many people think there is some great mystery to accounting.

You don't even have to make money to claim deductions. You can claim a loss for at least three years in a row before the IRS deems you to be a hobbyist rather than an author/publisher. Some companies such as Chrysler lose money for years and still take deductions. Keep good records and you will be able to prove you are in business. See the tax discussion in *Writer's Market*.

Raising the money you need to pay for the production and promotion of your book will take you into the world of finance unless you have a lot of loose, ready cash lying about. Insufficient capitalization is one of the greatest problems facing most new businesses. Money won't come looking for you. You have to find it by selling yourself and your book. But the money is there, it is available.

"High cash flow" is taking in lots of money but being unable to find any of it.

According to the *Wall Street Journal*, most entrepreneurs spend their own money to start their business. Forty-eight percent rely on savings, 29% borrow from banks, 13% shake down their friends, 4% look for individual investors, less than 1% strike deals with venture capital firms or government agencies, and 5% are successful with other sources.

In the beginning, you won't run up bills by hiring help or renting space, and you will even save some leisure-time money by staying home to write. So you will not have any immediate needs for large sums of cash. Most people have more money than they need for necessities; they throw away their disposable income on frivolous purchases. Going without booze, cigarettes and nights out is not only healthier, but the time can be better spent writing your book.

Some people advise the use of "OPM" (other people's money) rather than your own. Then if your business goes bust and you lose all the borrowed funds, you still have your own money in reserve. But as you tuck your prized manuscript under your arm and venture off, you are going to find that locating OPM takes some searching.

—The Small Business Administration has prohibited financial assistance to book publishers ever since it came into being in 1953. The SBA treats the whole opinion-molding media this way. This is to avoid financing radicals who might print seditious literature and then file for bankruptcy. This would leave the taxpayers with a social problem and the bill for starting it.

—Banks don't search for loan applicants in the publishing industry. They like "going" firms with upbeat balance sheets; like everyone else, they are in business to stay in business. Banks look on manuscripts/books as "speculative." Even armed with a detailed market research report on your product, you may find that you can't even get an appointment with the loan officer. A stack of books is not considered good collateral to a bank; if you defaulted, they would not know how to turn the books back into money. If you ask for money to go into business, the bank won't be interested.

You know you have arrived when you do not have to check the balance before writing a check.

Basically, there are two ways to borrow money from a bank. The first is the "term" loan, which is normally used to finance purchases such as a car. Term loans are paid back monthly and are usually limited to 36 months. The second is an ordinary signature loan with interest at the prime rate plus about 5%. A signature loan runs for a period of months and you pay it off at the due date. But while the loan is written for a stated period, it is common to pay just the interest and renew it. Many authors have been successful in acquiring money by leaving the manuscript at home and asking for a "vacation" loan.

You may need collateral, perhaps a second mortgage. If you have enough real and personal property, you will be able to get the money on your signature alone. Don't think small; large amounts are often easier to borrow.

All banks are not the same; shop around not only for loans, but for checking account charges. Banks are not doing you any favors, you are doing them a favor by storing your money with them and paying interest to them. Stop in at several and pick up pamphlets on their checking account and loan policies. Take the brochures home and compare them. Do they charge for each check deposited? You will be receiving a lot of small checks and any check charge will add up fast. Do they pay interest on checking accounts and if so, what is the minimum required balance? Will they let you bank by mail and will they pay the postage? Don't just think of your present needs, think of the future.

Incidentally, you may be better off working your new publishing company part time initially. Then if it fails, at least you are not out of a job, too.

—Altering your W-4 Form is advocated by some people as a way to have the IRS lend your withholding taxes back to you. If you have a regular job and a lot of money is being withheld from each paycheck, you may claim an exemption from withholding by making out a new W-4 form for your employer, early in the year. If you are in the 30% tax bracket, this is like getting a 50% raise. Of course, you must be serious about starting your business, keep good records and take deductions. Done correctly, you should be able to spend and deduct the formerly withheld money and "zero-out" at tax time.

Once you are working for yourself full-time, you will file estimated tax forms rather than W-4's.

—**Pre-publication specials** are often used to raise money. As the book goes to press, send out a brochure to all who might be interested in the book, and offer to pay the postage for a pre-publication order. Emphasize that the manuscript is complete and that the book is on the press. Tell them you won't cash their check until the book is shipped. Mention a shipping date but give yourself an extra month or two. Make another special offer to dealers. Pre-publication sales sometimes bring in enough to pay the printing bill.

—**Selling stock** in your business is another way to raise money, but there are a lot of problems. You are not big enough to make it worth your while so you should give money-raising a great deal of thought before sharing the rewards of your work. If you can find someone who will risk an investment in your book, you can find one who will give you a straight loan at a good rate of interest where his risk is lower.

—**Grants** are available from many foundations for worthwhile publishing projects. The Glide Foundation tells you all about them in *The Bread Game* (now out of print). Check your state arts agency, the National Endowment for the Arts, 1100 Pennsylvania Avenue NW, Washington, DC 20506 (Government), Alicia Patterson Foundation (private), and see the listings in *Grants and Awards Available to Writers*. Additional listings may be found in *Literary Market Place*, UNESCO'S handbook *Study Abroad*, as well as in magazines such as *CODA: Poets and Writers Newsletter* and *The Writer*. The Dramatists Guild and the Theatre Communications Group also publish useful periodicals. See listings in the Appendix and ask your librarian. Most of the grants and fellowships are for fiction and poetry. If your book qualifies, it can mean a large amount of money. But there is a lot of paperwork to go along with it.

—**Writers' colonies** often supply free room and board to support budding authors. Some have rigid rules limiting the length and number of stays. For a list, see *Writer's Market*.

> *You're the living, breathing, embodiment of the American Dream—free enterprise division.*

—**Your printer** may be interested in helping you in exchange for an interest in the book. Occasionally local printers take a personal interest in books, but do not expect a large national book printer to be interested. Typically, the printing company would absorb the printing costs and would receive 10-15% of the sales in return.

—**Parents** will often lend on a book. They often have faith in their offspring and want to see your name on a book as much as you do. But if you do borrow from friends or relatives, make the same presentation to them that you would to a bank. Talk figures and do not get emotional. Then write a loan contract and pay them the 10 to 15% interest that you would pay the bank. Put the loan on a business basis and keep the friendship.

—**Other possibilities** include credit unions, retirement plans, the Veterans Administration (if appropriate) and the Farm Home Loan Association, which is said to be very liberal in its definition of a "farm community." Send $23.50 for *Money Sources for Small Business* by William M. Alarid, Puma Publishing Co., 1670 Coral Drive, Santa Maria, CA 93454. Shop around. All these suggestions for borrowing money assume you have a good saleable product to begin with.

How much you will need is an important question, and this will take some research. Money will not be coming in right away. There is a lot of lead time for writing, printing and promotion, and the bookstores are notorious for being slow pay.

At 1989 prices, it might cost you $12,000 to launch a nice book. This would be 5,000 copies of a 5.5 x 8.5 softcover with 180 pages, some photographs and a four-color cover. Initially you might spend $2,000 for research trips, photographic work and office supplies. The typesetting and printing might cost $8,000 and then the shipping supplies and early promotion may run another $2,000. A book with fewer photos, fewer pages and a one-color cover could run much less, but without a good-looking book and some promotion money, the book will not sell. For details, see the chapters on pricing and promotion.

> *If you want your book to sell like a book, you'll have to make it look like a book.*

On the first venture, the printer will probably want his money in installments: 1/3 to start, 1/3 when the plates are made and 1/3 on the completion of the printing. After a book or two, he will no doubt give you normal 30 day terms, and want his money a month after he delivers the books to you. If he wants installments, agree to them and then request a "2% discount for cash." (2% of $8,000 is $160.)

In fact, you should always take cash discounts when paying bills, even if you have to borrow (at a lower rate) to do so. Invoices with terms marked "2% ten" mean you can knock off 2% if you pay on the 10th instead of the 30th day. This is the equivalent of 36% interest per year. If you pay money before it is due, you are financing someone else's business without receiving interest; unless they offer ten day terms, pay on the 30th day.

Realistically, not wishfully, project your other expenses. Then work up a projected income chart. How much money do you expect to come in, from where and how fast? Now you know what you will need.

If you wait until you need the money to approach the source, you have waited too long. If you can find the money at all at this point, it is likely to be more expensive. Line up your sources of credit now, but don't borrow the money until you need it. Borrow the funds for one, two or three years, whatever you project the needs to be, and make sure you will not be penalized for paying the loan back early.

Lean and mean. Run a streamlined, efficient operation. Do everything yourself and buy only those services you cannot perform. Avoid employees, they cost you time (management), money and paperwork. Print in small quantities to keep the inventory low. Once you have learned the business by doing every part of it yourself, farm out the repetitive and least enjoyable tasks. When contracting for services, remember that everyone is in business for himself first; you come second. The graphic artist, accountant and all the rest will try to sell you more than you need. They don't care about your business as much as you do because they have less to lose. Be careful taking advice from someone who is trying to sell you something.

Keep on top of costs. If you can save $1,000 per year by streamlining procedures and your net profit is normally 3%, the effect is the same as if you increased sales by $30,000.

Don't waste anything. Save the stamps from the incoming mail. Stamp collecting is big business and you may be able to sell them to stamp companies. Check the *Yellow Pages* and call several local stamp dealers for prices.

Machinery. As your publishing company grows, look for labor-saving machinery to multiply your efforts. Personal computers, photocopy machines, cordless telephones and postage meters will save you time. They are much better buys than an employee, and you will find that with depreciation, machines are not very expensive. As machinery accumulates, you will begin to understand the advantages of owning your own business.

The author has operated, and worked for, large firms but he opted to go it alone in 1969. It was 1983 before he decided to take on his first employee. In terms of both dollar volume and books sold, he was probably the world's largest one-person publishing company. Now Para Publishing is larger, but Dan has help.

Because he had committed himself to the luxury of a one-person enterprise, he had to operate efficiently. He concentrated on those areas which provided a maximum return on his investment of time and money: the highest profit and best results for the time and energy expended (invested).

Dan knows small business and small publishing inside-out because he plays both roles: He sets policy as management and implements it as labor. Consequently, he has developed simple systems to handle every task.

Dan is a small businessman. His background is in marketing and mail order. He did not come from the publishing industry and, consequently, he doesn't make their mistakes.

We think that small presses and self-publishing individuals frequently precede the market because they can more easily become involved in a new trend at the conceptual level and can bypass a lot of the red tape that slows things down in larger houses. - Bob Speer of Southwest Book Services

Manuscript to printer

Type set (composition)

You may proofread here but it is a waste of your time

Paste-up boards (layout)

Proofread

Corrections

Proofread again if there were a lot of corrections

Photograph boards

Strip negatives into masking sheet or "flats"

Burn blueline print and fold into signature

Final proofing: check page sequence, etc.

Burn plate

On press

Folding into signatures

Collating (gathering) signatures

Binding; installing cover

Trimming

Boxing

You are published

Chapter Four

Printing Your Book

—The Printing Process
—Design of Books
—Book Materials

Here is what you can expect when your book enters the production stage. This explanation of the printing process is meant to be brief, and yet provide you with enough information to deal effectively with your printer. There are many excellent books on the printing trade. Also see our Special Reports *Book Production* (on pre-press: composition, layout, editing and design) and *Buying Book Printing*. See the Appendix.

Information packaging. OK, you have the information and have written the manuscript. Now the project is to decide how to package the information to make it saleable. Some packages will bring in more money than others. You might print your information in a series of magazine articles, put it on cassette tapes, present it at a seminar or print it in a book.

Or you might concentrate on one of them, such as the book, and spin off parts to other formats. People are paying good money for well-packaged information today. Some manuals cost $75.00 and seminars may run $600.00 per day. Obviously, the "package" must appear to be worth the asking price. It must be a professionally run seminar, a nicely printed book or an attractive article in a prestigious magazine.

Printing processes. Almost all books are printed with the photo offset process today. Your original copy will be *typeset* with a computer-driven laser printer or a computerized photo composition machine. Your pasted-up "boards" will be photographed and the negatives will be stripped into a "flat." Then a bright light will be used to burn the thin printing plate through the flat. You may hear of other printing processes such as letterpress, which is old, and gravure, which is used for larger runs, but you will not use them.

A stripped-in flat

Conversely, there are also some less expensive, short-run methods. Wire stitched (stapled) booklets with up to about 60-5.5 x 8.5 pages can be reproduced very nicely on photocopy machines from typewritten material. Machines such as the

Xerox 8200 and 9500 will print both sides of the paper and collate them. They will even handle heavy cover stock. Short-run booklets may also be inexpensively produced by your local "instant print" shop.

Ask them for a brochure. To learn more about producing small runs of booklets with your instant printer, read *Publishing Short-Run Books* by the author. See the Appendix.

This book will concern itself with squarebacked softcover and hardcover books, those you normally see in a bookstore. If you have a book-length manuscript, one which will fill a book of 100 pages or more, you will want a clean, sharp, professional-appearing product, one that will sell. You want a book you can be proud of, and you want it to be acceptable to the stores.

Time. You can figure on four to five weeks to print, bind and deliver your books to you, but the work may take longer if your printer can't do all the work in-house and has to farm some of it out. Hardbound books will take a couple of weeks more because they take longer to bind.

The composition and layout should take less than a week if you do it yourself on a laser printer, and about five weeks if you give the work to a typesetter.

Book design. Go to a bookstore and a library to search for a book you can use as a model. Look for books in your subject area. Find one you like and buy or borrow it. If you can't find a book in your subject area that you like for looks and feel, try other subject areas that would appeal to your intended audience. If your intended audience is used to hardcover books, select hardcover. If they need a larger format book, select 8.5 x 11. If this is a reference book, select Smyth sewn pages. If the audience is conservative, you will tone down the back cover hype. Consider paper, binding, layout, everything.

Book printers will produce an acceptable book but that book will be boring unless you provide some direction. What usually happens is that the author-publisher spends a great deal of time on the text and the manufacturing becomes an afterthought. The package design is left up to the printer. What we see today are 5.5 x 8.5 softcover books that look the same. Printers can supply fold-out pages, gold foil on the cover, die-cut jackets, embossed covers and many other things. All you have to do is ask. So find a book you like and use it as a model. Do not just leave book design to the printer.

Note that chapters start on a right-hand page. If this leaves you with a blank on the left, fill the space with a photograph. Never leave a blank page, fill it with something even if it is just a page number. Books with blank pages sometimes are returned by buyers who think there is a manufacturing defect. Just supply the typesetter with a few extra photos and provide instructions to fill any blank pages with them.

Type may be set to *run-around* illustrations, but it is simpler and cheaper to make a break in the text and insert the photo or drawing full-width, from margin to margin. The width of the text in this book is 4.125 inches and most illustrations run margin to margin.

If all publishers thought alike, all books might look alike. Sometimes there is a good marketing reason to venture from the standard. This book is die-cut, nestled into a disc and shrink-wrapped.

Running heads are lines of type which appear across the top of the book page. Usually the title of the book appears on the left-hand page while the chapter title is on the right.

The "folio" is the page number. Folios may be placed in the top outside corner, bottom middle or even on the side. Usually, the folio is part of the running head. Traditionally, pages received Roman numerals in the front matter and Arabic numbers in the text. This was because the text was set separately and then the front matter was expanded or contracted to use up most of the pages in the signatures. But today, many publishers take a tip from the magazine companies and start the count, though not the numbering, from the title page. This makes the final page count higher and makes the purchaser feel he is getting more for his money. The argument goes: "I paid (the printer) for those pages, so I'm going to count them." See this book, for example.

Standardize and save money. If you vary from the norm, the creativity will cost you sales. Occasionally variations can be justified, as in a die-cut circular book on Frisbee play, but make sure the special work will contribute to the sales of the book. Remember, too, that libraries and bookstores have standardized shelving. You want your book to fit. Most short-run books are 5.5 x 8.5, perfect bound (glued) paperbacks with or without photos and drawings on a 50 or 60-pound paper stock. The cover is two or more colors on a 10 point C1S (coated one side) cover stock. Beyond this basic specification, a number of variations are possible.

Measurements. The conventional 5.5 x 8.5 size is suitable for both hardcover and soft; it is one of the most economical, fits a library shelf well and is by far the most popular. One hundred and twenty 5.5 x 8.5 pages make a much nicer book than sixty-8.5 x 11 pages. The only good reason to go oversize is if you have too much material. If you have large illustrations, such as charts, consider foldout pages. The printer can insert them between signatures; specify where you want the foldouts. If you have a lot of material, (over 500 pages, for example) in the 5.5 x 8.5 measurement, select the 8.5 x 11 size.

Whatever size you select, make all your books measure the same in order to standardize your shipping bags and cartons. If some books are 5.5 x 8.5 while others are 8.5 x 11, they will still stack well together. If some are 6 x 9, you will have packaging problems.

Number of pages. You need eight pages to qualify for the Post Office's "book rate," 50 to get a Library of Congress Catalog Card Number, 50 for a listing in Bowker's *Books in Print*, and 100 pages to qualify for a listing in H.W. Wilson's *Cumulative Book Index*. Over 100 is psychologically good, and will help to justify your price. So if you have just 90 pages, set the book in larger type, put more *leading* (space) between the lines, expand the Appendix or add some illustrations.

Your book will be printed on several very large sheets of paper which will be folded down into "signatures" (originally, the person who sewed the pages together *signed* his work). The number of book pages which will be in each signature will depend on the size of your printer's press, but 16 is common. This means that eight of the pages will be printed on one side of the sheet ("eight up") and eight will be printed on the other. Therefore, you will figure the pages in your book in multiples of 16.

If your type is not set yet, roughly estimate your pages from your computer printout or figure the number from the word processor's character count. Many authors like to write their books in a 5.5 x 8.5 printout so their manuscript looks closer to the finished page. Their text block measurements are 4.125 x 7.125. Naturally, you will have to adjust your figures to compensate for the different type styles between your computer type and the type the book will be set in, if different.

Often we want to have a page count before the boards are pasted up so that we can quote the number in our advertising. In your brochures, refer to the page count as: "More than 150 pages"; you don't have to be exact but people do like to know what they are paying for.

Poetry gets different treatment. Unless very short, each poem should have its own page.

Optima MEDIUM

Optima BOLD

Palatino SEMI BOLD

Plantin BOLD

Plantin BOLD CONDENSED

Salisbury BOLD

Serifa

Helvetica MEDIUM

Helvetica MEDIUM ITALIC

Helvetica BOLD CONDENSED

Helvetica BOLD

Helvetica BOLD ITALIC

Helvetica EXTRA BOLD

Helvetica OUTLINE

TYPE FACES are many and varied; no typesetter could stock all the styles and sizes. With the help of your typesetter, you will select the type size and style, the width of the columns (4¼" in a 5½ x 8½ book) and whether you want the right-hand side justified (even or ragged right margin). Books set with a ragged right don't look professional and find it difficult to gain acceptance in bookstores and libraries. Four type factors affect legibility: type style (sans serif, italics, etc. are harder to read), type **size, leading (rhymes with "heading" and is the space between the lines) and the column width (the eye was trained on narrow newspaper columns). To give your book some variation, you may use italics, boldface, small caps and larger sizes for chapter heads, captions, subheads and for lending emphasis.**

8/9
Helvetica
Light

10/11
Helvetica Bold
Condensed

Here are some more type terms to make you sound as though you know what you are talking about. "Point size" is the height of a capital letter (and its mount) as in "10 pt. type." There are 72 points to the inch. "Pica" is the printer's standard measurement for the length of a line and the depth of a page. There are 12 points to a pica and six picas to the inch. Therefore, "24 picas" means a four inch wide column. "Leading" or slug is the space between the lines. Printers used to use a strip of lead, hence the name. So, if you have nine points of type plus two points of leading, it would be written out as "9/11".

10/12
Bookman Light
Italic

9/10
Garamond
Book

Nine on eleven is about as small as you should go for a legible book. Ten on twelve is very common though children and older people with failing eyesight prefer a 12/14. What you will decide to use will depend to a great degree on the length of the finished book. Look through books you like and ask your typesetter for type samples.

10/11
Times Roman

Some composing machines put more type on a page than others using identical type face, size and leading. "11/13 Century x 24 picas" is not always the same; it all depends on how the machine was originally programmed. You will want a sample of your typesetter's work in order to estimate pages.

11/12
Chelmsford

Do not venture too far from the common typestyles such as Times Roman, Palatino, Baskerville, Caledonia, Bookman and Granjon.

8/10
Souvenir

Compare the various type faces

6 Helvetica
7 Helvetica
8 Helvetica
8½ Helvetica
9 Helvetica
10 Helvetica
11 Helvetica
12 Helvetica
13 Helvetica
14 Helvetica
15 Helvetica
16 Helvetica
17 Helvetica

18 Helvetica
19 Helvetica
20 Helvetica
21 Helvetica
22 Helvetica
23 Helvetica
24 Helvetica

**Character heights are measured in "points."
There are 72 points to the inch.**

"Leading" is the space between the lines of type

Headlines, such as chapter titles, which are larger than 12 pt. used to be set on a headliner machine, or with transfer type. Today, most computers with laser printers will print up to 24 point, which is large enough. Many print to 254 point, which is more than you need. While text type is usually set in a serif typeface such as Times-Roman, headlines are often set in a sans serif typeface such as Helvetica.

Illustrations will augment the text, enhance the appearance and aid the saleability of the book. Don't be cheap with illustrations. Each one is very inexpensive when the cost is spread out over the entire print run of books. If a photo or drawing will make the book more attractive, readable or useful to the buyer, include it.

Line drawing

Extra lines were crowded into this line drawing to give it the appearance of shading

**Photo printed
unscreened**

**Same photo
screened.
Study with a
magnifying
glass or loupe.**

　　Line art may consist of type, charts, sketches, etc. Draw-ings may be created on your computer or drawn separately and pasted in. If you draw your own artwork or have it done, use a fine-point felt tip pen with black ink. Reductions and enlarge-ments may be made on a photocopy machine.

　　"Clip art" is sold by the book or sheet and consists of line drawings on almost every possible subject. Clip art often lacks originality but it is less expensive than hiring an artist. Your printer or typesetter may have a good collection.

Art may be taken from old magazines and books, too. If the copyright has expired, the art is in the public domain. Prior to January 1, 1978, copyright protection was for 28 years. The new law makes the copyright renewable for an additional 28 years. Therefore, anything printed prior to 1937 is safe and anything in print before 1965 is probably safe.

Halftones must be made of any artwork, such as photographs, which is not solid black-white. The original photo is re-photographed through a screen and the resulting print is composed of dots of various sizes. The eye blends the dots together into a continuous tone. Making a halftone of a photo, pencil drawing, water color, etc., costs $5 to $10 each. This is a one-time charge if you save the negatives; you won't have to pay again to screen photos for the next press run.

Screens come in several values and are measured in dots per linear inch. The more dots, the crisper the printed halftone. Newspapers commonly use a 65- or 85-line screen (85 dots per inch) while books are commonly done in 120, 133 or even 150 line. Black and white photographs screen best. Color prints reproduced in black and white tend to get muddy.

Photos taken from other magazines and books have already been screened and may be pasted right onto the boards. However, if they are to be enlarged or reduced, they must be re-screened and this usually reduces the quality.

With both photos and drawings, reductions are preferable to enlargements. Reductions become sharper while enlargements only magnify flaws, losing clarity.

Photos will be added to the "boards" by the printer. Simply size them with a proportion wheel and leave space for them in the typeset text. Paste each photograph to a larger sheet of paper and list its page number. The first photograph on page 17 will be "17-A," for example. Use a red pen to write "17-A" on the blank space on the board.

Four color printing should be used on covers but it is normally too expensive for inside pages. To reproduce a color photo or slide, it is re-photographed (or laser scanned) four times, each time with a different colored filter over the lens. This produces four negatives consisting of the three primary colors (red, blue and yellow) plus black. The result is called a "four color separation." Then the paper is run through the press four times, each time with one of the colors, and the color photo is re-created. Naturally, four color printing is more expensive because of the additional camera work and press time. Always ask for a "color key" before your color pages are run through the press. When checking these four plastic color overlays, remember simply that the sky is blue, the grass is green, clouds are white, wood is brown, etc. What you see is what you get.

Paper is even more confusing than type faces, and while you should know what to look for, you will need the guidance of your printer to make a final choice. Most book printers stock a few basic types of book paper which they buy in huge quantities. They can get most any paper but other types will be more expensive because it must be special ordered in a smaller lot. Basically, you have four general paper choices:

1. Newsprint: Inexpensive but it looks cheap, it yellows quickly and the photo reproduction is poor.

2. Uncoated book stock: Looks good, photos OK. Most common.

3. Coated book stock (matte, coated or gloss): looks great, photos great, more expensive.

4. Fancy textured papers: May be hard to print, especially photos. Expensive.

Unless you are doing an art book, an uncoated book stock is what you need. Your printer will probably suggest a 50-pound or 60-pound "white offset book."

DELTA LITHOGRAPH COMPANY

TEXT PAPER COMPARATIVE COST FINDER

Many of our customers are interested in cost comparisons of the various weights and shades of text papers. The reasons for this are varied: weight savings, bulking, shade preferences and others. The cost trade-offs involved are often significant in reaching a decision. This Text Paper Comparative Cost Finder will help in these decisions.

The use of this chart is very easy. Using 50# Delta White offset book rolled stock as the base, or 100%, compare the other shades and stocking to calculate the comparative prices.

For example, if you have an estimate based on 10,000 copies of a book printed on 60# White sheets and want to calculate the approximate savings if printed on 50# White rolls, compare the 50# rolls listed below to the 60# sheets, or 100 vs. 130. Paper savings on the job would be 30%.

Text paper costs run between 28% and 50% of the total printing costs, depending on total pages in the book and the quantity of books produced. Therefore, in the example given, the overall cost savings would probably be about 15% (50% of 30%).

These figures cannot be used to calculate exact figures. They are only intended to give you a guide in figuring the comparative costs and specifications for your book.

STOCK	AVAILABLE IN	COMPARABLE PERCENT
50# Delta	Rolls	100
50# Delta	Sheets	112
60# Delta	Rolls	115
60# Delta	Sheets	130
45# Delta	Rolls	92
45# Delta	Sheets	105
70# Delta	Sheets	185
30# Omega Book	Rolls	78
35# Alpha Workbook	Rolls	65
50# Theta Natural Text	Rolls	115
50# Theta Natural Text	Sheets	130
50# Litecoat Beta Book	Rolls	110
60# Pica Matte	Sheets	215
60# Kappa Coated Book	Sheets	195

Paper comparison chart

Paper comes by the sheet or the roll (cut into sheets after printing). There are many criteria which must be considered when selecting paper.

1. Weight is expressed in pounds per 500 sheets but the measurements of the sheet vary according to the category to which the paper belongs. Sixty pound cover stock and 60-pound book papers are not the same. For example: 16 lb. bond = 40 lb. book; 20 lb. bond = 50 lb. book; 24 lb. bond = 60 lb. book and 28 lb. bond = 70 lb. book. Cover stock is rated in point sizes with 10 point (10/1000 of an inch thick) being very common.

Most books are printed on 50, 55 or 60 lb. stock. Generally, heavier paper is more expensive, though some of the newer lightweight papers, developed for combating Postal rates, are even higher in price. If the paper is too thin, the book will look and feel "cheap," if it is too heavy, the book may not fold flat. And, in either case, you have wasted your money.

In the metric system the weighing system is easier; all paper is simply weighed in grams per square meter of paper. There are no classifications.

2. Texture. Some highly textured paper does not accept ink well, especially halftones. Use a smooth paper such as "50 lb. white offset book."

3. Opacity. You don't want the type on the other side of the page to show through. Light-weight paper can be very opaque, especially when coated. Opacity may be tested by placing a printed sheet under the sample sheet to see how much type shows through.

4. Bulking factor is expressed in pages per inch (ppi). A 45 lb. paper may have a bulking factor of 640 pages per inch, while a 55 lb. stock might be 370 ppi. Heavier weight does not always mean thicker paper. Bulking depends on the fiber content of the paper and the milling process used; a high bulk may also be produced by whipping air into the paper during manufacture. Whipping produces a thicker paper without increasing weight. However, this fluffed-up paper allows ink to diffuse more, so halftones are not as crisp. PPI is measured by the even-inch. Once you know

the bulking factor of the paper you plan to use, you can calculate the width of the spine.

5. Grain in paper is similar to the grain in wood—it has a direction. Grain affects the way the text and cover lie. If the grain of the text is not parallel to the spine, the book will want to snap shut. Grain is also important if you plan to fold the paper, since it may fold better in one direction than another.

If the cover grain is perpendicular to the spine, the cover will tend to curl or pop open. Sometimes the cover will even crack on the folds. The problem is that some automated book machinery trims the books cleaner when the grain is perpendicular to the spine than when it is parallel. When the grain is parallel, the trimmer may make small tears in the cover stock where it curves around the spine of the book. With such machinery, the choice is between cover curl and cover tear.

6. Grade refers to the type of paper, be it writing grade, book, cover stock, envelope, gummed, blotting, chipboard, etc.

7. Coating is done with a clay-like material and produces a smooth, shiny finish. Since the ink dries on the surface of coated stock, rather than down in the fibers of the paper, the printed pages looks crisper and cleaner. Coated stock, while more expensive, makes halftones look much better. It is essential for art books. Smooth finishes may also be produced by drawing the paper over a blade edge, or through calendering (a heat and pressure roller process). The result may be a duller finish which is easier on the eyes.

8. Acid-free paper lasts longer and should be used for books of long-term interest. Some printed products, such as newspapers and magazines, are made to be read and discarded. There is no need to save them. Sixty percent of the university presses (which sell primarily to libraries) and 21% of other publishers produce their hardcover books on acid-free paper. You may wish to specify acid-free paper.

If you attend one of the many publishing seminars, you will probably be advised to purchase your own paper and "save about 15%." This makes about as much sense as taking your own oil to the gas station when you want it changed. The printer won't be happy about losing his markup and will probably charge you a "handling fee." Or he may raise your price later, claiming the job was "hard to print." If you buy your own paper, you will have to pay for it sooner, will be faced with storage and transportation problems and might lose it all if the printer botches a press run. It is far safer to obtain several quotes on the finished product and let the printer worry about the materials. After all, what you want is the least hassle and best price. Incidentally, printers and paper salespeople continually use the same pressure tactic, claiming there will be a paper shortage soon. Expect it. For more information on paper, see the *Pocket Pal*, listed in the Appendix.

Ink comes in a lot of colors and types, too, but both you and your printer will probably want black. If you are doing something special, ask to see his ink color sample books and run some tests. Remember that inks are transparent. If you print a drawing in blue and then overprint part in red, that part will become purple. Similarly, if you print blue ink on yellow paper, the print will be green. Unless you are doing a special art-type book, you will stick to the traditional black ink on white paper.

Hardcover or softcover. Traditionally, publishers printed in hardcover at a high price and would wait until sales dropped to come out with a cheaper softcover version. They might also publish a "library edition" with a supposedly reinforced hard cover, maybe an extra fancy "deluxe edition" on special paper, with gold stamped leather covers and even numbered and autographed. Then there might be a "large type" edition for both the elderly and visually impaired and, finally, an inexpensive "mass market paperback" edition. But what has emerged more recently is the very popular "oversize paperback," also known as the quality, trade, large format, large size, special or higher-priced paperbacks. These softcover books fill the gap between the mass market pocket-sized book and the hardcover version. Today, more and more books are being published in a softcover edition *only*. This is not because paper covered books are cheaper to manufacture, but because softcovers make more sense. Softcover books are printed on the same quality paper as the hardcover version. The differences are that the softcover edition is not normally sewn, has a thinner cover and usually does not have a jacket. So now your choice of covers is narrowed to the hardcover and the softcover.

Hardcover books are more expensive to produce and must carry a higher cover (list) price, and libraries used to prefer them. Today, however, libraries know how many times books can be lent out (about 18 for softcover) before they fall apart. If the price difference between the two is too great, it becomes less expensive to purchase copies of the softcover edition and replace them more often. The library may send softcover books out to be "Permabound" with laminated hard covers. It costs about $3.00 to extend the book's life in this manner. Hardcover bindings are often used for reference works and it is estimated that about 20% are purchased for gifts. Hardcovers do make a nicer presentation than a softcover edition.

By far, most of your sales will be the softcover, but you might produce some books in hardcover, not only for the libraries, but for those special presentation copies you will want for yourself. However, the problem with two editions is this: You want to make sure that they sell at the same rate so that you won't have a lot of one left over when you run out of the other and are printing a revision. If you publish both editions at the same time, you can expect to sell 10% to 20% in hardcover to 80% to 90% softcover for most books. On a 5,000 book press run, some publishers consider printing 4,000 in paper, 200 in hardcover and holding the texts of the remaining 800 to be covered later. But you must tell your printer to do this before the folding operation and you must print enough extra covers. Similarly, you must tell the cover designer you intend to use the same photo on both covers, so he will have the color separation made just slightly oversize. This allows for wrap-around on the hardcover while a small amount is trimmed off on the paperback.

The question is, just how long do you want a book to last? What good is a computer book that is five years old, even if its condition is perfect? The package lasts, but the content is out of date. Better the library or retail purchaser pays a lower price for a softcover edition and replaces it in a year or two with a revised edition or another title. Some reference books, such as dictionaries, should be published with more durable hard covers, but even annual references, such as the telephone directory, stand up very well in softcover. Another argument for the softcover book is that their covers last longer than the jacket on a hardcover book.

The major problem is that some reviewers still do not take softcover books seriously; they do not consider a title to be a real book unless it is published in hardcover.

More and more softcover books are showing up as school texts today. Paper editions are lighter in weight and take up less space, making them easier to carry and cheaper to mail. Their lower manufacturing costs result in wider distribution, thus bringing the author greater recognition. The cover of softcover books must be sealed. Traditionally, this was done with varnish. The cover made another pass through the press filled with varnish instead of ink. Today, ultraviolet-set plastics and plastic laminates are more popular. The extra treatment on the cover protects it against scuffing during shipment and provides a shiny or wet look. The additional cost is easily justified, as fewer books are returned damaged.

Workbooks and lab manuals must be durable enough to resist the flexing produced by constant use. Good results have been attained with Smyth sewing and perfect binding. The cover material may be 12 pt. C1S (coated one side) with a plastic laminate or a latex impregnated thick paper such as Lexotone or Kivar.

The cover of your book has two purposes: to protect the contents and to be a selling tool. According to *The Wall Street Journal*, the average book store browser who picks up a book spends eight seconds reading the front cover and 15 seconds reading the back. And this assumes the spine stood out enough to catch his attention, enticing him to pick up the book in the first place. Every word on the outside of your book must be used to sell what is inside. In mass market (small size, high volume) paperbacks, this "hype" consists of about 12 words on the front cover and 75 on the back. The blurbs use words like "stunning," "dazzling," "moving" and "tumultuous."

You can't tell—but you can sell—a book by its cover. - The Wall Street Journal

Alan Gadney commissioned covers for three computer books he planned to write. He had the covers printed in four colors and made into dummy books for display at the ABA Book Fair in Dallas in 1983. His books were the talk of the show and he took a number of large orders. Covers must be important, as he had not yet written one word on the subject.

The cover should include the title, subtitle (helps to identify the subject), the name of the author and a related photograph or drawing with impact. The print shouldn't be so fancy that it is hard to read at a glance. It is said that red attracts and sells best and many cover designers like to use it. Visit a bookstore and check the section where your book will rest. Consider what colors are there and pick something contrasting and bright that will stick out. Color sells, and the money should be spent to send the cover through the press four times. At the very minimum, two strongly-contrasting colors should be used. It depends upon your subject. For an action sport, an eye-catching color photo will sell more books than straight lines of type. The colors must contrast with each other. You will take black/white photographs of the cover for distribution with review copies. Darker colors may run together and look muddy when photographed in black and white.

Your cover must be bold, distinctive and intriguing to catch the eye and sell; it must stand out from the thousands of books around it. Important new information, such as a quote from a prestigious book review, may be printed on a sticker. Make the sticker a contrasting color and apply it at an angle so it doesn't look printed on.

The spine usually has the title, the name of the author and an eye-catching symbol. If it is a dog book, include the outline of a dog. The symbol may attract the buyer more easily than the printed word. If there is room, you may include the subtitle, but make sure the title is big enough to be legible. Traditionally, the name of the publisher was included on the spine, but in this case, you are the publisher and no one has heard of your company yet. Besides, people buy books by content or author, not by publisher. Some publishers also include the International Standard Book Number (ISBN) here. But beware of too much clutter. Your book will probably end up in the bookstore with only the spine showing from the shelf. Make the spine an eye-grabber.

The back cover layout was covered in Chapter Two. Many back covers have a photo and biographical sketch of the author. If you are a well-known celebrity, put your photograph there; but if you are not immediately recognizable, do not waste valuable selling space on an ego trip. Sometimes the back cover is used to promote other books by the author, but this valuable space shouldn't be wasted in this manner either; mention your other titles inside. Use whatever will sell the book. Make every word count on the front cover, spine and back cover.

Different markets are used to looking for different things on book covers. Target your primary audience and then try to cater to as many other markets as possible.

Mass market (smaller) paperbacks use a lot of color and "hype" because they have to compete with magazines for attention in supermarkets. It is assumed by some that these books are aimed at the less sophisticated people who don't frequent bookstores.

Mail-order books don't have to be flashy, but their type must be large and clear to show up well in photographs in brochures and ads. The back covers don't show in the ads so they are sometimes used to sell other books.

Trade books aimed at bookstores need a poster-like cover to aid in their sale. The back should also have a sales message, as it is the next place a potential customer will look after the cover.

Textbook covers must be much more conservative or they will "turn off" the educators who make the purchasing decisions. Don't make wild claims.

Don't be confined by convention. The unorthodox cover may catch the eye better. Unless the cover is offensive, it will be the first step in selling the book. But look over other books you admire. Most follow the same pattern in layout. There must be a reason, and you can bet it isn't lack of Madison Avenue imagination.

If the cover is not doing its job, consider changing it when you go back to press for a second printing. Once the book is in print the first time, you will come up with a number of ideas for changes.

Ask your printer to send you the overruns on the covers. You might even ask to have a few hundred extra printed. He will take these covers off the line before they are scored, folded and installed on the texts. These covers are beautiful and look very nice framed. You will be proud to hang one on your wall, and you might like to send a flat cover to those who provided you with a lot of help, such as the cover designer. Commissioned representatives carry covers to the bookstores rather than heavy books, so your distributor may need 20 to 30 covers. Many publishers use covers to make PR folders; they put all their sales information inside.

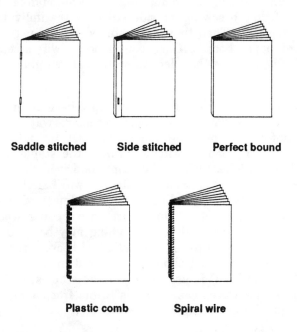

Saddle stitched   Side stitched   Perfect bound

Plastic comb   Spiral wire

Binding is your book packaging, the final touch. Consider your market (to whom will you sell it?) and the expected usage (will it be read once or used as a manual?). Because of the great expense of traditional hard binding, there may well be a cross between the hardcover and the paperback one day. In Japan, it is common to place a dust jacket on softcover books already. Give your buyers what they expect. If this is a higher-priced law book, select hardcover, but most nonfiction will be perfectly acceptable in softcover. The choices of bindings are many and here are the most common types:

—*Perfect binding* is the standard glued-on cover you see on most paperbacks. The pages are folded into signatures, often of 16 pages each, stacked, roughened on the edge and then the cover is wrapped around and glued on. The greatest advantage, besides lower cost, is that perfect binding presents a squared-off spine on which the title and name of the author may be printed. A text of more than 50 pages is required for a square spine, and you might have to use a high-bulk paper in a short book to achieve a sufficient thickness.

—*Cloth binding* (case binding or hard binding) usually consists of Smyth sewing, or side stitching the individual signatures together. Then they are installed (and glued) between two hard paper boards. Case bound books will accept a lot more flexing because they depend on thread, not glue, to retain the pages.

—*Wire stitches* are staples and may be used in binding paperback books. This is the least expensive way, and many highly automated printing plants are set up for it. Wire stitches may be "saddle stitched" where the staple is on the fold or "side stitched" where the staple is driven through from the front to back cover. Saddle stitching will handle 80 pages (20 sheets) or less, depending on the thickness of the stock, because of the amount of paper "lost" in wrapping around the spine. On the other hand, side stitching may be used to bind even several hundred pages. Side stitched books won't open to lay flat, so this method shouldn't be used in manuals. Some times "Holland tape" is used to cover the staples, making the book more attractive. The "stitches" come from a roll of wire and are adjustable in length.

—*Spiral wire* binding will allow books, such as automotive manuals and cookbooks, to open and lay flat, but spiral looks cheap. Spiral-bound books do not sell well in bookstores because the title doesn't show, and libraries don't care for them. It is possible to spiral bind pages *inside* a heavy cover stock. Some computer manuals are bound this way. But spiral still costs more.

—*Plastic comb* binding allows the book to open and lay flat and is often used for mail order books directed at professionals, short-run academic texts and industry manuals. This system may be used on books up to 1.5 inches thick. Comb binding is relatively expensive but looks cheap, the pages tear out and comb bound books don't stack well, making shipping a chore.

—*Velo-Bind* is similar to side wire stitches but uses melted plastic rivets. This method is very strong and may be used to install either special Velo-Bind hardcovers or soft document covers.

—*Cheshire* has an interesting hot melt hard and softcover binding machine, which is good for very short-run production.

—*Binders* are sometimes used for very expensive manuals directed toward professionals. They have the usual advantages of a binder but they are expensive, hard to ship and their pages tear out easily.

Typesetting is best done on your own computer. Using a word processing program, page layout program and a laser printer will give you complete control over the finished product, will be much faster and will save you a lot of money. See Chapter Eleven. To learn more about book pasteup, see *Publishing Short-Run Books* by the author. To learn about computer selection and how to set type with a computer, see the Special Reports *Computers For Publishers* and *Book Production* also by the author.

If you wish to have someone else typeset and layout your book or want a higher resolution than 300 dots per inch (dpi) laser type, look under "Typesetting" in the *Yellow Pages* and send out several requests for quotation.

Request for quotation. To calculate book production costs, send a request for quotation (RFQ) to a number of printers. Some printers set type and do paste-up, but many of the more price-competitive book printers do not. This means you have to set your own type or have it done somewhere else, usually locally. Most smaller and newer publishers today are setting type in-house with computers and laser printers.

Request that all quotes for printing, halftones, reductions, etc. be made on a per item and per page basis. If your quotes are not figured this way, reduce them to these page/item figures yourself. Then when the book is finished and the exact number of pages, photos, etc. are known, both you and the printer, individually and objectively, will come up with the same figure for the bill.

Here is a sample Request For Quotation or *RFQ*. To help you interpret it, specification examples and hints are in parentheses.

Request for Quotation

Please quote your best price and delivery in printing and binding the following book:

Identification

Title of book: (*Parachuting, The Skydiver's Handbook*)

Author: (Dan Poynter)

Specifications

Quantity: (3,000 and 5,000)

Number of pages including front and back matter: (352)

Trim size: (5.5 x 8.5)

Method of printing: (Offset: web press ok)

Copy: (Customer to provide pasted-up boards)

Illustrations: (Seven halftones, no bleeds)

Cover: (Print sides 1 and 4 only. Customer to supply color separations)

Paper:

Text: (50# white offset book)

Cover: (12 pt. C1S)

Ink:

Text: (Black throughout)

Cover: (Four color plus film lamination)

Proofs: (Complete bluelines)

Binding: (Perfect)

Packaging: (Shrink wrapped in stacks of six, or in a plastic bag lined, 275# burst test carton. Cartons shall be tightly packed and sealed and shall weigh no more than 40 lbs. each.)

Terms: (Net 30 days. Credit references available on request)

Deadline: (Please quote by   )

Your quote:

3,000: $

Overruns: $

Reprint of 3,000: $

5,000: $

Overruns: $

Reprint of 5,000: $

Price per halftone: $

Delivery charges: $

Discount for prompt payment:

Delivery time:

Other miscellaneous charges:

Remarks:

Signed:

For:

Date:

Quote valid for:

Any item in this RFQ takes precedence over any industry convention. The boards, flats and all artwork shall be returned to the customer on completion of the job.

Selecting your printer. There are three types of printers: full-service, specialty and instant. You want a specialty printer who concentrates on books. This is the age of specialization. Some printers concentrate on books, while others do business cards, magazines or calendars. General (full-service) job printers cannot compete with the specialists who are set up for one type of work, may run three shifts on the same presses and buy just a few kinds of paper in larger lots. See the list of book printers in the Appendix. More are listed in *Literary Market Place* and most of them are evaluated in the *Directory of Book Printers* by Marie Kiefer. For complete details on working with printers, from requesting quotes through trucking instructions, see the Special Report *Buying Book Printing* by Dan Poynter.

Solicit several printing quotes. You will find some bids to be three times higher than others. These price differences are amazing and make it obvious that it pays to shop around. Some printers are too big for you, some specialize in something other than books and some are too busy. You need a good printer who is hungry and specializes in "short-run" book printing.

If your state has an inventory tax, you might consider avoiding it by printing in another state and having the books shipped to you in small batches to avoid the date inventory must be taken. Shipping is not too expensive, as trucking companies give special rates for "bound books." Your printer may even be willing to drop ship large quantities for you so you can ship direct to major customers.

Some publishers have found considerable savings on color processes outside the U.S. They may have color separations made in Singapore, printing done in Hong Kong, etc. For more information on foreign printing, see our Special Report *Buying Book Printing*; information is in the Appendix.

Request for quotations should be sent to the printers listed in the Appendix. Add two local print shops to this list. Simply make up an RFQ like the one pictured, make enough photocopies and mail them to all on your list. Don't send your RFQ to just a few; the inquiry will not result in enough comparative data. The only way you will know you are paying the best price is if you get quotes from all. Don't worry about their reception of a photocopied RFQ, printers are used to making competitive quotes. Adams, Delta, Dinner & Klein, McNaughton & Gunn, Maverick, Morgan, Multiprint and some others provide "printing pricers" to help you estimate your costs.

When the RFQs are returned, spread them out for comparison. Some printers will fill out your sheet, while others will use their own form. Make sure the quotes are "FOB destination," that trucking to you is figured in. You will probably find that the distant printers quote much lower prices even with the trucking costs. If, however, the difference is small, you may wish to go with a local printer on your first book. A local job allows you to monitor the work at each step—a valuable learning experience. Next time, you will have more confidence to ship the job out of town.

Don't worry about hurting the feelings of your local printer. If his bid is not the lowest, show him the other bids. They are your excuse for not giving him the work. He will be interested in what the competition is quoting and will appreciate your openness.

Print it yourself. You might even decide to acquire a press and do the printing yourself. Be forewarned, however, that unless you have a simple job and are willing to sacrifice quality, the press run should be left to the professional. You have to decide whether you want to be a writer, printer or to concentrate on sales. Some people gain great satisfaction doing the whole job themselves. Unless you can use the printing press regularly, your own printing won't be competitive in price.

Get it in writing, get everything in writing. You are new to publishing and what you assume may not be the same as what your printer assumes. Good faith, trust and friendship are fine until the bill arrives. Ask for samples and show him what you like, what you expect. Get a contract with the printer explaining exactly what each part of the job will cost. Then if you have two more photos than your estimate, you and he will arrive at the same added figure. Count the books you pick up and get copies of the receiving slips. Monitor the production and make sure the book is coming out the way you want. If you see poor press work, tell the printer now. Don't wait to argue after binding. After the boards are pasted up and you have an exact page count, ask for a new quote on the press run. You should be able to calculate it using the original quote, but it is best to avoid any possible misunderstanding.

Make sure your contract includes a clause which states: "Any item in this contract takes precedence over any industry convention." You aren't familiar with the printing industry and aren't interested in how business is normally done. You simply want an attractive book and you want to know what it will cost.

Keep your artwork. Maintain a file with a couple of clean copies of the book and all your reproduction materials. If you need them again, and you do hope for many happy reprintings, you don't want to have to regenerate lost material.

Put all the artwork, photos, drawings, etc. into a large envelope. You want to be able to find them easily if you contract for a translation or other foreign edition. Keep the boards and negatives of all promotional material such as brochures and order forms.

The art boards for the book are the publisher's property. Many printers will tell you the large and thin metal printing plates, stripped-in negatives (flats) and boards belong to them, as they are the product of the printer's craftsmanship. A printer who argues this simply wants to make sure you return to him for reprints. The plates are difficult to store and printers often throw them out. Many also discard the boards, keeping only the flats. You may take possession of the plates and flats if you reserve their ownership in the printing contract. Fortunately, most book printers do not want to keep your flats and will charge you for storage if they have not been reused or returned within three years.

You should store the boards for future revisions. Find a cool, dry, clean place; they are subject to yellowing. If you think you might like to switch printers for the revision, you can always specify in the contract that you want the flats back after printing. On the other hand, allowing the printer to store the flats while you keep the boards is good insurance. If one place burns to the ground, you won't lose everything. If you will want to make revisions when you go back to press, it is more valuable to have the boards than the flats.

When the books arrive from the printer, count the cartons. Compare the carton count with the number on the bill of lading. Sometimes printers short-ship and sometimes books disappear in transit. Open random cartons and check for damage. If the books were loose in the carton, the top ones will be scuffed.

Do not stack cartons directly on top of each other. Overlapping them like bricks will provide a sturdier stack. Make sure the storage area is clean and dry and has a floor capable of supporting a great deal of weight.

Audio, video and computer disk formats. Since more and more information is being packaged in magnetic media format, they will be covered here at the end of the production chapter.

—Audio tapes. Over $100 million of non-music audio tapes were sold in 1985 and the figure is higher today. Eighty-five percent of all U.S. households and 60% of all cars have tape players. Audio tapes allow people to do two things at once, such as driving and learning. Many children's books are coming packaged with tapes now. For publishers, tapes mean high markup and low inventory; tapes may be reproduced in small quantities. See *Let Your Ideas Speak Out*. For audio editing, reproduction, packaging and advice, call Judy Byers at Audio Cassette Producers (303) 691-2225. Also see Bowker's *Audio Video Market Place*.

—Video tapes. Over 35 million households have a VCR and the number is increasing quickly. For publishers, video, like audio tapes, mean high markup and low inventory; tapes may be reproduced in small quantities. For more information on producing video tapes, get *Home Video: Producing For The Home Market* by Michael Weise, P.O. Box 406, Westport, CT 06881. For a directory of more than 40,000 available videos, get the *Video Source Book*, National Video Clearinghouse, 100 Lafayette Drive, Syosset, NY 11791.

—Computer disks. Certain products lend themselves to reproduction and distribution on disk. For example, Para Publishing has products titled *Publishing Contracts on Disk* and *Business Letters For Publishers*. There are 22 lengthy contracts on the contract disk, and some are over 12 pages of dense ten-point type. The disk format saves the buyer from typing the long contract, making it easily worth the $29.95 price. Perhaps you have a number of forms in your book that can be sold separately on disk. Bowker's *Software Encyclopedia* lists 25,000 software packages in 800 different subject areas (see your library). *Data Sources* (20 Brace Road, Cherry Hill, NJ 08034, or at your library) is a three-volume guide to software companies and hardware manufacturers. If you want help with software packaging and marketing, contact: Education Information Systems, Inc. Irv Brechner, P.O. Box 5125, Ridgewood, NJ 07451, Tel: (201) 445-7196, Fax: (201) 447-3972.

Para Publishing is a unique book business. It does not operate like a big traditional publisher and it doesn't lose money. Dan Poynter lays out the following reasons for the success of his company.

1. Publish your own material. Do not waste your time on, or split the money with, other authors.

2. Perform every publishing and business function yourself. After your first book, farm out those tasks you do not wish to perform.

3. Operate as a sole proprietorship, not a corporation, and keep your books on a cash basis.

4. Do not mimic the big traditional New York publishers. Many are not making a sufficient return on their investment. Some of their procedures exist for a good reason, while others are just convention (also known as a rut). The trick is to know the difference.

5. If you cannot "find a need and fill it," then create a need and fill it. Decide on your market before you write the book and write to that market.

6. Market your books like breakfast food, not like a film. This is not one-shot entertainment; go after a market share and keep selling that book year after year.

7. You will have to spend more time selling than you will writing. Concentrate on marketing rather than editorial functions.

8. Produce valuable information, aimed at a small target audience, and charge a fair price.

Chapter Five

Announcing Your Book

Telling The World You Are an Author and a Publisher

Getting Listed

Before you run off to promote your book to potential readers, you must announce it to the industry, the government and the world. In fact, some of these announcements must be made before you go to press. For a clear understanding of when each of the following should be done, see the Calendar at the beginning of the Appendix.

As you use this chapter, remember, if the people at some registration offices and directories reject your application, do not give up. Try to figure a way around their objection and file a new form. It is very doubtful they will remember your initial application rejection. Since these people may not have a lot of confidence in publishers with a single title (who may never publish again), it is best to represent yourself as being larger.

After all, this will not be your only book. Use different names for your company, publisher and author. "Deuel Publishing, Pam Deuel Publisher and book by Pam Deuel" is a sure tip off that you are small and new.

Getting listed in all the right places is easy with the use of *Publishing Forms,* a collection of applications and information for the beginning publisher. See the Appendix.

An ISBN application

The International Standard Book Number (ISBN) is a world-wide identification system which has been in use since the late sixties. There is a different ISBN for each edition and each binding of every book, so the number's use avoids errors in identifying the books ordered, shipped, received, etc. Publishers are finding that with the increased use of computers in the book industry, this system has become an essential element in the distribution of their books.

A typical ISBN might be 0-915516-21-7. Here, the initial "0" or a "1" indicates a book originating in an English speaking country. The "915516" identifies the publisher. The suffix 21 identifies this particular title and edition of the book, hardcover or softcover. The last number, "7," is a check digit, which is a mathematical function to make sure the rest of the numbers are correct, that they haven't been miscopied or transposed.

The ISBN is printed on the copyright page of the book and at the bottom of the back cover or jacket, above or below the bar code, in 12 pt. OCR-A type. Hardcover jackets should carry the number on the upper edge of the left-hand jacket flap.

Contact the International Standard Book Numbering Agency, 121 Chanlon Road, New Proividence, NJ 07974. Telephone: (908) 665-2883 and request a "Title Output Information Request form," and a "Verification form." There is a $100.00 charge for this service.

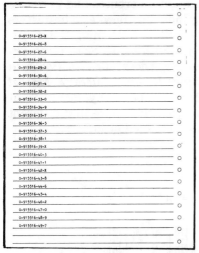

An ISBN log book sheet

You may request a number and a log sheet for 10, 100 or 1,000 titles. If you ask for 10, your publisher identifier number will be seven digits long and your suffix will be just one digit. If you ask for 1,000, your publisher identifier will be five digits, leaving you with three in the suffix. Many starting publishers modestly ask for ten, run out of numbers quickly and must apply for a new publisher identifier number—which is confusing. Ask for at least 100. The ISBN people will send you a card bearing your ISBN publisher identifier and a log book sheet with enough room for listing 100 different book editions.

Once started in the system, you will assign each of your new titles an ISBN suffix yourself. You do not have to start at the beginning of the log. The only requirement is that each title, revision and binding have a different number. If you use the first number on the log book sheet, the "00" will tip off those in the industry that this is a first book.

ISSN is for serials. Publications issued in parts, such as magazines, newspapers, annuals, directories, proceedings and any publication expected to continue indefinitely are called "serials." For more information on the ISSN, contact the Library of Congress, National Serials Data Program, Washington, DC 20540, (202) 707-6452.

R.R. Bowker. By now, you are probably finding there are a lot of agencies and offices catering to the book trade at 249 West 17th Street and 121 Chanlon Road. Bowker is a subsidiary of Cahners, which publishes many references and performs many services for the publishing industry. Bowker administers the ISBN and SAN programs as well as publishing the magazines *Publishers Weekly, Library Journal* and *School Library Journal*. Bowker publishes reference books such as *Books in Print, American Book Publishing Record, Literary Market Place, Publishers Trade List Annual* and many more. Treat each Bowker office separately, as though it were in a different building, so your mail won't get misdirected or lost.

The Bar Code

Bar codes. The bar code on a book identifies the ISBN, which in turn identifies the publisher, title, author and edition (hardcover, etc.). The ISBN itself is reprinted above or below the bar code. Now you can get both typeset at one place. Use the ISBN on invoices, catalogs, order forms, packing lists and the book itself. Use the bar code (with the ISBN) on the back cover of the book.

Beginning from the left, the first three symbols (978) identify this as being a Bookland bar code, that the product is a book. The next nine digits (091551661) correspond to the ISBN (less the check digit at the end) for the book. The last figure is a bar code check digit. In the smaller price extension bar code to the right, the first digit indicates the type of currency such as U.S. dollars. The next four digits indicate the retail price of the book.

Most bookstores are using price scanners now. Publishers, wholesalers and others in the distribution chain are scanning books, as the bar codes provide better inventory control.

Order a copy of *Machine-Readable Coding Guidelines for the U.S. Book Industry* ($5.00) from: The Book Industry Study Group, 160 Fifth Avenue, #604, New York, NY 10010, (212) 929-1393. Or, you may be able to get a copy free from: GGX Associates, George Goldberg, 11 Middle Neck Road, Great Neck, NY 11021, (516) 487-6370.

Bar code prints and negatives cost $10 to $30 and are available from the following suppliers: Landy & Associates, Marc Landy, 1049 Sudden Valley, #156, Bellingham, WA 98226, (206) 647-7494; GGX Associates, George Goldberg, 11 Middle Neck Road, Great Neck, NY 11021, (516) 487-6370, and Precision Photography, Inc., 1150 North Tustin Avenue, Anaheim, CA 92807, (714) 632-9000. Assign an ISBN to your book, order a bar code negative and give it to your cover artist for incorporation into your back cover design.

To order a bar code, call one of the above-mentioned suppliers and tell them you want a "Bookland EAN bar code with price extension." Then provide the ISBN, price, name of the book and any other information (e.g., hardcover edition) you may need to identify the negative they will send you. The bar code negative will be delivered in a couple of days.

Standard address number. The SAN identifies each separate address of every firm in the book publishing industry—from publishers, to wholesalers, to libraries, to bookstores. SAN's sort out the billing and shipping addresses and help to determine which "Book Nook" an order is going to.

A SAN may be requested when you apply for an ISBN. The seven-digit number should be printed on all stationery, purchase orders, invoices, etc.

The ABI form

Advanced Book Information is another Bowker service. By filling out their ABI form, your book will be listed in *Books in Print* and several other specialized directories. *Books in Print*, published in November of each year, is the most important directory.

Everyone in the industry turns to *BIP* first when looking for a particular book. This multi-volumed reference lists all available books by subject, title and author. Ask for it at the library and become familiar with this important work.

Contact the ABI Department, R. R. Bowker Co., 121 Chanlon Road, New Providence, NJ 07974. Telephone (800) 521-8110 and request an ABI guide book and a half-dozen ABI forms. There is no charge.

You should fill out an ABI form about six months before your book comes off the press, but don't be too anxious. On your first book, wait until you are about to ship your boards off to the printer. Some new publishers act prematurely; they list the book and then get delayed or never get into print. Your "publication date" will probably be six months away anyway, as discussed in Chapter Seven. Code your address on the ABI forms (see the discussion in Chapter Seven).

Always use the ABI guide sheet when filling out the ABI form. Some of the questions may mislead a person not familiar with publishing terminology.

Bowker will send you a computer-generated ABI checklist every other month to keep your listings up-to-date. This checklist must be returned every time even if all the information is correct. Failure to return the checklist may result in your books or company being dropped from *Books in Print*.

Library of Congress Catalog Card Number. LC numbers appear on the copyright page of each book and are also included in the lists and reviews appearing in the leading journals of the book trade. The LC number differs from the ISBN in that one ISBN is assigned to each different *edition* of a work (hardcover, softcover, etc.); the LC number is assigned to the work itself, regardless of the number of bindings. Use of the number enables subscribers to the Library of Congress' catalog card service to order cards by number and thus eliminate the searching fee. LC numbers are essential if you want to sell to libraries. About 20,000 libraries from all over the world subscribe to this service and some order almost every cataloged book. Additionally, most of the books are listed in *The National Union Catalogue*, issued several times a year in four editions. Most public and private libraries subscribe to it.

The Library of Congress card number must be requested prior to the publication of the book so that the number may be printed on the copyright page. They do not *preassign* numbers to books that are already in print since it is too late to print the number in the book.

Catalog card numbers are preassigned only to books which the Library of Congress assumes will be added to library collections, or for which they anticipate substantial demand for LC printed cards. The types of material which the Library collects only in a very limited way, and for which catalog card numbers are generally not available, include: calendars, laboratory manuals, booklets of less than 50 pages, brochures, advertisements, bank publications designed for customers, blueprints, certain kinds of light fiction, privately printed books of poems, religious materials for students in Bible schools, catechisms, instructions in devotions, individual sermons and prayers, question and answer books, most elementary and secondary school textbooks, tests except for standard examinations, teachers' manuals, correspondence school lessons, translations from English into foreign languages, picture books, comic strip and coloring books, diaries, log and appointment books, prospectuses and preliminary editions, workbooks, and vanity press publications. Since the people at the Library of Congress sometimes confuse self-publishing with vanity publishing, it is best to fill out the forms using different names for author, publisher, etc.

Library of Congress application Form 607-7

New publishers should write to the Library of Congress, Washington, DC 20540 and ask for "Procedures for Securing Preassigned Library of Congress Catalog Card Numbers" and their "Request for Preassignment of LCC Number," applications (Form 607-7).

The Library of Congress will send you your number typed on a 3 x 5 slip, giving the author, title, imprint and publication date. The catalog card number appears in the upper right-hand corner of the slip.

The first two digits of the LC number do not indicate the year of publication, but the year in which the card number is preassigned. If you register after January first, your book will appear to be a year newer. Ever wonder why the dates on films are in Roman numerals?

The Library of Congress must be advised of all subsequent changes in titles, authors, etc., and cancellations. This notification is important as it prevents duplication of numbers. A new number is not necessary when changes are made. Confirmations of changes will not be acknowledged unless requested by the publisher.

There is no charge for the preassignment of a card number. An advance complimentary copy of each publication must be sent to the CIP Office, Library of Congress, Washington, DC 20540. This copy is used for final cataloging so that cards may be printed before the book is released. The CIP Office provides postage-free mailing labels for use in sending these advance publications. The book is only for checking, so send the less expensive, softcover edition.

The Copyright Office is operationally separate from the CIP Office. But the CIP and Catalog Card Number offices are the same. Catalog card numbers may be applied for per the above information or when applying for Cataloging in Publication Data.

Apply for your numbers and listings in this order: ISBN, LC number and then file the ABI form.

Cataloging In Publication (CIP) is a program which enables publishers to print Library of Congress cataloging information on the copyright page of their books. Because the data block is already printed in the book, librarians are able to process new titles for library users rapidly and economically. First a publisher must be accepted into the program, and then he or she must request cataloging data for each new book.

For information on the CIP program, write the CIP Office, Library of Congress, Washington, DC 20540 and request: "Cataloging in Publication - Information for Participating Publishers" and some "Publisher's Response" forms. The CIP people are eager to help and can be reached at (202) 707-6372.

They even provide postage-paid mailing labels for the materials you are expected to send back.

Here is a line-by-line explanation of the CIP data block:

1. **Library of Congress Cataloging in Publication Data.**

2. Poynter, Daniel F.

3. Parachuting, The Skydiver's Handbook

4. 1, Parachuting. 2, Skydiving. I Title

5. GV 770P69   797.56   77-83469

6. ISBN 0-915516-16-0 Softcover

7. ISBN 0-915516-17-9 Hardcover

Typical CIP data block

1. The heading is made distinctive by setting in bold typeface

2. The author's name

3. The title of the book

4. The LC subject headings

5. The "GV 770" is the LC classification number. The "P69" is keyed into the last name of the author, in this case "Poynter."

The second number group is the Dewey Decimal Classification Number (see *The Dewey Decimal Classification and Relative Index*) and the last is the LC Card Number.

6&7. The International Standard Book Numbers.

Once you are accepted into the CIP program, you will send in information on each book prior to printing. Send photocopies of the front matter of your pasted up boards and a filled out LCC Data sheet to the CIP Office. This enables them to select the proper classification numbers. They also like to have any other information you might have, such as a descriptive brochure on the book, a photocopy of your ABI form and a biographical sketch of the author. Within ten working days, the Office will send the CIP data and the catalog card number.

Sometimes titles mislead and the CIP Office does not catalog the book correctly. For example, is *What Color is Your Parachute?* about job hunting or skydiving? If your book is miscataloged in every library across the country, readers will never find it. Give the CIP people as much information on your new book as possible and read their "Information For Participating Publishers" carefully. You may even supply suggested data. Pay particular attention to the "subject tracings" (line 4 above). How a book gets cataloged can be just as important as how it gets reviewed or advertised.

Form 607-6

To participate in the CIP program, you must be an established publisher, which is defined here as having published three books. For your first three books, make up your own data block and apply to the Library of Congress for just an LC number. Ask a librarian to help you with the numbers; they speak these book classification languages. Title your data block "Publisher's Cataloging in Publication Data." Lack of participation in the CIP program has no affect on obtaining an LC number or a copyright. Quality Books also supplies the service.

Copyright may be registered before your manuscript is published but, unless you are passing a lot of copies around for technical proofing and comment, you might just as well do as most publishers do: wait for books to come off the press. Your work is copyright protected, it just isn't copyright registered, yet.

Write to the Register of Copyrights, Library of Congress, Washington, DC 20559 and request three copies of Form TX (for registering books) and copies of Circular 1, *Copyright Basics* and Circular 2, *Publications of the Copyright Office.* Upon receipt, read over these publications and order any others you feel you need. The Copyright Office will also send you some business reply mailing labels so that you may send them the copyright form, your check and the books for registration.

Form TX

To register your copyright, follow these three steps:

1. Print the copyright notice on the copyright page (title page verso). The notice takes the following form: " © 1990 by Robert Howard." You may use the word "copyright" but the "©" says the same thing and it is necessary for international protection. Also add "all rights reserved" and expand on this if you like. Check other books. The copyright notice must appear in *all* copies of the book to protect you, so double check it and all the numbers on the copyright page every time you proof copy, boards, bluelines, etc.

The copyright should be in the name of the owner. The owner may be the author, the publishing company or whoever created or paid for the work.

2. Publish the book. Check for the copyright notice before any of the books are distributed.

3. Register your claim with the Copyright Office within three months of the book coming off the press. To do this, send a completed Form TX, two copies of the "best edition" of the book and a fee of $20. The "best edition" would be the hardcover if both the hardbound and softbound came from the printer at the same time. However, since the hardbound edition often takes longer to produce, the softcover may be the "best edition at the time of publication." If you enclose softcover copies with the Form TX, be sure to note that they were produced first.

The Copyright Office will add a registration number and date to the form and will send you a photocopy containing a seal and the Registrar's signature.

The new copyright term is for the author's life plus 50 years. Your ownership of the book is now a valuable part of your estate, so be certain your copyrighted material is mentioned in your will.

Copyrights protect you like a patent, but they are cheaper and much easier to secure. Like a patent, however, you must always be on the lookout for infringers. The copyright protects your text, photographs, drawings, maps, everything in the book except the title.

The Cumulative Book Index is an international bibliography of new publications in the English language. All the bibliographical information necessary to identify a book is provided: full name of author, complete title, date of publication, edition, paging, price, publisher, International Standard Book Number, and Library of Congress card number.

In addition to bibliographical information, the *Cumulative Book Index* also provides subject headings to describe the contents of the book. These headings can usually be determined by an examination of the table of contents and a reading of the preface; sometimes, a careful examination of the text is necessary. Books must have at least 100 pages and a minimum press run of 500 copies to be eligible for inclusion in the *Index.*

INFORMATION SLIP

Description of new book for FREE record in Cumulative Book Index, published by
The H. W. Wilson Company, 950 University Ave., Bronx, N.Y. 10452

The Cumulative Book Index is published monthly.   A copy of the book or descriptive
                                                                                        material will be appreciated.

Author ....
   (Full Name) (Please print)

Title ....
   (Verbatim)
....

Subject ....

Series and Number ....

Edition ... . No. of vols .... Size .... No. of pages .... Illustrations ....

Binding .... Retail price .... Date of publication ....
           (In your currency)   (Exact)

Name and Address of Publisher ....
   (From whom the book may be obtained)

For *IMPORTATIONS* the following additional information is *REQUIRED:* (a) Are you the sole U.S. agent for the book? .... (b) What is the U.S. publication date? .... (c) How many copies will be on hand in this country on the U.S. publication date? (or are on hand now)? ....

11-65—50M(2687)M.A.   Printed in U.S.A.

Cumulative Book Index Information Slip

A listing in the *Cumulative Book Index* gives your publication valuable publicity. Subscribers include most of the major libraries and booksellers around the world. No charge is made for a listing, but in order to record your book accurately, the H. W. Wilson Company needs a copy of the book. Wilson will also list your book in the *Vertical File Index.* Send books to: *Cumulative Book Index,* H. W. Wilson Co., 950 University Avenue, Bronx, NY 10452, (212) 588-8400. For more information on the *Vertical File Index,* use the same address.

Book Publishers in the United States and Canada is a directory in which you may have a free listing. For an application form, write Gale Research Company, Book Tower, Detroit, MI 48226, (313) 961-2242.

Small Press Record of Books in Print is a special *Books in Print* for smaller publishers. Contact Dustbooks, P. O. Box 100-P, Paradise, CA 95967, (916) 877-6110, for an application.

International Directory of Little Magazines and Small Presses is another place you will want to list your new firm. Contact Dustbooks, P. O. Box 100-P, Paradise, CA 95967, (916) 877-6110, for an application.

Directory of Editors & Publishers is a place to list yourself. Contact Dustbooks, P. O. Box 100-P, Paradise, CA 95967, (916) 877-6110, for an application. Request information on their other directories, too.

Publishers Trade List Annual is another Bowker publication. It is a multi-volume collection of publishers' catalogs used by the publishing industry to announce books. PTLA claims that 84% of the bookstores and 90% of the libraries use this publication when ordering. For information and an ad rate card, contact R. R. Bowker Co., 245 West 17th Street, New York, NY 10011, (212) 645-9700.

Publishers, Distributors, Wholesalers of the United States. Contact R.R. Bowker Co., 245 West 17th Street, New York, NY 10011. (212) 645-9700.

Any Book is a lower cost alternative to *Books in Print*, which is available on microfiche. To list your book, send for an application to The Library Corporation, Research Park, Inwood, WV 25428. Tel: (800) 624-0559 or (304) 229-0100.

Publisher's Catalog Annual will reproduce your catalog on microfiche cards and distribute them to bookstores. There is no charge for the service. Contact Chadwyck-Healey, 1101 King Street #180, Alexandria, VA 22314, (703) 683-4890, for an application form.

Publishers' International Directory is published by the K. G. Saur Publishing Co. Contact Saur, 121 Chanlon Road, New Providence, NJ 07974, Tel: (908) 464-6800, for information and a questionnaire.

ABA Book Buyer's Handbook is used by bookstores to find your shipping, discount, STOP and returns policies. A listing here will encourage STOP orders (See Chapter Six). Contact the American Booksellers Association, 560 White Plains Road, Tarrytown, NY 10591, Tel: (800) 637-0037 or (914) 631-7800, for an application.

The Book Buyer's Manual is published by the National Association of College Stores. For an application, contact them at NACS, P.O. Box 58, Oberlin, OH 44074, (216) 775-7777.

Literary Market Place is one of the most important reference books in the publishing industry. It lists every major publisher, publicity outlet and supplier. An inclusion here will help your customers and suppliers to find you. To be listed in this annual reference, you must publish at least three books a year. Send for an application form to *Literary Market Place*, 121 Chanlon Road, New Providence, NJ 07974, Tel: (908) 464-6800.

Writer's Market. A listing here means you want manuscript submissions from authors. For an application, write *Writer's Market*, 1507 Dana Avenue, Cincinnati, OH 45207, (513) 531-2222.

Directories In Print has over 10,400 listings and will accept your book listing if it has an extensive appendix. Send for a form to Contemporary Authors, Gale Research Company, Book Tower, Detroit, MI 48226, (313) 961-2242. Visit the library and look for other directories that might list your book.

Contemporary Authors is a large reference book containing over 91,000 biographical sketches. Authors of technical and vanity press books are not eligible. Send for a form to *Contemporary Authors*, Gale Research Company, Book Tower, Detroit, MI 48226, (313) 961-2242. Don't be modest, the more you write on the form, the more space you get in the book. After you fill out the application, make a few photocopies so you will be ready when someone else asks for extensive biographical information. The listing is free.

Who's Who in U.S. Writers, Editors & Poets. For an application, contact December Press, Curt Johnson, P.O. Box 302, Highland Park, IL 60035, (312) 432-6804.

Policies of Publishers: A Handbook for Order Librarians. Scarecrow Press, 52 Liberty Street, Metuchen, NJ 08840 (201) 548-8600.

Publishers Marketing Association (PMA) holds educational seminars, buys and shares advertising space, makes cooperative mailings and operates booths at major book fairs. Local affiliates of PMA are located all over North America. See the list of publishing associations in the Appendix. Write to PMA, 2401 Pacific Coast Highway, #102, Hermosa Beach, CA 90254, (310) 372-2732, for a sample newsletter and a membership application. Because of all the cooperative marketing programs, membership in PMA is a valuable investment.

COSMEP is the international association of independent book and magazine publishers. The name Committee of Small Magazine Editors and Publishers is, however, misleading. They publish a very informative monthly newsletter, and membership will establish many valuable contacts. Contact COSMEP, P. O. Box 703-P, San Francisco, CA 94101, (415) 922-9490, for a sample of the newsletter and a membership application.

Book Trade in Canada is the *LMP* of the Canadian book publishing industry. Contact Ampersand Communications Services, 2766 Sheffield Road, Ottawa, ON K1B 3V9, Canada. Tel: (613) 749-9998.

Canadian Books in Print is the *BIP* of the Canadian book publishing industry. Contact University of Toronto Press, Front Campus, Toronto, ON, M5S 1A6, Canada, Tel: (416) 978-2239.

Canadian Publishers Directory. Contact Key Publishers, 59 Front Street East, Toronto, ON, M5E 1B3, Canada, Tel: (416) 364-3333.

New & Forthcoming Canadian Books. Contact Key Publishers, 59 Front Street East, Toronto, ON, M5E 1B3, Canada, Tel: (416) 364-3333.

Forms. For a complete set of forms, including all those mentioned in this chapter, see the order blank on the last page of this book for *Publishing Forms.*

With listings in *Book in Print*, the *Small Press Record* and *Literary Market Place*, a membership in the Publishers Marketing Association and subscriptions to *Publishers Weekly*, *Small Press*, and *Writer's Digest*, you will begin to receive a lot of writing and publishing mail. See the listings in the Appendix.

The competition from the small presses, which have sprung up around the country, and which seem to be willing to take risks, has led some observors to conclude the New York publishing industry will eventually lose its primacy as the showcase for new talent and as the arbiter of literary taste. The rising cost of doing business in Manhattan, they argue, will force its firms to pursue only the most commercially promising manuscripts—blockbusters to sell through bookstore chains. - Richard Hartzell, Wilson Library Bulletin

Chapter Six

What is Your Book Worth?

Prices, Discounts, Terms, Collections and Returns

Book pricing is a complicated affair which strikes a compromise between a price high enough for the publisher to stay in business and low enough to overcome customer price resistance. There are, perhaps, three reasons people write books: reward (fame and/or fortune), love of writing and a desire to disseminate important material. While you may want to get the word out, your first book is usually for recognition, and once that is out of your system, the second is for money. Consequently, the author is likely to underprice the first book but work with a very sharp pencil on the price of the next.

Writing is like prostitution. First you do it for the love of it, then you do it for a few friends, and finally you do it for the money. - Moliere

The list price of your book will not be easy to set. Many first-time author/publishers ask themselves whether they want maximum financial return or maximum distribution, feeling they can't have both. Usually they wind up with a price on the cover which is too low. As a result, many small publishers have warehouses full of books which they cannot afford to market effectively. Without a sufficient price, there is not enough money for promotion and without promotion, the book will not sell. If the book fails to sell, there is no money for promotion, or even to pay the printing bill.

One major reason small publishers stay small is their failure to think objectively about pricing their books. Low prices make you work harder for less and limit your growth.

You must also consider that the price printed on the cover is not what you will receive for the book. Dealers require a percentage for their selling efforts. Your promotion costs, to let people know the book exists, are likely to be much higher than you originally anticipated—around 25% of the list price. Ten percent of the books may be shipped out as review copies and 10% may come back from bookstores damaged. Discounts, advertising and returns take a big chunk out of the list price.

Books are becoming more and more expensive; visit a bookstore and compare prices. According to *Publishers Weekly*, the average prices for books in 1991, the latest year available, were as follows:

Hardcover (eliminating those special books priced over $81): $31.86, and this compares with $17.32 in 1977. Some more specific areas were: Business $38.05, Science $45.43, Sports & Recreation $30.01, and Travel $28.61.

Softcover: $18.04, and this compares with $5.93 in 1977. Business books averaged $21.34, Science $27.31, Sports & Recreation $14.81, and Travel $14.08.

Mass market paperback: $4.85, and this is up from $1.72 in 1977. Business books averaged $8.02, Science $9.42, Sports & Recreation $6.77, and Travel $11.55.

The book *How to Beat Inflation* has just gone from $9.95 to $14.95

Some publishers like to test prices before deciding on them. There are times when a higher price will make a product seem more valuable and will make the book sell better. These publishers run identical ads, except for the price, and then check the returns. Mail order book buyers are said to be the least price-conscious of all.

Your book is unique. Like you, it is one of a kind. While a customer will not pay more than what he figures is a fair price, if your book is a good one and he wants it badly enough, he will pay what you ask. Underpricing a book to increase sales is often a very big mistake. In fact, it may even undermine the credibility of the book. And remember, price has a reverse impact when a book is purchased as a gift.

In a how-to book, you are selling exclusive information, not entertainment or stacks of paper; the selling price is not nearly so frightening to the buyer as it is to the author. According to *Publishers Weekly*, women are more resistant to book prices than men. Women buy most of the books on cooking, health, diet and gardening, as well as fiction.

Books you intend to sell through bookstores and mail order should be priced at eight times "unit production cost," textbooks at five times. Total production cost includes all composition, layout, printing, binding, etc. Pricing the book any lower than this is courting financial disaster. If the projected list price seems too high, consider cutting out some of the copy or photographs, or selecting a smaller type and narrower leading (space between the lines) to get more material on each page. Check with your printer for ways to reduce costs. Now, if the customer still won't pay that much, you picked the wrong subject to write about.

The 8X formula does not fit every case; there may be a few exceptions. Consider your audience and the cost of reaching them. If you write a pictorial history of your town and the Chamber of Commerce is buying all the books to give to tourists, your promotion and distribution costs will be much lower. For continuous-selling nonfiction aimed at a small target audience, you may be able to justify 8X the **reprint** costs (excluding the pre-press expenses). If 8X seems like a lot, you should know that audio-visual materials are often marked up 11X.

It may seem old and silly, but $9.95 still seems a lot cheaper to the subconscious mind than $10, and there is no good argument for a mid-price like $9.50.

Raising the price. Recheck your costs at reprint time; you may wish to raise the cover price. If you do raise the price, remember to change your ads, brochures, etc. and send off a news release on the reprint to *Publishers Weekly*. (Every little mention helps.) To ease the blow on your better dealers, who have you listed in their catalog, consider offering them a onetime buy on the new edition at the old price in order to protect their catalog listing. This offer will also generate quick cash to help you pay your printing bill.

Price on cover. Your book must have a price on the cover. The best places are on the bottom of the back cover on a softcover book and on the left jacket flap of a hardcover book. In the past, inflation prompted some publishers to remove the price from their books. The problem was that each print run had a different price, and stores would be returning older editions which could not be recycled into stock. Another problem was that if you did not print the price on the book, the store had to sticker it. If the book was returned, the sticker could not be removed without damaging the book. Today, all books must have bar codes and the price extension provides the price. Since the price is stated on the back cover in code for the industry, and since you probably have an order blank inside, the price might just as well be repeated for the customer.

How many books? You must consider both your purpose for writing the book and how many you can expect to sell. Do you want just a few books for family and friends? Will it be a high-priced mail order book with a small target audience? Or, will it be a popular book with a wide audience that should sell well in bookstores? How many will be used for review copies, gifts and other freebees?

Initial press runs should normally be limited to the number of books one can reasonably estimate will be sold in the first year. Unless you have a substantial number of prepublication sales, it is a good idea to limit the first printing to no more than 5,000. No matter how diligently you proofread, some errors will not surface until they appear in ink. Also, once you see the book in its final state, you will wish you had done some things differently. By printing a smaller number, you can use the next few months to catch your errors and make some design changes. Then you will be much happier about the revised second edition.

Set the first press run conservatively. It is better to sell out and have to go back to press than to find yourself with a garage full of unsold books. You will be spending a lot of money on promotion, so it is best to hedge your bets by tying up less money in the book, even though you have to pay a slight premium in printing costs to do so.

But do not be too conservative. All the books will not be sold, many will be used for promotion. If you print 1,000 copies and send 400 out to newspapers and magazines for review, there will be only 600 copies left to sell. Reviews are your least expensive and most effective form of promotion, and 400 review copies is a realistic figure (see Chapter Seven). Many publishers figure 10% of their print run will be used for review copies and promotion. Except for highly specialized topics, 3,000 makes a good minimum print run.

The economics of printing are as follows: the greater the quantity of books, the higher your bill, but the less each book will cost you. The "start-up costs" make the first press run much more expensive than reprints. The major expenses are the start-up costs of composition, layout, camerawork, stripping, etc. Once the type is set, you only pay for the paper, binding and press time. The more copies printed at one time, the lower the price per copy.

Economy of scale is only true up to a point, since the differences become smaller and smaller as the press runs increase. Each next thousand books becomes cheaper. The price breaks fail to maintain significance after about 9,000 copies. Normally, between 9,000 and 10,000 copies, you save so little that it isn't worth the storage space or the price of borrowing money. Therefore you do not want to print over 9,000 unless that number will move out within the year.

Book buyers are less influenced by price differentials than almost any category of customers. - John Huenefeld

For example, you might receive printing/binding quotes such as:

No. of copies	500	1000	3000	5000	7000	9000	10000
Total cost	$1495	1784	4485	6778	8750	10530	11300
Unit cost	$2.99	1.78	1.49	1.36	1.25	1.17	1.13

So it is to your advantage to order as many books as possible in order to get the best unit price. And you want the best price, as long as you are fairly sure you can sell the higher number.

Remember that a printer makes money on printing. Do not let him talk you into more books than you need. There is economy in scale but there are no savings in paying for books you can't turn into cash. Consider the total printing bill as well.

Print runs are never exact. Printers always run a few extra pages, expecting some to be spoiled. When all the sheets are gathered, there are still some which must be thrown away. Accordingly, it is customary in the trade to have overruns and underruns and your bill may be adjusted higher or lower, up to ten percent. A print run of 10,000 could wind up anywhere between 9,000 and 11,000.

Size of inventory. Consider reprint time, trucking time, seasonal demand, etc. Then, considering the size of your storage space, amount of money you can invest, need for future revisions, inventory tax dates, etc., print a one-to-two-year supply. One great advantage of these annual printings is the ability to make revisions, keeping the text up-to-date.

Retail price should depend more upon the value the buyer places on the product than on cost to the producer. - Leonard Shatzkin, author of *In Cold Type*

Estimating sales for that first year will be difficult with your initial book because you don't have other books with which to compare it. You may get an idea from your own previous work experience and may be able to find out what similar books have done. But remember that bigger publishers have more clout in the bookstores and already have the connections for placing their titles; you will not do as well initially. Check with anyone you may know in other publishing companies for their educated estimate and get a copy of *Financial Feasability in Book Publishing* by Robert Follet. It contains guidelines, worksheets and rules of thumb for estimating sales. See the Appendix. With proper promotion, any reasonably good nonfiction book, aimed at all but the tiniest markets, should sell 2,500 copies in its first year (plus up to 500 promotional copies). Do some market research. How many associations, magazines and conventions are there in this activity? How many people care about this subject? If you cannot objectively project moving 3,000 copies in the first year, you will have to raise the price to justify printing the book.

Reprints have to be timed just right. If you order a reprint too early, you may tie up more money before the first run is paid for. And, many of those books could be sitting on the shelves in the stores—unsold. It is a good idea to make some telephone calls to find if the book is actually moving. On the other hand, if you wait too long to reprint, you run the risk of being out of stock and losing the all-important sales momentum the book is enjoying. Reprints usually take three to five weeks. Coordinate with your printer so you can get a fast reprint if necessary. It is much better to be out of books for a few weeks than to have the truck arrive with 5,000 more as bookstores are returning copies.

Discounts must be set down in a definite policy right from the beginning. Discount structures have to be clear to both you and your customers to avoid any misunderstanding.

Ultimate consumers placing individual orders usually pay the full retail price and send cash with their order (CWO). When an order is received without a check, it is best to return it with a copy of your brochure and a short note requesting payment in advance. Circle your prices and terms on the brochure; some people order asking to be billed, because they don't know what the full price will be. Asking for payment in advance will lose a few orders but it will stop credit losses and cut billing costs. See the order blank at the end of this book. COD shipments require too much paperwork for a small sale and the collection charges often upset the customer.

Dealer discounts. The terms publishers extend to booksellers vary so much from firm to firm that the American Booksellers Association publishes a loose-leaf handbook trying to list them all. Discounts are supposed to be based on the theory that there is a saving in bulk shipments. However, bookselling tradition has based the discount rate on the category of the wholesale customer, arguing that certain middlemen need a greater discount because they are passing part of it on to retailers.

—**Wholesalers** get 50% to 60% off on the theory that they purchase large quantities for resale to retailers and libraries. Often they are regional suppliers providing stores with both one-stop-shopping and a short supply line for quick and easy restocking. They allow bookstores up to 40% off depending on the size of the order, but stores are usually allowed to mix titles. In order to maintain large library accounts, they usually extend discounts of 20% to 33%. Wholesalers sometimes pay the shipping (FOB origin) when purchasing from the publisher.

Some wholesalers will not handle a small press book unless the publisher is willing to take out a space ad in their catalog. This may be little more than a disguised bonus discount, and each request must be considered on its own merits. For example, the charge for inclusion may be $250. If they agree to order $5,000 worth of books at 50%, and normally you would give 55% for this large quantity, then the $250 can be justified as it is 5% of $5,000. It all works out the same to you. Sometimes these are first-time-only charges to get you into the system and to test your book. Also, some wholesalers offer to give one-line listings to the rest of your books if you will pay for display space for one of them.

—**Retail bookstores.** Discounts to bookstores start at 40% for single orders and this comes as a shock to many new publishers. But one has to consider the high overhead retailers have in the form of rent, taxes, salaries, utilities, insurance, etc. They need at least 40% to stay in business. Incidentally, bookstores enjoy a smaller markup than gift, sporting goods and other stores which often get 50% or more. The publishing industry has been able to justify the lower discount by making the books returnable if they aren't sold. Fortunately, books are uniform in size, easy to store, simple to ship and unbreakable. Shipping is added to the bookstore's bill (FOB origin).

—**College bookstores** get 20% to 25% off on (text) books to be sold to students. The quantity is often large and any books not sold after the school term begins are returned. There is very little risk, as the store is just acting as an order taker. The "short discount" results in a lower price to the consuming student.

These short discounts are sometimes applied to regular books and when this is done, all sales literature should be clearly marked. The book trade will not be too enthusiastic about the poor discount, but they can't complain if they are buying in ones and twos and have been informed of the short discount in advance.

—**Libraries.** Some publishers and wholesalers give libraries a 20% discount, but most libraries do not expect a discount and many orders will arrive with a check made out for the list price. Libraries are only ordering one book so there is no justification for a discount. Most small publishers are charging the libraries full list price and shipping postpaid (at library rate).

The Federal Trade Commission (FTC) requires that the discounts you offer one dealer be offered to all dealers who are purchasing the same quantity. You are not required to extend credit, but if dealers are paying cash and want the same quantity, you must sell at the same discount.

Discount schedules are being used by many publishers in deference to discriminatory tradition. It is based not on the classification of the customer, but on the order quantity. The universal schedule works well for larger publishers since they have several books and allow titles to be mixed to achieve higher discounts. Smaller publishers will use the universal schedule for bookstores.

Before you can sell a person anything you have to make him or her want it more than the money it cost.

Dealer Bulletin

January 1, 1991

Featuring new and better discounts as well as a greater selection. See brochures for descriptions and list prices.

Discounts

1 book	no discount
2-4 books	20% off
5-9 books	30% off
10-24 books	40% off
25-49 books	42% off
50-74 books	44% off
75-99 books	46% off
100-199 books	48% off
200 or more books	50% off

STOP orders earn a 40% discount. Please add $1.75 per book for shipping. Order using full title and/or ISBN for identification.

Terms. Our terms are net 30 days from date of invoice. A finance charge of 1 1/2% per month will be added to all overdue balances over 60 days.

Credit. Please submit orders on your purchase order form or letterhead. Orders over $50.00 must be prepaid—or send three trade and one bank reference.

Resale Numbers. California dealers must mention their resale number with their order.

Shipping. Books are best shipped via the Post Office's "book rate." We can ship via truck, UPS or Federal Express but do not recommend them for long distances, as the rates are considerably higher. Shipping is FOB Santa Barbara.

Shortages or non-receipt must be reported to us within 30 days of the order date.

Promotional materials. We can supply photographs of all our publications for your catalog work.

Book Trade. Our books are available from major wholesalers such as Baker and Taylor, Publishers Group West, Bookpeople, Pacific Pipeline, the distributors and others. See their microfiche.

Orders may be sent to P.O. Box 4232, Santa Barbara, CA 93140-4232. Telephone orders may be made to (805) 968-7277 9:00 a.m. to 5:00 p.m., Pacific time. Purchase orders may be FAXed to (805) 968-1379 at any time.

Example of discount schedule

The theory of the universal discount schedule is that the wholesaler will earn a better discount by buying in larger quantities. Bookstores and libraries ordering smaller quantities get a "courtesy discount." This encourages the purchasers of small quantities to order from wholesalers with a great title mix, where they can get a better deal and reduce their paperwork with one-stop shopping. Remember that these small quantity special orders from the stores are not getting your books on the shelf for all to see. The book has already been sold and will go straight to the customer.

No single plan fits all types of publishers. For example, if you have one book or a single small line of specialized books, cater primarily to a specific class of people, and expect to have several large dealers who purchase hundreds of books at a time, you may wish to consider a simplified discount schedule. The simplified schedule works best for sales to stores other than bookstores.

1-2	no discount
3-199	-40%
200-499	-50%
500 and up	-40% -25%

Simplified discount schedule

"Less 40%, less 25%" amounts to 55% off. First you deduct 40% and then take 25% off what is left. Wholesalers reselling to retailers make 25% on their investment, which is a good amount.

The simplified schedule gives every dealer the 40% they need, allows you to serve the non-book industry with large orders while not upsetting the book trade with its small orders, and leaves you with just three figures to remember. Whatever discount schedule you choose, make it simple. You will have to use it to compute each order.

Prices are offered on assorted titles, except where there is a great difference in price. You wouldn't mix a $1.50 title, normally wholesaled 500 at a time, with a $30 book usually purchased three at a time.

Don't confuse "discount" with "markup." A discount of 50% from $2 to $1 is the same as a 100% markup from $1 to $2.

When figuring your discounts, total the order and then subtract the discount. You will come out with a slightly higher figure than if you figure the discount per book and then extend it out. For example, buying 200 $5.95 books at 50% off, there is one dollar difference. $5.95 x 200 - 50% = $595.00, but $5.95 - 50% = $2.97 x 200 = $594.00.

Your discounts and terms should be printed in your dealer bulletins, listed in the ABA *Book Buyer's Handbook* (560 White Plains Road, Tarrytown, NY 10591), etc. where they will be easily found by your dealers.

Once you have published your prices and terms, stick to them. Besides the need to obey the FTC rules, it just is not profitable to deviate from those figures which took you so long to calculate. Some dealers will be asking for a better deal, and some publishers feel that any sale above their cost is a good one. But it is not fair to give one customer a better deal than another. You have to draw the line somewhere. Your valuable time should be used to generate additional net income, not more marginal gross.

Consignments make you into a banker as well as a publisher. Consignment is when the dealer takes delivery on the books, but doesn't pay the publisher until they are sold. The biggest problem is that since this inventory is free, the dealer may push his paid-for inventory harder. He has no incentive to move your book when he can move another he has paid for. Wholesalers/distributors are an exception; many of them operate only on consignment and pay 90 days after they ship. On the other hand, with the returns policy peculiar to the book industry, all sales really amount to "consignment."

"Delayed billings" are a little of the same thing and only constitute a loan from the publisher to the dealer. Money costs money. You can check today's price for it at your bank.

> *We are in a consignment business that pretends it is not.* - Sol Stein, President of Stein and Day

Shipping charges are usually included in the price charged on individual retail sales. The book may be advertised at "$9.95 ppd" (postpaid). While you have made an allowance for postage in the list (cover) price, the buyer feels he is getting something for nothing. Occasionally, the publisher will pay the shipping when a dealer has sent cash with order (CWO). Normally, however, the dealer pays the shipping (FOB origin).

Book rate postage is spiraling upwards and both publishers and booksellers are becoming very conscious of the shipping expenses. Similarly, the cost of packing materials and labor are high and some publishers try to offset some of these with a "handling charge." The term "handling charge" is sure to evoke a nasty response from the customer no matter how small it may be. If "postage" is not the same as the amount on the package, you will also hear about it. So, if you do plan to tack on a little extra to pay for the invoice, its First Class mailing, envelopes and shipping supplies, call the postage and handling charge "shipping."

Some publishers tack a processing charge of 50 cents onto all orders. This is a lot on a single book, but it is only a penny each on a carton of fifty. Processing the orders costs the same.

Those dealers who object to any figures higher than the postage on the carton usually just scratch it off the invoice when paying the bill. Invoice altering becomes more frequent after each Postal rate hike.

STOP stands for "Single Title Order Plan" and, like SCOP or "Single Copy Order Plan," it consists of a special multi-part order form which arrives with a check. Because the store is paying in advance, they assume a discount of 20% to 40%. The check may be filled in or blank and restricted to a certain maximum amount. Sometimes the order asks that the book be shipped direct to the customer and other times to the store. Part of the purchase order may be used as a shipping label.

Contact the American Booksellers Association for an application form for a listing in their ABA *Book Buyer's Handbook*. When you fill it out, indicate that you wish to participate in STOP and list your terms. Many publishers agree to accept STOP orders based on the list price, less a 40% discount plus $1.75 for shipping.

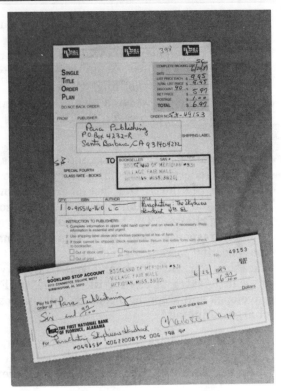

A STOP order

Terms and credit are different in the book trade. Most wholesalers and bookstores routinely take 60 days to pay, many take 90, and some get around to mailing out checks in six or eight months. This forces the publisher into a frustrating banking situation. There are very few small publishers who can afford to finance the inventories of their dealers.

The customary terms for the book industry are that invoices should be paid within 30 days of an end-of-the-month statement (30 EOM). This is up to 30 days longer than "net 30 day" terms. Some publishers, eyeing other industries, offer "2% ten day" terms, but the dealer usually pays late and still takes the 2%. Another way to get most of your money faster is to offer 5% for "cash (or check) with order" (CWO). Unfortunately, this offer is usually taken by the financially sound "good pay" customer who would pay on time anyway, not by the slow pay customer you will have to chase for months. Many of the newer small publishers don't subscribe to the 30 EOM terms or discounts for fast pay; they quote strictly "net 30 days."

"Advance dating" of invoices is sometimes done for seasonal businesses and catalog houses. The invoice is dated a couple of months later. This provides the dealer with the opportunity to get the books into stock before the rush—important where timing is critical and sales will be late.

Ship your invoices separately via first class mail; don't just enclose them in the carton with the books. The longer it takes the invoice to reach the customer, the longer the customer will take to pay it.

Once you have decided on your terms and have published them, stick to them religiously. Any sign of relaxation will be evidence that you don't mean what you say and some dealers will take advantage of you. You are a publisher, not a banker, and if you were in the loan business you would charge interest.

Credit. It is only practical to extend credit and ship quickly to new accounts. You will receive all sorts of small orders from distant bookstores and it is not worth the time and effort to run a credit check on each one. It may cost $50 or more to run a credit check, even if you do it all yourself by telephone, and it will take a lot of time. On one- and two-book orders, credit checks are not worth the effort for the occasional bad pay or bankruptcy.

If a large order out of nowhere seems too good to be true, it probably is. A few people have ordered large quantities of books (200 of a title) from small publishers without ever intending to pay for them. They turn around and sell the books to stores and remainder houses at a great discount.

In 1982, the author suffered a bad accident just prior to the ABA book fair. He was in the hospital for five weeks and could not work for almost six months. While in the hospital, he received a very large order from someone who pretended to be a big wholesaler in Michigan. The buyer even had the nerve to write across the bottom of the purchase order: "Missed you at the ABA, get well soon." It took several years to put the jerk out of business and at last report even his bankruptcy trustee couldn't collect from him.

Set a limit of, say $50, for any dealer order coming in on a letterhead or purchase order. Enclose your brochure, statement of terms and return policy with the invoice. You might also like to slip in a form letter welcoming their account, explaining that you are happy to extend credit and that prompt payment of this invoice will raise their limit to $100. Beyond that, you will require trade and bank references. Those who do not stand your test, or who are awaiting a credit check for a large purchase, may be urged to pay in advance via a "pro forma invoice" (you make out a complete invoice to include shipping charges but you don't ship the books until the invoice is paid). Another clever trick is to ask for 50% of a large invoice in advance—then ship just 50% of the order.

Schools, libraries, state and federal governments are "good pay" but often "slow pay." They have taxing authority so it is hard to go bankrupt no matter how badly they are managed. Just make sure their request comes on their purchase order. Too often someone in the Park Department will write to you on city letterhead asking for a book, with no mention of money. This may well be an unauthorized order.

Sometimes schools or government agencies will telephone or fax an order and then will follow with a written purchase order. If you are lucky, they will mark the second message: *Confirming order—do not duplicate*. Otherwise, you may wind up shipping twice.

Join a local publishing association and meet some of the people in other book firms. If you question an account, often a call to one of your contemporaries will provide the credit information you seek.

Foreign orders may be treated in the same way as domestic ones. There will be a difference in shipping charges, sometimes higher and sometimes lower. Unless they pay in dollars drawn on a U.S. bank, there may be a check cashing charge. Foreigners have about the same payment history as U.S. customers.

Some publishers place a surcharge on foreign orders, and it might be appropriate to add a small paperwork fee to very large orders requiring customs forms. But since most foreign orders do not require more work than domestic shipments, a surcharge discourages foreign sales and insults foreign customers.

Statements. Wholesalers and bookstores are accustomed to receiving end-of-the-month statements of their accounts; they want a recapitulation of the many small orders they have placed. Statements are not a requirement, but they may speed payment when these customers are waiting for one. You can type up statement forms but initially it will be far cheaper, easier and faster to photocopy your invoices. Often the copy shops near colleges charge as little as five cents each for photocopies. Check the *Yellow Pages* and make some calls. Once you are computerized, printing statements will be easy.

Photocopy the invoice and stuff the copy into a windowed #10 envelope. This system avoids separate statements, transposition errors, small envelopes, typing and collection stickers. Hand-write your collection message on the copy. The collection messages may include:

1. Is there any reason why this past due bill has not been paid?

2. If you are unable to pay the whole bill, won't you evidence your good faith by sending us a partial payment?

3. We subscribe to Dun and Bradstreet's Commercial Collection service.

4. If payment is not received within ten days, we will be forced to turn this matter over to our attorney for collection.

Enclose brochures on new books with the statements. You might as well fill up the envelope to its full postage limit.

Collections. When the money does not come in on time you have to exercise your collection process.

When keyboarding invoices, always include the name of the person signing the order on the second line. This focuses your claim on a specific individual, where it will have more impact than if you simply send invoices and statements to the company. Now pen a nice personal note on the bottom of the statement to this particular person.

If the account goes another month without a response, pen a stronger note on the bottom of the statement. Then wait two weeks and make a telephone call. If they don't pay in 90 days, cut them off. You don't need customers like them. In most other industries, 30 days would be the limit; the book industry is much slower.

After this, there are a couple of options. You may arrange with your attorney to send a standard collection letter which will be typed out automatically on a word processor. The charge may be $10 to $15 and the attorney may give you a better price on a quantity of collections. You may also consider a collection agency. Your local firm will have affiliates all over North America or you might contact a large firm with many offices, such as Dun & Bradstreet. Collection agencies usually take one-third as their collection fee and they prefer the easy cases. They have little power and usually get their money through a personal visit, which embarrasses the bookseller. They will threaten legal action and will turn the case over to a local attorney if they fail to collect. Generally, the older the debt, the harder it is to collect.

SKO-Brenner-American is a collection agency that specializes in the book trade. They publish a monthly confidential list of delinquent bookstores and wholesalers. They will also handle collections. For information on their services and a subscription to their newsletter, contact SKO-Brenner-American, Phyllis Ball, 196 Merrick Road, Suite 101, Oceanside, NY 11572, (516) 764-4400.

The telephone is a powerful collection instrument and a good supplement to dunning notices. Many callers use guide scripts to make sure they get their complete message across quickly.

Remember, it is better to have the books returned unsold than to have the books sold and not get paid.

If a customer has been bouncing large checks on you, put the next one in "for collection." Your bank will send it to the customer's bank with instructions to hold the check until there is enough money in the account to pay it.

To collect a large bill from a foreign customer, try calling the cultural attache at the nearest embassy or consulate. Often the attache will relay your message and this puts pressure on the foreign debtor.

The higher your markup, the better you can afford mistakes.

Whatever collection system you select, make it automatic so that you can be objective and will not allow deadbeats to negotiate delays. Let customers know you mean business. See *Business Letters For Publishers* for some suggested collection letters. See the Appendix.

**Matching checks
to Invoices**

The accounts receivable operation is one of the most pleasant because it is always fun to count your money. As the checks arrive to pay for due bills, match them with the invoices (if only everyone would note the invoice numbers on their checks!). Mark the invoice with a date stamp to indicate when the payment was credited. Put this pink file copy in a record storage box or binder. See the invoice handling discussion in Chapter 10.

Checks will be received made out to the publishing company, the author or the name of the book. Name them all on your check deposit stamp. Pay a little extra for a self-inking stamp, it will save you a lot of time.

Deposits may be made up every week or so. Endorse the checks with a rubber stamp and list them on an adding machine tape. If your bank wants you to list each check individually on the deposit slip, threaten to go to another bank. Big corporations do not have to do this and you won't either if you stand your ground. Keep it simple!

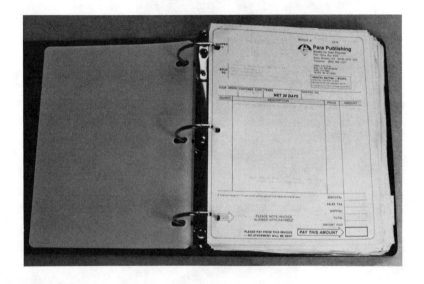

Invoices may be stored in a binder

Returns are one of the biggest controversies in the book business. Both wholesalers and bookstores expect to be able to return all books they do not sell, and they return 15 to 20% (figures for the chains are higher). If this sounds like a lot, then consider that the figure is so high for mass market paperbacks that the dealers save shipping by stripping the books and sending back only the covers for credit.

Make effective use of your most valuable asset, your time.

Book Return Policy

1. Our books are returnable. If a title isn't moving in your market, we want to get it back before a new edition makes it obsolete. Thank you for giving it a chance on your valuable shelf space. Our return period is normally between 90 days and one year of the publisher's invoice date; however, we will accept the book for return after one year as long as the edition is still in print. To keep our products current, we update our titles every one and a half to two years.

2. Return permission must be requested so that we may issue detailed packing and shipping instructions.

3. Notice of shortage or non-receipt must be made within 30 days of the shipping/invoice date for domestic shipments; 60 days for foreign.

4. Books damaged in transit are not the responsibility of the publisher. Please make claim to the carrier.

5. Returns must be accompanied by your packing slip listing quantity, title, author, original invoice number and invoice date. Books returned with this information will be credited with 100% of the invoice price, minus shipping. Otherwise, it will be assumed the original discount was 60%. Some books have been returned to us when they should have been directed to one of our wholesalers; books should be returned to their source.

6. Routing: Ship books via parcel post (book rate) prepaid or UPS prepaid to Para Publishing, Attn: D. Poynter, 530 Ellwood Ridge, Santa Barbara, CA 93117-9700. Note, this is not the same as our order address.

7. To qualify for a refund, returned books must arrive here in good resaleable condition. If they are not now resaleable, please don't bother to return them. If the books are in good condition but you are not willing to package them properly for the return trip, please don't waste your time and postage.

To package the books so that they will survive the trip, we suggest you wrap them in the same way that they were sent to you. There are two important steps in successful book packaging: Keep them clean and immobilize them. Place the stacked books in a plastic bag. This will separate the dirty newsprint and greasy Styrofoam peanuts or discs from the book edges and will prevent grit from creeping between the pages. To keep the books from shifting (which causes scuffing), cut a shipping carton to the right size and stuff it tightly with dunnage.

Since it has been our experience that books shipped loose in oversize "Jiffy bags" always arrive scuffed, it is now our policy to refuse them at the Post Office so that they will be returned to the bookstore. Do not use Jiffy bags!

8. A credit memo will be issued toward future purchases.

9. Industry tells us that it now costs more than eight dollars to write a letter. Correspondence, packaging and postage cost us all a great deal in money and time (and time is money). Years ago when postage was cheap, it made sense to return slow moving books. Today, however, many bookstores are finding it is more cost effective to mark down the books and move them out.

Thank you for contacting Para Publishing.

Sample return policy statement

The returns system almost amounts to consignment and the publisher is caught in a bind, because if the booksellers did not have the return privilege, they would be far less likely to carry his books. The publisher wants his books displayed and so has to take the chance of having several of them come back. Therefore, there is little difference between consignment and a no-strings return policy. Returns result in zero profit transactions (ZPT's). The books went out with paperwork, and came back with paperwork; everyone was busy but nothing was sold.

From time to time, people in the book industry suggest changes to the system of returns. One recommendation which is often heard is to eliminate the returns and to pass the savings on to the bookstore in the form of higher discounts. Because we operate in a free-market economy with a lot of competition, none of these suggestions have ever caught on.

Make up a return policy and send it to anyone who requests it. Baker & Taylor and some of the other wholesalers will probably ask for your return policy when they first open an account with you. Also send the policy when a bookstore or wholesaler requests permission to return some books.

Most publishers will allow returns between 90 days and 12 months of the invoice date. They specify 90 days because they want to make sure the books were given a fair trial on the shelves, but 12 months because they do not want them sitting around too long; the title may go into a new printing.

Most publishers require the bookseller to request permission and specific shipping instructions first, but few stores do. They just ship the books back.

The paperwork with the return should identify the original invoice number under which the books were purchased. You want to credit the bookseller with the correct amount, the amount they paid. You also want to make sure the books came directly from you. If the books were purchased from a wholesaler, they should be returned to the wholesaler.

Books must arrive back at the publisher in good, unblemished resaleable condition so that they may be returned to stock. This is the biggest failing of the bookstores. They almost never pack the books properly. They just throw them in a carton, often without cushioning material, and send them back. During the long trip, the books chafe against each other and the carton and, consequently, they arrive in a scuffed, battered condition.

Large publishing firms usually do not send refunds on returns. They issue credits because they are dealing with the customer on a continuing basis. Small publishers, with few other titles to offer, should send a refund check.

The worst thing that can happen to a new publisher is to have a phenomenally successful first book. They think they know the secret and that publishing is easy. - Tom Drewes, Quality Books

Never skimp on your research. So-called writer's block is invariably the result of too little research. If you know enough, you won't have trouble filling as many pages as you want to. - Louise Purwin Zobel

Chapter Seven

Promoting Your Book

Making the Public Aware of Your Book Without Spending For Advertising

As an author, whether you self-publish or go with a large publisher, *you* must do the promotion. If you intend to be a successful author, you will measure your success with money. To make a profit, you will depend on good promotion and marketing. This chapter covers promotion: those methods which require some time and effort but no big advertising dollars. Of course, there will be a certain amount of overlap.

Your most important reference book will be *Literary Market Place*. While you may use the copy in your local library, this reference will be used so often, you should buy one for use at your desk. Also recommended is *The Publicity Manual* by Kate Kelly.

> Do not spend a nickel on paid advertising until you have exhausted all the free publicity available.

The secrets to book sales are, first, to produce a good product and, second, to let people know about it. Most small publishers receive very little publicity for their books. This lack of attention is not because of any great conspiracy between the big (New York) publishers and the media; it is simply because the neophytes do not ask for coverage. Many small publishers are good at publishing but haven't any experience in marketing. They seem to have little interest in their books beyond the editorial work and production; they do not want to sell, they just want to create. Some beginning publishers seem to feel the marketing end of publishing is "too commercial" and this becomes their excuse for neglecting the most important part of any business: informing the buying public of your wares. For, obviously, if you cannot sell your product, you will not be able to afford to produce more editorial material.

Cost to advertise. Selling books through space advertising is expensive because books are a *low ticket* (low selling price) item. If you were selling airplanes, one sale would pay for a lot of ad space, and if you were selling less expensive candy, you would sell to so many people that the ads might pay. It is tougher to break even when advertising a low priced product to a small and scattered group of people.

For example, a one-half page ad in a national book-oriented magazine could run you $1,370.00. Using round numbers and assuming you printed the book for $1.00 and are selling it for $10.00, you would have to sell 153 books at retail, or 274 books at wholesale, just to break even on the ad. Experience tells us you will not.

Do not spend money on advertising when you can get publicity free. Put your time and money into less expensive review copies and news releases. Use the free publicity to find which magazines are right for your book. Then spend your advertising money there. Always test before you spend money. Too many publishers start with large ads and blow their promotion money in the wrong places.

Just as a parent's responsibilities do not end with giving birth, an author's do not end with publication. The child must be raised and the book must be marketed.

Publicity vs. advertising. The major differences between *publicity* and *advertising* are cost and control. Publicity is free while advertising is not. On the other hand, you may control your advertising, while your publicity may be rewritten by the editor or not run at all. The public is usually more receptive to publicity because editorial copy is viewed as news. Advertising is perceived as self-serving. An industry rule-of-thumb is that editorial coverage is seven times as valuable as paid coverage.

Competition for free space is a tough proposition. Over 100 new books are published for every day the bookstores are open; the crowd is thicker in the fall than the spring. You have to compete for attention in a crowded field and against much larger, more knowledgeable firms. But you will be surprised at how successful you can be when you jump into the fray, exploiting the media through news releases, review copies, radio and TV appearances, feature stories, lectures, etc.

Large publishers are lucky if 40% of their titles make money, and they have departments of experts to launch their promotion. They also have built up thousands of key contacts during their many years in the business. You have only one book, your first, and therefore, you have only one chance to make it. But look at the brighter side. The big firms often work through routine and without imagination. Your overhead is much lower and you are cutting out the middlemen by publishing yourself. You will do a more effective job of promotion because you have a greater interest in the book than a publisher who is looking after several titles at one time.

By doing the promotion yourself, you are avoiding the most common problem in author/publisher relationships: differing views on the amount of effort which should be invested in each area of promotion and advertising. The author cannot be objective about his product and is convinced that the book would sell better if only the publisher would promote it. The publisher, on the other hand, needs more sales to convince him it is worth investing more dollars in advertising.

Before we plan the attack, we have to analyze the current state and trend of the industry. We have to understand its approach to selling books. During the late 1970s, many of the big New York publishers were absorbed by the bigger multinational conglomerates such as ITT and Gulf & Western. Normally, the main interest of these larger companies is to serve their stockholders by generating maximum return on their investment. To do this, they employ sophisticated marketing techniques to move books. These conglomerates concentrate their efforts on sure bets and high volume, often tying in films and merchandise offers to build public interest. Their marketing dovetails perfectly with the approach by the large chains such as Walden and B. Dalton. Most of their manuscripts come from well-known celebrities or are custom written for a pre-defined audience.

Some small publishers, on the other hand, accept "good literature" manuscripts and then try to interest the public in the book. Because of this approach, the book often lacks a well-defined audience. The problem is compounded by a lack of resources for proper promotion.

It is nearly impossible to compete with the large publishing firms on their ground because you do not have their connections or clout. You do not want to follow the small publisher because he is not making much money. But there is a lot of room for the very small independent publisher with imagination, initiative and a well-defined target market.

Analyze the market by determining who might purchase your book and then figure the best way to reach them. If your book is on auto repair for the car owner, one prospect is the car enthusiast. What does he read? You will want to send news releases, review copies, ads and maybe even articles to auto magazines. Since there aren't too many little old ladies who are going to purchase such a book, you won't send review copies to women's magazines. Where do car enthusiasts congregate? Auto supply stores, car rallies, auto shows? If this repair manual covers a single type of car, you may be able to find a highly targeted mailing list of male owners of that type of car. The trick is to think about who the buyer might be and then think about where this type of person can be found. Rarely is the answer: bookstores or libraries.

Analyze carefully the type of person who is a prospective purchaser of your book. This is perhaps the single most important thing to consider.

As you read through the next few chapters, think about your book and its market. Make a list of, or underline, those ideas mentioned that best fit your book. Then go back and work out a promotional schedule, by the week, for several months. List ad deadlines, dates for mailings, etc. Set a schedule so you won't lose sight of it later when you are busy typing orders and stuffing boxes.

A common complaint by those who use a Hi-Liter felt tip marker to indicate the important parts of this book is that their copy of *The Self-Publishing Manual* winds up completely yellow.

If you are approaching book stores, college book stores, public libraries or school libraries, you want to determine their seasonal buying patterns. If you are pursuing direct mail sales, you will want to set up a system of mailings and emphasize the program in certain seasons. The keys to your promotion are market targeting and timing. More on all these later.

Binder organization. Organize your thoughts and record your work by setting up a binder for your book. Use a 2" or 3" three-ring binder with dividers for five sections. The red *slant-ring* binders with inside pockets are best. Now set up each section, as follows:

—*Section one* is where you record your promotional plan. Type up your initial plan and check off the items when completed. Whenever you have a new idea, turn to the second page of section one and make a note. Use the balance of this section to store every news release you write, every ad you place and every brochure you design. Date each promotional piece and review what you have done months later.

Our book marketing philosophy. We firmly believe the best way to sell most nonfiction books is with book reviews, news releases and a limited amount of highly targeted direct mail. Then once you have established your book in the U.S., it is time to explore the foreign markets. Book reviews and news releases result in free publicity while direct mail delivers your sales message directly to potential customers.

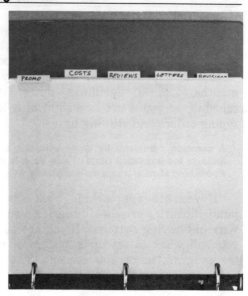

Set up a red promotion binder for each book

—*Section two* is for all your costing information. Store copies of all the printing, artists', trucking, etc. bills as well as all the printing quotations. With this information all in one place, even after six printings you will know exactly how many books have been printed and what each print run cost.

—*Section three* is where you store the reviews, testimonials and other publicity you have generated. All the good things which have been said about your book are kept in one place so that when you want to make a list of testimonials, they will be easy to find.

—*Section four* is for any important correspondence. Here you will store some of the more interesting letters which do not fit in the other sections.

—*Section five* is the revision section. As you come across new material or think of something that should be included in the next edition, make a note and store it here. Also take one copy of the book and mark it "Correction Copy" and keep it near your desk. Cut off a corner of the front cover so that it won't walk out of your office or find its way back into stock. As you find small errors or want to make changes, mark this book. Then when it comes time to return to press, all your revision information will be in the correction copy and the fifth section of your binder.

You will appreciate the promotion binders even more after you publish several books. All your costing, promotion, review and revision information will be easy to find.

Rate of sale. You can expect your sales to take on an airfoil shape if your promotion is well organized. Sales will climb rapidly, level out, taper off and become steady. Thereafter you will notice bumps in response to seasonal changes, or when your advertising or promotional work is successful. The big initial jump is due to your pre-publication publicity.

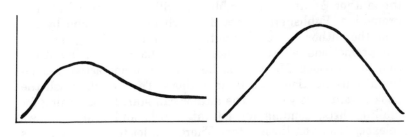

Your sales chart   **Typical big firm's sales chart**

The big New York publishers market books in the same way Hollywood sells a motion picture. They throw it out on the market to see if anyone likes it. If it gets a response, they dump in a lot of promotional money. Then they push it for a couple of months. When the interest cools, they bring out another product and start all over. As a small publisher, it makes more sense to market your book like breakfast food or soap. Develop your product, pour on the promotion, carve a niche in the market and then continue to sell at the same level for years. This can be done with a nonfiction book which is revised at each printing.

> *The main difference between marketing a book and marketing soap is that a book is a one-shot deal . . . a book usually has only 90 days to make it or it's dead.* - Carole Dolph, Promotional Director, Doubleday & Company

"**Best sellers**" are only a name, a myth. This is not like a gold record in the music industry or another service to the trade, run by Bowker. National best seller lists (there are several and they do not often agree) are assembled from certain bookstore and other sales reports. Even if you move a million books via mail order distribution, you won't make a best seller list. On the other hand, you may calculate that your book is the best selling book in its field and there is no reason you can't mention this in your advertising.

Promotion is up to you. Whether you are the author or both the author and the publisher, it is up to you to make your book a success. If you have a little of the ham in you, if you are "mediagenic," so much the better.

One of the major problems in traditional publishing is that the author assumes the publisher will take care of all the promotion. Publishers do not do much promoting, and by the time the author figures this out, the book is "not new," making any promotional efforts too late. The media does not pay attention to old books. Many publishers will welcome active promotional participation from their authors. They want to sell the book as much as you do. The author can start by searching for mailing lists, sending for ad rate cards and drafting news releases (more on these later). There is a lot to learn from this chapter even if you aren't self-publishing.

Bookstores make your book available but they do not promote it. These outlets provide availability, but you must encourage people to go into the stores. If your book is a hot seller, the bookstores will want to carry it. If no one asks for it, the stores will not touch it. You must create the demand.

Key contacts are those people who can help you move the greatest volume of books with the least expenditure of time and money. These contacts must be developed if you are going to promote your book properly. The only difference between you and a professional book publicist is that the professional already has the media contacts. There are many wholesalers, TV people and subsidiary rights buyers who are just waiting to "discover" you and your book. While most are very busy, they want you; that is what their job is all about. You will meet a great number of nice, helpful people, but only a few "key" contacts will do you a great amount of good. What you have to do is to locate and then carefully cultivate them. Some of the people will be listed in *Literary Market Place* and other directories available at your library. For others, you may have to call the company and ask for the name of the "small press buyer," etc. Tell the company operator who you are and ask who you should properly correspond with. Write or call this contact and field your sales pitch; establish a rapport. Maintain credibility and remember that they are everyone else's key contact, too. Do not expect them to return calls. Send review copies of your book and follow up in a few days with a telephone call asking "have you received it?" If this is a chain or a wholesaler, be bold and ask for an order.

Start files on these key contacts and fill the folders with letters and notes of your telephone conversations. Note the personal likes and dislikes of your contacts so you can bring them up in future conversations. Treat contacts well and they will be there to help you with your next book, too.

Address codes. Tracing each order you receive back to a specific promotional effort or paid advertisement provides you with important business intelligence. Without this information, you may be unknowingly spending your energy and money in the wrong places. Waste becomes tragedy when you continue blind promotional spending because you are not certain which projects are paying off by bringing in book orders. Both your time and money are limited; you must spend them in those places which will bring maximum return. The trick is to add a code to your address.

To code your address, just add an extra letter or number to your street address or box. Code everything! Every brochure, ad, order blank, press release, directory listing, everything. Then, you will receive only a few orders you cannot trace. Some people will be influenced by your promotion and will seek your book through their library or bookstore. But coding will indicate the source of most of your orders.

Show me a publisher who says you can never tell which book is going to make it and I'll show you a publisher who evaluates manuscripts without considering the market.

List your address as *4759 Walker Street, Suite 712*, or in a classified ad where every word costs, *4759-712 Walker*. Many customers figure out the obvious codes and, knowing they aren't important to the address, leave them off. So, if you are advertising in *Popular Science* in August, 1989, don't use *4759 Walker Street, Dept. PS-8-9*. Use a plain number or a *suite* number; they appear important to the address. Never use a *department* number which is an obvious code. Careful coding is even more important with news releases and those items not going directly to the general public, because the media are conscious of these codes and often won't repeat them. An address code is of no value to you if it doesn't get used.

List all the places to which you are mailing news releases and other promotional material and give a short code to each. Letters are good for a start but there aren't enough of them and some can be confused when rendered in script on an envelope. Avoid "I" & "1", "u" & "v", "G" & "6", "Z" & "2", "0" &"O", and "4" & "H".

Many people ask "But won't the Post Office object to all this added information?" The answer is no, as long as the essential addressing information is there so they may easily determine where to direct your mail. On the other hand, you may confuse visiting customers who drive down your street looking for a building tall enough for a *Suite 712*.

If you have more than one title (book) or edition (binding) and are advertising or promoting two or more in the same market, make a notation on each envelope as you process orders, indicating which book was ordered. Then total up the responses at the end of the month and record them by code letter or number on a ledger sheet. Also enter on the sheet when certain advertising and promotion hit, so you can better visualize the reasons for the results. These tallies aren't hard work and can even be done spread out on the floor in front of the TV set.

Where some of your orders come from is terribly revealing. How else would you know, for example, that a mention in a *Changing Times* article brought in 140 orders? Or that most foreign bookstores find you in *Books in Print?* With this information, you will be able to assess what works and where you can most effectively spend your time and money to generate more sales. After a few months you will wonder why address coding wasn't obvious to you from the beginning.

Promotional materials take many forms and many are already at hand. Think of the ways you can use photocopies of your manuscript, folded and gathered pages, overruns on covers, photocopies of the boards, etc.

Consider combining the jacket of your book with a cover letter and an order blank for a mailing. Another successful and popular promotional piece is to make press kit folders with overruns of the cover. Just ask the printer to print a few hundred extra covers. Then fold them, tuck in your promotional materials and mail them out. The result is an inexpensive yet impressive, professional-looking press kit.

Professional book promotion services are available for those who haven't the time or desire to do their own work. These professionals can be a great help, especially on your first book when you are just learning the ropes. Book publicists write and place news releases, organize autograph parties and place authors on TV. Typically, they charge a flat monthly fee, plus expenses for all services. For radio and TV they might ask for $750 for the first city they service, such as a big one like Los Angeles, and $250, plus expenses, for each additional city. In each city, you might do four radio and TV shows each day for two days. If you decide to hire a professional publicist, start early. Do not wait until the pub date.

Large publishers have their own in-house promotion departments, while *Publishers Weekly* estimates there are close to 200 independent book publicists. Some are listed in the Appendix. More may be found in *Literary Market Place* under "Public Relations Services."

Testimonials and endorsements. Many people feel that there is no better promotion than a recommendation from a satisfied customer. Testimonials and endorsements will be used in two places: on the back cover of the book and in your sales literature.

Being an author is 5% writing and 95% promotion. - Russ Marano, *Hi-Tek Newsletter.*

—**Back cover**. Endorsements may be gathered from peer reviewers who read and comment on chapters or complete manuscripts. You want their comments as peer reviewers to double check your work, and you want their praise to quote since they must be opinion molders. This means you want people known in the book's field or known to the general public. They should be people with recognizable names or recognizable titles.

Please do not ask Dan Poynter to endorse your book unless it is on publishing or sky diving. His endorsement on other subjects would not be appropriate or valuable.

—**Sales literature**. You will want to add testimonials and excerpts from your reviews to all your brochures, as well as to your "review and testimonial" sheet. The rev/test sheet is an important piece of publicity in that it indicates that other people like your book. This sheet should be sent to later reviewers, prospective dealers and anyone else you are trying to convince the book is a winner.

You may need endorsements on a particular point or you may need a variety of endorsements. You do not want all the endorsements to say the same thing, or to be very general, such as *it is a great book*. After someone has reviewed your manuscript, approach them again. Write out an endorsement making a particular point and ask the peer reviewer to look it over and edit it. Say that you need a quote in this area. Editing is much easier than creating and most people will accept the prompting quickly.

The best way to collect testimonials is to ask for them. It is easier than you think, because people like to see their name in print. As long as your book is good, experts in the field will jump at the chance to be mentioned. If they sell products or consulting, the exposure is valuable to them. Whether due to vanity or possible financial gain, recognizable people want to have their names in print. Do not pay for endorsements; quotes cannot be considered valid if payments are involved.

Unsolicited testimonials will arrive after the book is published. They should be answered and filed for future use.

Books do not sell themselves. People sell books.

Your publication date is a place in the future, well after your books are off the press, when your promotion hits and your books are available in the stores. The publication date is a means of focusing attention. The idea is to have the product accessible when public attention peaks in response to your promotion. You want to time book reviews, TV appearances, space advertising, autograph parties, etc. to hit after bookstore deliveries.

The publication date has nothing to do with the date your book is published—the day it comes off the press and you have finished books in hand. It is the date you list on the ABI (Advance Book Information) form but it is not the *day of publication* you list on the copyright form. The publication date is a *fiction* for the benefit of a few big, important pre-publication review magazines such as *Publishers Weekly*. There is nothing to stop you from selling or shipping books. Due to the high cost of storing inventory, even many large New York publishers do not hold their books from the market until the pub-date. In fact, sometimes entire print runs are sold out prior to the publication date.

After your publication date has passed, remove mention of it from your review slip, news release, etc. There is no need to remind the media that your book is no longer new. Let them focus on the issue and the quality of the book.

The big, important pre-publication reviewers need 12 to 15 weeks lead time, so you will have to pick a publication date at least four months after the books are scheduled to roll off the press. *Publishers Weekly* and the other *wholesale trade* review magazines need this time to evaluate your book, assign it to a reviewer, write the review and get it into print for the benefit of the stores. Monthly and bimonthly magazines such as *The Kirkus Reviews* need even more lead time. The stores, in turn, need time to order the book and receive it into stock so it will be available to the public on or before your publication date. When planning your publication date, remember that book rate shipping can take three weeks from coast to coast.

There is no way anything you send to PW can be too early. - John Baker, Editor-in-Chief, *Publishers Weekly*

Newspapers have shorter lead times than magazines. Since they are dailies or weeklies, they require books just a few weeks prior to the publication date.

Production is always subject to delay, so it is recommended that for your first book, and until you learn the problems exacted by the printing trade, you wait until the book is off the press before you set your publication date.

If you have achieved sufficient pre-publication momentum, you should make a significant amount of sales before the printing bill arrives. It is a matter of planning, scheduling, timing and work. The big publishers expend 90% of their promotional effort by the publication date. You, of course, will keep up the pressure.

The best publication dates are probably in the first quarter of the year. Most of the big publishers aim for October and November to take advantage of the Christmas gift-buying season. Avoiding the last quarter of the year will decrease your competition for publicity.

Some publishers will tie their publication date to a significant date in order to hitch on to publicity naturally occurring on that date. For example, if you have a book on Spike Jones, you might want to schedule your publication date for his birthday. If your book is on an aspect of World War II, you might tie in to D-Day. People will be thinking about the war on this date so your book will benefit from the memorial publicity. If you know your book and its subject area well, finding a date to link to should be easy. If you need help, check *Chase's Annual Events* and Beam's *Directory of International Toiurist Events*.

It is always smart to take advantage of a prime selling season. A book on a summer sport should come out in early spring when people are making plans for the summer. A book on skiing should come out in the fall.

Book reviews sell books. Reviews are not difficult to get, while they cost you very little in time and money. But there are two major types of book review media: *pre-publication date* or *wholesale reviews* and *post-publication date* or *retail reviews*. They cater to separate markets and the approach to each is different. In addition, there are early reviews and continuing reviews. Review order and breakdown looks like this:

1. Pre-publication date reviews aimed at the wholesale market.

2. Early reviews, copyright and listings.

3. Post-publication date reviews aimed at the retail market. These include:

 a. The sure bets; those that will probably review the book.

 b. The rest; those that might possibly review the book.

4. Continuing review program.

—**Pre-publication reviews** are directed toward the industry. Certain magazines will review your book prior to publication so that the bookstores and libraries will have the opportunity to stock it before patrons start asking for it. Since over 100 new titles are published for each day the stores are open, there is no way a store can stock every book. In fact, booksellers can't even spend the time to evaluate them all. Consequently, many book dealers and librarians depend on the concise summaries in industry review magazines when making their purchasing choices. Pre-publication reviews are directed at the trade and should not be confused with the regular book reviews aimed at the ultimate consumer/reader. Good reviews in the pre-publication review magazines will bring you more good reviews in other publications later.

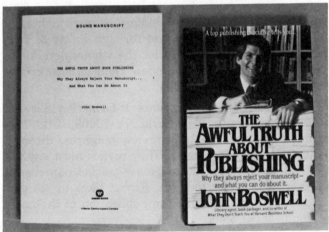

Bound galley and finished book

If your book fails to sell, you don't know your market.

Ninety or more days prior to your publication date, send bound galleys with a cover letter and a news release to the following pre-publication reviewers. Galleys may be just photocopies of the pasted-up boards but you stand a much better chance of review if the pages are perfect bound with a plain cover. Pre-publication reviewers are used to receiving bound galleys in a book-sized format. For instructions on preparing galleys or *Cranes*, see the Special Report titled *Book Reviews*. See the Appendix.

1. *Publishers Weekly*, Forecasts, 249 West 17th Street New York, NY 10011, (212) 645-0067, 463-6758. *PW* is directed at the book trade (bookstores, libraries and publishers). A good review here will result in many bookstore orders; most will come through wholesalers. *Publishers Weekly* gives priority to books with broad general appeal. They review new books only, no reprints, reissues or new editions. Send galleys. Circulation 38,000.

2. *Library Journal*, Nora Rawlinson, 249 West 17th Street, New York, NY 10011, (212) 645-0067, 463-6758. *LJ* is a magazine directed to general public librarians. They review 5,000 books each year specifically to assess their value to the library market. For many nonfiction books, a good review in *Library Journal* will sell over 1,000 copies. A rave review on a high demand topic may move 5,000. Most of these library orders will come through a library wholesaler, and some 80% of these through Baker & Taylor. Therefore it is important to let the wholesalers know about your book, too. *LJ* will review from galleys or the finished book. Circulation: 28,000.

3. *Kirkus Reviews*, Library Advance Information Service, 200 Park Avenue South, New York, NY 10003, (212) 777-4554. *Kirkus Reviews* is a book review magazine directed toward libraries and bookstores. They review most any fiction and nonfiction except poetry, mass-market paperbacks and children's books for toddlers. *Kirkus* likes to see galleys three to four months prior to publication of the book. Circulation is about 5,400.

Book reviewing is one of the few activities in the world that could be said to depend largely on love. - Jack Beatty, Literary Editor, *New Republic*

4. ALA *Booklist*, Up Front, Advance Reviews, 50 East Huron Street, Chicago, IL 60611, (312) 944-6780. *Booklist* reviews books for small and medium-sized public libraries. They review fiction, nonfiction, reference, young adult and children's books. This does not include textbooks, workbooks, pamphlets or coloring materials. Send galleys or finished books. Circulation is 31,500.

5. *The New York Times Book Review*, 229 West 43rd Street, New York, NY 10036, (212) 556-1234. *The New York Times* is one of the most prestigious of review publications. *Times* reviews are also syndicated, so a review there may appear in papers throughout the country. *The Times* does not review very technical, specialized or juvenile books. Send galleys and then send books when printed. Circulation is 1,600,000.

6. *The Los Angeles Times Magazine*, Linden Gross, Times Mirror Square, Los Angeles, CA 90053, (213) 237-7811. *Times* editors look for books which are of general interest to their newspaper readers. Circulation: 1,100,000 daily, 1,300,000 Sunday.

7. Quality Books, Inc., 918 Sherwood Drive, Lake Bluff, IL 60044-2204. (708) 295-2010. Quality is a distributor of small press titles to libraries.

8. Chicago Public Library, Mary Ellen Quinn, Collection Department, 1224 West Van Buren, Chicago, IL 60607.

9. American Library Association, Sandy Whiteley, *Reference Book Bulletin*, 50 East Huron Street, Chicago, IL 60611-2795. (Two copies.)

10. Major book clubs. Send bound galleys to the major clubs, such as Book-Of-The-Month and Literary Guild and those specializing in the book's field. See *Literary Market Place* for a list of book clubs and the Appendix for a book club mailing list.

"F&G's" are the folded and gathered signatures of the printed book ready for binding. F&G's used to be sent to the publisher for approval prior to binding the print run. *Bound galleys* are F&G's with a generic perfect-bound cover.

11. Presentation copies to opinion molders. The best way to get sales moving is to get the book talked about by the right people. These may amount to just a very few people to hundreds. Sometimes the publisher uses these special bound galleys to get the public talking about the book. Many people feel receiving an advance bound galley is much more impressive than receiving the actual book. Some opinion molders should get bound galleys, while others should receive the finished product.

—Early reviews, copyright and listings. In anticipation of your new book coming off the press, address shipping bags to those places listed below and stuff them, as appropriate, with: cover letter, review slips, photocopied Advance Book Information form, and a 4 x 6 or larger black and white photograph of the book's cover. Stuff in brochures, copies of early reviews and other materials to convince reviewers the book has been accepted by others. Do not skimp here. Then when the truck arrives from the printer, stuff the books into the bags and ship them off.

Note what is said about each of the addressees below, as some may not be appropriate to your book. If yours is an adult scientific text, do not bother to send it to the *Horn Book Magazine* which reviews children's books.

1. One copy to *Publishers Weekly*, Weekly Record, 249 West 17th Street, New York, NY 10011, (212) 645-0067, 463-6758. You should have sent bound galleys to *PW* some months earlier. This is a confirmation copy to show the book has been published.

2. One copy to *Library Journal*, Bette-Lee Fox, 249 West 17th Street, New York, NY 10011, (212) 645-0067, (212) 463-6758. You should have sent bound galleys some months earlier. This is a confirmation copy to show the book has been published.

3. Two copies to *School Library Journal*, Attn: Trevelyn Jones, 247 West 17th Street, New York, NY 10011, (212) 645-0067. *SLJ* will consider for review any book appropriate to school library use. This monthly has a circulation of 43,000.

4. One copy to H.W. Wilson Company, Attn: *Cumulative Book Index*, 950 University Avenue, Bronx, NY 10452, (212) 588-8400, (800) 462-6060 in NY, (800) 367-6770 outside NY. For a description of services offered by the H.W. Wilson Company, see Chapter Five.

5. Send one copy to H.W. Wilson Company, Attn: Martha T. Mooney, *Book Review Digest*, 950 University Avenue, Bronx, NY 10452, (212) 588-8400, (800) 367-6770, (800) 462-6060 (NY). This monthly publication (except February and July) publishes some 6,000 abbreviated reviews annually.

6. One copy to *The New York Times*, Attn: Daily Book Review Section, 229 West 43rd Street, New York, NY 10036, (212) 556-1234.

7. One copy to *The New York Times Magazine*, 229 West 43rd Street, New York, NY 10036, (212) 556-1234.

8. One copy to *Choice*, Attn: Patricia Sabosik, 100 Riverview Center, Middletown, CT 06457, (203) 347-6933. *Choice* is a publication of the Association of College and Research Libraries, a division of the American Library Association. Monthly except August, circulation 4,800.

9. Two copies to ALA *Booklist*, American Library Association, 50 East Huron Street, Chicago, IL 60611, (312) 944-6780. You should have sent bound galleys to *Booklist* some months earlier.

10. One copy to *Kirkus Reviews*, 200 Park Avenue South, New York, NY 10003-1543, (212) 777-4554. You should have sent bound galleys to *Kirkus* some months earlier.

11. One copy to the *Horn Book Magazine*, Attn: Anita Silvey, 41 Beacon Street, Boston, MA 02108, (617) 227-1555, (800) 325-1170. *Horn* reviews about 500 books each year for children and young adults. It is published bimonthly and has a circulation of 24,000.

12. One copy to *Small Press Review*, Attn: Len Fulton, P.O. Box 100-P, Paradise, CA 95969, (916) 877-6110. *The Small Press Review* specializes in fiction and poetry.

13. One copy to Gale Research Co., Attn: *Contemporary Authors*, The Book Tower, Detroit, MI 48226, (313) 961-2242, (800) 521-0707, (800) 877-GALE.

14. One copy to The Library of Congress, Exchange and Gift Division, Gift Section, Washington, DC 20540.

15. One copy to the Baker & Taylor Company, Academic Library Services Selection Department, P.O. Box 6920, Bridgewater, NJ 08807, (908) 218-0400 for their New Book Approval and Current Books for Academic Libraries plans. Enclose a photocopy of the Advanced Book Information (ABI) form. See Chapter Five.

16. One copy to Dan Poynter, P.O. Box 4232-P, Santa Barbara, CA 93140-4232, autographed. Yes, the author receives six to ten books each week from new authors who have used this book to publish. That is why *The Self-Publishing Manual* has been called "the book that has launched a thousand books." All books are acknowledged.

17. One copy to American Library Association, Attn: Deborah Robertson, *Openers*, 50 East Huron Street, Chicago, IL 60611, (312) 944-6780, (800) 545-2433, (800) 545-2444 (IL), (800) 545-2455 (from Canada). *Openers* covers features tied into books, music, television and reading. This quarterly publication has a circulation of 250,000.

18. One copy to *Small Press Magazine*, RR#1, Colonial Hill, Mt. Kisko, NY 10549. Tel: (914) 666-0069. Bimonthly, circulation 7,000.

19. One copy to *Kliatt Young Adult Paperback Book Guide*, Attn: Doris Hiatt, 425 Watertown Street, Newton, MA 02158, (617) 965-4666. Kliatt annually reviews some 1,400 softcover books for young adults. The magazine is bimonthly and has a circulation of 20,000.

20. One copy to Newspaper Enterprise Association, Attn: Carol Felsenthal, American Library Association, 50 East Huron Street, Chicago, IL, 60611.

21. One copy to the *San Francisco Chronicle*, Attn: Patricia Holt, Book Editor, 275 Fifth Street, San Francisco, CA 94103, (415) 777-1111. Holt looks for books of interest to her local readers.

22. One copy to the *Small Press Book Review*, Attn: Henry Berry, P.O. Box 176, Southport, CT 06490, (203) 268-4878. Books are selected for review, not only for merit in their respective fields, but for their standard of writing, editing, design and production. Bimonthly.

23. One copy to *Newsday* which reviews general-interest books such as history, politics, biographies and poetry. They do not review how-to books. *New York Newsday*, Jack Schwartz, Two Park Avenue, New York, NY 10016. (212) 251-6623.

24. One copy to the *New York Review of Books*, Attn: Barbara Epstein, 250 West 57th Street, New York, NY 10107-0001, (212) 757-8070. This biweekly magazine publishes reviews, prints excerpts and buys serial rights. Circulation is 12,000.

25. One copy to *USA Today*, Books For Review, 1000 Wilson Blvd., Arlington, VA 22229. (703) 276-3400, (800) 368-3024. This daily national newspaper prints reviews under special subject areas such as sports, money, lifestyle, or art and entertainment.

26. One copy to each of the eight to ten major wholesalers. See Chapter Eight and the Appendix. Use the forms in *Publishing Forms*.

27. One copy to each of the six to ten most important opinion-molders in your field. If these people talk up your book, you will be off to a good start. Enclose a letter or note.

28. One copy for Library of Congress cataloging if you are in the CIP program. CIP Office, Library of Congress, Washington, DC 20559. Once you have published three books, you are eligible to participate in the CIP program and receive library cataloging data for printing on your copyright page. See *Publishing Forms* and Chapter Five.

29. Two copies to Register of Copyrights, Library of Congress, Washington, DC 20559 for copyright registration, along with your check for $20.00 and copyright Form TX. See Chapter Five.

30. One copy to LC Acquisitions and Processing along with your brochure and dealer discount schedule. Library of Congress, Attn: Jane Collins, Acquisitions and Processing Division, Crystal Mall Annex, Washington, DC 20540.

31. One copy to Chicago Tribune Books, Dianne Donovan, 435 North Michigan Avenue #400, Chicago, IL 66011-4022, (312) 222-3232.

32. One copy to the *Los Angeles Times Book Review*, Jack Miles, Times Mirror Square, Los Angeles, CA 90053, (213) 237-7000.

33. One copy to *Rave Reviews*, 163 Joralemon Street, Brooklyn Heights, NY 11201, (718) 237-1097.

34. One copy to *Voice Literary Supplement*, M. Mark, 36 Cooper Square, New York, NY 10003, (212) 475-3300.

35. *The Washington Post*, Book World, 1150 15th Street NW, Washington, DC 20071, (202) 334-6000. A favorable review in *The New York Times* or the *Washington Post* tends to stimulate good reviews in the book sections of smaller newspapers. Send a finished book. Circulation 770,000 daily, 1,000,000 Sunday.

36. One copy to *The Bloomsbury Review*, 1028 Bannock, Denver, CO 80204, (303) 892-0620.

These early review copies must be sent out as soon as the truck arrives from the printer. Reviewers like *new* books and books are dated so it is easy to tell when they are not new. Equally important, most of your initial sales will come from these reviews. So if you do not get moving with your review copy program, that inventory will not move out. Meanwhile, the dated books are getting older every day.

—Reviews to the ultimate consumer. Now that the pre-publication and early review packages are out, it is time to get to the *retail* reviewers. These are the rest of the book review magazines, the rest of the newspapers with book review columns, freelance book reviewers, radio & TV stations with talk shows and book programs, and last but not least, periodicals which cater to the book's field.

It would be very expensive and terribly inefficient to send review copies to every reviewer, and yet a lot of publishers do this. Many of the larger publishers automate their review book process. The result of taking the human touch out of the loop is that some reviewers get more than one package, while others receive the types of books they do not review. Reviewers who request a specific title are often ignored by big publishers because the promotion people are currently concentrating on a new line of books. Smaller publishers tend to be smart enough to send out a requested title knowing there is a very good chance of it being reviewed.

Since reviews are very effective, yet review copies are very inexpensive, it makes sense to spend more time and effort on reviews than on most other forms of promotion or paid advertising. For most books, it is not unusual to send out 300 to 500 review copies. This may seem like a lot, as many publishers circulate less than 100, but it is a sound investment. First, the complete review package will probably cost you on the order of $3.00 for the book, promotional material, shipping bag and postage. Several inches of space in magazines, major and minor, are extremely valuable. And this is editorial copy, far more credible than advertising puffery. For example, 94% of the librarians rely on reviews they read in *Library Journal*, while only 35% believe the ads.

If only 30% of the magazines review your book, you are way ahead on your investment. Considering that reviews return so much on their investment, it is wise to follow these two simple rules: 1. Do not be stingy with review copies but do not waste your money either, and 2. When in doubt, ship it out.

There are different kinds of reviews. A *summary* review relates the contents of the work without issuing an opinion on its value. These reviews help potential readers select books for their particular needs. An *evaluative* review decides whether the author has covered the topic and compares the book with similar works. It usually ends with a favorable or unfavorable recommendation.

Your book is a product of yourself. You poured your time, heart and soul into it. But just because you were interested enough to take the time to write it doesn't mean a reviewer will be interested enough to take the time to read it all. A book critic will read your book, but a book reviewer will probably only check the front matter. Some reviewers write up 10 to 15 books a week. Most of the reviewer's work will come from your news release and other enclosures. Make them good.

It helps to understand the lot of the editor and/or reviewer. Whether they are full time or freelance, they have one thing in common: They are very busy. Neither time nor room are available to review all the books that come in and there just aren't enough book review columns to go around. Even the prestigious and prolific Sunday supplement of the *New York Times* can only cover about 10% of the books received. All books are not assigned; most reviewers select the ones they want to review. You can't change the situation so you might as well understand and take advantage of it.

A few years ago, this author was dropping off a load of books at the loading dock around back of the Post Office in Santa Barbara. He saw a young man (not in a Postal uniform) with a cart full of packages over near the dumpster and his curiosity mounted. As he watched, the man ripped open the cartons, took out what appeared to be books and placed them in a large carton. Then he threw the wrappers in the trash. Unable to stand it any longer, he approached the man and asked if these were *lost-in-the-mail* books. Turns out the packages were for Los Angeles book critic Robert Kirsch. This gigantic load of books was being received at his home address (imagine what showed up at work) and he not only didn't have time to pick up the books himself, he didn't have room for the wrappers. There is a second lesson here, too: Much of the material you ship with review copies is likely to become separated from the book.

Ruth Coughlin of the *Detroit News* says "I arrive at my office each Monday morning to find 200 books in unopened mailing envelopes stacked outside my door." Alice Digilio of the *Washington Post* says "We have somebody here 20 hours a week, whose only job is to tear open book packages."

If your book has special area appeal, you can greatly increase your chances for review by submitting your book to the special publications reaching that particular group. For example, if your book is on hang gliding, you would send review copies to *Hang Gliding* magazine and *Glider Rider*. Then you would consider every aviation, outdoor, sport, recreation, do-it-yourself, teen, men's, etc. magazines you could find. There are some 60,000 magazines being printed in the U.S. today (and a lot more foreign). There must be some reaching the groups you want.

Be prepared for delays with the smaller associations' publications. They want to review your book but they have certain staff and budget limitations. Usually they rely on outside free help for book reviews. Typically, the editor will only scan a book before sending it off to an appropriate expert requesting him or her to review it. Often, the reviewer is very busy too. If you know the editor or reviewer, usually the case in an industry publication, give him or her some help. Offer to write the review yourself, sending it to the reviewer for additions or changes. They usually simply sign your work and send it in.

Selecting periodicals. Selecting magazines and other media for potential reviews and news releases is fun. Go to the library and search through the racks for appropriate magazines. In a large library in a major city, this could take all day. Look for book review columns and copy down the name, title and address of the reviewer.

Pick your publications carefully. Select only those likely to review your book because it relates to their publication and the interest of their readership. In other words, don't send an aviation book to *Solid Waste Management* magazine until you see garbage trucks with wings. Be objective and realistic.

Once you have a feel for the wide range of magazines and how they review books, stop by the bank for a roll of coins for the public library's photocopy machine. Then visit the reference desk at the library and ask for directories such as:

1. *Standard Periodical Directory* (thousands of magazines)

2. *Ulrich's International Periodical Directory* (many U.S. and foreign periodicals)

3. Hudson's *Newsletters Directory*

4. Gale's *Newsletters in Print*

5. *Literary Market Place* (with many good lists such as book review syndicates, book review periodicals, book columnists, cable networks, radio & TV stations with book programs, book clubs, news services and newspapers with book sections)

6. *Bacon's Publicity Checker*

7. Gebbie's *All-in-One Directory*

8. *Editor and Publisher's International Yearbook* (the key radio and TV personnel)

9. *Working Press of the Nation* (lists media people at newspapers, magazines, radio, television, syndicated columnists, etc.)

10. *Directory of Literary Magazines* by the Coordinating Council of Literary Magazines. (666 Broadway, 6th Floor, New York, NY 10012.)

11. *Writer's Market* (directed at writers in search of magazine publishers)

12. *Encyclopedia of Associations* directory (lists 18,000 special-interest trade and professional organizations)

13. *National Trade and Professional Associations* (6,000 associations, unions and societies)

14. *The Pocket Guide* (lists major trade, business and general interest magazines and newspapers. 33 pages. Free from Media Distribution Service, 307 West 36th Street, New York, NY 10018)

Address review books to a *person* or your book may get ripped-off by someone else on the staff. When this happens, you not only waste a book, you lose out on a review. Also address review books to the *position*, not just the name of the editor or reporter. If your recipient is on vacation, your mailing might be pigeon-holed for weeks—and no longer considered news once rediscovered upon his or her return. If you cannot find the editor's name in one of the above-listed references, call and ask, or address the package to *The Review Editor*.

Depending on your subject, you may find 200 to 400 potential reviewers for your book. Don't be surprised if you come up with 600. On the other hand, if the topic is very specialized, the print run is short, and the cover price is high, you may find there are only a few dozen interested and qualified potential reviewers. The best rule is to contact everyone who might possibly review the book. Divide the periodicals into two groups:

1. The good bets; those that will probably review the book and

2. The rest; those that might possibly review the book.

Some magazines will be perfect matches for your subject, and some will have such a large circulation that they cannot be ignored. Send books to the small group of good bets, but send only the literature and a reply post card to most of the rest. When the cards come back, send out the books and the literature. You are fishing at this point; you won't hook a fish with every cast but you have narrowed your odds with the post cards.

Para Publishing

P.O. Box 4232, Santa Barbara, CA 93140-4232 USA
Telephone: (805) 968-7277   Fax: (805) 968-1379

Dear Book Reviewer:

Are any of your readers frustrated authors? How would you like to help them, by revealing the secrets of breaking into print?

The Self-Publishing Manual has just been published in an all-new, expanded fifth edition. Known as the book that has launched a thousand books, it brings publishing within the reach of nearly everyone.

Help all your readers, who have a book inside them, by **returning the enclosed post card today.** <u>You</u> might encourage a future Zane Grey, Mary Baker Eddy, Whitman, Poe, Thoreau, Shaw, Paine, Kipling, Sandburg or Twain (all self-published.)

Sincerely,

PARA PUBLISHING

Daniel F. Poynter
Publisher
DFP/ms

REVIEW BOOK REQUEST

I would like to receive a review/examination copy of

Book title _____

PLEASE SEND THE BOOK(S) TO:

Name of publication or broadcast station _____
Name of reviewer _____
Full job title _____
Mailing Address _____

Circulation _____ Frequency _____ Av No of Pages _____
Brief description of publication _____

Audience profile _____
Comments (optional) _____

**Cover letter and
request post card**

Go through the directories and make up lists of newspapers, weekly magazines, review journals and specialized periodicals. Many smaller newspapers do not have reviewers on their staffs; they use syndicated columns. So be sure to send review copies to all syndicated reviewers.

Next, go through trade magazines and newsletters in the book's subject field and hunt for reviewers or contributors who have reviewed books.

If you do not have time to go through the above-mentioned educational exercise of compiling your own lists, some may be rented—ready to go. Paralists (P.O. Box 4232, Santa Barbara, CA 93140-4232) maintains several up-to-date lists. Write for current list counts and prices.

Reviewer addresses should be entered into the computer so they can be reproduced for use again. A simple mailing list program will do the job, but a data base program such as dBASE IV will allow much more flexibility. Add a code to each record in the address file to indicate what type of review publication it is (e.g., aviation magazines, parachuting magazines, ballooning magazines, in-flight magazines, soaring magazines, etc). The narrower your classifications, the more valuable your lists.

Most label programs will allow you to print one-across pressure sensitive labels or four-across Cheshire labels. The pressure sensitive labels are handy for smaller in-house mailings, while you will want to use the plain paper Cheshire for the larger mailing-house mailings.

The review package sent to reviewers should include a book, brochure, review slip, sample review/news release, reprints of other reviews, cover letter, reply card and a photograph of the book. Here are the details:

1. Book. Do not send a damaged book or *selected second* as some publishers do. You want to put your best foot forward, hoping to get the attention of the reviewer. Pack the book as you normally do so that it will arrive in good condition.

Some reviewers still assume that in real publishing the hardcover edition comes out several months prior to the softcover. If they receive a paperback, they assume the title is old. Today, with the increasing dominance of the *quality* or *trade paperback,* this barrier is beginning to be breached and many books are being selected for review on their own merits, rather than be sorted by their wrapper. If you are publishing in softcover only, make sure the point is clear in your review package.

2. Brochure. Use the brochure you have drafted for the retail buyer and make sure it looks professional. There is no need to print a special brochure for the reviewer.

Para Publishing

Presents for review

Is There a Book Inside You?
A Step-By-Step Plan For Writing Your Book

Publication date: March 1991 (shipping now).

Edition: Third, completely revised with new cover, price, ISBN and bar code.

Number in print: 20,000

Specifications: 236 pages, 5.5 x 8.5 trim with four-color and laminated Kivar cover.

CIP/LC: 90-46852.

ISBN: 0-915516-68-3, book alone: $14.95
ISBN: 0-915516-73-X, book with audio cassettes: $69.95
> An unabridged six hour reading of the text. Album contains six cassettes and a copy of the book.

Subsidiary rights:
> Writer's Digest Book Club main selection
> British rights to Exley Publications

Promotional plans:
> Foreword by Barnaby Conrad
> $35,000 promotional budget
> Space advertising, direct mail and major author tours

A copy of your review to the address below would be appreciated

Para Publishing, P.O. Box 4232, Santa Barbara, CA 93140-4232 USA
Tel: (805) 968-7277, Fax: (805) 968-1379

Book review slip

3. Review slip. Many books are sent with book review slips listing vital information, while a lot of others also have the title, publication date and price(s) rubber stamped on the inside of the front cover. Most publishers slip the loose sheets into the book. Pasting them inside the cover will make sure they arrive *with* their books. Some reviewers want the information stamped on for identification in case they lose the book review slip, and many publishers stamp the book to prevent the reviewer from selling the book to a bookstore. Review slips may also be made by computer-generating the information on mailing labels and pasting them on the inside front cover or flyleaf of each book.

Book review for *Choices: A Teen Woman's Journal for Self-awareness and Personal Planning*
by Mindy Bingham, Judy Edmondson and Sandy Stryker.

For Immediate Release:

"As a little girl, did you ever wonder what became of Snow White, Cinderella, and Sleeping Beauty after they married their princes and retired to their respective castles?"

And so begins a revolutionary new book, **Choices: A Teen Woman's Journal of Self-awareness and Personal Planning** by Mindy Bingham, Judy Edmondson and Sandy Stryker (Advocacy Press). This refreshing book is a welcome change from the traditional offerings for teenage girls. While the publishing industry continues to produce more and more romance novels for adolescent girls that reinforce the "they-lived-happily-ever-after" Cinderella syndrome, **Choices** gives the message, at a critical time, that the teenage girl has to take charge of her life—that she can't just drift and hope for some Prince Charming who will take all her burdens away.

Example of a sample review

4. Sample review in the form of a news release. Many reviewers use releases verbatim. In fact, it won't hurt to write up two samples, a short one and a long one.

Example of pasted-up pre-publication and early reviews

5. Other reviews. Reviewers are cautious people. They are more apt to review your book if it has been treated favorably in pre-publication reviews by big name reviewers. One way to convince them your book is worthy of their attention is to include copies of these early reviews. Cut out each review, paste it on a piece of plain paper and cut out the masthead or title of the magazine and paste it in for source and date identification. Underline the best parts of the review to draw attention to them. Make photocopies for your review kit.

Take advantage of a good review. Besides being very good for the ego, it can be used to further stimulate your promotion program. You want your wholesalers to know you are promoting the book, so send them a copy. If a review appears in a local newspaper, send copies to the local bookstores. Keep these pasted-up reviews on file and send them out with future review copies, letters to foreign rights buyers or for use any time you need more promotional material.

6. Cover letter. The cover letter should be short and to the point. If you plead for a review, you will sound as though you need something from them. Make your letter sound as though you are helping the reviewer find something his or her readers will be interested in. Stress benefits to the recipient, not to you.

Mention that you are enclosing a review copy. Suggest an interesting or unique (perhaps local) angle. Introduce the book and its contents. Tell why the book is important to today's reader and ask for a review.

Some public relations people like to get very personal in review copy mailings. They jot a little personal note to the reviewer hoping to snow them into thinking they have met before, or that the reviewer may have made some long-forgotten promise at a cocktail party.

7. Reply card. Include a self-addressed reply post card so reviewers may indicate the response they plan. You want to be ready to collect the clippings for your files and future promotion. Don't be too upset by the return rate on the reply post cards. Some cards will take a long time and others will not be returned at all. Many reviewers just don't know when the review will appear.

It is not necessary to use a business reply indicia or a stamp on the post card. Reviewers in significant periodicals do not buy their own stamps. They throw outgoing mail in the out basket for the mail room.

PLEASE ACKNOWLEDGE

We have received the complimentary review book or galleys you sent of

Book title: _____

☐ We expect to review this book on (date): _____

☐ Please send a photograph of the book

☐ Please send a photograph of the author

☐ We did not find this book suitable for our review.

Name of reviewer: _____

Full job title: _____

Name of publication or broadcast station: _____

Mailing address: _____

_____ Zip: _____

Comments (optional): _____

_____

Review book acknowledgement post card

8. Photograph. Artwork will get you a lot more space and make the review more attractive—resulting in a higher degree of readership. Enclose a photograph of the book and, if the book is well-illustrated, samples of the artwork. Send photos of the book whenever you feel they might be used, and always offer the photos at the end of your news release. A clearly typed taped-on identifying caption should hang below the photograph. When placing the order for prints, specify that they are *for reproduction*, glossies, and 4 x 6 (or larger) in size. Unless you have a readily recognizable face, send a photograph of the book, not of yourself. Remember what you are selling.

Rubber stamps. Some publishers stamp their review copies *Professional Review Copy, Not For Sale* while others just use an address stamp. Rubber stamp the edge of the book so that the marking is visible without lifting the cover. It is embarrassing when a review copy finds its way back into your for-sale stock. Reviewers often suggest the price, publication date and other important information be rubber stamped inside the front cover in case the review slip is lost.

REVIEW COPY
NOT FOR SALE

Review book rubber stamp

The rubber stamp or pasted slip will not stop the sale of a review book but it will insure the book will not be returned to you by a bookstore for credit.

In mid-1979, the newspaper and book industries were scandalized when ten newspaper book reviewers were accused of selling review books to the Strand bookstore in New York. Apparently, several bookstores send form letters to reviewers soliciting books. Typically, the stores buy the books at 25% of list price and resell them at 50% of list. One reviewer estimated he received 30,000 review copies in seven years. Many periodicals have a policy of donating review copies philanthropically; to hospitals, charitable book fairs, foreign libraries, etc.

Certainly the ability to sell review copies may promote the requesting of more books with no intention of considering them for review. There is nothing wrong with a reviewer requesting a book if he or she plans to review it. But it is wrong if they plan to sell the book without first considering it for review.

Review/Testimonial sheet. The rev/test sheet lists excerpts from reviews and testimonials along with pertinent printing and rights information.

Unsolicited testimonials. There is no better promotion than a recommendation from a satisfied customer.

Save all those unsolicited testimonials and nice letters; bank them for future use. When you have ten to twenty of them, photocopy them, cut them apart and arrange their best, most quotable parts in a logical order. Put duplicate praise aside and try to arrange the testimonials so that they flow, tell a story and follow one-another. Then either get permission to use their signatures, or paste the testimonials to a sheet of blank paper omitting the name and address of the writer. Start the page off with "What readers are saying about *(name of the book)"* Since all the typewriter and handwriting styles are different, the page will have good credibility.

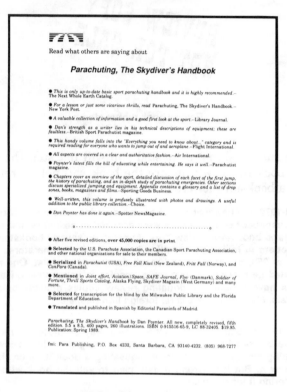

Read what others are saying about

Parachuting, The Skydiver's Handbook

● *This is only up-to-date basic sport parachuting handbook and it is highly recommended.--*
The Next Whole Earth Catalog.

● *For a lesson or just some vicarious thrills, read Parachuting, The Skydiver's Handbook.--*
New York Post.

● *A valuable collection of information and a good first look at the sport.--*Library Journal.

● *Dan's strength as a writer lies in his technical descriptions of equipment; these are
faultless.--*British Sport Parachutist magazine.

● *This handy volume falls into the "Everything you need to know about..." category and is
required reading for everyone who wants to jump out of and aeroplane.--*Flight International.

● *All aspects are covered in a clear and authoritative fashion.--*Air International.

● *Poynter's latest fills the bill of educating while entertaining. He says it well.--*Parachutist
magazine.

● *Chapters cover an overview of the sport, detailed discussion of each facet of the first jump,
the history of parachuting, and an in-depth study of parachuting emergencies. Other sections
discuss specialized jumping and equipment. Appendix contains a glossary and a list of drop
zones, books, magazines and films.--*Sporting Goods Business.

● *Well-written, this volume is profusely illustrated with photos and drawings. A useful
addition to the public library collection.--*Choice.

● *Dan Poynter has done it again.--*Spotter NewsMagazine.

● After five revised editions, over 45,000 copies are in print.

● **Selected** by the U.S. Parachute Association, the Canadian Sport Parachuting Association,
and other national organizations for sale to their members.

● **Serialized** in *Parachutist* (USA), *Free Fall Kiwi* (New Zealand), *Fritt Fall* (Norway), and
CanPara (Canada).

● **Mentioned** in *Joint effort, Aviation/Space, SAFE Journal, Flyv* (Danmark), *Soldier of
Fortune, Thrill Sports Catalog,* Alaska Flying, Skydiver Magazin (West Germany) and many
more.

● **Selected** for transcription for the blind by the Milwaukee Public Library and the Florida
Department of Education.

● **Translated** and published in Spanish by Editorial Paraninfo of Madrid.

Parachuting, The Skydiver's Handbook by Dan Poynter. All new, completely revised, fifth
edition. 5.5 x 8.5, 400 pages, 260 illustrations. ISBN 0-915516-65-9, LC 88-32405. $19.95.
Publication: Spring 1989.

fmi: Para Publishing, P.O. Box 4232, Santa Barbara, CA 93140-4232. (805) 968-7277

Review/Testimonial sheet

Approaching other periodicals. Now that you have mailed books to the *good bets*, those periodicals that match your subject and are very likely to review the book, it is time to approach others. Your second list may total 1,000 or more.

Send a cover letter, brochure, news release and a reply card. The reviewers will request a review copy if the book looks as though it might interest their readers. Some will print your release without asking for a book.

A mailing to 1,000 reviewers may bring a response from 200 or so. The mailing and the resulting book shipment will be far less expensive than sending books to the original list of 1,000.

—Continuing review program. Your review copy program will not end at the publication date. Requests will come in as other reviewers hear of your book and you should be on the lookout for new reviewers. For example, keep an eye on the Media section in *Publishers Weekly.*

There were 1,733 daily newspapers in the U.S. at last count; 458 are morning and 1275 are evening; 783 newspapers publish on Sunday. Only three papers have Sunday book review sections: *The New York Times, The Washington Post* and *the Los Angeles Times.* They were discussed earlier under pre-publication reviews. There are approximately 7,700 weekly newspapers. Then, there are magazines. There are a lot of possibilities.

Three to four months after your initial review copy mailing, hit those sent the cover letter, news release and reply card, again. Send them the same package (deleting any reference to the publication date) but this time, hand-write across the top of the release: *This book is available for review.* A lot of reviewers will have missed your first mailing or they may decide to look at your book because they have read of it elsewhere. You will be amazed at the response. A year later, re-slant your release and try this again.

In 1983, 19 publishers joined in a *Books for Review* program. A very attractive brochure offering 29 books was sent to 1,800 reviewers. The participation cost was $46 per book or about 2.5 cents per contact. Approximately eight percent of the reviewers responded by requesting some 700 books. Over fifty requests were received for some of the more popular titles. The publishers were able to approach reviewers inexpensively, while not wasting books or material on reviewers who were not interested. The *Books for Review* program is a good example of how publishers can band together to exploit free publicity while keeping their promotion costs down. *Books For Review* was turned over to the Publishers Marketing Association and is currently being mailed to 1,700 daily metropolitan newspapers.

Be on the lookout for review possibilities outside the book pages of magazines and newspapers. Depending upon your subject, contact cookbook editors, lifestyle editors, sports page editors, etc. Watch for special sections.

Unsolicited requests. From time to time, you will receive unsolicited requests for review copies. You may wish to look up the periodical for its frequency, circulation and audience match, as well as whether this person is really on the staff or a bona fide stringer. Is the request on credible media letterhead? However, since the review package costs you so little, the better procedure is probably just to respond cordially. Certainly the free publicity a review can provide is worth many times the cost of the book. When in doubt, ship it out.

Press clipping services have people who regularly read all major publications and clip out mentions of their clients. You may subscribe to one of these services (see listings in *Literary Market Place*) but it probably is not worth the expense. The clipping services cannot read every periodical; they often send clippings which mention your key word but not you, and you do not need all these clips anyway. Many smaller periodicals will send you copies of their magazine containing the review. Some people enclose a clipping with their order. So there will be very few reviews you do not hear about.

Advertising. Never suggest to an editor that you might be willing to advertise in the magazine as a way of gaining a review. Most editors do not sell advertising—that is the job of the advertising department. Petty bribery will repel most review editors who view themselves as independent. On the other hand, when the ad sales representative calls it is OK to say that you are *waiting for the review to test the match between your book and the magazine's audience.*

Once you receive a card notifying you a review will appear in a given publication, you may like to advertise in it, too. Some publishers feel this double impact is worth their while though others do not. Many like to see how the review pulls before investing in an ad. They let the review test the medium and then they quote the review in the ad. The major advantage of the ad is that it is more likely to have specific ordering information. Since it isn't likely your book will be reviewed twice in the same publication, advertising is the only way to continue contacting the readers.

Many book reviews are mean-spirited. Even if a reviewer likes a book, he or she must find fault and write snide and/or patronizing little asides about the author's character or motives that demonstrate the reviewer's intellectual and moral superiority. - Author Andrew Greeley in *Publishers Weekly*

Bad reviews. Some of your reviews may be negative, and one reason (but not the only reason) is that some reviewers are negative. Some of these critics are frustrated writers who try to bring all other published authors down to their level. They take cheap shots or use the book as a springboard for lofting their own views.

Reviewers tend to be very cautious people. Even a very favorable review will probably contain one negative sentence or paragraph. This is a cover to save the reputation of the reviewer in case the book turns out to be a loser.

In smaller publications aimed at a select target audience, the author will probably know every qualified reviewer. Skydiving books have to be reviewed by experienced parachutists. In this case, the author may ask a colleague to review the book. Some reviewers write negative reviews on purpose. In an effort to find a qualified reviewer, the editor will look for someone with a background in a book's subject. Books are sometimes unknowingly assigned to a reviewer who has an ax to grind with the author.

Don't worry about a negative review. Any review is better than no review because people tend to remember the subject more than the details of the critique. Even a bad review will arouse reader curiosity. Libraries must cover every subject and acquisition librarians are always searching for something new.

When you quote the negative review, just use the good parts. If there are no *good parts*, just say . . . *as reviewed in the* Washington Post or . . . *find out why* Consumers Reports *hated this book*. Do not edit out the bad words so that the review appears to be favorable. According to Brigitte Weeks, editor of the *Washington Post* Book World: *Ellipses are often the enemy of truth*. It is flagrant misrepresentation to edit out less desirable phrases if they change the meaning and intention of the review. Reviewers and editors are writers, too, and most have excellent memories. If you misquote them, they will probably catch you and will certainly remember you when next you send a book for review.

Learn from negative reviews. Perhaps your promotional approach is misleading. Think about changing your news release. Help the reviewers to understand the book. Try to direct their thinking. The same goes for good reviews. Focus on the praise—the parts of the book reviewers like. Emphasize these parts in your news release.

Why reviewers review books. Many reviewers will spend some ten hours reading a book, a couple of days thinking about it, and perhaps six hours writing up the review. Some reviewers are paid a small amount and many do not get paid at all. They get the book and the satisfaction of being on the inside of publishing and/or their area of specialty, expertise or profession. To add insult to injury, the Internal Revenue Service has attempted to tax some reviewers for the value of the books they have received.

Local newspapers, magazines, radio and television almost *have* to cover you because you and your book are local news. Get out the *Yellow Pages* and make up a list of local media. You will probably find more than you first thought. Send a review package to each periodical, addressed to a particular features editor. They may not have a book review section but you would rather have a half-page feature on yourself and your book anyway. Follow up in a few days with a telephone call to the most important ones. Next, do the same for local radio and television stations.

If you know a freelance or staff reviewer personally, send him or her a review copy. Use every possible *in* you might have. Hit all your home towns, where you live now, where you grew up, where you went to school, all of them. You may get not only a nice review, but a special feature story as well.

Follow-up calls increase your chances for a review. Don't be a pest but it is acceptable to call to see *if a book has been received.* You may find your package has not been received or that your book or news release should have gone to another editor.

> *Someone once remarked that we have the power of life and death over a book. Life perhaps, but not death. We could devote our entire section to loathing the latest Sidney Sheldon, and it would make no difference.* - Stefan Kanfer of *Time*

Acknowledge all reviews with a personal letter. Praise and thank the reviewer. They will remember you when you send your next book. A small amount of time spent on letters here is an investment in the future. Annotate your computerized list of reviewers to indicate that this reviewer has performed for you.

Some publishers save time by writing *thank you!* across a photocopy of the review and mail it to the reviewer.

How to ship. Review copies may be sent to most reviewers via the Postal Service's Book Rate. If the author lives near any of the reviewers on the list, hand delivery never hurts.

When the *Frisbee Player's Handbook* rolled off the press, Santa Barbara co-author Dan Poynter made up a list of reviewers in ZIP code order. New York co-author Mark Danna made the systematic rounds of reviewers in Manhattan and *threw the book at them.* The unique circular book was brought to their attention, made an impression and was very well reviewed.

If the reviewer requested the book on one of your reply cards or on letterhead, make a photocopy of the card and place it on top of the book. Everyone recognizes and takes an interest in their own handwriting. Seeing their own writing will make a reviewer pay more attention to the book and the rest of the package.

Credit the reviewer. Reviewers like credit for their work, so mention their name as well as that of the publication. For example, end the quote with "Kevin Gibson, *Parachutist Magazine*". In fact, if the reviewer really likes the book, he or she will try to provide a few quotable lines, hoping for a mention.

Permission to quote. Reviews are written to be quoted. You do not have to contact the reviewer or periodical for permission.

Put a lot of effort into reviews. Far less expensive than display advertising, they are the best promotional investment you can make. For more details on setting up your review program, see the Special Report titled *Book Reviews*. See the Appendix.

News releases. Most small publishers receive very little free publicity for their books. This lack of attention is not because of any great conspiracy between the big (New York) publishers and the media, it is simply because the neophytes do not know how to ask for free coverage. News releases are used to announce products, promotions, and events. They accompany galleys and review copies of books, and are included in press kits for radio and television stations. Sometimes a release accompanies other promotional or informational material, and sometimes a release is mailed alone.

News release is the modern term for *press release*. Your message will be sent to all forms of media such as radio, television and other opinion molders, not just the print media.

The media are in the news gathering/publishing business; they want to hear from you. Publicity is not expensive advertising, it involves the use of inexpensive news releases. News items receive a much higher degree of readership than advertising, and greater readership leads to more response (sales). News releases generate publicity and invite book reviews. Releases may be used to announce publication of your new book to newspapers, magazines, libraries, radio and TV. In fact, they should be sent to anyone who will listen.

Many of the articles and news items you read were written by the people mentioned in them. Editors may use only one news release in ten but news releases make up 20% to 25% of the editorial space in many newspapers and magazines. Some of the smaller, more highly-targeted publications use an even higher percentage.

Editors would use more outside material if the news releases they received were more interesting. Your challenge is to draft copy that is irresistible to the editor—to come up with interesting information the editor will want to pass on to his or her readers. You want the editor to open your monthly mailings first while thinking: "I wonder what good material John is sending me today?"

Remember, you are providing a service to editors. As an author-publisher, you are an expert in your field and an information source. You are providing important, timely and interesting information to the editor and his or her readers.

While publicity misused can be nothing but an ego trip for the author, well used it can be a powerful sales tool. - Al Lind

On your first book, while you are still learning about the printing trade and your own schedules are apt to slip, it is probably best to send out your first news release when the manuscript is actually delivered to the printer. When you are writing your next book, you may start sending out the releases earlier. These early releases should contain a more generalized publication date such as "March, 1990." Later it may be moved, or the specific day may be added. Do not send early releases to newspapers. Publicity is wasted when mailed before your books are in the stores.

Some authors do not like to reveal their project too early, and hold off on their releases. They are afraid someone might pick up on their good idea. But other writers purposely get their release out very early in the hope of scaring off the competition. Whichever approach you take, someone will call to say "Don't write it, my book is at the printer now!" "At the printer" usually means they may sit down at their typewriter soon. The four steps to placing your news releases are:

1. Develop an interesting angle that shows how your book will benefit the reader.

2. Locate and cultivate the appropriate media contacts.

3. Deliver the information in the proper form.

4. Be persistent and follow up.

News release layout. Give the editors what they want and need; deliver the information in such a way that it is useful and newsworthy. The less re-writing your release requires, the more chance that it will be used. You will draft some releases for distribution to a single publication. Study the publication, imitate the writing style and follow the same article layout. The secrets are to know what the editor considers good news value and to know how to write in good press style.

Releases should, like all writing, be accurate, consistent, clear, concise, persuasive, interesting, and above all, correct in spelling, punctuation, and grammar. (I didn't say this would be easy!) - Rose Adkins, past assistant editor of *Writer's Digest* magazine

(Letterhead)

NEWS RELEASE

For Immediate Release...

Contact: Joyce Ready (805) 968-7277

Headline
Type a descriptive, clever and catchy headline in capital letters and center it. Lure the editor to read more. Then space down four lines and get into the body of the release.

Issue or problem
The lead paragraph is designed to invite the largest number of people to read the article. It must have broad appeal; make it interesting. The release should be *issue oriented*; write about the *problem*, not the book. The release should begin by stating the problem and telling why this is an important subject. Make it provocative.

Development
Spend a second paragraph developing the message. Put the most interesting information first to keep the reader reading. Recite the most important items in descending order so that if some are cut from the end, the most important will remain. Provide interesting facts and statistics.

How the book solves the problem
Now move from a *what* orientation to the *how* orientation. It is not necessary to dwell on the book. Anyone who finishes the article will be interested in the book. Then describe the contents of the book; mention it as a resource. Continue with some background on the topic and show why your book is unique, useful and timely. Recite benefits to the reader.

Author
Spend a paragraph on the author and tell why the author is an expert on the subject.

Ordering information
Give the price and mention that the book is available from the publisher as well as the stores. List your address so the reader will know where to send the money. Code your address.

End the release with the newspaper termination sign: *-30-*.

News release outline

One reason the demand for books is constant is that the book-buying public is not static. It is constantly changing. New readers are entering the bookshops all the time, while old readers are going to that big library in the sky. - Max Alth

Para Publishing

P.O. Box 4232, Santa Barbara, CA 93140-4232 USA
Telephone: (805) 968-7277   Fax: (805) 968-1379

For immediate release . . .

Contact Monique Tihanyi (805) 968-7277

Skydiving = A New Way to Fly

Skydiving! Not just falling out of an aircraft in a rapid vertical tumble for thousands of feet, but exhilarating horizontal flying; the closest we humans have ever come to unencumbered bird-like flight.

Skydivers can deflect the air to fly horizontally. In fact, they can achieve an angle of 35 degrees or more from the vertical, or approaching 1:1. This means that on a sixty second skydive from 12,500' providing 10,000' of freefall, a jumper can cover 7,000' of ground, or 1.35 miles.

Skydiving also takes place at controlled vertical speeds between 110 and 190 mph. This is why the *Guinness Book of World Records* awards skydiving the record for the world's fastest non-mechanical sport. Freefalling jumpers spread their flying surfaces (arms and legs) to fly prone like Superman or sweep them back to stand on their heads. Since their weight remains constant but their drag area can be changed, skydivers can go up and down--relative to each other. They pile out of aircraft one-after-the-other and then swoop down to make a formation on the same level.

Today's parachutes are exciting too. Gone are the traditional round canopies which were purely drag devices. The new airfoil-shaped, ram-air inflated wings provide lift and are flown like a glider. They have a 20 mph. airspeed, a ten foot per second sink rate and can be flared for tip-toe landings. Whether you want to try another aviation activity or learn more about parachutes, where can you find more information?

News release example (first page)

I never said starting your own publishing company would be easy. I only said it would be worth it.

Word processors make news release tailoring easy. Most of your release will remain the same, but you will tailor the headline and lead paragraph to the target audience. For a book on publishing, we would have different pitches for magazines sent to publishers, writers or printers. Just change the headline and lead paragraph and let the machine copy the rest of the previous release.

—**Format.** The format of the release is standardized. The easiest way to design it is simply to type "NEWS RELEASE" on your own letterhead stationery. The release will look fancier if you have special forms typeset. By using your own stationery, you automatically have the important information such as company name and address at the top. Then just type in the release date (*For Use the Week of September 17th*) or (*For Immediate Release*).

Place a contact name with telephone number in the upper right-hand corner. If your name is Tom Drewes, the book is authored by Tom Drewes and the book is published by Tom Drewes Publishing, make your company look a little larger by selecting another (*pen or PR*) name for the contact person.

—**Layout.** Double space on 8.5 x 11 paper. Some publicists use legal size paper which has the advantage of sticking out of a pile of papers—they are more easily noticed. Begin a third of the page from the top and leave one-inch margins on the sides and bottom. The release may be any length but one page is usually best. If the release runs more than one page, identify the story with a header in the upper left-hand corner of the second page. Or excerpt a portion and place it in a separate background release or author biography. One way to condense a release to a single page is to use the word processor's ability to change from double space to 1.8- or even 1.5-line spacing. Do not use a staple to bind pages together, use a paper clip. Never type on the back of the sheet.

An alternative format is to set the type one-column wide on slick stock so that your piece is camera-ready. This format is useful to smaller publications since they may strip-in your piece without resetting the type. The difficulty is that you must submit several formats, as magazine and newspaper columns are not of uniform width.

—Style. Observe basic journalistic style: Keep your sentences to 23 words or less; *3 p.m.*, not *4:00 P.M.*; commas and periods inside close quotation marks; no capital letters for anything in the text but initials, first letters of proper names and first words of sentences (exception, TV, not tv); no extra space between paragraphs (double space same as the rest of the text); the first mention of the author should include first name, middle initial and last name (subsequent mentions should contain last name only). Magazines like book titles in italics while newspapers place quotation marks around them.

Use the fewest number of words to communicate any thought. Circle all repeated words in a paragraph and select alternates. Cut unnecessary words. Never use a less common word when a familiar one will convey your meaning. Use simple sentences; complex sentences can be hard to read. Do not make judgements. If you say the *book is the most important contribution to literature since the Bible,* the editor will cut it out or trash your release. On the other hand, it does not hurt to quote someone else who says something nice about your book. Proofread and re–proofread!

Take your time and compose a good release. Not all news gatherers do their own work all the time, so your release may appear verbatim in print. It may even be reprinted word-for-word as a book review.

A release which starts out "Festival Publications is happy to announce . . . " is self-serving. There is a much better chance your release will be used if the headline begins "Breakthrough found in . . . " The release is being written for the readers of the periodical, it isn't an announcement for your company picnic. When drafting a news release for a specific section, such as *Publishers Weekly* "Back to Press" column, write it in the same format, no more and no less. Do not make the editors rewrite the release, they may round-file it instead.

If possible, include a photograph. One from the book illustrating the point you are making in the release is best. Remember, you want the release to push your program; the book is secondary—almost subliminal.

Never talk about what you are going to do until after you have written it. - Mario Puzo

Type up the release and have it duplicated at the "instant print" shop by photocopy or offset, depending on the number you need. Ship them off with a photo of the book and enclose a reviewer response card (below).

Send the releases to all appropriate magazines, book clubs (see Chapter 8), to subsidiary rights contacts (Chapter 8), wholesalers, libraries, sales representatives, hometown papers, etc. Don't forget alumni, fraternal, trade or church publications with which you may have a connection. Spread them around. Follow up with a telephone call to the most important periodicals.

News releases to local periodicals may be hand-carried. Personal delivery not only receives more attention, meeting editors will be a great education for you.

Use news releases liberally. Every time you go back to press, issue a release to herald it. Magazines such as the prestigious *Publishers Weekly* will give you a few lines if you just let them know. Releases should also be issued to announce speaking engagements, TV appearances, autograph parties and any other newsworthy event. If business slows down, think up a newsworthy event and write a release on it.

```
                    PLEASE ACKNOWLEDGE

    We have received your News Release about (book title): _____
    We will take the following action:
    ☐ Your book will be featured on (date): _____
    ☐ Your book will be featured in the near future
    ☐ Please send a photograph of the book
    ☐ Please send a photograph of the author
    ☐ Please send a complimentary copy of the book


    Name: _____
    Full job title: _____
    Name of publication or broadcast station: _____
    Mailing address: _____
    _____ Zip: _____
    Comments (optional): _____
    _____
```

Release Response Reply Card

An enclosed Release Response Reply Card will provide instant feedback. The cards will tell you if you are writing good releases and if you are sending them to the right people. You won't have to wait months wondering if the articles will appear. You will be ready to collect clippings and the responses will provide leads for possible book reviews. Always respond to *PW's* requests for information for their spring and fall announcements issues. Once you register for an ISBN, you will be on Bowker's mailing list and should receive these requests automatically. If you are going on tour, send a short release listing the places and dates to PW's "Author Publicity" column. Also be on the lookout for special editions of *Publishers Weekly* and other magazines. Some of the special editions are on cookbooks, travel books, sports books, etc. Listings are usually free.

Remember that media people work in a pressure-cooker world. Be polite, they won't expect it. You will get a lot of mileage out of one kind word.

For more information on news releases and paint-by-the-number instructions for drafting and using them, see the Special Report *News Releases and Book Publicity*. See the Appendix.

Press kits. Some publishers like to get fancy and issue a "press kit." While it isn't necessary to send a kit with a review book, there are other events where you may like to hand a kit to a reporter. The press kit is a pocket folder containing news releases, early reviews, letters of endorsement, author biography, cover letter, touring dates, testimonials, photographs, a business card, etc. The folder may be from a stationery store or, if the book measures 8.5 x 11, may be made from book cover overruns.

Notify your friends of your new book by mailing them a news release and an order blank. Send these mailings to friends, relatives and influential people in the field covered by the book. They are prime prospects and will help to promote your book by just talking about it. Influential people in the field should receive a complimentary copy; you want these opinion molders on your side.

Radio and television talk shows offer tremendous exposure for a new author. They provide an audience in the millions at no cost to you. Talk shows are constantly looking for fresh material and authors are a prime source. As an author, you are an expert on a particular subject, you are interesting.

—**Television.** The big television shows are best, of course, as they reach more people. The "Today," "Tonight," " Phil Donahue Show," and "60 Minutes" are the most influential in bookselling. The best plug for a book is when Johnny Carson or Phil Donahue takes a personal interest. According to *TV Guide*, an appearance on *Today* will sell 3,000 copies of a book, while a few minutes on *Donahue* can move 50,000. But these bigger shows are hard to crack. They have lots of material because they are deluged with news releases, visits and other personal contacts by the public relations departments of the big publishers. The competition is great and there just isn't enough air time to go around.

But there are ways to get on the big talk shows as well as to crack the other media; it depends on your subject. For example, if your book is on Frisbee disc play, you might approach the Wham-O Manufacturing Company, which makes the Frisbee disc. Of course, you already know them because they gave you a lot of the material for your book. They have a public relations firm on retainer and it is to their advantage to give your book a lot of promotion. You may be able to use their muscle free. You are actually doing them a favor, since your book gets their foot in the media door so they can promote their product. Incidentally, such a company would be a prime customer for your book. A Frisbee book would make an ideal corporate gift and could be used in promotions.

Do not overlook the smaller and local shows. They are much easier to get on and you may use them to work your way up. Many stations have special shows for interviewing authors, and most have at least one talk show. The local station will want you on its community affairs program. Depending on your subject, the station may even produce a short clip for their news broadcast. Once you have appeared on one local station, don't give up on the others. Use another interesting angle.

The publicity departments of publishers would kill for five minutes on the Johnny Carson Show. - Ron Nessen, press secretary to past President Ford

To get on a show, find out who the producer is. Locally, you may simply call the station and ask the switchboard operator. For other stations, call the station or consult the directories in your library.

—**Radio** talk shows can be handled from home. There is no need to get dressed or to travel. Use smaller radio shows to learn the medium and work your way up to larger radio shows and television.

Example of a media brochure

Let the talk shows know you are available by sending them a *media flier*. The media flier stresses an interesting *issue* and offers you as an expert to explain the subject. The back of the flier may describe the book. But the book is not the main subject, it is simply giving credibility to the expert.

The show's producer will call you to set up an appointment and then will call you at the appointed time (always clarify whether they will be calling at 7 p.m. your time, or their time).

Respond by sending a copy of the book, your news release, and photocopies of any reviews you have received. If you send a list of questions, most hosts will use it.

Lists of talk shows are available in *Literary Market Place*, other directories and from ParaLists. See the Appendix. You may also take out a listing in the *Radio-TV Interview Report*. For an application, contact Bradley Communications, Bill Harrison, 135 East Plumstead Avenue, Lansdowne, PA 19050-8206. Tel: (215) 259-1070. .

When you go on the air, be prepared. Do not use a telephone with *call waiting*. The clicking is annoying. Since several months have passed since you wrote the book, reread it. Practice public speaking. Think over the best answers to the questions most likely to be asked. Rehearse the stock answers and use high-impact words. Go over the main points you want to make and slip them in no matter what the questions. The talk show host may frustrate you by bouncing from subject to subject, so don't be caught with nothing to say. Push the subject, not your book. Do not mention the book at every opportunity—it turns off listeners and wears out your welcome.

On the morning shows, you will be lucky to have 60 seconds on the air. Later in the day you may have four to eight minutes. Evening shows may run an hour.

A few years ago, this author was listening to a local radio station while running errands. He heard a disc jockey talking about making his first parachute jump. Since the author had written several books on skydiving, he called the disc jockey, who spoke to him between record breaks. An invitation was extended and the author dropped by the radio station for an impromptu interview which lasted all afternoon.

Media people are busy and are under a lot of deadline pressure. While your book is the most important thing that has happened to you lately, it is just another news item to them. They are not easily impressed, they deal with newsmaking personalities all the time. Be polite, they won't expect it. Everyone around them is tough and short. A kind word from you will go a long way. A thank you note afterwards will leave a nice memory and you will receive great treatment for your second book.

The biggest problem all authors have with interviews is that their books are not in all the stores. Listeners may make one attempt to buy the book and then forget about it. The best way to handle this potential disaster is to tell the host you will send a free *information kit* to any listener who will drop you a card. Talk show hosts love to give things to their audience and most will repeat your message and address again and again. Now the responses will come directly to you so that you may add these hot prospects to your mailing list and send them a brochure and other information on the subject.

For more information on talk shows, see *On the Air* by Al Parinello. See the Appendix.

Author's tours are the way you promote your book out of town and they are very hard work. There was a time when all the author did was to deliver his manuscript to the publisher and then go home to await his royalty checks. However, with the advent of TV and more hype in the book business, the major effort for the writer now is in criss-crossing the country, selling the book. According to *The Wall Street Journal*, "For the publisher it is publicity at low cost. For the author it is an endurance test." It's a tough, grueling experience and it isn't inexpensive, but there is no cheaper way of reaching so many of the book buying public.

Author tours mean going on as many radio and TV shows as possible and visiting bookstores between shows. It is terribly discouraging to find that most of the stores do not have your book in stock. Some self-publishers fill their van with books so they can make store deliveries before going on the air.

Mail your itinerary to *ABA Newswire* several weeks before you are scheduled to leave. The American Booksellers Association publishes this newsletter for the book stores. Then when you call the stores, they will recognize you.

> *When promoting your book, speak proudly about it. You worked hard on it and should be proud. False modesty will get you nowhere.* - Mark Danna.

You may try to book the shows yourself or hire one of the publicists listed in the Appendix. Most book publicists feel Los Angeles is the most cost-effective city for a touring author.

For more information on author tours, read Peggy Glenn's book: *Publicity for Books and Authors*. See the Appendix.

TV giveaway programs will provide you with great exposure and all you have to do is donate a book. These programs are presented to raise funds for charitable organizations. Be on the lookout for them.

News conferences are often staged by big firms by hosting a lavish party for the press. But there is nothing wrong with a small gathering. If you have something provocative to say on a timely subject, if it would normally be mentioned as a news item, you may be able to draw out the media. You do not have to rent a hotel suite. News conferences may be called in a friend's home or in a public meeting place. Press people just want the information as quickly as possible. Be prepared with press kits.

Featured articles on yourself are another way to gain publicity. Local papers, company magazines, alumni publications, etc. are always looking for interesting news about their people. Let them do a story on you and they will mention your greatest accomplishment— your book. You are now an expert, an interesting person just because you are a published author.

You are news to every publication with which you are connected, from a national association to a local newspaper. Take advantage of them. Remember, book reviews sell books but featured stories sell more books.

Book promotion through magazine articles is another way to gain publicity for your book while furthering your writing career. It is easy to spin off articles from the chapters of your book. You can sell the articles, build your reputation and help to sell the book, too.

First of all, you will be pleased to find that you have less difficulty selling articles to magazines now that you are a published author. You are an expert, and magazines want authoritative articles. Of course, you will want to end the article with "Editor's note: Jan Nathan is the author of . . . which

is available from . . . " and type the notice in just as you want
it to appear; do not leave this up to the editor. Those who read
the article will be interested in the subject or they wouldn't be
reading about it. Many will want to know more and will seek
your book. So, while you are making sales on books, you might
as well get paid for the article.

Most national magazines do not pay a great deal for articles—usually just a couple of hundred dollars. However, the
exposure is more important to you than the money. You even
might like to consider that if you offer the article free, you
have a better chance of its seeing print. Write to the editor,
enclosing a few applicable pages from your book, and offer to
write an article with the magazine's editorial slant. Offer to
send an outline or include it with this first mailing. If your
book is in a word processor, it will be easy to extract a section,
add an introduction and a conclusion and edit it slightly.

Speaking engagements are another way to publicize your
book. As an expert on your subject, you are in demand by service organizations, adult education programs, church groups,
PTA's, the Chamber of Commerce and others. Many of these
groups feature a guest speaker at every meeting. Sometimes
they rotate the responsibility among the membership to find a
speaker. Your call to them may actually get someone off the
hook.

The possibilities will become obvious once you begin to
think of your topic from the marketing standpoint. If yours is a
carpentry how-to book, a hardware store or lumber yard might
like to build a seminar around you. Your presentation might
turn into an annual affair. Think of the nurseries which hold
pruning classes every spring. You will make good contacts and
develop new ideas; it is stimulating.

When you make your speaking appearance, always mention
your book. Have one on display and make several copies available for sale and autographs in the back of the room. Authors
often make more on book sales in the back of the room than
they do on the speech. Prepare a short, powerful speech on one
small, very interesting, related item and leave plenty of time
for questions and answers. Always write out your introduction
so the host won't stumble around trying to explain who you
are.

Speaking engagements will do three things for you; they promote your book, you may receive a fee for speaking and they add to your professional portfolio. Now, in addition to being an author and a publisher, you are a lecturer, too. You must be an expert!

Seminars are speaking engagements you organize yourself. You set up the day-long program and collect the admissions. A General Motors study found approximately 40,000 seminars are given in North America each year and generate revenues of $100 to $160 million.

Use your book as a text for the seminar and include it in the admission fee. Display related books in the back of the room and sell tapes of your lecture. If you have an idea, you can get $20 for the book, $80 for the tape and $300 or more for the seminar. For information on setting up seminars, write Communications Unlimited, Gordon Burgett, P.O. Box 6405, Santa Maria, CA 93456.

Autograph parties are a good ego trip when successful and can help to make your other advertising more effective. Normally these events are scheduled by the publisher for the benefit of the author. However, unless the author is well-known, the autograph party rarely pays. The best scheduling is to tie in with a radio or TV appearance and some local advertising.

Contact a local bookstore and ask if you may set up a table, erect a sign and provide some refreshment. The bookstore may be reluctant to sponsor such an event unless you are willing to underwrite some of the cost. The expense won't be small because, in addition to the refreshments and sign, you will have to consider a good deal of advertising via mail and space ads. But the store may pay half. Even if they fail to sell a lot of your books, this "event" you are staging will bring new customers into their shop. Once introduced to the bookstore, they are more likely to return in the future.

Once you know a local paper is going to review your book or do a feature article on you, visit the bookstores. Suggest they might like to place an ad in the same edition to draw readers into their store. Offer to stage an autograph party—another fine tie-in.

Don't overlook fund-raising event autograph parties. Here, you would do the selling and would donate part to the club or organization.

To make an autograph party successful, you must pour on the publicity. Send out large numbers of news releases and invitations. Make the event sound big and important. Make everyone in town think that everyone else is going, that if they don't go they will be the only one not there.

Book awards. There is probably no greater satisfaction to a writer than having his book selected for an award. Some book awards are big and well known and some are small. There are those that are general while others are quite specialized, but all are awards and just being nominated for one looks good in your advertising.

Awards may be mentioned in advertising, and announcement stickers may be applied to the books. These stickers are a bit of extra work but they get attention. In later printings, the "sticker" may be printed on.

Book awards, contests and grants are listed in *Literary Market Place* and *Writer's Market* available at your library, and in a pamphlet entitled *Grants and Awards Available To American Writers* published by P.E.N. American Center. See the Appendix.

Related book lists can be used to plug your other books. Each of your books should carry a list of all your books and these lists should be updated at each reprinting. The list may appear on the rear jacket flap or in the appendix of the book. This is a way to get your sales message to potential buyers in the same field at little cost.

Be prepared to move when your book takes off. Have your promotional plan organized so you will be able to gain maximum mileage from your publicity. Capitalize on each piece of publicity. Have your releases, ads and letters drafted.

Take advantage of every possible market. Pursue the most lucrative but don't overlook the marginal ones. It costs very little to service more markets once you have done the initial organization.

The secret to successful publishing is not to produce more books but to market effectively those books already published.

Chapter Eight

Who Will Buy Your Book?

Distribution Channels

Your marketing effort is vital to the success of your book. Yours may be the greatest tome ever written, but if your sales message fails to reach its intended customer, your book won't sell. People just will not line up automatically to purchase your book. You have already expended a great deal of effort in writing and publishing your book but it is the energy you expend now that will make your earlier effort pay off.

Unfortunately, many creative people recoil at the thought of selling their own product. But they must promote their book. It makes no difference whether they went with a large New York publisher or elected to do their own publishing. If the book is to sell, the author must do the promoting.

> *The writing of a best seller represents only a fraction of the total effort required to create one.* - Ted Nicholas Peterson

The role of marketing is to return maximum sales on minimum promotional investment, "to get the most bang for your buck." You want to invest your money where you will get the best return. This means placing promotion and advertising where you receive the best response per dollar and hour invested.

An often heard rule of thumb for response percentages—for example, the number of orders received from a mailing—is 2%, and there are many entertaining stories of much better returns. What really counts is the return in sales on the advertising investment. A cheap ad becomes expensive if it fails to bring in any sales. To determine your results, you must total your alternatives before you sign up. The woods are full of ad salespeople and their primary mission, like yours, is staying in business. They will promise you anything to get into your advertising budget.

Consider the amount of work which will go into the promotion. Total up your office expenses ("licking and sticking") and the direct costs such as stamps and envelopes or ad bills, and balance these against the selling price (if to wholesalers, you will get less per book) and the expected response. Total these up and make the decision, but try to be objective. Run small tests before rolling out into a large investment. Code your address in all marketing efforts as described in Chapter Seven, so you can trace the source of your orders.

The size of the industry. Book publishing is a $9 billion industry. Each year some 47,000 books are published in the United States. Nearly 4,000 are mass market paperbacks while some 13,000 are softcover. The percentage in softcover is increasing. The balance of 30,000 titles are hardcover. Roughly 30,000 titles are new and 17,000 are reprints. There are some 12,000 retail bookstores where the shelf life for a book is six months or less.

In *adult trade hardcover* sales during a recent year, 46.6% of the books were sold through retailers, 39.6% through wholesalers, 7.9% directly to libraries and institutions, 3% through special sales and 2.5% directly to customers. Over 5% were exported, about half to Canada. But professional books, those including technical, professional, scientific, medical and business titles, went directly to consumers 30% of the time.

According to a 1985 Gallup survey, 55% of *all book purchases* were made in bookstores, 9% (mostly mass-market paperbacks) from supermarkets, 8% from department or discount stores, 7% from book clubs, 6% via mail order, 4% from drugstores, 1% from newsstands and 10% miscellaneous. There is also other evidence that the number of books sold directly to the consumer via mail order has been on the increase in recent years.

In Canada, some 65% of the books sold are imports, 25% are Canadian published and the rest are foreign books adapted and manufactured for the Canadian market.

In a *Publishers Weekly* article, a poll revealed that only 5% of the population buys six or more books per year (hardcover and paperback) and most buyers were between 18 and 45 years old. Women buy more books than men and prefer fiction, while men buy more nonfiction. The better-educated buy more nonfiction and the lesser-educated, more fiction. While 40% would consider a book as a gift, they weren't sure a book was appropriate and thought it would be difficult to choose one the recipient might like. They did feel, however, that books are very personal.

Research and experience will help you select the best places to spend your advertising money. Some of these markets are obvious and you should start planning around them. Then you will want to branch out into the non-traditional markets where there may be less competition. For example, Warner Publishing cracked a new market in 1978 when Karen Lustgarten's *Disco Dancing* was sold in record stores. Your options are so numerous and varied that it is difficult to concentrate on the important areas.

Audience specialization is concentrating your promotional efforts on those most likely to buy. Before you wrote your book, you analyzed your potential audience and then you slanted your text toward them. In producing your book, you considered how it might be marketed and made your product attractive in this medium. Perhaps you put extra effort into the cover. The selection of your marketing channels is very important. For example, the chains seem to concentrate on fast moving books. If your book does not have a wide audience, you do not want to be in the chains. The unsold books will only come back. Even if you get your book into a non-book market where there aren't any returns, you want the books to sell, not to sit on the shelves forever. So consider who patronizes each of the various outlets and be objective in considering whether they are your audience.

There has been little market research in the general segment of the book industry. Most of the sales effort is based on past personal experience. In analyzing the market, you will consider your principal marketing concerns, your customers (individuals, schools, libraries, international markets, subsidiary rights, industry, government, etc.) and your distribution channels (mass market outlets, wholesalers, bookstores and book clubs). Your marketing tools are book reviews, space ads, direct mail advertising, sales representation, etc.

With a specialized nonfiction book you can avoid the expensive traditional big publisher methods of marketing to everyone and concentrate on the more profitable areas. Work smarter, not harder. Define your core audience and then get to work. Select your special audience and find a way to reach them. You will find your target group is served by magazines, stores, catalogs, broadcast interviewers, specialized book clubs, columnists and others. For example, if your book is on skydiving, you know you can reach your customers through the U.S. Parachute Association, the Para-Gear catalog, *Parachutist* magazine and at the national championships. Who is your customer? What is his profile? Where can you find him? Where does he congregate with others like him? What magazines does he read? What clubs does he join? Where is he?

You do not have to attack the whole group, you can go after just the cream off the top. Mail to the libraries with the biggest budgets, visit the buyers of the larger chain stores and select the wealthiest of the direct mail purchasers. Ads and mailing lists can be purchased selectively by region and other criteria; you do not have to buy the whole country.

Hedge your bets by balancing your markets. Put most of your energy into selling your target group. Sell to the rest, too, but don't spend a lot of time courting them. Invest your time and money wisely.

> *There is no secret formula. It is simply a good item for which there is a need, at the right price, offered to the right market.*

Repetitive audience contact is your mission once you have identified your marketing area. A repeated promotion in direct mail advertising, space ads, etc. will normally bring the same response as it did the first time. Naturally the returns will drop off if done too often, but many agree that six weeks is sufficient spacing. And there is some value to repetitive exposure; after a while, people begin to recognize and become comfortable with you. It is wise to change your message occasionally as some in your audience will pass over it, having seen it before. But don't change for the sake of change. Repeat what works, go with a winner.

You must test each type of advertising on a small sample of the group you are trying to reach. One initial ad rarely produces a bonanza. But each customer who bites is a prime target for similar books on the same subject. People who buy how-to books on a specialized subject collect them all. Slowly build your clientele and your product line.

Multiple markets will cost more in time and money but will stabilize your financial position by smoothing out the peaks and valleys. It is wise not to have all your eggs in one basket. With a how-to nonfiction book, you may concentrate on wholesalers, catalogs, and direct mail. Some of your effort will depend on you. If you like personal contact, you might do more talk shows and visit more bookstores. If you like your privacy, you might use the mail. Book promotion should be fun, so do what you enjoy most.

Seasons will affect your sales and you should plan your major marketing efforts around them. The big publishers bring out most of their new titles in the fall, targeting them at Christmas. Their second major season is in the spring. There is a good gift market but the competition is rough. June graduates are a good market. Business books move best in the late spring and late fall, not during the summer. Outdoor books do best in late winter when people are confined indoors and thinking about the activities of the coming summer. Travel books will do well a few months before the applicable travel season.

The fact is, do-it-yourself books have never been more popular than they are now, and their popularity is growing steadily. - Arnold F. Logan, Petersen Publishing Company.

Most publishers find December and late August to be slow. Business picks up after the first of the year and after Labor Day.

The Public, or ultimate consumer, may be approached directly. Books have been sold door-to-door, hawked on street corners, at street fairs and flea markets. The advantage of selling direct is the elimination of the middlemen; you keep the entire list price for yourself. But approaching the ultimate consumer requires greater effort and the books are sold one at a time.

The other method of reaching the public is by mail. Direct mail advertising is less personal but more private; it appeals to many authors. Pre-publication offers to the consumer usually pull very well. Direct mail advertising and mail order distribution are discussed in detail in the next two chapters.

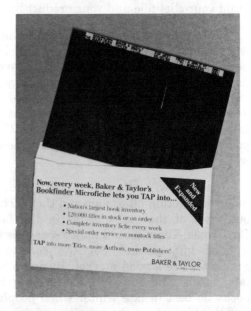

Now, every week, Baker & Taylor's Bookfinder Microfiche lets you TAP into...

New and Expanded

* Nation's largest book inventory
* 120,000 titles in stock or on order
* Complete inventory fiche every week
* Special order service on nonstock titles

TAP into more Titles, more Authors, more Publishers!

BAKER & TAYLOR

Microfiche card

Microfiche systems. Some of the larger distributors, such as Ingram, Baker & Taylor, Publishers Group West and Bookpeople have instituted microfiche systems. They ship these 4 x 6 film negative "fiche" inventory lists to the stores each week or so. Now when a customer asks for a book not on the shelf, the bookstore can look it up, verify that it is available, make a toll-free call and have it delivered by UPS in a couple of days.

The customer may pay for the book then and return to pick it up, or have the book delivered to his or her home. Bookstores like making sales when they do not have to inventory books. Even the chains use the system because it is sure and fast.

While you cannot place your book in every bookstore, you can make it available through every store with these microfiche systems. Some distributors want a larger discount to include you in their system, but this investment is well worth the added exposure. Visit a bookstore and ask to use their microfiche reader—see for yourself.

Divisions of the industry. The industry has divided itself by concentrating on certain areas of the product, marketing areas and marketing methods. The balance of this chapter will concentrate on the various marketing channels.

As you read about the industry, you will come to the conclusion that the best way to handle the book trade (bookstores and libraries) is through various wholesalers and distributors. Distributors consolidate shipments to bookstores, providing a lower per-unit shipping cost; they recycle returns back into stock and sweat the collections. The last thing you want is an order from 1,250 Waldenbook stores. It would take weeks to invoice and ship three to five books to each store. Often the cost of the shipping supplies alone will be more than the difference in discount. It takes just as long to ship one book as it does a carton. Better to ship cartons to a wholesaler than many small parcels to individual stores.

Mass market paperback distributors, about 450 in number, merchandise the smaller pocket-sized paperbacks along with magazines. No more than ten independent distributors ("ID's") account for 90% of the total volume. They service some 80,000 outlets, including newsstands, drugstores, department and college stores. In 1988, they sold over 500 million books at a median price of $4.58 each. At 4,000 to 5,000 new titles each year, there are just too many for the rack space available. Print runs usually begin at 50,000 and paperbacks are treated like magazines. If the books do not sell, the covers are ripped off and returned for credit (to save postage). It is estimated that 36% of all mass market paperbacks are returned but 50% on a particular title is not unusual.

These mass market jobbers own their racks and refill them each week. There is no buying decision by the store. If the books do not sell in two weeks, they are pulled and replaced. If they do sell out, the space is filled with something new; the title is not reordered. Again, these books are treated just like magazines.

It would be nice to have your book in every supermarket in the country but the gamble of low price, high return rate and high print run is too great. To be successful in this market, your book must have vast general appeal.

Book Wholesalers and Distributors. Most bookstores and libraries buy from middlemen. Initial bookstore orders may go through a rep. but reorders are faster through a wholesaler. These firms ask for a 50% to 60% discount from you and sell to their customers at 20% to 40% off, depending upon quantity (titles may be mixed). With regional warehouses, wholesalers offer fast service and one-stop shopping. Even the big chains make use of wholesalers when they run out and are desperate for a book. Often, with a call and UPS service, they can get the books in a couple of days. Many wholesalers cater only to libraries. They provide a valuable service by combining orders and saving the library from thousands of single orders.

There are a lot of people in the book business who have visualized the big buck and have gone into wholesaling. While the gross may be big, the net is small and it takes a very large and highly efficient operation to be profitable. A number of distributors have folded.

With wholesalers, the important mission is to get into their system with a large stocking order. This does not mean you should oversell them. They will return what they can't move, so it is always safer to go low. This approach also maintains your credibility with the buyer, who is more likely to take your suggestion for an initial stocking order next time.

Selling to wholesalers is most effective with a personal visit, but you can often make a sale by mail. With a single book, your first, it won't pay to fly across the continent, but some wholesalers may be close by and you might be able to get to others while on a business trip or vacation. The best months to approach wholesalers are January and July in anticipation of the peak selling seasons.

You will find these contacts very educational; these visits shouldn't be left to sales representatives. Make an appointment so your trip isn't made only to find the buyer on vacation. Be prepared. Take copies of your book, in both softcover and hard if available, your dealer price list, copies of your reviews, your return policy, photographs of the book, everything. Prepare a summary of recent purchases and returns if they have already ordered from you. A lot of small orders may indicate a demand warranting a larger single order. Remember that the buyer is not there to help you and won't be judging your book on its literary merits. He or she is thinking about whether the buying public will respond; will it move and if so, how many?

A good reorder rule of thumb is to take half the quantity the distributor has sold during the last three months. If you make the suggestion, it will ease the decision making. Don't shoot too high or the buyer will have to lower the number. If the buyer can get a discount break by adding a few more books to the order, mention it. Don't forget to offer any catalog or display materials you may have, such as photographs, posters or dumps (shipping cartons that become display stands).

Familiarize the wholesaler with your terms and return policy and have an order blank ready with his name and address already filled in to save time. Get a purchase order number and always leave a carbon of the order.

Make up a "call report," just as you would demand one from a sales rep working for you. It is a good working habit and, filed away until you next have to contact that buyer, will provide revealing information which may have slipped your mind.

Then follow through by mailing your brochure and other materials to the buyer with a note. Follow up later with a telephone call to ask if he or she is ready to reorder. Look up the buyer at book shows, establish a person-to-person contact. Whenever you receive major television or print coverage, send the information to the buyer. Let him or her know if you are going on a major talk show. Let the buyer prepare for the demand. Some publishers make monthly mailings to their distributors.

If the distributor has purchased from you before, check their stock. They may even let you into the warehouse. Some wholesalers have very poor inventory feedback systems and aren't even aware that they are out of your book until you mention it. You will build a lot of good will by suggesting they return stock that isn't moving.

Wholesalers don't often return books, since when one is returned by one bookstore, it simply gets recycled off to another one. Your book may fail in one store because of its unusual clientele or because the book was "lost" under the counter and not displayed.

Many distributors operate on consignment inventory and pay 90 days after they sell the books to the bookstore. This means they have very little invested in their operation. While publishers should avoid selling to small accounts on consignment, there are good arguments for these terms with distributors. Book manufacturing requires large print runs, so the inventory might just as well sit in a few other warehouses as your own. Remember, however, title to the books is still yours. If the books are lost or damaged, if the wholesaler does not have insurance, the loss could be yours.

Most of your volume will be through a half dozen wholesale accounts if you have a general interest book. These distributors move quantity; that's maximum books for minimum processing paperwork. Accordingly, they are very important to you. In fact, if your dealer price list requires a large number of books for a discount, it will force more stores to order from wholesalers, which may simplify your business. Remember that wholesalers only fill orders, they don't create demand. Even if you don't contact them, they will order from you sooner or later. Then you will know that your promotional efforts have encouraged one of their clients to order. But single copies are not enough, you must get into their system. Once they place a number of small orders, bring this to their attention and suggest a larger stocking order.

Wholesalers are often reluctant to open accounts with a publisher with only one book. Therefore, you must be persistent. You must convince them this is the first book of many and that this book will move. If they turn you down at first, do not be discouraged. Work on your sales to stores and then go back and try again. Wholesalers want to take on winners. Show them you have a book that is selling and they will want you.

The two big stocking wholesalers with multiple regional warehouses are Baker & Taylor and Ingram. Smaller stocking wholesalers are Bookpeople, Publishers Group West, Inland, the distributors (always with a small "d") and Pacific Pipeline. The many other library wholesalers rarely stock books. Coutts, Blackwell, Bro Dart, Ballen, EBS, Midwest, and Scholarly only respond to orders from libraries. You can find these wholesalers listed along with others in the Appendix and in *Literary Market Place*. The *American Book Trade Directory* also has a list and even provides contact names. Here are brief profiles of some of the wholesalers.

Wholesaler vs. Distributor. Should you select a true wholesaler or a true distributor? Select a single distributor if you want to hire a company to take over your promotion and fulfillment. Select several wholesalers if you want to maintain control of your warehousing and shipping. Most publishers will be happier handling their own fulfillment and dealing with as many wholesalers as possible.

Wholesaler and *distributor* are used interchangeably here. Technically, wholesalers stock books for many, many publishers on a non-exclusive basis. They do not push books with sales reps and most place orders with publishers only when they receive an order from a bookstore or library. Distributors act like an arm of the publisher. They represent a few publishers on an exclusive basis, warehouse the stock, and send sales reps to the stores. So, distributors serve the publisher by handling his warehousing and shipping while wholesalers serve the bookstore and library by finding books for them.

The problem is that many of the wholesalers and distributors have reformulated their businesses so they have moved out of their original mold. Many do not even know which one they are. Therefore, we will use the terms interchangeably.

Ingram Book Company is headquartered in Nashville, Tennessee, with six regional warehouses. Ingram stocks fewer titles (some 95,000) than Baker & Taylor but stocks the books in greater depth. Ingram carries the books of some 700 publishers and serves 18,000 bookstores and libraries. They shipped 60 million books in 1988. Ingram does not promote books, they make them available to retailers.

Ingram is very business oriented: they want to know about your promotion. You must convince them there will be demand for your books. Be prepared to answer their questions about what you plan to do to make your book sell. Their decision to buy or not to buy your book will be based on your promotional plans as much as the quality of the book itself. Most of the buying for the regional warehouses is controlled from Nashville. There are several buyers, each responsible for a particular area. Try to get to the computer books buyer, the trade nonfiction buyer, etc. as applicable, or you may wind up with the small press buyer (a less prestigious classification). Call Ingram for the name of the current category buyer. Ingram usually gets a 50% discount and pays the freight, though some new publishers have been held to 55%, FOB destination.

Ingram mails its microfiche listings to over 9,000 bookstores each week. Getting on the fiche is a respected accomplishment, but staying on it through reorders is more difficult and a more accurate measure of your book's success. Ingram also publishes *Advance* magazine and *Paperback Advance*.

Ingram runs special promotions. For a price, your book can be featured in a circular mailed with the monthly statements or microfiche mailings (cost was about $1,150 in 1992), or the book can be mentioned by the order operators.

Ingram does not like to deal directly with new publishers or small publishers. They will, however, consider your books if carried by a wholesaler such as Publishers Group West. PGW visits the Ingram buyers several times a year to present new titles. You want wholesalers to present your book but you may also make your own presentation and let a wholesaler fulfill the orders. Send a copy of the book, with a brochure and any other promotional materials, to Ingram Book Company, Ann Mogensen, 1125 Heil Quaker Blvd., LaVergne, TN 37086, (615) 793-5000. To get the book listed in Ingram's Title Data base, send a book brochure to Ingram Book Company, Title Data Base—Dept. 96, 347 Reedwood Drive, Nashville, TN 37217, (615) 793-5000.

Baker & Taylor is headquartered in Bridgewater, New Jersey, with nearly autonomous warehouse branches in Somerville, New Jersey; Reno, Nevada; Momence, Illinois and Commerce, Georgia. While the company is education-oriented and much of their effort is directed toward finding books for libraries, the bookstore market is serviced with a microfiche system. Baker & Taylor is a mirror of library demand. If you receive a good review in *Library Journal*, for example, some 75% of your library orders will come through B&T.

Baker & Taylor stocks more than 120,000 different titles. They will require a 55% discount to put your books into their system as a *stock publisher*. Agreements vary. If you do not choose to be in the system, you may allow Baker & Taylor any discount you wish. Since they are usually waiting for your book to complete a large order, they won't quibble over the discount and will even pay a pro forma invoice (in advance). Being a stock publisher with a listing on the microfiche makes your books available to many more stores and buyers, which is easily worth the 55%. There is a $100 listing charge.

Baker and Taylor attends the ABA Book Fair as both seller and buyer. Sellers staff the booth on the floor while buyers meet with publishers to review new titles in a room in the convention center or a nearby hotel. When visiting the fair, find out where the buyers are, make an appointment and keep it.

Contact Baker & Taylor in Bridgewater and ask for a copy of their *Information Outline For Publishers*. This multi-page document explains all the Baker & Taylor programs. Fill out and return their *vendor profile questionnaire* and their *new book information* form. Baker and Taylor, Publisher Services, P.O. Box 6920, Bridgewater, NJ 08807-0920, (908) 218-0400.

Publishers Group West accepts your books on consignment, FOB destination (you pay the shipping), takes 24% of the net (what they receive from stores), and pays you 90 days after they ship to the stores. Sales reports are sent to publishers each month. Located in Emeryville, California, they have several sales reps. PGW is very selective, runs a tight ship and pays on time.

PGW will represent your book to Walden and Dalton. They make periodic treks east to pitch books to both major chains. Selling the chains can be a major coup. Bookstores are served with a microfiche system.

Contact PGW for their contract, announcement card and *editorial fact Sheet*. Fill out the sheet, sign the contract and return them with a review copy. Publishers Group West, Elizabeth McGreevy, 4065 Hollis Street, Emeryville, CA 94608, (415) 658-3453, (800) 982-8319.

Bookpeople started with the small press movement in 1968 and is known throughout the industry for stocking small press books. They carry some 15,000 titles from more than 1,500 publishers to service over 4,000 bookstores, health food outlets and women's stores around the world. Fifty percent of their customers are on the west coast, 35% in the east and 15% outside the U.S. Bookpeople has a microfiche system, publishes a catalog and issues *Bookpaper*, a monthly listing of new titles.

Bookpeople accepts books on consignment, FOB Oakland, takes a 55% discount and pays 90 days after the books are shipped. Sales reports are sent to publishers each month. Contact Bookpeople for a copy of their Small Press Distribution Agreement. Bookpeople, Randy Beek, 7900 Edgewater Drive, Oakland, CA 94621, (510) 632-4700, (800) 999-4650.

Inland Book Company was founded in 1981 by David Wilk and Stephen Hargraves and was designed to be a *Bookpeople of the East*. They specialize in small press titles and literary works and warehouse some 20,000 titles from 1,600 publishers. Send a copy of the book and promotional materials to Inland Book Company, David Wilk, 140 Commerce Street, East Haven, CT 06512, (203) 467-4257.

The distributors (always with a small "d") was founded in 1970 and warehouses some 15,000 titles. They make regular trips to pitch B. Dalton and other chains. Contact The distributors for a copy of their Consignment Agreement. Send a copy of the book and promotional materials to The distributors, Linda Speckman, 702 South Michigan, South Bend, IN 46618, (800) 348-5200.

Golden-Lee Book Distributors is headquartered in Brooklyn with distribution centers in Atlanta and Los Angeles. Send a copy of the book along with promotional materials to Golden Lee Book Distributors, Attn: (hardcover, mass market or trade paperback) Buyer, 1000 Dean Street, Brooklyn, NY 11238-3393, (718) 857-6333, (800) 221-0960.

New Leaf specializes in health and metaphysical titles and sells to health food stores as well as bookstores. Contact

New Leaf for a copy of their *Information for Small Presses* and their *Consignment Contract*. Send a copy of the book and promotional materials to New Leaf Distributing Co., 5425 Tulane SW, Atlanta, GA 30323-3636, (404) 691-6996.

Nutri-Books specializes in books and tapes for health food stores, gyms and health studios. Founded in 1955, it warehouses some 2,500 titles. Send a copy of the book and promotional materials to Nutri-Books Corp., Roger Willbanks, P.O. Box 5793, Denver, CO 80217, (303) 778-8383.

Pacific Pipeline is a regional wholesaler to bookstores, libraries and specialty retailers, that is very strong in the northwest. Founded in 1974, they specialize in regional and outdoor books and warehouse some 45,000 titles. Pacific Pipeline publishes their inventory on microfiche and also publishes a catalog. Contact Pacific Pipeline for a copy of their *Consignment Agreement*. Send a copy of the book and promotional materials to Pacific Pipeline, Helen Ibach, 8030 South 228th Avenue South, Kent, WA 98032-3898, (206) 872-5523.

Wholesaler contact. Contact each wholesaler for submission forms as mentioned above. Or get all the forms and more from a single source in *Publishing Forms*. See the Appendix. Send the forms with a copy of the book. Send brochures to the rest of the wholesalers and distributors so they will know where to find you when they receive an order. See the list of wholesalers in *Literary Market Place*. For a mailing list of over 1,600 book wholesalers, distributors and exporters on pressure sensitive labels ready to peel and stick, see ParaLists in the Appendix.

Ingram and Baker & Taylor move the most books, and Ingram will probably only deal with you through a wholesaler such as Bookpeople or Publishers Group West.

Exclusives. Some book dealers, usually wholesalers, may request an exclusive. They argue they need this protection for all the sales effort they plan to put into your book. The problem is that exclusives usually make people lazy. They don't have to work because they are receiving credit for all the sales anyway.

Exclusives are appropriate for true *distributors* but not for true *wholesalers*. One of the problems is that some of the companies that began as wholesalers are reformulating their businesses by demanding exclusives, but not choosing to represent your entire line of books. They are *cherry picking* the best titles.

It is difficult, if not impossible to know in advance which wholesaler or distributor will represent each of your titles in the best way; and it can be financially disastrous if you place all your eggs in the wrong basket.

Remember that a contract is nothing more than an offer. You can always make a counter-offer by inserting *non* before the word *exclusive* and returning the contract for their new signature.

If a distributor wants an exclusive, ask where they are strong. They probably want only the book trade: bookstores and libraries. Narrow them down to that and reserve all other markets (gift stores, single-book mail order, etc.) to yourlself.

Chain Bookstores concentrate on the fastest moving books rather than the specialized. Waldenbooks, B. Dalton/Barnes & Noble and Crown together do about 30% of the $4-billion retail book trade; Walden (1,228 stores in 1989) and Dalton (1,143 stores in 1989) alone account for 16%. B. Dalton and discounter Pickwick are owned by Dayton-Hudson Corporation, while Walden is part of K mart. Crown is a discounter (228 stores in 1989) owned by Dart Drug and Thrifty. Walden, Dalton and Crown are growing rapidly. There are some sixty other smaller chains. If you are publishing bookstore-type books, the chains are too large an outlet to be ignored.

The chains buy for all their stores from their headquarters. According to *Publishers Weekly*, Dalton is the largest hardcover retailer in the U.S. and they have the lowest unsold book return rate in the industry. Their operations are computerized, so they know what is selling and can plan reorders. They purchase by category and demographics, matching books to the store's clientele. B. Dalton stocks more titles than Walden but not in as great a depth.

Establish and maintain key contacts at the chain headquarters but don't overlook sales visits to their individual stores. Most local outlets are authorized to make small purchases and they are especially receptive to regional books. Walden does not permit local managers to make purchases but headquarters does listen to them when they request a local publisher's book. Most chains expect a 40% discount, FOB origin, and many pay in 60-90 days.

The chains are easy to reach since each has a single buying office. Call and ask for the name of the current appropriate category buyer and send a copy of your book along with promotional materials. See the Appendix for a list of the major chains. More chain stores can be found in the *American Book Trade Directory*. See the Reference Librarian at your local public library.

Bookstores, individual but not necessarily independent, are a diverse group of retailers. They include the downtown bookstore, the college store, the religious bookstore and others. Over 12,000 in number, they come in all sizes: some sell books exclusively while others carry books as a sideline, some stores are general and some are specialized, and some are attached to museums or libraries. With the introduction of new marketing techniques, the stores are proliferating, but their quality is dropping as some confine their selections only to the fast-moving titles. They do not stock in depth.

—Bookstore patron profiles consist of the regularly purchasing book addict and the occasional buyer. These are people who are used to plunking down $19.95 for hardcover fiction. Fifty percent of the customers in a bookstore are looking for a particular book. These particular book seekers are more likely to be younger and female. Forty-seven percent are looking for a nonfiction title, 27% for a particular book of fiction and 28% want textbooks. While 20% do not find the book they are looking for, 54% buy one or more books before they leave. Then there are those people who never visit a bookstore.

If selling books through bookstores was good business, the stores might be paying their bills.

Modern booksellers are faced with trying to attract and sell to all these people. To do so, they have to locate in high rent, heavy-traffic areas. Stores report an inventory turnover of two to five times a year, with an average of 3.3 times. If a book hasn't moved in six months on the shelf, it is usually returned. The newer and smaller publisher is trapped between the Scylla of wide exposure and the Charybdis of massive returns.

Many small publishers tolerate, but don't pursue, small individual bookstores. The major problems with stores are that they order just a few books at a time, complain about the 40% discount, seldom pay in 30 days and often return the books for a refund—damaged. You wind up processing a lot of paperwork for many small orders and returns, while making very few sales. The best approach is to let the wholesalers handle the stores. Once the wholesalers make your book available to the stores, you may spend your energy creating a demand.

Publishers reach the bookstore market through personal sales visits, direct mail and space ads, particularly in *Publishers Weekly*. But a lot of orders are generated by customer requests from those influenced by an ad, a television appearance or other promotion.

Large publishers with many titles send their sales representatives to call on bookstores. With one or two titles, it is hardly worth your time. But these sales calls can be a good learning experience for you. The big publishing reps carry only the (lighter weight) covers or dust jackets of new books to show the buyer. You have an advantage by carrying in the actual book. You can also offer to drop off the books and save them the postage. The best time to visit a store is between 3:30 and 4:30 in the afternoon when there are the fewest customers. Always call for an appointment; buyers usually do not have time for drop-ins. Ask to speak with the store manager or buyer.

Bookstores rely on sales reps for recommendations, so the buyer should be receptive. He or she may ask about your promotion plans. Tell them you are a local author and, therefore, local people will be interested in your book. Mention any local publicity such as talk shows which are planned. Stores want to know if the book will be promoted. Reviews and author appearances are more important than advertising. If the book is professionally produced, a sale should not be difficult. Be ready with the stock phrase: "I can offer you the books at a full 40% discount, without delivery charges, and they are fully returnable, of course." The whole pitch will probably run five to ten minutes.

If you still can't persuade the buyer, you might like to try "consignment." Here the store pays for the books only after they are sold; that is, when they need more of them. With consignment, the discount should be dropped to 25% to 35%. Keep the initial order small. It won't help to overload the store only to get the shelf-worn books back in a few months. It is better to keep the inventory turning over.

—**College, school and textbook stores** also respond best to face-to-face sales calls. There are some 2,800 college stores serving 2,200 U.S. colleges and universities with over 11-million students. These stores are on their own schedule, depending upon whether they are on the semester, quarter or early semester system. Don't put too much energy into college stores. Students don't spend money on much more than assigned texts, recorded music and beer. About one-third of school store orders are through wholesalers, so wholesalers may be a better way to reach this market.

—**Approach.** If you like personal contact, load up the car and visit the stores. If you would rather stay home, you can hit more bookstores via direct mail advertising. A list of stores can be found in your library in the *American Book Trade Directory*. Once you have established an account, you can use the telephone for a certain amount of restocking, but you can't beat a personal visit for keeping your book on the shelf.

During your visit, help the store to put your book on the proper shelves. If your book is poetry or fiction, place some copies in those areas and more in the subject matter area. For example, if your poetry is about the outdoors, place a few copies with the outdoor books.

You might like to try offering posters, displays and racks but most stores won't have room for them. Experiment with your local store.

You might try sending a free sample copy to a few more distant stores. It will get their attention and is cheaper than a

234 The Self-Publishing Manual

visit. Be sure to stamp the book "Review copy, not for resale" so you don't get it back as a return.

To get your message to bookstores, use co-op mailings, targeted mailings and trade magazines, but let the wholesalers do the fulfillment. The Publishers Marketing Association makes co-op mailings to the 4,400 members of the American Booksellers Association. Your message can be included for a reasonable charge and you do not have to do all the licking and sticking. PMA's address is in the Appendix. Targeted mailings may be made to bookstores with special-interest sections. For lists of these stores, see *Buy Books Where, Sell Books Where, Specialty Booksellers Directory, Directory of Specialized American Bookdealers* and *Directory of Specialist Booksellers in the U.K.* See the Appendix. Read *Publishers Weekly, American Bookseller* and *Small Press magazines* and look for up-coming special editions. Send in your listing information so that your book will be included.

Libraries come in several types: public, private, special, school, government, etc. There are almost 15,000 public libraries, Three thousand more can be found in colleges, 15,000 are special (including 1,700 law), 20,000 libraries are in high schools, 50,000 in elementary schools, 1,000 are governmental, and over 1,000 formal libraries exist in larger churches.

Even though orders are for smaller quantities, libraries offer greater potential to the small publisher than bookstores. The size of the market is hard to verify, however. Some 76% of the libraries that respond to your mailings will order from a wholesaler, and 75% of those orders go to Baker & Taylor. Rather than place thousands of orders with individual publishers for single titles, libraries save time by sending all orders to a wholesaler. They are extended a 20% to 33% discount by the wholesaler, so they are receiving both price and service. Their problem is money. The cost of ordering and processing a new title can cost as much as the book itself. In many libraries, personnel expenses make up half the budget. Many libraries are spreading their already tight budgets even thinner now by adding audio-visual and other non-print items.

> *Many librarians view the publisher as being the money-grubber between the author and the reader.*

—**Market size.** Libraries spend around $1.4 billion each year for books, buying some 14% of the books published. Public libraries buy 23%, el-hi school libraries 33%, college libraries 27% and special (e.g., law, medical) libraries 17%. Many of their purchases are for books with press runs under 5,000, which would not get published without their support.

Most of the libraries with purchasing budgets over $2.5 million are members of Association of Research Libraries. Five percent of the university libraries have $1 million to $2.5 million to spend on books, 40% have $300,000 or more and 40% have $100,000 or more. Most community and other two-year colleges have only $20,000 to $100,000 However, university libraries spend 40% to 80% of their budgets on books, with most of the rest going for periodicals.

As could be expected, children's books and fiction aren't of any great interest to college libraries. And, no fill-in books--librarians do not want people writing in their books. Send your brochures to the right type of libraries.

If libraries bought one copy of every book published in the United States, they would each need a budget of over $2 million per year. Yet less than 2,600 public libraries have an annual book budget of $25,000 or more and most have much less. They have to be selective in their purchases. Contact only those libraries that can afford to buy your book. Do not waste your energy and money pursuing the rest.

Many libraries buy more for topic than quality. They have to justify their budgets to the community (if public) and try to get something for everyone. It is said that better judgment is shown in the purchasing of children's books and fiction. One librarian recently explained: "When material is scarce on a topic and interest is high, we will often buy any reasonably-priced new book through an ad in *Library Journal* or even a flier. However, we usually don't buy if the book receives a bad review."

—**Do library orders kill sales?** Some book publishers will not sell to libraries on the theory that this one sale will kill several others when many people read the book free. They note that many magazines charge libraries a higher price for a subscription on the theory that more people will read the periodical.

Other book publishers feel the libraries are show-casing their book—and are paying to do it. At least four orders for *The Self-Publishing Manual* are received each week with a letter starting "The library will not let me check the book out again so I guess I'll have to buy my own copy."

Library loans may hurt sales of fiction, which is only read once, but not reference books which are used over and over. Mailing a free copy of a new book to major libraries might even be a good promotional investment.

—Approval Plans. Some wholesalers serve their library accounts automatically by sending collections of books in specific categories *on approval*, allowing the library to return the unwanted titles. Because the wholesaler has *pre-screened* the books and matched them to the library's special collections, few are returned. Academic and special libraries may buy 30% of their books this way, while public libraries buy some 10% of their books through approval plans. Obviously, it is to your great advantage to have your book included in these computer matched offerings, especially in the Baker & Taylor system.

—Ordering cycles. Libraries tend to do most of their ordering around the beginning/end of their fiscal year (usually December 31 or June 30) when they try to use up their old budget or break into a new one. This is when they may show slightly less buying discrimination. Your book might be selected at this time even if it is an afterthought, not a first choice. At the three-quarter point in their fiscal year, libraries are often out of book purchasing funds. School libraries usually use the slow summer months to work on ordering.

—Acquisition librarians. Some libraries have acquisition librarians, while in others book selection is done by committee. Because more than one person is often involved in acquisitions in the larger libraries, it is wise to send more than one copy of each piece of literature.

Do not send your promotional material to the *head librarian* or *acquisition librarian*. In large libraries, it is best to direct mailings to the subject area supervisor who makes the actual buying decisions. These supervisors are in charge of areas such as: *children's books, adult fiction, reference*, etc.

It helps if you build consumer demand, as most libraries respond when a title is requested by a library patron. For example, school libraries are responsive to the wishes of their faculties. Mailings to teachers often result in school library orders.

Many communities have both city and county libraries. Large library systems will need copies of your book for every branch and these multiple orders are very nice.

—Books wear out, they can be lent out only so many times. The life span of most books is one-and-a-half to two years. Unless a worn out title has seen a lot of recent use, it usually isn't reordered. On the other hand, if the book has been very popular, the library may order several copies. Books are also stolen—some 20% of the collection is lost each year. So many books are kept past the due date that librarians do not have time to look up their price. Many libraries have a flat fee, say $10, for any overdue or lost book.

In 1979, when *The Self-Publishing Manual* was first presented to a librarian in Santa Barbara, she said "We will have to order several of these. This is the type of book our patrons keep." During the next few years, the library went through more than 20 copies, and this is despite the fact the book is available for sale in several bookstores, instant print shops and office supply stores around town.

—Dealing direct. Some publishers have elected to deal directly with libraries instead of using wholesalers. Most of these publishers specialize in higher-priced reference books for which libraries are their largest market. They make regular mailings to libraries, count on getting full price and like to stay close to their market. But only 24% of the public libraries and 55% of the school libraries will deal directly with publishers. The rest prefer to use wholesalers.

While librarians don't throw out as much mail as bookstores, they are likely to purchase only one book per branch. It is hard to justify a mailing when more often than not, the library will order it through a library wholesaler to whom you give 40-60%.

When you receive an order direct from a library, add the address to your list and include the contact name. Send periodic mailings. Librarians react like any other clients to your direct mail advertising.

Some publishers say price is not a major consideration because the librarian is not spending his or her own money. The librarians say they buy to cover a subject; they will buy a higher priced book if it meets the need and is the only one available. Libraries do not expect a discount unless they order several copies. Some publishers follow a universal discount schedule giving 10% for an order of five, 20% for 20, etc. Some big city public libraries will take advantage of quantity deals because they are buying for several branches.

—**Your local library** should buy your book just because you are part of the community. Some even have a special private room for books by indigenous writers. If so, it may be appropriate for you to donate a copy to this reference section. If you do make such a donation, be sure the local paper is notified with a news release so you can get some promotional mileage out of your largess.

Dan Poynter donated a couple of his new books to the local public library when he lived in Quincy, Massachusetts. The books were placed in a special room reserved for local books. This was quite an unexpected honor in the hometown of two presidents.

Marketing plan for libraries. The best way to handle the library market is to strike a deal with Quality Books, become a stock publisher with Baker & Taylor, let all the library wholesalers know where to find you by sending them a brochure, join the PMA library mailing, make your own mailings to libraries with special collections, and prepare a great review package for *Library Journal*. Here are the details:

—**Quality Books** uses sales reps to sell books to libraries. In the business over 20 years, they have some 6,000 active library accounts. Quality needs 100 new titles each month, and actively seeks new books. They sell to libraries at list price or at a 20% discount.

Quality wants 55% off, consignment, returnable and 90 days to pay. If you will agree to a 60% discount, they will pay in 60 days. Fifty-five percent may sound like a lot but Quality buys by the carton and pays on time. Returns to publishers average two to three percent and Quality pays the return shipping.

Write to Quality for a *New Book Information* form and a sample *Distribution to Libraries Agreement*: Quality Books,

Inc., 918 Sherwood Drive, Lake Bluff, IL 60044-2204 (708) 295-2010.

Quality rejected *Parachuting, The Skydiver's Handbook* **when it was initially published. The selection committee just didn't believe the library market was large enough for such a specialized sport. Quality was handling a number of the author's other books and gave the handbook another look soon after Tom Drewes took up skydiving in 1983. Everyone has been pleasantly surprised—Quality has moved several hundred copies.**

The Quality Books Selection Committee looks for the following when evaluating a book for library use:

a. Adult nonfiction.

b. New—copyright in current year. The book must not have been exposed to the library market previously. Publisher's primary market must be outside the library market. Book must be submitted to Quality books prior to official publication date.

c. Book is well organized.

1. Good title and subtitle. Must be informative, not cute. Must clearly and instantly convey the book's purpose. Title must be the same on cover, spine and title page.

2. Includes table of contents and index.

3. Book is clearly different from others in its field. Librarians like to fill information gaps.

4. Information is readily accessible—the book is *user-friendly*.

d. No fill-in books. The book must be usable by several customers.

e. Cataloging in Publication data to help in cataloging the book.

f. ISBN to aid identification of the book.

g. Binding. 34% of the books purchased by libraries today are softcover. The less-expensive edition allows librarians to order more books from the same budget. However, the perfect binding must be durable. The book must have a spine to display the title and must be shaped to fit a library shelf, not long, low or round.

h. A topical subject. Book must be the type customers want to borrow from the library.

i. Sales aids. The publisher should supply extra covers for the reps to show to the libraries.

The selection committee turns down 700-800 titles each month. Some books do not meet the selection criteria above, but most rejected submissions are older books from larger publishers. Think about these criteria when writing/designing your next book.

The secret to having your book accepted by Quality Books is to notify them of the new title early. Quality has to get the jump on the regular wholesalers if they are to be effective in moving books for you. The time to send in the *New Book Information Form* is before you go to press. Then books may be shipped directly to Quality from the printer. It is a great feeling to go to press knowing that 400 books are already sold.

—**Baker & Taylor.** Become a *stock publisher*. Contact should have been made as you worked through the previous bookstore section.

—**Notify other library wholesalers with a mailing**. This mailing should have been done as you worked though the previous bookstore section.

—**Book Reviews** in library review magazines. Since a good review in *Library Journal* or *ALA Booklist* will move around 1,200 copies of most books, book reviews are worth some extra effort.

Book reviews are librarians' overwhelmingly most popular tool for making selection decisions. Acquisition librarians just do not have the time to read and evaluate the more than 100 new titles available each day. Librarians rely mostly on *Publishers Weekly, Library Journal, ALA Booklist, Kirkus Reviews, Choice* and *The New York Times Book Review*. Ninety-four percent of the librarians rely on reviews in *Library Journal* while 91% read the reviews in *ALA Booklist*. Only 44% believe the ads in *LJ* and 35% have confidence in the ads in *Booklist*. The figures for *Publishers Weekly* are 75% and 53%. See the addresses for the magazines in the Appendix. Also see the *Book Review, Selection & Reference* section of *Literary Market Place*.

Follow up on review packet mailings to the above-mentioned library review magazines with a telephone call. Never ask if they plan to review the book but rather if they have received the book. If not, or they can't find it, get a name and send another.

—PMA mailing to libraries. Four times each year, The Publishers Marketing Association mails a flat envelope containing individual book fliers to 2,600 public libraries across the U.S., which have a purchasing budget of $25,000 or more. These are just public libraries, and then only those that can afford to buy. Cost for participation is $110 plus your flat (unfolded) flier on one or more books. Contact PMA; the address is in the Appendix.

Consider the type of library most likely to buy your book: Maybe you just want school, medical, or law libraries, or maybe you have a regional book and just want public libraries in New England. Then make a mailing either alone or in cooperation with other publishers.

—Mailings to Special libraries and libraries with special collections. Look for special libraries or regular libraries with special collections. If yours is an aviation book, send brochures to libraries with an aviation section. Do not go to the expense of mailing to all libraries when you can isolate those that have a particular interest in your topic. Gale Research rents lists of libraries with **special collections**. Gale Research Company, Judy Graham, Book Tower, Detroit, MI 48226, (800) 223-GALE, (313) 961-2242.

For a list of **special libraries**, contact the Special Library Association, Elsa B. Williams, 1700 Eighteenth Street, NW, Washington, DC 20009, (202) 234-4700.

Many individual library associations will rent their mailing lists. For example, The American Association of Law Libraries can supply a list of 2,300 law libraries on labels. For more information on contacting special libraries, send for *Marketing to Libraries Through Library Associations* from the American Library Association, Sandy Whitely, 50 East Huron Street, Chicago, IL 60611, (312) 944-6780.

When you plan to make a mailing to specialized libraries, invite other publishers to join you. Co-op promotions can save a lot of money and help justify otherwise marginal mailings. Contacting other publishers is easy. Just send a notice of your proposed mailing for listing in the Publishers Marketing Association *Newsletter*.

For a great deal of inside information on mailing to libraries, see Nat Bodian's *The Publisher's Direct Mail Handbook*. See the Appendix.

—Magazines. *Library Journal*, *ALA Booklist* and other trade magazines run special editions and special sections throughout the year. Areas covered are travel books, children's books, metaphysical books, cookbooks, religious books, etc. Listings are usually free. Advertising and listings should be planned for these special editions where attention is being drawn to a particular subject.

Write to each magazine for ad rates and announcements of special editions. The addresses are in the Appendix.

The school market spends over a billion dollars each year for text books, and while most of these books are developed especially for certain courses, many are regular books developed for other markets but adopted as supplementary educational aids. While educators want the very latest information, most are leery of being experimental. Teachers need to be assured that the book is up-to-date and has been accepted by experts elsewhere. Educators are the most price-conscious of all the book markets, even though they aren't spending their own money. Textbook publishers respond by keeping their prices lower than normal and extending only a 20% (short) discount to the school bookstores.

—Elementary and secondary schools. In the U.S. there are some 64,000 public elementary, 24,000 public high and 1,800 combined schools in 18,000 school districts. Additionally, there are some 14,000 private elementary and 4,000 private high schools. Together they employ 2.3 million teachers.

In 22 states, schools purchase texts under a state adoption system, where titles are approved by a board for a five-year period. State adoption is a hunting license and allows the salespeople to try to sell the book to the schools. Even where there is no state adoption system, planning seems to follow a five-year cycle. In some areas, publishers have to ship to central depositories where the schools draw on books as needed. This usually means a consignment inventory and the publishers aren't paid for the books until requisitioned by the schools. The school market is tough and very competitive.

In recent years, publishers have had to use larger type in their school texts—not for the students but for the teachers. The median age for teachers in the United States is over 40 years, 49 in California.

—**Colleges and universities.** Colleges are changing. There are more students over 25; more women are going back to school; and more people are turning to continuing education courses in their specialty.

There are three types of college bookstores. Some are owned by the institution, some are private and some are college stores with a private lessee. Those connected with the institution may take advantage of "library rate" postage schedules.

Textbook publishers concentrate on wooing the instructors who must select books for their courses in more than 3,000 schools. This decision is easy for some professors as they pen their own. Normally the purchasing is done by the local bookstore and the instructor notifies them of his or her choice by April for the fall term. Of course, there are problems. The choice is made late and the estimate of the number to be needed is frequently wrong. Then some students avoid buying the text by sharing, or making repeated visits to the school library. The result is a return rate on textbooks of more than 20%.

Teachers expect to get free examination copies of books, and while some treat this privilege with respect, others just collect books or sell them to the bookstore. The bookstore, in turn, sells the book to a student or returns it to the publisher for a refund. The bookstores even supply the educators with blank "Desk Copy Request Forms" designed to be sent to the publisher. Often the younger instructors are trying to build up their libraries. The older professors, who have more say in book selection, do much less collecting. Some publishers like to request more information about the size of the course, the requester's academic position, etc. Sol Marshall of Creative Books answers desk copy requests with a form letter offering the book at a greatly reduced price. This way he at least covers his costs.

During the last 20 years, this publisher has sent out scores of re-quested "desk copies" and so far only two have resulted in large bookstore orders.

To attack the college market, analyze your book's subject and determine which course might find it useful. The educators are easy to find, and direct mail advertising is the most effective method of reaching them. In fact, some publishers find the lists so specialized that they use them to send free, unsolicited examination copies.

Mailing list information can be found in your library. See the Standard Rate and Data Service's directories, *An Advertiser's Guide to Scholarly Periodicals* and *Direct Marketing* magazine. Check the *Yellow Pages* for local list brokers and see the listing of mailing list sources in the Appendix.

Another way to reach the educational market is through book exhibits at academic book fairs and conventions. With only a title or two, you may like to share a booth with someone else, or turn your book over to a firm which will represent you for a small fee. These exhibit services are listed in the Appendix and *Literary Market Place*. See the paragraph on book fairs, elsewhere in this book.

College buying patterns are affected by school schedules, depending on whether they are on the semester, quarter or early semester system. The best months to make mailings to colleges are February, April, July and October. Once you make contact with an instructor, add him or her to your mailing list; they are valuable. Once a professor has adopted one of your books, some say he or she is twice as likely to do it again.

Pre-publication sales will bring in some money early and help you pay the printing bill. But it isn't wise to start too soon on the pre-publication publicity for your first book. The first time around is a learning experience and there will be count-less delays. You do not want to find yourself spending all your time answering the question: "Where is the book?" With the first book, hold your announcement until it is on the press. The next time, adjust and start earlier.

Once you learn the promotion ropes, you should be able to sell enough books through pre-publication sales, to both wholesale and retail customers, to pay the print bill.

Write up a news release, send in your ads and make a mailing. Offer an early wholesale deal ("to be shipped direct from the printer") to associations and specialty dealers. It is nice to have a pile of orders on the desk when the book comes off the press. But timing is important; these orders must not pour in too early or too late.

If your book is specialized and you are able to find an appropriate mailing list, you should consider a pre-publication retail offer. Tell the potential buyer the book is being printed, and if they want one hot off the press, to send their money now; that you will be shipping on a first-come, first-served basis. Include an early order deal such as "postage free if you order from this ad." This mailing should also be sent to all your friends and acquaintances; many will respond and be pleased that you thought of them. If a prospect is mentioned in the text or the acknowledgments, he is sure to buy one.

Specialty (non-book) outlets offer many nonfiction publishers their largest market. For example, a book on mountain climbing may sell better in backpacking shops than bookstores and the size of the store's purchases will be larger. Sales to stores other than bookstores are often called *non-traditional sales* or *special sales*.

At Para Publishing, we tolerate but do not pursue bookstores. The only relationship between nonfiction books is their packaging; the subject matter of each book is unique. Nonfiction should be sold where customers for it can be found. Boating books should be placed in nautical shops, tourist books in tourist shops and football books in sporting goods stores. Sell your books where the highest concentration of potential customers can be found. Most of your prospects probably never go into a bookstore. So, make your books available through bookstores but do not confine your sales efforts to these shops.

—**Stores**. Many specialty shops will want a 40%, 50% or more discount but they usually buy outright. There are no returns.

Bookstores are lousy places to sell books.

In these specialty shops it is very important to establish, cultivate and maintain as close a personal relationship as possible with the management. It is of the utmost importance that they like you and your book so they will promote it at every opportunity. Selling them the first time often requires a personal visit to prove the sales potential of the book. When making a direct mail promotion to these firms, remember their peak selling seasons and the required lead time.

One innovative book marketer is Bruce Lansky of Meadowbrook Press. He is good because he markets books the way he used to market candy. His (then) wife Vicki wrote a book on nutrition for babies called *Feed Me, I'm Yours*, and the Lanskys decided to publish it themselves. First Bruce tried a local children's clothing store. They bought, so he approached a wholesaler of infant items but was turned down flat. He had to offer consignment and counter racks to let the wholesaler prove to himself the books would move. The wholesaler called three days later and ordered 12 dozen more—they were in business. Next Lansky created a mailing stuffer for the wholesaler to put in with the statements sent to his 1,000 accounts. Sales soared. Lansky's secrets are:

1. Play dumb. Visit the account and learn all about terms, key accounts and trade reps in that field.

2. Don't act like a publisher; act like you are in the same business. Bruce was in *infant accessories* that day.

3. Use success to breed more success. Do your research, run small tests and learn the industry. Subscribe to their magazines, join their associations, exhibit at their trade shows. Make a mailing to distributors and retailers and follow up with calls.

Other non-book retail channels include gift shops, hardware stores, garden shops, sporting goods stores, etc. Many are establishing book corners for an additional profit center, as well as to lend prestige to their line.

Run a test in a few local shops. Develop your approach (posters, counter displays, price, etc.) before rolling out in a wider promotion. Just as there are wholesalers servicing the bookstores, there are those who cater to the non-book outlets. Check these stores and look for books. Find out who distributes them to the store.

> *The smallest houses were relatively more successful in using non-book retail outlets than the largest houses were.* - Judith Appelbaum in *Publishers Weekly*

If books are not being carried, you will have to reach the stores through direct mail, advertising in their magazines or sales reps of other lines. Search for lists of that type of store. Ask the local store manager for names of hot sales reps and rep groups who handle other lines of products. Sales reps will want 10% to 15% of the *net billed amount* (a commission on the books after discount, not the shipping charges).

If the specialty shop is a franchise, make a pitch to the headquarters. Many franchisors do not control the buying of their franchisees and even if they do, the sale will not be easy. However, the hope of making one large sale to the whole chain is worth some of your sales time.

> A few years ago, the author was in a local instant print shop when the owner began asking about *The Self-Publishing Manual.* Forty percent off sounded good, and the printer wanted to put some books on the counter. The author doubted the books would sell, but brought in eight copies in a (cut-down carton) counter display to humor the printer. Three days later, the printer called for more. Apparently, the types of people who frequent copy shops are the types who work with the written word—a good market after all. This lesson resulted in an expansion into other instant print shops and to a book on how to paste up. Some outlets for books may not be obvious at first.

If you receive an inquiry from a market you never thought would be interested in your book, draft a letter to similar stores or groups saying *this store or group ordered the book and we thought you might be interested too.* The mailing may be just 100 pieces—no great investment—and there is a good chance of a payoff.

If the Appendix of the book has a source directory, make a mailing to each firm saying *you are mentioned in the book; thought you would like to know; and we think you might like to offer this book to your customers.* Build up a strong, reliable dealer network.

—Selling to the U.S. Government. There are 2,300 libraries in the federal government library system and 80 agencies which purchase books, according to *Publishers Weekly.* Most of the libraries come under the Defense Department. Some of the Army's libraries must be approached through central offices while others deal direct. The Office of the Director of the Army Library Program procures hardbound books for Army libraries around the world and paperbacks for distribution in the field. Of approximately 60 clothbound titles chosen monthly, some 60% are nonfiction. About 100 paperbound titles are procured each month and distributed in 900 kits; selections are highly recreational. Centralized purchases are made under annual contracts with wholesalers. Navy libraries spend over $3 million each year. The U.S. Information Service runs 129 libraries in 110 countries with 6,000 to 25,000 volumes each, and devotes about $2 million each year to procurement. They like to see brochures and review copies. The Veterans Administration operates 392 libraries with a budget of more than $2 million. For addresses of government procurement offices, see the Appendix and contact your local congressperson's office. Start by sending book brochures to U.S. Government acquisitions offices.

The U.S. military has 2.2 million active-duty personnel, 49,000 Department of Defense civilians, 2.8 million military dependents, 3.9 million military reservists and dependents, 4.6 million retirees and their dependents, for a total buying power of 13.6 million. The military payroll is over $58 billion. They are stationed at 250 installations across the U.S. and several overseas bases. They do most of their shopping in base commissaries.

Since military personnel are transient, they are hard to reach via direct mail. One of the best ways to influence buying is through base newspapers and magazines. For a detailed report, see *Selling Books to the Military Market* by Michael Sedge: Strawberry Media, 2460-P Lexington Drive, Owosso, MI 48867. See the list of military procurement offices in the Appendix. Another source of orders is from targeted groups within the government or military services.

The author's *The Parachute Manual* would be of interest to parachute riggers, both civilian and military. A mailing made to all military parachute lofts generated private sales and the brochure was passed on to procurement offices, so that the book could be ordered for the library or the loft. Brochures sent to the ultimate user often get a much better response than those sent to procurement offices.

—**Premiums** are products which are given away or sold at a discount to promote business. Premiums may be given away by a store or other businesses to attract customers, or used as incentives for salespeople as prizes for achieving sales goals. According to *Potentials in Marketing* magazine, 16.8% of the companies using premiums, use books. The premium market is estimated to amount to $11.5 billion annually and about 1/2-

billion is spent on books. Books make especially good premiums and incentives, as they may be customized by printing a special cover and because they are held in higher esteem than some other premium trinkets. In fact, in some areas, regulated industries such as banks are prohibited from giving away certain items, or the value of the items they may consider is limited.

If your book covers a regional topic, try local businesses. Small quantities of books may be rubber-stamped with *Compliments of Valley National Bank,* as an example. If you cover a subject with wider appeal, such as a book on beer can collecting, contact the beer, aluminum, steel, can and packaging companies. Such a book would make an ideal corporate gift or might be worked into a promotion. A tour guide book might be sold to a motel chain.

Judy Dugan was working in a graphic arts shop when the first edition of *The Self-Publishing Manual* was being typeset. As she pasted up the pages, she read the book and became increasingly interested. She had been toying with a local history-geography manuscript for years, and began asking the author all sorts of questions about the possibilities for her book. One problem she had was a lack of money to invest.

The author noticed that Valley National Bank was moving into a building in downtown Santa Barbara. He explained that they were a prime candidate for a regional book, as it would tie the out-of-town bank to the local community. A premium could be used to lure potential patrons into the bank.

In two short visits, she walked out with a purchase order for 5,000 copies in softcover and 1,000 copies in hardcover. She was paid one-half on signing and one-half on delivery, at full list price. She had 30 days to deliver, but had not finished the book yet. Fortunately, Judy was a graphic artist and there was a printer right next door. *Santa Barbara Highlights and History* was delivered on time. The money allowed her to print 11,000 books so she could service the local tourist market with her 5,000.

The bank's copies had special back cover printing: *Compliments of . . .* and the bank advertised in newspapers, on radio and television. They invited people to come into the bank for a free autographed copy of the book. They set up a table and a sign, and Judy spent the week greeting people and signing her name. Judy's book became a valuable traffic-builder for the bank.

Premium orders are large, usually 1,000 or more books, and the customer may ask for 60% off. Such a discount can be justified for a large order which eliminates the problems of financing, storage and individual shipping. A typical premium discount schedule might look like this:

Number of copies	Discounts
25-99	20%
100-299	40%
300-499	45%
500-999	50%
1,000-14,999	60%
15,000 up	Cost of printing plus 10% of list price

Discount schedule for premiums

If you can strike some premium deals before going to (or back to) press, you may increase your press run and achieve a smaller per-unit cost. Early sales are also a great help in paying the first printing bill. Be prepared to do a lot of leg work. Premium sales are tough and time-consuming, but the payoff is big.

—**Nonprofit organizations** are always running sales to raise money for their cause. These flea markets, bake sales and auctions, promoted by church and civic groups, can provide you with an opportunity to move some books. Try approaching some local organizations first to get a feel for the way they operate. If you are successful, consider a mailing list to similar groups. Don't forget to tell them of your past good track record for sales and assure them that the unsold books may be returned. Local clubs and local chapters of national organizations raise funds too. If your book is appropriate, you might strike a deal. A gardening book might be sold by a gardening club, for example. By making the nonprofit organization a dealer, they raise money for their group and you gain access to a new audience.

—**Educational campaigns** conducted by special interest groups offer another market for books. These people range from helpful social agencies to business interests promoting their side of an issue. Be careful to remain objective in order to maintain your credibility. You don't want to become too closely associated with either side; you want the use of their name, you don't want to let them use yours.

To find organizations with "causes," consult *National Trade & Professional Associations of the U.S. and Canada* and Gale's *Encyclopedia of Associations* available at your library. Write to these organizations, enclosing your brochure, news release, etc. Tell them why your book would be valuable to them but hold off on the price until you get a bite. The price will depend on the number they want, and the number could be in the thousands.

Subsidiary rights. Essentially, subsidiary rights give someone else permission to reproduce (re-package) your material. They include book clubs, mass market paperback, film rights, translations, etc. The two major classes of subsidiary rights are *print* rights and rights to *non-print adaptations*.

Subsidiary rights are so important to the big publishers that the rights are often auctioned off before the original book is printed. However, most publishers report that less than two percent of their income is derived from subsidiary rights sales. A condensation or small book club sale usually brings more fame than fortune. For example, selling the condensation rights to a magazine might bring $400. However, the endorsement is worth a great deal more. *Condensed in . . . magazine* can be used in brochures and other promotions and these endorsements beget more subsidiary rights sales, as well as more book sales.

Such a sale is also a great morale booster for both the author and the publisher, not only for the money but because someone else obviously likes the book.

The main reason publishers can sell the subsidiary rights for so little is that they are not paying production costs to their printers or, more important, royalties to their authors. Most author-publisher contracts call for a 50/50 split of subsidiary rights *revenues*. Some contracts give 90% of revenues to the author on any non-print (e.g., film) subsidiary rights. The publisher gets 10% as an *agent.*

A publisher's attitude toward a manuscript ought to be similar to a coal mine operator's attitude toward coal: get every last bit of value out of it. - Sol Stein, President of Stein and Day

Some subsidiary rights require only a continuation of the same printing (book club rights), but don't let your customer get away with just paying for the additional press time. They should pay for all your set-up and overhead costs. If you aren't familiar with negotiating rights, get a literary agent or an attorney who understands the publishing business, when a book club or other subsidiary rights buyer becomes serious. The agent will get 10% to 15% of whatever he or she brings in, while the lawyer will work for a percentage or a straight fee for checking the contract. Agents are listed in *Literary Market Place*. Media attorneys are listed in *Publishing Contracts on Disk*, from Para Publishing. See the Appendix.

—**Mass market reprint rights** are for those pocket-sized books selling from $1 to $5 in the supermarkets. This is the one market where it is easier to sell fiction than nonfiction. Mass market publishers like 7-year contracts with renewal options, and initial print runs of 30,000 to 50,000 copies. Mass market publishers offer 4% to 7.5% in royalties, the cover price is low and the scale does not slide up until sales reach 150,000 copies. Advances are usually just a few thousand dollars. Unless you have a *very* popular book, the mass market firms won't be interested.

Mass market publishers may be contacted after your book has been out for a year or so.

—**Periodical rights.** Serializations and excerpts by magazines and newspapers may be *first serial rights* if before publication, or *second serial rights* if afterward. Both generate a lot of good publicity. Big publications pay more than small ones, and the first rights are more valuable than second. The subject matter has to be of great interest to the publication's readers.

Serializations help generate sales for the original book. Always request the periodical print ordering information for your book. Place exact wording in your contract or letter as well as on the material submitted, such as:

"Reprinted with permission from *The Self-Publishing Manual* by Dan Poynter, copyright © 1989. Available from Para Publishing, P.O. Box 4232-802, Santa Barbara, CA 93140-4232 for $21.45 postpaid."

Such a notice will generate a lot of individual mail order sales. Anyone who reads the whole article will be a prime customer.

Magazines will probably contact you regarding serializations after receiving a review copy of the book. However, you should make the offer to *appropriate* magazines prior to going to press. Send a Crane-type galley to those magazines with good readership-to-book match. For specific details on Cranes and galleys, see Special Report titled *Book Reviews*. See the Appendix.

—Condensation rights. Book condensations in magazines do not normally pay a lot, but the publicity they provide will sell more books. Make sure the magazine is a quality product, one you will be proud to be associated with. Check their past condensation work and call the publishers of the subject books. Ask if they are happy with the way they were treated, with the quality of the condensation, and compare the price they were paid with the one you have been offered. The name and number of the person in charge of subsidiary rights at each publishing house can be found in Section One of *Literary Market Place*.

The magazine normally farms out the rewrite, and the work should be a condensation, not a reprint of the two meaty chapters. You can expect them to offer a couple of hundred dollars, up to several thousand, depending upon the publication. Expect an offer of $400. Remember, they have to rewrite the text and that costs money. Sell the condensation rights on a non-exclusive basis; the magazine will be first in print but you want to retain the right to sell again to other publications. Always obtain *text approval*. They could completely miss your point in making the condensation. Read the draft over carefully and make corrections; your name is on the piece and the condensation will be a major sales tool for your book. You want it to be right. Make sure the condensation includes information where the original book may be purchased, complete with price and address. See the example in *Periodical Rights*, above.

Without subsidiary rights, publishers would operate in the hole. - John Dessauer

Magazines will probably contact you regarding condensations after receiving a review copy of the book. However, you should make the offer to appropriate magazines prior to going to press. Approach just a few magazines with a good book-to-readership match.

—Anthology rights. An anthology is a collection of selections of writings from one or more authors, usually on one theme. Editors of anthologies may offer you a flat fee or a percentage of a normal royalty. If ten authors are each contributing a chapter, each might be offered 1% of the list price or one-tenth of a ten percent royalty.

You might decide to spin-off a piece of your book into your own anthology by contacting authors in the same field for submissions.

—Book club rights. Book clubs offer you some money and a great deal of prestige. Since they were established in the mid-twenties, the Book-of-the-Month-Club (BOMC) and the Literary Guild (each with over a million members) have been helping their members by selecting the best books of the thousands available, at lower than normal prices. Now there are more than 200 book clubs moving over $500 million worth of books each year, most of which cater to highly specialized groups.

The usual book club royalty is 10% of the list price plus production expenses. For example, say it costs you one dollar to print the book and the list price is $10. The clubs like to discount to their members, so knock off 20% and you have $8. You will receive $1.80 per book representing one dollar for production and eighty cents as a 10% royalty on the $8 selling price. If the book club invests in the printing, you get just the *royalty* of 10% of the club's selling price. Book club purchases are usually non-returnable.

Larger clubs will make their own printing or join you in your original print run. Smaller clubs will want to buy from your finished stock. Those doing their own printing or joining yours should benefit from a 10% royalty deal. Book clubs buying 500 to 1,000 books from your stock should be treated as a large dealer and be given a discount of around 60%.

The larger clubs usually want an exclusive; they don't want other clubs to carry the book too; at least not at the same time. Smaller clubs aren't so particular because their memberships do not overlap.

A book club sale is an important endorsement. If you can make the sale before going to press, the endorsement can be noted on the back cover as well as on all your promotional materials. For example: *Writer's Digest Book Club, Main Selection.*

Do book clubs hurt regular sales? Absolutely not! They help you start off with a large number sold, provide you with a valuable endorsement and draw a lot of attention to the book in their promotions.

Approach book clubs when you have a completed manuscript or galleys to show them. If they don't respond, write them again after publication and enclose photocopies of your reviews. They have to be convinced it is a desirable book, and that is where clippings of reviews can help. Send a letter to every club that might possibly be interested. Check *Literary Market Place* for book clubs and make up a list for a mailing. Or, as a quicker alternative: A list of 225 book clubs, on labels ready to peel and stick, is available from ParaLists. See the Appendix.

—Performing rights cover stage, motion pictures, radio and television. Film rights will be somewhat unusual for a nonfiction book but it does happen.

The usual royalty rate is 15% of the **net** and this is a very bad deal. Film companies are notorious for their unusual accounting procedures, which result in a very small net; some have been known to write off everything possible against the film. Always insist on a smaller percentage of the **gross**. The gross figure is much more objective.

Performing rights involve complex contracts and should not be negotiated without special advice. If you receive a firm offer, see a media attorney.

> *The bottom line makes it abundantly clear; subsidiary rights have become less and less subsidiary.* - Nancy Evans

—**Translation rights**. Translations offer good possibilities, and here you will want to deal with a foreign publisher. These foreign publishers will pay you a royalty and take care of everything. Normally you supply the photos and a couple of copies of the book with late changes noted. They translate the text, change the measurements to metric and take care of all the printing, distribution, etc. Royalties may be 5% to 7% for hardcover rights and 5% to 10% for softcover.

Foreign publishers and foreign rights representatives are listed in *Literary Market Place*.

When negotiating a contract, consider the number of copies to be printed, the printing schedule, cover price, royalties for both hardbound and softcover editions, the advance and the government tax, if any. Some countries impose a tax on exported royalties; Japan, for example, charges 10% of the remitted amount.

For complete details on foreign sales, see the Special Report titled *Exports/Foreign Rights, Selling U.S. Books Abroad*. See the Appendix.

—**Merchandising rights**. If the subject of your book suddenly becomes hot, customers will beat a path to your door with offers to put the character or words on tee shirts, decals and coffee mugs.

See *Literary Market Place* for more subsidiary rights possibilities. See *Publishing Contracts on Disk*, available from Para Publishing, for actual subsidiary right wording. See the Appendix.

Write to likely subsidiary rights prospects well before publication and ask if they would like to see photocopies of the manuscript. Then follow with a telephone call. Mail out a lot of inquiries simultaneously, don't go at them one-at-a-time. There isn't enough time for this luxury.

Remember: A book not submitted is a book not chosen.

Co-publishing is a way for two firms to spread the risk and reward in a new book. Usually one publisher is large and the other small, or the two concentrate on different markets. Usually the larger publisher handles the bookstores and libraries, while the smaller publisher sells direct to user groups and handles the individual mail order sales.

Selling out. Those smaller publishers who do sell their book to the big publishers usually sell too cheap. Editors from major houses make the rounds of the booths at book fairs, such as the American Booksellers Association Book Fair in the spring. These acquisition editors are hunting for good books to add to their lines. Small publishers are usually thrilled to be courted by a big house and often make the mistake of selling for the same 10% royalty an author gets for a manuscript. Ten percent of the cover price is small reward after expending so much time and money to package and promote a book, as well as to test the market. The big publisher is exploiting the little publisher at 10%, because all the risk has been removed. Successful books should cost more. The large publisher must understand the book is coming from another publisher; this is not just a manuscript from an author. A fee should be paid to the small publisher for packaging and market exploration, as well as a royalty to the author.

When a large publisher buys a book from a small publisher, the price should be for two or three times the production costs, plus 10% of projected sales. They should pay for all your time, work and financial risk. The deal should be made "royalty inclusive" which means receiving your money up front—not waiting until months after their books are sold.

Sell only the *North American rights* to the *book trade*. Retain all rights, except to the bookstores and libraries in the U.S. and Canada. Always keep the non-exclusive individual sale, mail order rights. The big publisher will not be interested in individual sales anyway. Make sure you can buy books for the printing cost plus ten percent. Normally you will be required to buy in lots of 500 or more, but this is a great deal for you because you do not have to invest in a large print run. Make sure all rights revert to you once the publisher lets the book go out of print. In evaluating a contract, consider the royalty, advance, when you will get paid, who gets what part of other subsidiary rights, the duration of the contract, and free copies to the author.

Small publishers and self-publishers would be better off to cut a distribution deal rather than a co-publishing deal with a larger publisher. In a distribution arrangement, the big publisher would buy several thousand books for 60%-70% off list price on a non-returnable basis with payment in 30 days and would have an exclusive in the book trade: bookstores and libraries. Insist on a large quantity so the large publisher is in deep and has to promote the books. With the book trade covered, the author/publisher is now free to concentrate on the retail mail order sales and the non-book markets. But be forewarned, if you do sell out, you will probably make less money while losing control of your book.

Exchange title promotion. Mail order customers interested in a certain subject tend to purchase every book which covers the area. Unfortunately many small publishers do not have titles in any depth on any particular topic. When two or more publishers of like material handle each other's books, their customers get a wider range of choices and the publishers get an improved response rate to their advertising. This cross-distribution, formerly common only in other sales channels, is now becoming more familiar in mail order book marketing.

Approach publishers with books that complement yours. Trade cartons of books based on their list price, and add them to your brochure. If you do not wish to take on products from other publishers, at least make an agreement to stuff each other's brochures into outgoing packages.

Bookshelf books. Offering other books in the same line as the anchor product will spread costs and make you the *information center* for your interest area. For example, Para Publishing has six books on various areas of publishing with *The Self-Publishing Manual* as our anchor product. We have special reports on very narrow publishing subjects, a newsletter, *Publishing Poynters*, and we host publishing workshops. But there are a lot of good books we did not write which will help publishers. So we buy them from their publishers and offer them to our book publishing customers. See the list of the books we recommend in the Appendix.

Keep your bookshelf focused on a particular topic. Most of your orders will be for your own books. The bookshelf books will sell well, but they will not approach the sales of your own books.

Recordings and Braille editions are published for the blind. If your book is well-received, you may be approached by a library for permission to translate your book into Braille or to put it on tape. When you fill out the copyright form for your book, you will have the opportunity to give the Library of Congress a non-exclusive right to reproduce your book in recorded or Braille form.

The international market. Foreign sales of books exceeded $916 million in 1988 with most going to Canada, Great Britain and Australia. Since English is the commercial and aviation language of the world, as well as one of the most used tongues in the fields of science and technology, there is a good demand for books in our language.

Be advised that adding a country will not double your sales. For example, expanding from the U.S. to Canada may increase sales 7% to 10%. You must compare the sizes of the English-speaking populations.

The most common way to cater to the international market is to fill and mail foreign orders in the same way you fill domestic ones. Most of your export sales will come with the daily mail. They will be just like your domestic orders except for their lighter-weight stationery, strange addresses and pretty stamps. Most of the foreign bookstores will get your address from Bowker's *Books In Print*.

Postal rates for foreign shipments may be higher or lower than domestic rates, depending on which rate has been raised most recently. There is a 5 kg. (11 lb.) weight limit for books. But if you are shipping more than 15 lbs., you may qualify for "Direct Sacks of Prints" at 72 cents per pound. Since it is so inexpensive to export, it makes little sense to print the book abroad in English unless the press run is huge.

One way to reach foreign bookstores and libraries is to look for them in *International Literary Market Place*. Look for publishers that concentrate on your same field.

Sponsored books are those you are almost commissioned to write. There may be an institution which wants your book printed badly enough to give you a large advance order. For example, if you wrote a book on the Frisbee® disc and there were no others on the subject, the Wham-O Manufacturing Company, which makes flying discs, might want the book to be published because the publicity would help their sales. With this sponsorship, they might want some sort of cover credit, such as: "Published in association with Wham-O." Such an endorsement is to your advantage as it would only lend credibility to the book.

Some industries need favorable publicity and find that sponsoring a book is much less expensive than placing full page ads. A book is also much more effective promotion as it appears to be more objective.

Specialty shows, such as sport and boat exhibitions and trade shows, are rarely worthwhile for a small author/publisher. However, you can make sure that your book is carried and offered for sale by someone in the show. Find a booth with related merchandise and offer them some books on consignment. Give them a carton of books and an examination copy for the table. They get a piece of the action and you get the exposure while moving books.

Book fairs provide important exposure to your book. The major national U.S. shows are sponsored by:

1. The American Booksellers Association, 560 White Plains Road, Tarrytown, NY 10591, (often in late May and attended primarily by bookstore managers)

2. The American Library Association, 50 East Huron Street, Chicago, IL 60611 (late June and attended primarily by librarians)

3. The National Association of College Stores, 528 East Lorain Street, Oberlin, OH 44074 (usually mid-spring and attended by college bookstore managers)

Write to the listed organizations regarding the fairs and then attend a nearby one yourself to assess how you might fit in to your advantage. The big associations also sponsor regional and local book fairs.

International book fairs are held all over the world with the most important being in London and Frankfurt. They can give good exposure and may lead to subsidiary rights, but probably are not worth your own exhibiting effort.

Conventions and conferences of professional, academic and trade associations will present you with a "qualified" audience for your books, if you match your subject matter to the show. Educational books do well at educational exhibits and these conferences are especially fun as they provide an opportunity to meet with authors as well as customers. For more ideas, consult *National Trade & Professional Associations of the U.S. and Canada Directory* and Gale's *Encyclopedia of Associations* available in your library.

Exhibiting at a book fair is often an inspiring experience; it will recharge your batteries. You will learn more about the industry, meet some great people, make valuable contacts, sell a few books and, perhaps, even some subsidiary rights. Typically, the show's management provides a space measuring about 10' x 10', a draped table, curtained side and back panels, a sign, carpet, and a chair or two. Check their brochure closely. Get some book stands and take a good supply of books and brochures.

Shows cost money. Booth space at the big American Booksellers Association fair runs $1,520 and up. The ALA is much higher. But they also have a small press section at $450. In addition to booth expenses, you must consider your personal travel, book shipping, hotels, meals, etc. You can spend $1,000 exhibiting, but $3,000 is not unusual.

Exhibiting services will put your books on display with those of other publishers very inexpensively and some do a very good job of representing your wares. Write to several of them to compare prices and see which fairs they plan to attend; some offer package deals if you sign up for the whole season. There is a list of exhibiting services in the Appendix.

For more information on book fairs, read *Book Fairs, An Exhibiting Guide for Publishers* by the author. See the Appendix.

The best book is a collaboration between author and reader. -
Barbara Tuchman, *Practicing History*

Chapter Nine

Advertising Your Book

A dvertising may be used to create an awareness of your new book, and even to stimulate an interest in it. But advertising is expensive and must be approached slowly. Nonproductive advertising will deplete your bank account fast. It is a cold, hard fact that most advertising doesn't pay. This is often because the approach is wrong. So, feel out each of the many areas and test them before you jump in with lots of money.

It is said that advertising will make a good book sell better, but it can't turn a poor one into a success. We will have to assume that more people besides just you see some value in your book.

First we will talk about advertising in general and then we will discuss the details of your brochure, direct mail advertising, classifieds, telemarketing, space ads and radio/TV. Much of the information is overlapping and may be applied to more than one area of advertising, so it is advisable to read the entire chapter.

The success of your advertising campaign will depend upon the sales potential of your book, whether you contact the right market and whether your ad is effective. You must select your markets (buyers) and then find the least expensive way to reach them. Target your primary market but do not overlook the secondary ones. Concentrate on one medium of advertising (e.g., direct mail) but do not dismiss the others (e.g., space ads).

In each ad campaign, figure the cost of the campaign "per sale" (how many books did this ad sell?). The cost "per contact" is interesting, but it is the cost per sale that tells you if you are winning or losing. Ads placed in magazines to promote wholesale sales to bookstores must generate sales of five times their cost to be worth your while. For example, a $10 ad must sell $50 worth of books. Ads directing the orders to you (mail order) must produce 2.2 times the cost of the ad, minimum. The difference is because you are giving the bookstore 40% of the list (cover) price, whereas the mail sales come directly to you at full price. These figures are quoted by the industry and may vary depending on the original production cost of your book. Keep them in mind as you plan your ad strategy. Do not run unprofitable ads! They waste money and make you work for nothing.

Determining an ad's potential profitability is not the place for wishful thinking. You have to calculate all the possibilities, the types of advertising and the places it might be put; this comparison will help you to choose where to place your money.

The people selling advertising talk about the "number of impressions" and "accumulative impact" when they try to get you to spend more on promotion (or try to explain why your ad wasn't successful). A series of good, consistent ads may be of some help, as a prospect may remember that he has heard of the book before, but remember that you are selling a $10 or $20 book, not a $10,000 or $20,000 automobile. You have to sell a lot more product to pay for the ad and you can't even justify as much need.

> It is easier to promote one book twice than to write a second book.

If you are pushing bookstore sales, and your book is on a popular subject, space ads may be best. If your subject is normally sold to business, professional and/or educational markets, direct mail should get more of your attention. In fact, many small publishers put most of their efforts into direct mail.

Ted Nicholas (Peterson), author of several money books, describes his advertising system as pyramiding revenue derived from sales. He suggests putting up a small amount of money for advertising, running good space ads (and he tells you how to write them), waiting for the money to come in and then re-investing it in ever greater amounts of advertising.

If you have a good method, don't deviate. Creativity for creativity's sake is dumb. Whatever worked before will almost certainly work again. All marketing methods must be tested, not just direct mail advertising. Once you find a good system, stick with it.

The most-recommended book in this area is *Successful Direct Marketing Methods* by Bob Stone. See the Appendix.

Direct response marketing is any promotion or advertising that provokes a measurable response or order from the individual to whom it was targeted. In book publishing, direct marketing consists of order blanks in books, catalogs, package inserts, radio, television and direct mail.

Creating ad copy. You will need a good basic description of the book that will appeal to the consumer; this material, altered as required, will then be used over and over. Come up with a very few words to describe the book. This becomes its "handle" and might even be the subtitle for the book. This handle will be expanded for brochures and catalogs while it is directed toward the intended audience. Some small ads will only have space for the handle and a small amount of hard-hitting copy. Once this is done, the future copy writing is easier, as you are not starting from scratch each time.

I know half my advertising is wasted but I do not know which half. - William Wrigley

Direct Mail Advertising. Most people like to receive mail, and one book out of four is sold via direct mail advertising. Most of this volume goes to book clubs but they don't get all the business; there are about a half billion dollars left. Direct mail offers the small publisher an opportunity to sell the customer without competing with the big publishers. Mail provides equal treatment, something you may not get in the bookshops.

> Don't confuse *direct mail* with *mail order*. Direct mail is a form of advertising which competes with space ads and television spots, while mail order is a delivery method or form of distribution which competes with store fronts.

—**This is the age of** *specialization,* of target marketing, of the narrow focus. As consumers, we have the advantage of buying only those products that are specific to our wants and needs. As entrepreneurs, we *tailor* our products to special segments of the population and then *tailor* our pitch to bring the product to their attention.

Direct mail advertising allows you to pinpoint your target market with a specialized pitch. For example, the people you target with your mailing might be skydiving instructors. Skydiving instructors have different needs and desires than skydiving students, or jump pilots, or parachute riggers, or drop zone owners. Each is involved in skydiving in general, but each requires a different pitch.

—**Target marketing**. Direct mail advertising is another target shot at the customer. This is not a shotgun blast at every household in the neighborhood, hoping to find a couple of people interested in your books. It is (hopefully) a mailing only to those who have expressed a past interest in your type of merchandise. They have not only expressed an interest in books, but in your type of books and have responded before by sitting down, writing out a check and sending for something.

What can be more fun than going to the Post Office and finding 500 envelopes, each with a check in it, from people who want to buy what you have created? - Jameson Campaigne, Jameson Books

Unless you have several related titles, priced over $25 each, to share your brochure, you won't make money regularly in direct mail advertising. The smaller and newer publisher will only be successful using direct mail for pre-publication offers and occasional mailings to (often smaller) highly-targeted lists.

—Think long term. Very few mailings make a killing from outright sales the first time out. With each mailing, you are trying to add qualified buyers to your house list for future orders. A *qualified buyer* is someone who has sent money to you before, and this person is more likely to respond again and again. So, the objective is to develop a customer, not just to make a sale.

Your house list also becomes a valuable asset and a new profit center as you will be able to rent it to other firms. More on renting your own list later.

Direct mail advertising is one very effective way to contact potential buyers for your book. The mailing usually includes a cover letter, brochure, order form and a reply envelope, but it may also direct the addressee to a nearby store.

—The economics of direct mail. One must understand the economics to put direct mail advertising of books into perspective. If you tell enough people about your book, a certain percentage will buy it. The challenge is to keep costs down by telling just that certain buying percentage. A general-interest book advertised to a general consumer audience is lucky to generate a return of 1.5% to 2%. That is just 15 to 20 orders per 1,000 pieces mailed. In fact, only 10% of the recipients will even remember the mailing piece.

The cost, on the other hand, may be quite high (probably around $400 per thousand or 40-cents per piece). The amount depends upon the price of the list (the more selective ones cost more), the postage, the type and number of inserts and other expenses such as mailing house stuffing fees. A high response rate is required just to break even. So, it is tough to make a living selling a single title through direct mail. But now you have a customer who may buy again. And that means you need more than one product.

The direct marketing formula. What makes direct marketing successful is the offer of the right products via the right medium with the most enticing propositions, presented in the most effective formats, proved successful as a result of the right tests. The successful direct mail campaign is made up of planning, list selection, copy, layout, timing and testing.

—**Repetition.** One rule of direct mail is that if you re-mail to the same list anytime after a couple of months the response will be almost as great as the results from the first try. Many marketing people use a list four times a year and if it fails to break even or better each time, it is time to change the list. They say that repetitive mailings have a cumulative effect and the message is strengthened. Good lists have a certain amount of turnover. Names are continually being added and deleted.

—**Timing.** The best time for your mail to arrive is on a Tuesday, Wednesday or Thursday. A lot of mail arrives on Mondays and the day after holidays, and your piece could be lost in the clutter. Friday's mail is often put aside as the recipient is about to leave for the weekend. Unfortunately, it is difficult, if not impossible, to time delivery of mailing pieces to a day of the week when using Bulk Rate.

The best times of year for offers to arrive, according to some experts, are after the new year and after Labor Day. The Direct Marketing Association compares the months for response (assuming your book is not season-related, such as a Christmas book or a year-end holiday gift offer) as follows:

January 100%	July 73.3%
February 96.3%	August 87%
March 71%	September 79%
April 71.5%	October 89.9%
May 71.5%	November 81%
June 67%	December 79%

Best months based on January

A good test of the worth of a book is the number of times we can read it with profit.

Other months are compared with January, the best month. Some say that March to April (income tax time?) and May to June are the worst months. Other experts warn against the summer months when people are away and the mail piles up. Most agree December is bad because the Post Office is jammed and the potential customer is busy with family and holiday activities.

The subject of your books will determine the best months. For example, if your books are on outdoor sports, the best months are January through May, with a peak at March, and September through November. During the summer, the prospects are out doing what they were reading about during the winter. The best time to mail to Federal libraries is March and April when they are preparing for their next fiscal year. May appears to be the best month for schools. Professional books seem to sell better in the first quarter of the year. The third quarter is second best. All factors must be considered in relation to your specialized subject and audience.

Many DM professionals like to test in September so they can roll out in January. And remember, what counts is when the mailing is delivered, not when it was posted.

— **Foreign mailings**. The United States is a culturally *influencing* country. The world consumes great quantities of U.S. information and thought. With the increase in both the standard of living and purchasing power in many other countries, the potential for book sales is increasingly good. There is a demand for books on leading edge subjects.

English has become a world language in this century. In fact, while 3,000 languages are spoken in the world, 40% of the knowledge base is in the English language. English has replaced German as the scientific and technical language, replaced French as the diplomatic language and is the international language of aviation. English is also the world language of business. Business books from the U.S. have done very well in the last few years with the surge of worldwide interest in U.S. management thought.

When you are ready to draft an ad, stimulate your creative juices by reading a couple of articles or a couple of chapters on copy writing.

Naturally, books in English should be promoted with brochures in English and prices should be quoted in dollars, as it is customary to settle international accounts in U.S. currency.

The problems in mailing outside the U.S. aren't any greater, they are simply different. Check the postal regulations for foreign mailings. Send for a copy of the Postal Service's *International Mail Manual*.

Foreign mailing lists are available though, generally, they aren't as sophisticated as those in the U.S. When renting foreign lists, specify one inch Cheshire format, or you may receive a printout you can't use.

In the book industry, direct mail to foreign potential buyers is the most under-used marketing technique. It has great potential and is waiting to be properly exploited.

—Bulk rate. Any serious direct mail campaign will use the Postal Services *Third Class Bulk Rate*. The annual bulk mailing fee is $50. Once paid, you may mail for .198 cents per piece up to 3.3667 ounces each, as long as you are mailing 200 pieces or more. See Chapter Six of the Postal Service's *Domestic Mail Manual*.

—Line of books. One way to increase your return on a mailing list is to promote more than one book, but don't confuse the customer with a cluttered brochure. Concentrate on those books in a single interest area. Don't bury the gems in garbage; the recipients may not take the time to dig out the books they need.

Publishers should concentrate on a single line of books, such as aviation, regional subjects or waste water treatment. Then all the books in your brochure or catalog will relate to each other. There is no need to make up a separate brochure for each book. Think like a specialized book club and define your audience.

—Order blank in book. Every book should have an order blank for the same and/or other books on the last page—facing out. Turn to the last page in this book as an example. It is important to ask for an order and that is what order blanks are designed to do. It is not enough to hope a potential buyer might find your address on the copyright page, because he or she still won't know how much to include for shipping and sales tax. The order blank says: *Yes, we accept orders, will take your check or credit card and here is exactly what the book will cost.*

Why would anyone buy a book they already have? For a friend! At Para Publishing, we receive more orders on our back-of-the-book order blank than from any other direct response effort we make. We have over a million books out there and each is selling more books for us.

—**800 numbers.** It is generally accepted in the industry that a toll-free 800 order number will increase the response to an offer, but the 800 number is not usually cost-efficient when selling books because books do not cost enough. The major benefit of the 800 number to publishers is to raise the level of customer service.

800 numbers work best when paired with credit card charge arrangements. Today, people are prepared to place a call and charge a product to a credit card.

—**Charge cards** make buying much easier and will bring both more and larger sales. They are particularly handy for telephone orders. See the discussion of credit cards in Chapter Ten.

—**Lettershops** have machinery so they can do your envelope stuffing and mailing faster and cheaper than you can. Check the *Yellow Pages* and call a few for prices. Save your time and let the lettershop do the licking, sticking, stuffing, sorting, sacking and posting.

If you deal with a mailing house, they will deliver the stuffed and addressed envelopes to the Post Office. The Post Office will send you their receiving form, detailing the quantity delivered, with your bill.

Always give the letter shop a folded and stuffed example of your mailing piece. You want to make sure the envelopes go out with the inserts in a certain order and facing the right direction.

If you want a response, you have to ask for it. - John Huenefeld.

—**Book pricing.** Direct mail advertising is expensive so, generally speaking, the book must be priced at $25 or more to make the project viable. The price of the book may be lower if it will appeal to a highly targeted group that is easy to reach. Professional books tend to carry a higher price. Law and many engineering books are over $80. Lower-priced popular books positioned for trade distribution are rarely profitable to advertise by mail.

—**Piggyback offers**. One way to reduce costs is to place more than one offer in an envelope. Direct mail advertising is the most obvious place to piggyback. You want to be sure the extras don't detract from, and dilute, the main offer. Many publishers piggyback by simply including a brief backlist of other related books rather than another fancy brochure.

—**Bookshelf.** The additional books you offer may be yours or they may be from other publishers. You should be able to buy books wholesale from other publishers at 50% off through their Special Sales department. To learn all about how to carry complementary books, see the Special Report *Bookshelf, A New Profit Center for Publishers*. See the Appendix.

—**Sell non-book items**. Ray Teagarden has a very successful book in his *The Muffler Shop Manual*, but it is his first and only book. So he drafted another flier for specialized muffler tools, many of which he designed himself. Now he is the source for muffler information *and* tools. Every book he sells establishes his credibility and leads to sales of other products.

—**Weight limits**. You can get a #10 envelope, four sheets of paper, a stamp and a label under the one ounce First Class Mail limit, and you can send more if you are using the 3.3667 ounce Bulk Rate. Be careful, staples and stamps add to the weight, too. But you can get twelve or thirteen 3 5/8 x 8.5 slips into the envelope. They provide the recipient with an easy reading/sorting format similar to a card deck. He or she is more likely to look over each offer when it is presented separately, than to inspect a page with several offers jumbled together.

For a more-accurate measure and to get the maximum out of your postage, weigh up several stuffed envelopes at the same time. Ten should be just barely under 10 ounces on the scale, for example. That is cutting it close!

To calibrate your scale, use nine unworn *solid* copper pennies (not the new sandwiched ones). Nine pennies weigh one ounce. Calibrating a scale to zero without weight is not accurate.

—**Sales tax on printing**. Some states, such as California, do not charge sales tax on the printing of direct mail packages. Direct mail brochures, letters and envelopes must be delivered directly to the mail house by the printer to qualify. This can be quite a saving so it is worth checking the laws in your own state.

California also does not charge sales taxes on shipping supplies such as cartons, bags and tape. Presumably the purpose of the exemption is to promote exports.

—**Response formulas** are used to speed testing. They are also useful when the orders are coming in and you want to know what can be expected over the next few weeks.

If you mail **first class**, you can assume that within two weeks of receiving your first response, you will have received 50% of the total responses you will receive. So plot mail receipt on your calendar. Two weeks after the first order arrives, double the orders received so far and that is the number you may expect over several months.

If you mail **Bulk Rate** you will receive half your responses within four weeks of your first response. Ninety-eight percent of the responses to a mailing will come within 13 weeks.

A newer method, which some feel is more accurate, is the *add the last week projection* method. Take the book sales of any number of weeks, then add the last week's sales again to the total. The result is the least number of orders you will get. For example: You mail 100,000 pieces and receive 2,000 orders in the first three weeks; 1,000 came in the last week. Add 1,000 to 2,000 and you can expect a total return of 3,000. The more weeks you are into the mailing, the more accurate the projection, but three weeks should be accurate enough.

The heaviest day for response should be the second Monday after the first order arrives. Mondays are always a heavy mail day because you are receiving three days' worth. Tuesdays are always light because few people mail over the weekends. In fact Tuesdays often have a higher percentage of foreign mail (which was mailed the previous week).

With an ad or book review in a **daily newspaper**, you can expect 80% of your orders within a week.

The response formulas, mentioned above, are generalities. Direct mail is an art, not a science. There is no substitute for your experience in your own field. Keep response analysis records so you can develop your own response rates.

—Echo effect. Every promotion campaign you wage for a book will bring in some sales that are not directly attributable to that campaign. Some people find it easier or faster to buy your product somewhere else, such as dropping by a retailer. There are many ways people can get the book besides returning the order form. Professors who receive interesting mailings often request their libraries to order the book. Echo effect is difficult to measure, but some direct marketers claim it often exceeds the direct orders.

Since over 75% of libraries deal with wholesalers, most of the orders from a mailing to libraries will come to you through Baker & Taylor. Sometimes, publishers even help the potential customers in this direction and, in effect, give him a choice of purchasing by mail or visiting a bookstore. The brochure might say: *Available at your local Walden Bookstore or direct from the publisher.* Some publishers imprint circulars for bookstores, to be mailed to the bookstore's mailing list.

—White Mail. Orders not traceable to any promotional effort or source are called "white mail." The longer you are in business, the more orders you will receive that are not traceable to any specific promotion.

—Profit analysis. Direct mail marketing is a process of looking where you have been, seeing how you got there and deciding where to go next. Past mailings and testing are the tools for future decisions. Profit (or loss) may be determined by taking your book sales, less returns, less your cost of books and fulfillment and less your direct mail costs of postage, printing and letter shop fees. A P/L sheet might look like this:

Direct Mail Profit/Loss

Gross sales $_____

Less returns $_____

Net sales $_____

Less cost of sales

Product (production cost x units sold) $_____

Royalty $_____

Cost of fulfillment (wrapping and postage) $_____

Total cost of sales $_____

Less promotion costs

Mailing list rental $_____

Printing $_____

Letter shop fees $_____

Your time $_____

Total promotion costs $_____

Profit (or loss): (Net sales less total cost of sales and less total promotion costs) $_____

Most small press publishers lack an understanding of mailing lists. So many firms waste so much money on lousy lists. They buy "mail order" lists not knowing what those people bought, how much they paid, what their profile is, how many times the list has been rented, when they bought, and on, and on. - Galen Stilson

—**Follow the rules.** Finally, direct mail advertising is no place to be innovative. The margin for error is slim; you cannot afford mistakes. Read the books and magazines and do what everyone else is doing. Advance into direct mail advertising slowly by testing small numbers. Direct mail advertising works for books only when the book is specific and the list is highly targeted.

—**Mailing Lists.** While many elements are required for a successful direct mail package, the list is the most important part. The best package mailed to the wrong list can't do well. Conversely, the worst package mailed to the best list often does acceptably well. Obviously, the goal is to mail a good package to a good list.

Mailing lists make the difference between success and failure in direct mail marketing. The list must target the appropriate group and be up-to-date. Posting your offer to the wrong person is a waste you cannot afford; the margin is just too slim. You want quality, not quantity. People get new jobs, move, die, lose interest in certain fads and trends, forget hobbies, etc. Yesterday's prime prospect may have other interests today, or may have moved.

In late 1987, the author wrote and published *The Expert Witness Handbook.* He rented the list of experts from the National Forensic Center. The 4,400 names came from an expert witness directory where each person listed had filled out a questionnaire to be listed. The response was a whopping 11% and there were very few nixies (bad addresses). Based on these heady results, he rented another list of 22,500 *experts and consultants.* The return was a disappointing one percent and there were hundreds of nixies. When selecting lists, you need perfect matches and the list must be clean.

—**List categories.** The real purpose of direct mail advertising is to build a list of qualified buyers. These are people who have ordered books by mail and have ordered from you.

Direct mail mailing lists fall into three categories, sometimes called *yours, theirs* and *compiled:*

1. **House** lists

   a. Sales. Past buyers.

      1. Premier list. Multiple order past buyers

   b. Prospects

2. Mail **response** lists. Lists of people who have responded to offers similar to yours. These are lists you rent from list owners or list brokers.

3. **Compiled** lists. These lists are developed from membership lists, directories, etc. These are lists you rent from list owners or list brokers.

—House list. The highest quality list is normally your own. This is your list of customers—those who have contacted you. Your house list should pull two to ten times better than any you might rent. The people on your list know you and your product, they look to you as an old friend, they feel comfortable doing business with you and they have done business with you before.

The people who were your best customers last month are most likely to be your best customers this month. They should be contacted repeatedly. These customers will buy from you again and again as they experience changes in their needs, mood and financial condition. You may not change (with something new to sell them) but they may change.

Think of using your house list in three ways:

1. Identifying the best customers on your house list.

2. Find more customers for your house list by using outside lists.

3. Selling books to your house list at a maximum profit with minimum waste.

You should maintain two house lists: A *sales* list (those who have bought something) and an *inquiries* list (those people who have contacted you for information but have not sent money). All other lists from other people contain only *prospects*.

Your sales list is by far the most important. The only people who should be added to it are those who have paid to get on it by buying something.

New customers have to be bought (through list rental), existing customers are free.

There are several ways to build your house list. The common way is to rent another list, make a mailing and then add the names of those who respond to your own list. Names of good prospects may be found in various directories, depending on the subject of your book. Some firms have used contests to generate interest and more inquiries, while others have sold merchandise at a loss to attract attention. Just be sure to segregate all responses into the sales or inquiries lists, as appropriate. Do not corrupt your lists with untested names.

You may begin compiling your own retail prospect mailing list by going through your Christmas card list. Include all family, friends and acquaintances. Include anyone who might conceivably purchase your book.

Also start your **commercial lists:** bookstores, libraries, wholesalers, big non-book accounts, people and companies in your industry.

And work on your **promotion mailing lists:** magazines, newspapers, radio and TV stations. Check reference books such as *Literary Market Place.*

Keep your lists for your next book so you will be prepared when it comes time to send out pre-publication announcements, review copies and other promotion.

—**List maintenance.** Lists must be kept up to date if they are to maintain pace with our mobile society and remain valid. This means keeping the list in mind and continually being alert for address changes and returned mail.

Some publishers just clean the list, except for recent buyers, every couple of years. Even though a name was well qualified as a former customer, if he hasn't responded again in the last year, he probably never will.

Your house list should contain computer fields to indicate recency, frequency and amount of purchase for each customer.

It costs more to sell a book to a new customer than to an existing customer.

If you mail via first class, the letter will be forwarded, and if it can't be delivered, it will be returned. The problems are that first class costs more than bulk rate and you won't get a new address to update your file.

There are several endorsements you may place on the envelope. Each will solicit different treatment from the Postal Service. Some, which may be used alone or in combination, are:

1. Address Correction Requested
2. Address Correction and Forwarding Requested
3. Forwarding and Return Postage Guaranteed
4. Do not Forward, Address Correction Requested, Return Postage Guaranteed

Read the excerpt from the *Domestic Mail Manual*. It is important to understand the services and prices before you mail. Do not use *Address Correction Requested* on a rented list. Do not clean someone else's list.

A certain percentage of bulk rate mail never gets delivered. Some estimate the amount to be as high as 10% to 20%. Five percent of the bulk rate mail is undeliverable due to a lack of a room number in large buildings. In a big city, 25% of the bulk rate mail may be discarded rather than delivered. Print the whole mailing address.

In one delivery test by Doubleday, a first class re-mail was made of 1,948 pieces of returned third class bulk rate mail. Eighty percent of the so-called nixies were either delivered or forwarded. First class mail gets better treatment.

—**Recency**. Lists, whether yours, theirs or compiled, must be recent. Any list not mailed to within the last three months will not be *recent*. Since 20% of our population (over 50-million people) moves every year, there will be too many nixies. When renting, ask when the list was last *cleaned*.

—**Guarantee**. Most lists are guaranteed to be 90% deliverable. That means the owner or broker will send you a refund for all undeliverables *over* 10% of the list rented. Let us say you rented 10,000 names, mailed First Class at 25 cents and 1,020 pieces are returned as undeliverable. You get a refund of $4.40 or 22 cents for twenty pieces—not much when you spent $220 to mail to the other 1,000 bad addresses.

—**Turned down?** Sometimes we approach a magazine or association to rent a list only to be turned down. We are told they are protecting their subscribers or members from junk mail. Any list can be rented if you can provide a sufficient *benefit* to the list owner. Try this approach: Tell the list owner that if he will give you the list on labels, you will pay all the mailing costs and will stuff his brochure for nothing. You get the list (free) and the list owner gets a mailing free. A win-win situation.

—**List brokers.** List brokers specialize in bringing list owners and list renters together. The broker receives his fee (usually 20%) from the list owner. Brokers can be a good source of direct mail advice.

Lists and list brokers can be found in *Direct Marketing* magazine, *Direct Mail Rate and Data*, *Klein's Directory*, your local *Yellow Pages*, and several are listed in the Appendix of this book. Send to all the brokers in the Appendix for their catalogs.

One thing you will find is that the same lists are handled by many different brokers. You will see the same list in catalog after catalog. Many lists are small and brokers will have a minimum. And, since the broker is obtaining the list from several different sources, they cannot be merged or totaled to meet minimums.

—**Copying lists.** Copying lists violates the rental agreement, normal business ethics, is against the law and is a waste of money. List *rentals* are for one time use only and you are obligated not to add the names to your file. The list owner guards against second usage by sprinkling the list with decoy names. Stealing an unproven name from a list will only dilute the quality of your own house list. You are, however, authorized to add a name to your list once you have qualified it, once it has resulted in an order.

Lists go out of date fast because people move. Over 20% of our Gypsy-like population moves each year, and address changes are even higher with younger people. Almost 47% of the population is not living in the same home they occupied five years ago. In the western U.S., the figure is over 56%.

Since you probably won't rent the same list more often than every six months, it is cheaper and more accurate to rent the list again than to copy *and* maintain it. We are assuming, of course, that the list owner is cleaning out the nixies regularly.

—**Hotline names** are new additions to the list. If you are selling books on beginning skydiving, why rent the whole membership list from the U.S. Parachute Association when you can rent names of just the new members? Hotline lists tend to be 60 to 90 days old.

—**Rent parts of lists.** You don't have to rent the entire list. Why send to all libraries when you are likely to get a better return from those with a higher book acquisition budget?

One co-op mailing operated by the Publishers Marketing Association is made to 2,600 public libraries with purchasing budgets of $25,000 or more. They could mail to 6,600 libraries with purchasing budgets of $1,000 or more, but most of those libraries cannot afford to buy. Be selective.

—**Testing a list.** The big direct mailers must be successful or they would not continue to mail. The main reason they are successful is that they test before investing large sums of money in a mailing.

Testing is a preliminary mailing or distribution intended as a preview or pilot before a major campaign. Test mailings are used to determine probable acceptance of a product or service and are usually made to a specially selected list.

Unless the list is very small or you are very sure of it, test it first. This is done by renting just part of the list and sending your mailing to every *nth* (e.g., tenth) name. Nth name testing provides a better sample than renting names from A through D or Zips from 0000 through 03000. A safer variation to Nth name rental is *last digit Zip* or *last two-digit Zip* selection. Just ask for names with Zips ending in a specified number. These variations stop list owners from slipping in *hot* names to enrich the tested list (in the hope you will be back to rent the entire list). Another advantage to Zip selection testing is that you can eliminate the tested names when mailing to the entire list.

A minimum sample should be 3,000 names (some experts say 5,000) and remember that you are testing the mailing package as well as the list; they both affect the results. Since you will need 30-50 responses for your test to be statistically valid, you may have to mail to 3,000 to 5,000 names (if you can realistically project a 1% response). In testing, it is the responses that matter, not the number mailed.

Keep working with the small quantities until you are satisfied that you will get a good return if you use the whole list. If a mailing to a sample group produces a 2% response, statistics show that a mailing to the entire list will result in a 1.4% to 2.6% response, and it is usually just under 2%. Realizing these probability limits will help you to evaluate a list and make the decision whether to risk a big mailing.

A lot of things can go wrong with a test mailing. A list can be non-representative or out of date. Or your book could be bad, and the word may have circulated between the test and the big mailing. Keep good records; only with statistics can you effectively evaluate a mailing. Note all your costs. If a test is inconclusive, run another test. Most tests fail; expect it. When one fails, be thankful you didn't mail to the whole list. Then drop that list and don't try it again.

Roll out mailings to the entire list do not always reflect your test results. There are just too many variables: time lapse, season, change in economics, weather, consumer behavior and many more. The test mailing benefits from pass-along readership. Some recipients who are not buying send the brochure on to a friend they know has an interest in this book. When you mail to the entire list, you also hit the pass-along readership and they have already seen your offer.

If you are committed to marketing your book by direct mail, you will need a continuous program, one that can be constantly adjusted as needed. When a test list works, expand its use. When it fails, get rid of it.

It is a good idea to remain flexible by continually testing your mailing piece with small changes. Never make two significant changes at once in the same package, or you won't know which one is responsible for the change in response.

—**Address format**. Should you address your labels to the individual or the company? This depends upon the product and your approach. The question is whether you want the offer to go to the individual or the person in that particular job. People change jobs quite often these days.

The Postal Service now likes to have the *attention* part of the address on the first, rather than the last, line. On the other hand, you should decide if you are mailing to a company with an employee or to an individual or wants to receive mail at work rather than home.

> Company name
> Person's name
> Street Address
> P.O. Box address
> City, State, Zip Code

The Postal Service delivers mail to the address on the line immediately above the city-state-Zip line. If the customer provides both a street address and P.O. Box, use the street address for UPS shipments and the P.O. Box for Postal shipments. If you use both, put the street address above the P.O. Box.

Some people have more than one address or get mail at work addressed different ways. You might be sending two pieces to *Richard Stands, Zeller Mfg. Co.* and *Zeller Mfg. Co., Attn: Richard Stands.*

—**Finding lists.** As a small publisher, you are probably also the author. You are a *participant* in the subject you write about. While a book is just a product to a large New York publisher, you have a mission and are closer to the book's subject matter. If, for example, your book is on skydiving, you know there are two magazines, one national organization, and one national championship catering to your group. You know how to reach your readers because you are one of them. Associations have direct lines to people interested in their mission. Most have a membership list, magazine, annual function, etc.

Direct Mail Lists Rates & Data lists 80,000 mailing lists. Ask for it at the reference desk of your public library.

If a space ad in a magazine has pulled well, consider renting their subscription list for an expanded offer. Compare list rental costs with the cost to buy space advertising in the magazine. Consider renting select portions of the list or the hotline; (just recent subscribers).

Your competitors may not be interested in renting you their house list but they may be willing to trade for your house list on a name-for-name basis.

—Costs of lists. Most lists run between $40 and $100 per thousand or four to ten cents per name. Cleaner, more highly targeted lists tend to cost more.

—Sell your mailing list. If you maintain your mailing list by noting which book (subject area) the customer purchased, it becomes very selective and quite valuable. These are people who have taken the time to sit down, get out the check book and mail away for a book. They are very good prospects for similar offers.

You may handle your own list or work through a broker. To contact a broker, see the lists in the Appendix. Most brokers will be interested in handling your list when you reach 20,000 names; some want 50,000.

Start by getting listed in *Direct Mail List Rates and Data*. This directory provides the details on over 80,000 lists. Send for a listing form to Standard Rate & Data Service, Inc., *Direct Mail List Rates and Data*, 3004 Glenview Road, Wilmette, IL 60091, (800) 323-4601, (708) 441-2345.

Your brochure lies at the heart of your promotional campaign and it may be produced long before your book is off the press. The brochure should describe the book, tell about you, and answer most of the recipient's potential questions. The basics are the book's measurements, number of pages, type and number of illustrations, binding and price. The contents should be summarized to provide a clear understanding of the book's coverage. Do not use too much detail or the buyer may find too much material he or she does not want—sell the sizzle, not the steak. Excerpts from reviews will demonstrate that others like your book, too. Follow the proven, standard formats.

The brochure will be stuffed into most of the letters you send out daily to friends, associates and relatives, used with your other pre- and post-publication mailings, and sent to those who respond to your ads inviting them to "send for a free descriptive brochure." Yes, your brochure is more important than a business card and has a lot more information.

The best way to answer inquiries is with your brochure. If the writer asks particular questions, the simplest way to answer is by circling the appropriate parts of the mailing piece. Many publishers like to return the inquiry letter with the brochure to remind the writer that he asked for this advertising matter. If you aren't over the postage limit yet, it is nice to stuff in other related information. For example, if the inquiry is about hang gliding, enclose a membership application from the hang gliding association. You will build valuable good will.

Brochures provide you with an opportunity to say nice things about yourself that you can't say in face-to-face selling. It is almost as though someone else wrote the copy. Be direct, clear and give the reader as much information as possible.

Your local instant print shop can give you the best deal on black and white 8.5 x 11 brochures. If you need more space, they can handle 8.5 x 14 and you can fold it four times to fit a standard #10 envelope.

Every pass through the press costs more money, so some people like to use colored paper and another color ink. This gives the appearance of a lot of color but it is still a one-color print job. Use good materials and make the brochure slick. If you send out a mimeographed brochure, people will assume you are selling a mimeographed book.

Some publishers have produced very nice brochures by printing their ad copy on the back of book cover or jacket over-runs. Ask your printer for any "overs" and/or ask him to print a few hundred extra covers.

People like to see what they are buying, so a photo of the book should appear in the brochure. You don't have to wait for your book to be printed to take a photograph of it, however. Photograph the cover art and have the print blown up to book size (e.g., 5.5 x 8.5). Then make a dummy by wrapping the print around another book. Take several photos with different settings and from several angles. Then select the best print and have some 4 x 6's made up. At this point, you may not know exactly how many pages the book will have, but you can estimate and then use a description like: "over 180 jam-packed pages."

Once the brochures arrive, use them everywhere. Stuff them in every package, letter, news release, mailing, etc. Carry some in the car, leave them at the barbershop, in the seatback pocket on the airplane, at the dentist office, etc., and carry some with you at all times. Pack one in with every book you mail out. A brochure has to be distributed to do any good.

Pre-publication offers are often in black and white as time is of the essence. For short press runs, you may be better off going with a black and white flier and dealing with your local quick printer for quality, price and quick delivery. Over 10,000, it pays to go color and at 50,000, the price drops again significantly.

Printers specialize, and a number do nothing but four-color *catalog sheets*. These catalog sheets may be called a *flier* if flat and a *brochure* if folded. These specialists buy large quantities of the same type of paper at a lower price and have all their equipment set up in–line for greater operating efficiency. They are standardized at 8.5 x 11 inches on 70 pound or 80 pound white slick paper, with four colors on one side and one color on the other, or four colors on both sides. You may also use 11 x 17 inch stock, folded.

Here are some typical 1993 prices from Econocolor for a flier 8.5 x 11, four color one side, one color on back:

> 10,000: 8 cents each
> 30,000: 4 cents each(enough for web press)
> 50,000: 3 cents each

You do not always have to buy a large quantity to get a good price. Some of the catalog sheet printers run specials such as 1,000 sheets with one color separation for $395.

> *Tell not what the recipient can do for you, tell what you can do for the recipient.*

When you are ready to work on your brochure, see the Special Report *Brochures for Book Publishers*. See the Appendix.

In a direct mail piece, the circular, flier or brochure is introduced by your cover letter and all pieces work together. Until you get into big mailings with specially designed packages, you may use your *regular* brochure with a cover letter tailored to the list to be used. In a very large mailing, it won't cost any more to print up a specific circular for that mailing and it will bring greater results. Remember that the circular has a photo of the book while the letter does not—and photos sell. Circulars are more likely to be filed for future action whereas letters have a more limited life. So don't send a letter without a circular.

—**Benefit copy**. State your primary benefit in your headline. Capture the reader's attention by promising something the reader wants and can relate to.

Make the benefits believable. Readers will be skeptical. Make the benefits specific. The reader must be able to relate to your offer. Use *you* copy. There should be at lease twice as many *you's* as *I's*.

—**The "AIDA formula"** is the oldest and most widely used method of reader motivation. It is designed to lead the recipient to the offer and impel him to take action. AIDA stands for: get ATTENTION, arouse INTEREST, stimulate DESIRE, ask for ACTION. Some people have modified AIDA to: ATTENTION, INVOLVEMENT, DECISION and ACTION. AIDA is just as effective today as it has always been.

—**Drafting the brochure**. Follow these steps when drafting your brochure. To lay out the circular, start with a blank folded dummy and plot the location of each part of it: the teaser copy, order form, photos, etc. Set up the brochure and then write the copy to fit.

The circular should have big impelling headlines that give the recipient a chance to see himself in the mailing. He will respond favorably if he identifies subconsciously with the product. Always include a photo of the book so he can see how big and nice it looks. Make the copy easy to read: one thought to a sentence, short words, short paragraphs and don't overdo it. Make the type big and bold and use the layout to lead the reader from start to finish in one logical, flowing sequence. Special emphasis may be given to the more important paragraphs by setting them in italics, bold face or by indenting them. Use subheads. Use all the information necessary and end with an order form. Look over the slick promotions you receive in the mail every day and analyze them.

Most mailings succeed or fail within about ten seconds after they are opened. If they don't catch the recipient's attention in that time, they go into the round file. We are bombarded with thousands of advertising messages from the mail, billboards, TV, etc. everyday and we tend to build up a defense toward them.

Little grabbers can also help. Words like *you* and *new* and *save* and *free* still work. And gimmicks like offering to pay postage if they order today from this form invite action, even though it may be your policy to ship all retail sales postpaid anyway.

Highlight the important aspects of the book in the rest of the copy. Relate to the reader and use testimonials, which are more objective, if you have them. Keep the message brief or the reader will get lost in the copy and give up. He feels his time is valuable so don't insult him by wasting it. Give details on the number of pages, illustrations, chapter titles, etc. Facts, not words, sell books.

If your brochure is mixed-up and illogical, what will the recipient think you are capable of doing in a book? Be specific. If yours is a technical manual directed at a select audience, the package doesn't have to be terribly fancy but it should be very detailed.

—**Self-mailers** are brochures mailed without envelopes. While less expensive to produce, they usually don't pull as well as offers arriving in envelopes. Self-mailers may not be used in international mail; letters going out of the U.S. must be in an envelope.

If you use a FREE offer, be sure there are no strings attached. People get mightily fed up with "free" offers that cost them money.

—**Consider a post card** with a photo of you and your book as an inexpensive way to reach prospects. Post cards are not as expensive to print as a full mailing package and they cost less to mail. Some publishers have cards printed when their covers are printed. The cards wind up being 12 pt. C1S cover stock with four colors and a plastic coating.

—**The Direct Mail Package** has five main elements:
1. Graphics. What does it look like?

2. Offer. What is the deal?

3. Copy. How well have you described the product and offer?

4. List. Who is the offer being sent to?

5. Timing. When will the mail be received?

—**The offer or "order form."** While it usually comes last in the direct mail package, the order form should be written first, as it is the cornerstone around which the rest of the mailing is built. The purpose of your mailing may be to solicit an order or to request some descriptive literature and you must guide the recipient to take the specific action you want. By preparing the order form first, you will assure coordination of all the parts of the mailing and will keep all copy headed in the same direction. Make the offer simple, clear and easy.

Many people don't read the whole brochure, they are sold early in the package and turn straight to the order form. If you have more than one title, print a check-off list. Don't ask the customer to write the title in; he may lose interest or may write in the title of only one book because you have not prompted him with more titles. If you use the words "I enclosed $_____ for:" you are making it easy for him. If the order form is printed on colored paper, it will be easier to locate.

It is a good rule to have your name and address on every piece of a mailing package. One piece alone sometimes makes the sale.

Make the order form easily detachable or on a separate card. Note the deadline, shipping costs and sales tax, if any. Always include a money-back guarantee, an unconditional one. The form should have enough room for the customer to write in his or her name and address; make this area big so you will be able to read the handwriting. Make sure your name and address appear on the front, back or both. Pre-addressed envelopes are expensive but they are probably worth sending to non-business people (who may not have an envelope handy). Some advertisers like to call their order form a "trial order card." Refer to it in the text of your letter to remind the customer that it is there.

If you are offering air mail delivery for an additional charge, add a box where the customer may make a check mark. Note on the form that *Book Rate* may take three to four weeks while an air shipment will be three to four days.

—The cover letter. Each mailing should start with a cover letter to personalize the message and to bring attention to your offer. The letter is your prime selling tool; it encourages the recipient to read the flier and to use the order card.

The direct mail letter should be interesting and easy to read. It has to grab attention and relate to an interest of the reader in three to five seconds or it will go straight into the round file. So, draft your letter to the type of person on the list.

As with any personal message, it should be friendly but not insincere or disrespectful. Sincerity is hard to define but insincerity can be spotted instantly. Make sure the letter is clear and complete by having a friend read it both to himself and aloud. Write as you talk, don't search for big words. The letter may run one to four, or even more, pages, whatever it takes to make the pitch. Be concise and don't use any more space than necessary. Keep the paragraphs short; five sentences should be the limit. Sentences should be short and simple; ten to twelve words are enough.

Your opening sentence has to be dramatic. It has to make the reader want to read more. Stress **benefits** to the reader. What can your book deliver to him or her? Change *we'll help* to *you will*. When you find yourself writing: *This book will help* *you* . . . Stop and change it to *You'll discover how easy it is to .* . . . Change *if you* copy to *when you* copy. Do not give the reader a yes/no option. *If you order before the end of January, you will receive* . . . should be changed to: *When you order before the end of January, you will receive.* . . .

Do not make broad, generalized claims; be specific. *This could be the greatest book you will ever encounter* should be changed to *With this book, you will be able to* . . . .

The ten words with the most magic in copywriting are *Free, New, You, Now, Win, Easy, Introducing, Today, Save,* and *Guarantee.*

The offer of a bonus will increase response. On a **pre-publication mailing**, say: *And if you will order from this form, we will pay the postage and will send the book as soon as it comes off the press.* On pre-publication offers, emphasize that the book is on the press and assure them you won't cash the check until the book is shipped. Mention an expected shipping date, but give yourself an extra month to six weeks.

End your sales letter by telling the reader exactly what you want him or her to do. *Grab your pen and checkbook right now and fill in the order blank. We absolutely guarantee your satisfaction. The book must meet your expectations or your money back. You can't lose!*

Your letter should have a date so it will look like a letter. Use wide margins; the eye is trained to handle narrow newspaper columns. Small margins make a letter look too detailed, too much of a project to read. It is nice to address the recipient such as *Dear Dr. Brock* but this requires time and some automatic equipment. A *Dear Friend* or *Dear Fellow Skydiver* may be printed on. Some people like to use a headline to grab attention, even though it is much less personal. Important points may be set off from the body of the letter with indented paragraphs, underlining, or italicized type. But don't overdo it or the value becomes diluted. If your audience tends to be older (with poorer eyesight), be sure to use 12 or even 14 point type. If you run the letter in two colors, say black and blue, you may use the blue ink for your signature.

If you print on both sides of the letterhead, put *Please turn over* at the bottom. It is surprising how many people never think to turn the paper over. Don't end a sentence at the bottom of a page. Keep the reader hanging. Carry him over to the next page with some provocative copy.

The *second chance letter* increases sales. It is the one which says: *Don't read this unless you have decided not to order.* You get mailings with second chance letters every day.

Type out your letter—don't have it typeset, it won't look like a letter. Fold the letter—printed headline side out so the recipient doesn't have to unfold it to start reading. Use a letter fold, not an accordion fold or the stuffing machinery at the lettershop may have trouble inserting the letter into the envelope.

Always include a letter in your direct mail advertising package. There is an old saying: *Let the flier do the telling and the letter do the selling.*

Make your letter easy to read. Keep your words, sentences and paragraphs short. Use subheads or bolding to ease skimming. Many readers skim the letter first to see if it is worth reading. Break the copy into units. Do not put more than two commas in a sentence and no more than six commas in a paragraph. Do not put two sentences with commas back-to-back. Include a personal P.S. Many feel the P.S. is second in importance only to the headline.

—Letterhead. Your letterhead is you. It is a matter of image since most of your customers and suppliers never see you in the flesh. A nice design costs little more to print than a poor one and you want to instill trust and confidence. If you wish to appear successful, you might like expensive paper with an engraved and/or embossed letterhead.

If you use the same list very often, it is a good idea to change your letterhead and package so that the offer doesn't get stale. You don't want the recipient to take one look, recognize it and toss it out unopened.

It takes hard writing to make easy reading. - Robert Louis Stevenson

You can give the impression of color by using ink of one color and paper of another and still pay for only one press run. There are a lot of types of paper and you should look through the catalogs at your print shop. The letterhead for promoting a carpentry book might be printed on a wood grain paper and you could even add scent. How about cedar?

—Envelope. If the recipient does not open the envelope, then all your creativity, work and expense on the inside goes to waste.

Galen Stilson, the famous copy writer, has a research assignment for you: Take two or three hours on a slow day and visit the Post Office to observe people going through their mail. See how many people pick up their box mail and head straight for the waste basket to sort out the pieces they don't want to carry home. After a couple of hours of seeing ad mail being quickly glanced at and discarded, unopened, you will gain a new appreciation for the importance of the envelope. In the future, you will spend more time trying to figure out how to make that envelope do what it is supposed to do for you—get opened.

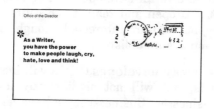

Doesn't this message make you curious?

The envelope is often used to arouse the recipient, inviting him to open it by exciting him with some printing on the outside. This printing is called *teaser copy*.

Teaser copy by way of words, photos, etc. is used to suggest a strong and clear **relevance** to an immediate need. To be effective, the teaser must be directed to the type of people in the specific list. The teaser must relate to the recipient. Individual buyers want to know what the book can do for them, librarians want to know what it can do for their patrons and a bookstore owner wants to know if it will sell (as opposed to why it may be a good book).

The teaser copy is located on the outside of the envelope or self-mailer, but it should also be repeated on the inside to help the recipient find the place to start reading and to reassure that you are going to deliver on your promise. Even if the recipient keeps the contents, he or she will surely discard the envelope and you don't want them to lose the teaser.

If you are offering something free, say so on the envelope. Do not tell too much. The purpose of a teaser is to get the envelope opened. Do not try to sell the book on the envelope. Get the letter opened so you can sell the book on the inside.

To get the recipient's attention, your envelope must stand out from all the rest. Many things affect whether the envelope will be opened, such as color, artwork, size, stock, etc. Go through the mail you receive and ask yourself what your reaction is to various possibilities.

Most smaller publishers do not have to be preoccupied with tricking recipients into opening their envelope. Since they know this group of people (because they are one of them) they know the recipients are interested in their company and product. When you receive an envelope from someone in the book industry, don't you open and read it? Of course. You may not buy every time, but you are interested enough to read the contents because you are a publisher.

—**Business reply envelopes** (BRE) will increase response from individuals, but will not significantly improve the response from businesses. Businesspeople have less trouble finding envelopes and stamps. The cost of business reply service has increased so much, it probably is no longer worth the expense when selling low-priced books. A business reply mail permit is $75 per year. Each letter returned will cost you the First Class postage plus 9-cents for a total of 38-cents per piece (in 1992).

—**Testimonials**. People are overwhelmed with exaggerated claims and hype. Therefore, it is important to incorporate a confidence factor into your promotional copy. Testimonials will help justify your claims for the book and draw attention to your customer service. Testimonials help build the reader's perception of believability, stability, honesty, and value. Testimonials may be placed in the circular or on a separate sheet.

To be valuable, the endorsement must be from someone who has a *name* or *title* recognizable and important to the reader. For example, if you have a book on golf, you might want a few nice words signed by Arnold Palmer or a testimonial from (John Doe), Executive Director of the PGA.

There are two ways to gather testimonials: Wait for them and ask for them. Collect the testimonials from your *happy letters* and book reviews. You may ask for testimonials with a letter or an evaluation form enclosed with the book.

Save your testimonials and use them when writing up your next mailing. Be sure to get permission if you use an endorser's full name or enough information so he or she could be identified.

—The guarantee. The guarantee card may be separate, part of the brochure or part of the order card, but the guarantee itself should be mentioned several times. Some publishers leave their address off the guarantee card to make it more difficult to find (the address is on the order card and that was mailed). Some ask that books be returned via insured Parcel Post which is more expensive than Book Rate and makes the customer go to the Post Office to mail the book back. A general complete satisfaction guaranteed is preferable. You want to build your customer list and are aiming for repeat customers, not just a single sale. Unless your book is worthless, you will experience few returns.

A money-back guarantee may boost a response as much as 25%. People are more likely to give the book a try if they feel they have nothing to lose. A *15-day free examination* usually boosts sales without increasing returns.

At Para Publishing, we offer an unconditional money-back guarantee at any time, no questions asked. We want customers to be happy with their purchases. If they return a book, we are glad they took the time to look it over. The theory behind the no-time-limit guarantee is that without a deadline, such as ten days, a customer may never get around to making the return. Either the theory is valid or we have very good product because we have very few returns.

You will probably find that the stronger refund policy will increase up-front profits without an increase in requests for a refund. A strong guarantee reduces customer fear and less fear means more orders.

—**The order of insertion**. The order of insertion will be the way you want the recipient to read the material. The most logical way is: cover letter, brochure, testimonial sheet, order card and return envelope. And remember, people open envelopes from the back, not the front. In foreign mailings, check the local custom. Do their envelopes normally close on the top or the end? Always make up an example of the mailing for the letter shop to follow.

—**Alternative packages**. There are several alternatives to the standard package mentioned above, such as card decks, co-op mailings, statement stuffers and catalog bind-ins.

—**Card decks**. There are several ways to get your message to potential customers and one is with card decks. You may join another deck or start your own. If you join another deck, make sure the lists are well-targeted to your book's audience.

Standard Rate and Data Service lists over 600 card decks in its *Business Publication Rates and Data Directory*. Ask the reference librarian for it at your local public library. You may find a deck going to a list well-targeted for your book.

Decks are printed and packaged by special machinery. If you decide to run a card deck mailing yourself, a deck printer will give you a better price than a local job printer.

—**Co-op mailings**. One way to reduce mailing costs is through cooperative mailings. Several publishers may share a list by stuffing their flier into one envelope. This system works when publishers of like books are approaching the same market. Co-op mailing is offered by a number of companies which combine your brochure with other related solicitations and mail them to a selected list in a single envelope. The postage savings can be considerable. Each firm operates differently and uses different lists, so you should write to them all and compare their deals.

Revlon makes cosmetics in the factory and sells hope in the drugstore. - Charles Revson

Magazine and newspaper advertising can be broken down into two subgroups: *classified* and *space* (display). Unless you are covering a very broad or strictly local subject, you probably won't consider newspapers. Their audience is general and the life of the paper is short. Most new entrepreneurs start with the cheaper magazine classified, and then graduate to space advertising as their business expands and their expertise increases. Space ads cost more but pull better: greater risk, greater potential reward. Your problem is that a book is a low-priced item. You have to sell a bunch to make an ad pay.

Bookstores respond to face-to-face approaches by sales people, not ads. Librarians rely on reviews. But space ads can work with proper direction. The last few years have seen a great proliferation of highly specialized magazines which cater to particular groups. The costs are usually lower, the quality of the prospect better and the response ordinarily higher. If your book is on parachuting, you would want a monthly ad in *Parachutist* magazine. If your book is about left-handed people, advertise in their magazine. Since 10% to 12% of the population are lefties, an ad in any other magazine will be wasted on 88% to 90% of the readers.

Be your own ad agency and save over 15% on your space ads. Advertising firms make their money through the 15% commission they get on all the space they write for a magazine or newspaper. Normally commissions apply only to space ads, not to classifieds. And if you place your own ads, you can get even more. For example:

Cost of ad	$100
Ad commission (15%)	-15
Cash with order (2%)	-1.70
Total ad cost	$83.30

They all want the same thing—a magic button to push that will make them thinner, more beautiful, richer.

```
AGENCY:                    INSERTION ORDER

A.M. FURMAN ASSOCIATES

527 Madison Avenue
New York City, NY 10022
(212) 421-3707

   PRODUCT:                        DATE

   ADVERTISER:                     THIS ORDER APPLIES TO OUR CONTRACT
                                   NO.


   TO:


Dates of                                      Space
Insertion    Times    Caption    Key   Ordered    Position




Special Instructions:



RATE: _____    LESS FREQ. DISC. _____ PERCENT
      _____    LESS AGENCY COMMISSION _____ PERCENT OF GROSS
      _____    LESS CASH DISCOUNT _____ PERCENT ON NET
                       NET AMOUNT THIS ORDER $ _____
BY: _____
```

**Example of
an advertising
insertion order**

Being a new account, the periodical probably won't extend credit anyway, so simply write up your ad insertion order like the one above, take the 2% deduction for cash and enclose your check. It is very unlikely that they will reject your terms.

Check to see if the magazine offers MasterCard or VISA. By charging your advertising, you won't be billed until the magazine appears. This can give you use of your money between then and when you placed the ad order.

To establish your own ad agency, there will be a small investment necessary to give the appearance of a completely separate entity. You will need a different firm name, letterhead, telephone number, check book, etc. Make sure that all are signed by people outside of your publishing company. Many publications, such as *The National Enquirer*, will not allow commissions to "in-house" ad agencies. Some will even spend quite a bit of time trying to match up telephone numbers, signatures, etc.

> *The ad worked because it attracted the right audience . . .
> because it aroused curiosity and because it offered a reward. -*
> John Caples

Per inquiry ads require no investment and are a good way for you to try out new advertising media. Many smaller newspapers, magazines, radio and television stations will run your ad for a share of the results. The orders are sent to them with the checks made out to you, thus giving you both a check on each other. Their cut is usually 33% to 50% of the order, about what you would give any retailer. The reason they do this is to fill unused space or time, making blank areas generate some income.

Normally you have to prepare the ad. This means nice "camera-ready" artwork for newspapers and magazines, or tapes for radio and television. A one minute videotape may run $100 originally and about $25 for each duplicate. Many authors (and other entrepreneurs) prefer doing their own shows to hiring an actor at $50 or more. An author is very much a part of his book and the personal touch can go a long way.

The best approach is to write the station, paper, etc., describing your book and asking if they accept *Per Inquiry* advertising. They want sure deals, so if you have done this before, recite your good track record.

If you have already tested a medium and experienced a good return, it may not be worth your while to offer them a P.I. deal. It is usually better to pay for your ads and get all the money, than to go P.I. and take only part. On the other hand, even free advertising is wasted if it fails to generate business; it is a waste of your time and energy.

Piggyback promotion consists of attaching information on additional books to your regular promotional work. While not a major part of your promotional effort, this element is worth constant consideration as it leads to bonus sales; it moves more books at little additional cost or effort.

Add brochures and fliers to your outgoing mail. Filling up the monthly statement envelopes may have less value. Some of these people are "slow pay" and it is questionable whether you want to encourage any more of their business. Secondly, the statements go to the business office, not to the buyers. So unless you have an office procedures-type book, the brochure may never get to the right person. Some accounts are with small firms where one person handles everything; here a stuffer will get to the right person. If they want your new book badly enough,they may be encouraged to pay the old bill.

Exchanging brochures with other firms works well. This mutual promotion operates on the theory that once you have sold a customer your book, you have nothing more to offer. But you and another small author/publisher with a similar book can pat each other on the back and give each other a hand by each stuffing the other's brochure. It is like exchanging mailing lists except that it is easier and cheaper (no licking, postage or envelopes). When a brochure arrives in a mailing from another publisher, it is an implied endorsement of your book.

Dustbooks (P. O. Box 100-P, Paradise, CA 95969) will pay you $3.40 for each copy of their *International Directory of Little Magazines and Small Presses* which is sold via their piggyback stuffer.

Bookstores are sometimes receptive to stuffing your brochures in their outgoing mail. They will want their address on the fliers and they may agree to use a rubber stamp. To make a rubber stamp imprint look nice, it must be clean and used firmly, often slowly. So you might offer to do it. When your printer is running your brochures, have him run a batch for you with your address and then opaque out the address and run the rest blank.

Blank back matter pages may be used to announce your other titles. Book copy and signatures rarely come out even, there are usually a few blank pages at the end. These pages should be put to work rather than wasted. This principle is so common in Germany that the last section of many books looks like a catalog. When the book is being pasted up, be prepared to add some additional promotional copy to fill up the last signature. This will also add to your mailing list, since it will bring in sales from those who have purchased books before, not directly from you, but from bookstores and other indirect outlets.

"Pass along" approaches work well in large organizations such as libraries and schools, particularly when you aren't sure who you should be contacting or if more than one person is involved in the decision-making process. Just send two or three pieces of the same brochure (consider postage again) and ask the recipient to pass the others on to someone else.

Envelopes can be used for piggybacking by printing teaser ads on the outside. Some firms use their envelopes to promote "hot" forthcoming books with an exciting blurb. Then they use these envelopes for all their mail. When you grow big enough for a postage meter, you can order your message on an imprint slug.

Remember that the piggyback principle is an "add on" to other promotion only. While it will generate more business from existing customers, it will not bring in new clients. Every time you make a contact with a potential customer, you want to show him everything you have to offer. Hopefully, at least one will appeal to him. But remember that stuffers cost money and must not be wasted. Send them only when there is a chance of an order.

Co-op advertising is a popular way the big publishers direct sales to bookstores with local space ads. Typically, the publisher pays 75% of the ad cost (but no more than 10% of the value of the books shipped to the store) and the bookstore pays 25%. If the store is a regular advertiser in the local papers, they usually get a slightly better rate. The procedure is to have the store place the ads, but the tear sheets and bills go to the publisher. Then the publisher credits the store with 75% of the bill toward book purchases.

To justify co-op advertising you have to anticipate that the store will move a lot of books. And, while the stores may be the major outlet for the big publisher, they are usually a minor one for a small firm which concentrates on mail order sales.

The Federal Trade Commission (FTC) regulations insist that any deal offered to one dealer must be made available to all. A small publisher who tests co-op ads with one store could find himself in great financial difficulty being obligated to advertise for everyone else.

Many small firms feel that co-op advertising is just too complicated and too time-consuming and they routinely answer all inquiries in the negative. They save time, money and stay away from the FTC.

Doing business without advertising is like winking at a girl in the dark. You know what you are doing but she doesn't.

Ad participation may be worked to benefit both you and another firm with a similar book or product. It allows you greater flexibility while your participant gets a sure bet. You place your own ads and then supply him with a mailing list of those who responded, but at a higher per-name price. This is not just another random mailing list. These are people who have sent for a related product lately. For example, if you are routinely offering a hang gliding book in general magazine ads, you are attracting customers from outside the sport and you are selling them on the activity with your book. A list of these prime prospects would be very valuable to a hang glider manufacturer and he should be willing to spend 50 cents per name for them. It is a good idea for him, because he doesn't spend time on this part of his advertising program and he pays only for results. It is a good deal for you because it allows you to advertise in more places and to continue with marginal-return ads.

Point-of-purchase sales aids include bookmarks, dumps, posters, etc. Posters can be very useful in specialty shops and booths but there just isn't any room for them in a bookstore. Librarians like posters but they rarely buy more than one book. Free bookmarks with advertising are used 30% to 38% of the time by bookstores. Dumps are special shipping cartons/display units which are used by 38% to 40% of the stores, depending on the available counter and floor space. Many larger stores suggest and request them. Some clever publishers have designed small dumps with directions for detecting counterfeit bills on the back. This assures premium display space on the counter near the cash register.

Dumps can often be found in dumpsters behind bookstores. Many publishers ship their books in counter dumps, floor dumps and shippers (cartons). Bookstores do not need the dumps because they have shelves. So they toss both the dump and the shipper into the dumpster. You will find a variety of colors, sizes and shapes. Use the dumps for testing new (non-traditional) markets.

Show how your book solves problems and enhances the stature of the user among his or her contemporaries.

Catalogs, whether for books or related specialty goods, offer a prime market to publishers. Some catalogs list general interest books, some concentrate on a line of special titles (for example, business and finance), while others may carry a line of merchandise and a section on related books. Catalog orders are large and the mail order firm is usually committed to your product for a full year.

Special merchandise catalogs are those featuring a line of merchandise, but which devote a page or two to related books. Since you are already in the field (having written about it), you probably know who they are.

For more, go through the ads in related-field magazines. After you send for a few, you will find yourself on the mailing lists for most of them. See your reference librarian for directories of catalogs.

A brochure may get you into a catalog sooner. For example, if you have a book on sport parachuting, the mail order parachute supply firms will want to carry it. However, your publication dates may not coincide with their catalog deadlines. If you supply them with a brochure, which they may insert into all catalogs, outgoing mail and packages, they will be offering your book immediately. Of course, they will want their name printed on the brochure. This approach may be used in certain cases as a sneaky sales tool. Sometimes you can't convince a firm to handle your book. But if you take them a bunch of free brochures to stuff, the orders will come in. Soon they will become convinced of the book's sales potential and be forced to add it to their line.

Your catalog is probably a long way off. After you have published ten books, you will need a catalog just to maintain organization. A catalog is a good reference and a public relations tool. With just a few books, a much cheaper brochure for each book is all you will need. Fliers on individual books will usually out-pull a catalog, which is too big and takes too much time to read through.

Good judgment comes from experience, and experience—well that comes from poor judgement.

The big publishers separate their catalogs into two distinct sections: the new titles or *frontlist* and the *backlist*. The catalog may be titled "Books for Spring" and will feature all the current offerings up front. Last season's titles which are still available will be in the less-prominent backlist in back.

If you want to publish a catalog but have only a few titles, you might consider carrying related titles from other publishers.

Commission sales reps offer to do for the smaller publisher what the sales force does for the larger ones. Their job is to call on bookstores to brief the buyers on new titles, straighten up the stock, take orders and otherwise service the account. The orders are sent to you, the reps do not stock books.

Commission reps get 10% of the amount of the sale to retailers and 5% of the sale to wholesalers; and they will ask for more. Since the rep has many books and too little time in the bookstores, he will push only the sure-fire sellers in order to maintain credibility with the book buyer. If you want to better understand what a commission rep can do for you, visit a bookstore yourself and give selling a try. Compared to direct mail, reps are quite a luxury; many publishers don't feel they are worthwhile.

Even if you have a line of a half-dozen titles, most of the bookstore orders generated by the sales reps will be small. Since many books will be returned by the stores, it costs a lot of money to service these small accounts. There is a lot of paperwork and book counting.

When you get a telephone call from a sales rep, don't be snowed by his request for "exclusive world distribution rights." Tell him you won't give exclusive territories, explaining that if you had given an exclusive to someone last week, you couldn't consider his offer. Don't make any deals over the telephone; you are under too much pressure. Always ask for the offer in writing. Then you will have several days to evaluate it.

The author tried sales reps for a year and a half. While sales increased some 20%, over $2,500 was virtually uncollectible. When he let the sales reps go, his sales dropped 20% but his headaches dropped 80%.

If you are still interested in locating commission salespeople, there is a good list in *Literary Market Place*. Also check the classified ads in *Publishers Weekly* and look for reps. at book fairs.

Telephone selling, or *telemarketing*, may be used to complement your other promotion. It should be used aggressively on both incoming as well as outgoing calls to stimulate business. Time is money and travel takes a lot of time. While the most important wholesale accounts almost have to be sold in a face-to-face presentation, there are others which may be handled by telephone. And with the telephone, those important accounts may not have to be visited so often. This approach is particularly important to the small author/publisher who is pushing a single title. Many buyers appreciate a call instead of a visit, as it uses less of their valuable time.

Plan your call. What is your objective? What do you plan to accomplish? If you want to make a sale, get organized. A written script is the best way to start. Write it up the same way you would an ad, by starting with the most important point to get their attention. In calls to the trade, emphasize how well the book is selling and invite them to get in on the action. Offer to send a review copy, tell them about your return policy, get it all in there. Say: "Shouldn't I put you down for ten copies at 40%, fully returnable?" Then practice your delivery until it becomes smooth and natural. You don't want to stay on the line longer than necessary to get what you want.

Make a written record of every call incoming and outgoing. Keep a pad near the telephone and write down who, the date and what. Keep these slips on file. Before calling an account, pull their file and review your past contacts. This will make the contact more personal.

Always call the same person. Look them up when making a visit or touring a book show. If you establish your credibility and treat them right on your first book, they will probably take the second book sight unseen.

Important book reviewers should be contacted by telephone after you send the complimentary copy. A good opening line is "Have you received the book?" They are more apt to review books by authors they know, and the telephone is an easy way to reach them.

Subsidiary rights, remainder offers, etc., may be negotiated over the telephone, but always ask to get their offer in writing. This delay of a few days will provide you with some breathing room to think it over and, perhaps, even to find a better deal.

When customers call to order one title, use this opportunity and *their* telephone money for an add-on; tell them about other related titles which are new and might appeal to them.

Check your telephone directory for the rates for both intrastate and interstate calls. Clip out the charts and stick them on the wall next to the telephone. A 7:30 a.m. call from California is much cheaper than one made a half hour later, and it reaches New York at an ideal 10:30 a.m. East coast publishers can use the reverse by calling the west coast after 5 p.m. when the rates drop again.

Many large firms have toll-free 800 numbers. To find whether the company you are calling has one, simply dial (800) 555-1212 and give the operator the company name and address.

Used properly, the telephone can be a great sales tool without significantly increasing the communications bill. Telephoning is much cheaper and easier than travel.

Remainders are overstock books which are sold off to remainder dealers at greatly reduced prices. The big publishers are only interested in books while they are maintaining a certain level of sales. When the demand drops, out they go. Your situation is different because you are storing the books at home, have a lower overhead, like the prestige of having a current book and can get by on the occasional sales. Initially, each book in your brochure adds to your size. You will have to have a number of titles before you will be interested in dropping any. You can always run off another 1,000 copies; there is no reason to go out of print. If it is a good how-to book and you have kept it up-to-date with revisions at each printing, it should continue to sell.

John Huenefeld offers this rule of thumb for determining when to dump a title: Multiply the quantity on hand by the list price. Then divide by 20 to get 5% of the list price value of the stock. Now compare this 5% figure with the net sales for the

last 12 months. If the sales were not greater than this 5% figure, it's time to call the truck.

You might be able to move the books more profitably with a
sale via your own mailing list at, say, 50% off. Also make an
offer to the big chains; over 65% of them purchase remainder
stock.

Remaindering is big business. Twenty thousand titles go
out of print each year and some 25 million copies are
remaindered. A lot of big firms are in this business; many
wholesalers carry remainders and they may account for one-
third of a bookstore's gross. Some books see their sales pick up,
once they have been remaindered. The new price and marketing effort has turned books completely around. Remaindered
books have sold out and have gone back on the press.

Notify your wholesalers before remaindering a book and
offer to take their stock back. Wholesalers are needed customers and are too valuable to upset and lose. You might start
by offering them a special buy on the books for, say, 60% to
70% off.

Lists of remainder dealers may be found in *Publishers
Weekly, Literary Market Place* and *American Book Trade Directory*, all at your library. Write to a number of remainder
dealers, indicating the quantity, list price, title, hardbound or
paperback, condition, location and whether they are prepackaged, and if so, in what increments. Enclose a copy of the book
and your sales materials. Establish a closing date and announce that you will accept the best offer for any quantity.
Shipping is FOB your warehouse, terms are net 30 days and
the books are not returnable. Once you have selected the
highest bidder, call him and make sure you have a deal.

Your offers may be between 5% and 10%, but don't be
surprised at hearing 20 cents each. Since your name is on the
book, it is worth your while to get it out to the field and onto
peoples' shelves, rather than to throw them into the dumpster.
Even at 20 cents, they are still "sold." Most remainder dealers
will want 1,000 to 5,000 books, minimum, and they want your
entire stock so as to have an exclusive. Some will take your
slightly damaged stock—those scratched copies returned by
bookstores.

For detailed information on remainder and other forms of inventory reduction, see the Special Report *Beyond Remainders*. See the Appendix. Hopefully, you won't have to deal in remainders.

Donate damaged returns to a charity. You may deduct the value of the book at its original acquisition cost plus the postage out. Prisons, foreign libraries and church bazaars will be very happy to accept your books. By donating your scuffed books, you recover your original investment in them.

For details and addresses for donating books and taking tax deductions, see our Special Report *Beyond Remainders*. See the Appendix.

Your book is a success when people who haven't read it, pretend they have.

Chapter Ten

Fulfillment

Moving Your Book Out The Door

Book order *fulfillment* consists of invoicing, inventory storage, picking, packaging and shipping. These routines involve opening the mail, sorting it, typing the invoices, wrapping the books, affixing the shipping label, applying postage to the package, making the trip to the Post Office (or other delivery system) and maintaining a record of the sale. *Inventory management* includes storage and stock monitoring so you will know when to order another printing.

Fulfillment is expensive. According to John Huenefeld, most small to medium sized publishers spend about 10.5% of their gross on fulfillment. All costs, including labor, storage and shipping materials, amount to $2.44 per order handled or 66 cents per book. If your business is mostly wholesale (many of the same book to fewer customers), you should be able to drop your fulfillment percentage to six or seven.

Mail order selling offers you the opportunity to run a high volume, worldwide business without a large cash investment in multiple facilities. To compete with larger companies, all you will need is a better product and more efficient promotion. Since we are far from most of our customers, book publishing is in the mail order business.

Mail order businesses are those which deal with their customers at a distance, without personal delivery. The product may not be delivered by the Post Office; a large shipment might go by truck. Mail order is particularly appropriate for the distribution of books. In fact, over half of the business and professional books are shipped directly from the publisher to the ultimate consumer.

Smaller publishers are attracted to mail order selling because it is easier than getting into bookstores. They ship to wholesalers and stores, but they don't spend the money on visiting them. In fact, there are many stories about books which have done poorly in the stores, which, when properly promoted, sold well through mail order.

Mail order buyers probably do not frequent book stores and it is likely they do not even think of themselves as *book buyers*. In a *Publishers Weekly* article about Bantam, it was noted that geographically, mail orders line up proportionately with population figures. Most orders come from the most populated states, California and New York, not from the states with fewer bookstores. Mail order purchasing is a habit. Many people prefer to buy informational books this way. Once they begin, they often buy everything they can find on the subject.

Order Processing. Once your business grows to where you have numerous titles and several employees, you will require a more elaborate fulfillment system. But initially you will do it all yourself so you can keep it simple. One way to keep it simple is to streamline the workload to avoid any duplication of effort. For example, typing up an invoice and then typing a separate label is a waste of time and money (cost of label, etc). A number of pieces of information must be recorded to process an order. By using carbon copies, all may be done at the single initial invoice typing. This *one-writing* also avoids transposition errors in figures and addresses.

To enable you to visualize the distribution system, the fulfillment process will be discussed in sequence.

—Postal orders. Open the mail and check the contents but do not take the orders and checks out of their envelopes. Sort the stuffed envelopes into piles according to whether they are individual retail sales, book dealers (stores or distributors), libraries or special accounts, such as associations, sport centers, etc. Make up a separate pile for inquiries—you will want to send these people a brochure. Other separate piles will be for accounts receivable, letters to be answered, etc.

When a retail order arrives without a check, make a note of the omission (such as "check not enclosed") on the envelope. Then send a brochure with a note requesting money in the correct amount. Occasionally, you will get a letter back saying that a check was enclosed with the original order. But you will have your note on that envelope to confirm your suspicions and jog your memory. Make a photocopy of the envelope with the notation, and request the sender recheck his or her records and/or send you a photocopy of the cancelled check.

—Telephone orders. Telephone contacts are important opportunities for sales and increased sales. They take place when you have the attention of the prospect and they are (usually) paying for the call. Consequently, telephone calls should not be handled by an untrained employee. Make sure everyone knows who is to take calls, except in case of overflow, or train every staff member to take calls. Have an order form ready, or route orders to the order entry computer operator for direct punch-up. Order pads prompt questions, so that all information, such as the *ship to* address, is obtained.

As you grow, you may investigate **credit cards** sales and accepting orders via toll-free **(800) telephone numbers.** But initially, Postal and regular telephone communication will be sufficient. For details and addresses, see the Special Report *Book Fulfillment*. See the Appendix.

—Answering machines are very useful in business, as they can take orders after business hours. Answering machines are a great convenience to both you and the customer. They may order at any time and it is nice when you return after a weekend away to find a number of orders waiting for you.

Many people like our recording which says: "Para Publishing, this is Dan Poynter. If you would like an information kit on publishing or parachuting, please leave your name and address. If you would like to charge a book to your Visa, MasterCard or American Express card, please leave your name, address, telephone number, the name of the book, type of charge card, the card number and the expiration date. Thank you." *(beep)*

—**Telex** is useful for accepting international orders. If you have one now, keep it. If you do not, get a fax machine instead.

—**Fax.** Facsimile machines are the latest rage in office equipment. Faster than FedEx and cheaper than a stamp, the fax machine is replacing the Postal Service.

Since even basic *personal* facsimile machines can send the first page in less than a minute, and since transmissions can be made automatically after hours when telephone line rates are lower, one page can be sent coast-to-coast for 16 cents. That is less than a stamp. No wonder more and more mail order companies are accepting written orders on fax. Major publishers are now accepting bookstore orders on fax.

Facsimile machines are typewriter-sized boxes that plug into your telephone line. Anything you can put on a sheet of paper, from typewriting to handwriting and drawings to photographs, may be transmitted to any other fax machine. They provide instant written communication. Customers may fill in an order blank, note their credit card numbers and send the order at the speed of light. Their machine even confirms that the order was received and issues a "receipt."

Publishers may also use a fax for instant copy proofing with printers. You can't transmit a book's bluelines but the fax will save time proofing miscellaneous pages and illustration positions. Even more time may be saved proofing brochure and newsletter copy with local typesetters and printers. With a fax machine, you don't have to leave the office and run down to the printer.

Virtually every foreign printer and publisher uses fax today. If you do business overseas, you need a fax machine.

Facsimile transmissions do not replace the telephone; they replace the Postal Service for delivering letters, purchase orders and drawings. When you think about it, paying someone to hand-carry a letter across town or across the country is a waste of time and energy resources. Now your typed letters will go into two piles: one for the Postal Service and one for the fax machine.

Fax has a sense of urgency. Facsimile transmissions get read before the morning mail. If you want to get the recipient's attention, fax will do it.

Your fax machine prints a transmittal report after sending a document, to confirm that the letter was received on the other end. It is like getting a *Return Receipt* for every piece of mail at no extra charge.

Credit cards will increase sales and increase the size of the sale while cutting down on collection problems. People have become accustomed to telephoning an order and placing the charge on a credit card. Visa and MasterCard are used the most in telephone orders, with American Express, Discover and the others used to a much lesser extent. While the bank will want 2% to 7% of each sale, depending upon the average size of the sale and your monthly volume, it credits your account immediately. So credit cards will increase your cash flow and may decrease your need for expensive short-term borrowing.

Credit card orders take more time to process because you must fill out a charge slip and call in for approval. But the sale always comes out even, so there is no additional billing or difference to refund, and there are no accounts receivable collection problems.

The problem is in getting the Merchant Card privilege from the bank. Because of high losses to fly-by-night boiler room telephone operations, the banks have stopped offering Merchant Card privileges to mail order and telephone order businesses. About the only way for a publisher to qualify today is to convince the bank that most of your sales will be from walk-in traffic. For this, you need the appearance of a store front, and it also helps if you own your property or can show you have been around for a while. You will also have to agree to credit anyone who contests a charge. Since you are offering a *satisfaction guarantee*, this requirement should not be a problem. Start by contacting your bank for Merchant Service. If they will not cooperate, approach other banks in town. They will want *all* your business including checking accounts, and may be more helpful if they can get all your business. The best advice is be persistent. Let your banker know you are serious and will keep trying until you get merchant status. It will be easier and cheaper for the bank to give in now rather than later.

See our Special Report *Merchant Card Status* for details and numbers for taking credit cards. See the Appendix.

Individual Orders from retail customers who are sending cash or check with their order (CWO) are handled best initially with a sheet of 33-part address labels (e.g., Avery Label #5351) with pressure sensitive adhesive. Make a carbon copy using carbon paper backed with ordinary typing or mimeo paper.

Type the date on the first label in the upper left-hand corner of the sheet of labels. Going down the column, as you pull each order out of its individual envelope, type the check number, the amount of the check without a decimal ($21.45 becomes 2145), your code for the book being shipped and any special shipping instructions, if applicable. Then space down typing the customer's name and address.

```
1234    2345    AIR
Dustbooks
Len Fulton
P.O. Box 100
Paradise, CA 95969
```

A typed label might look like this. The check was #1234, the amount of the check was $23.45, the book was *The Self-Publishing Manual* and it is to be shipped via air instead of book rate.

As you grow, you may install a personal computer with with an inexpensive order-entry/accounting program such as *QuickBooks* (Intuit, P.O. Box 3014, Menlo Park, CA 94026) With the computer you will be able to do much more with the collected information. Later you may invest in an even more sophisticated order entry computer program. See the Appendix.

The labels are easy to affix to the shipping bags. The carbon copy is your permanent record for tax and other management (planning) purposes. This label system is much faster, simpler and cheaper than using individual invoices for each order.

If you have another need for this individual order information (perhaps you are selling the mailing list), make another carbon or photocopy your file copy. If you want to send brochures out to past customers, photocopy the carbon sheet onto 33-part label stock. There is no need to re-type the address.

If you use a computer, it will capture and store all the information for later use. Then you may take advantage of pin-feed labels, and carbon paper will be unnecessary.

—**Shipping labels** come in three basic styles:

1. Individual 33-part labels in sheets for occasional typewriter use

2. Rolls for continuous typewriter use

3. Fan-fold stacks with pin-feed holes on the sides for computer use. Here is an example of a 3 x 5 label:

Para Publishing
P.O. Box 4232, Santa Barbara, CA 93140-4232 USA

Printed Matter—Books • Forwarding and Return Postage Guaranteed
Special Fourth Class Book Rate or Library Rate

Fan-fold label

Fan-fold, custom printed labels are available from label manufacturers. One is Discount Label, P.O. Box 709, New Albany, IN 47151-0709. Tel: (800) 457-2400.

Do not order labels on slick stock. Addresses will smear and ink takes much longer to dry.

—**Save the envelopes** with their enclosed orders. At the end of each week or month, rubber band the envelopes and date the pile. Save them for 12 to 18 months in case a customer contacts you about the order, or the package is returned as undeliverable. If a book is returned by the Post Office as undeliverable, check the postmark to determine when the shipment went out and then go through the envelopes to find the original order. The book may have been sent to the address on the check rather than the one on the envelope, numbers may have been transposed, etc.

If a customer complains that the wrong book was shipped, he or she did not order the book or a check was enclosed, a check of the original order will confirm or deny the claim. When replying, enclose a photocopy of the original order so the customer can see what he or she did.

—**Books not received.** Occasionally a customer will write complaining that he or she has not received the book. Check back through the original order envelope and label carbon or computer record to make sure you received the order, that the book was sent and when. Then write to the customer stating the date the book was shipped and that it was sent via slower, but cheaper book rate which often takes some 30 days in the U.S. and 90 days to foreign addresses. Remind him the package had a return address and mention that the parcel was not returned to you. Rarely does the Post Office lose books. Tell him if the book does not arrive in a couple weeks more *to return this letter and you will ship out another book*. When you ship the second book, write up the transaction on an invoice and note on it that if he receives two books to *refuse delivery* of the second one. This way the Post Office will return the book to you with only postage due. If the customer accepts delivery, he may never get around to sending the book back and you are out a book. If he has already received a book, the chances are very good he will refuse delivery of the second one because he does not need two.

—**Ad codes**. At the end of each month, total up the orders responding to each address code and record the responses on a spread sheet. See the discussion of address coding in Chapter Seven.

—**Short slips** may be used to collect small amounts. Some customers will not send enough to cover the book, shipping and sales tax. Sometimes the shortage is not worth the cost to collect it. Very small improper payments (high or low) are not worth haggling over. Just ship the book.

Short Slip

Your order was short $ _____

We know you will appreciate our shipping the books now rather than holding up the shipment pending payment of this small amount.

Please return this slip when you make your payment— now OR with your next order or payment. THANK YOU.

Your name: _____

Check number: _____

Send to Para Publishing

Accounting Department

P.O. Box 4232

Santa Barbara, CA 93140-4232

Tel: (805) 968-7277

Fax: (805) 968-1379

Short slip

Short slips may be used to collect these small amounts, but set certain limits such as:

0 to 40 cents short: Forget it.
40 cents to $4.99: Enclose a short slip.
Over $5.00: Cut an invoice for the balance.

You must compare the costs of collecting small amounts with the amount that can be collected. Most people are good about short slips and will pay, but it is not worth badgering them for 30 cents if they must use a 25 cent stamp to send it to you. Collect these small payments as they come in and bank them once a month. The small amounts add up and are worth collecting.

Rick Hartbrodt read the previous paragraph in a library copy of the second edition of *The Self-Publishing Manual*. Testing the author/publisher, he sent just $9.95, the price at the time and not enough for sales tax or shipping. Dr. Hartbrodt moved to Santa Barbara and went on to write and publish his first book. Later, he confirmed to the author that he had indeed received his book for just $9.95.

—**Overpayments**. If the customer sends a little too much, ship the book a faster way such as UPS or Priority Mail. If he or she sends a lot too much, issue a refund check for the balance. Fortunately, credit card orders come out even.

—**Bad checks**. Checks rarely bounce, and it is not worth the record keeping and loss of customer good will to delay shipments until a check clears the bank. When a check is returned, check the original order envelope to see if there is more than one address. Send off a photocopy of the returned check and the bank notice that came with it. Write across the photocopy *Please send another check* and circle the bank charge and the new total amount. Perhaps half of these paper hangers will make the bad check good. You may always include a short, direct letter but this photocopy technique is faster and simpler. Since books have a high markup, it probably is not worth your time to expend more effort trying to collect these few, small debts.

—**Insurance.** Insuring books is a waste of time and money. Books lost or damaged in the mails should be replaced by the shipper. Your only alternative is to insure each parcel. It is far cheaper to *self-insure* and replace the occasional lost or damaged book. There will not be many lost books and the cost is small, compared to the price of insurance and the paperwork involved, to say nothing of the value of a happy customer.

—**Refunds** should be handled promptly. *The customer is always right* or, at least, he must be treated as though he is. A cheerful, fast refund will let him know he can trust you and there is a good chance he will be back.

Unlimited Guarantee

We guarantee your satisfaction. Order any book and look it over. You may return it at any time if you are not satisfied and your full purchase price will be refunded, no questions asked. There is no 10 day or 30 day limit; you may even return it after a year.

Set up as few barriers to ordering as possible. If your product is good, most customers will keep it. Since there is no limit on the free trial period, most unsatisfied customers will put off the return—forever.

The customer usually pays the shipping on an order and on a return. This means that you refund or issue a credit only for the price of the book.

Dealer orders from commercial wholesale customers and those individual retail customers who must be billed are handled best with a multiple copy, carboned (or NCR) invoice. Initially, when your business is slow and you have to keep stationery investments small, you may use standard invoice forms with your address rubber stamped on them. Next you may wish to order a more attractive imprinted standard invoice form. And finally, you will graduate to your own custom designed invoice.

—**Invoices** should be typed to insure clarity but, unfortunately, most standard invoices are not laid out for typewriter use; they require you to tab and index all over them to insert the necessary information. The most often needed information should be on the left-hand margin to eliminate tabbing.

				INVOICE #		DATE	

Para Publishing
Books by Dan Poynter
Post Office Box 4232
Santa Barbara, CA 93140–4232 USA
Telephone: (805) 968–7277

ISBN: 0-915516
Fed. I.D. #95-6532235
SAN: 215-8981
DUNS: 09-141-9358

SHIPPED TO

SOLD TO

PRINTED MATTER — BOOKS
SPECIAL FOURTH CLASS
BOOK RATE OR LIBRARY RATE
Forwarding and return postage guaranteed

YOUR ORDER	CUSTOMER CODE	TERMS		SHIPPED VIA	
		NET 30 DAYS			

QUANT.	DESCRIPTION	PRICE	AMOUNT

A finance charge of 1 ½% per month will be applied to all balances over 60 days

SUBTOTAL

SALES TAX

SHIPPING

INVOICE NUMBER

PLEASE NOTE INVOICE
NUMBER WITH PAYMENT

TOTAL

AMOUNT PAID

PLEASE PAY FROM THIS INVOICE
— NO STATEMENT WILL BE SENT

PAY THIS AMOUNT

Example of an invoice

Invoices which must be typed should have the book name, edition, ISBN and price printed on them, so that this identifying information does not have to be typed repeatedly. Computer-generated invoices may be like the example.

Invoice forms may be purchased with or without sequenced numbers. Some publishers like to add their own invoice numbers and work a code into them. On the other hand, others like the pre-numbered forms, as typing in numbers only takes valuable time. A computer will automatically add the sequenced number and the current date.

Do not forget the customer's purchase order (P.O.) number; they want it on all invoices, packages, etc. Make sure you are sending the invoices and packages to the correct addresses. They may be different and the addresses are particularly hard to find on military and government purchase orders. Some purchase orders have three to five different addresses (originating, billing, shipping, etc.) on them.

The Invoice route

Send the first (white invoice) copy via first class mail (or fax) by simply folding and slipping it into a windowed #10 envelope. Include your brochure and other promotional information. The yellow second copy goes to your shipping area and the third (pink record) copy is stapled to the purchase order, hole-punched and placed in your accounts receivable three-ring binder in invoice number order. Use this same system even when the invoice is generated by computer.

If you have another need for all this invoice information, you may use a four-piece invoice. Occasionally, orders will be received with requests for *four copies of the original invoice*. But publishers usually just send one copy, with the thought that if the purchaser really needs more copies, he can use his own photocopy machine. Why spend your money for both photocopies and postage? On the other hand, some publishers feel they may be paid sooner if they provide the number of copies requested.

—Accounts receivable. When payment arrives, match the check with the pink invoice, and date stamp the invoice to give you a record of when payment was received. Then move the pink invoice to a binder of a different color for storage.

Sales tax will have to be added onto the invoice on those *retail sales made within your state.* Do not collect sales tax on books sold *for resale* to bookstores and other firms in your state. When you sell to another re-seller in your state, you must record their state *resale number.* The point is that the ultimate purchaser will pay the tax. You must either collect it or get a resale number to indicate who will collect it. In most states, libraries are not exempt from sales taxes; after all, they do not re-sell the books. Usually, the sales tax is not collected for any sales made out of your state. The sales tax is on the merchandise only, not the shipping charges. The time may come when we will have to collect sales taxes for all retail sales because Congress periodically considers a national sales tax.

The bottom of the invoice may be used for any other pertinent information or even nice personal notes.

Continuous forms save a lot of computer printer loading time. Order continuous form invoices through your local printer.

Credit. The customer may send a check, authorize you to charge his or her credit card, or you may extend credit (e.g., *Net 30 days*). Most publishers require check or credit card from individuals and extend credit to bookstores, libraries and wholesalers, but there are exceptions.

—Individuals usually send a check when ordering by mail and authorize a credit card charge to Visa or MasterCard when making a telephone order. More and more people are ordering by card and expect to do so. Many publishers have the rule: *no credit sales to individuals.* Get a check, credit card or ship COD. This rule eliminates many small receivables and occasional uncollectibles.

—Businesses expect terms but many small ones are using credit cards. Though the interest rate is high, cards offer simple credit to the small business.

For those businesses that insist on sending purchase orders without money, you may extend 30 day credit terms or send a *pro-forma invoice*. This is a regular invoice listing the books, shipping charges, sales tax (if applicable) and the total. Once they pay the invoice, you ship the books. Most small publishers routinely extend credit to bookstores, libraries and businesses as long as the orders are not too large.

—Wholesalers. The book industry is not known for fast pay. Sixty, 90 and even 120 day payments are not uncommon, and since books have to be sold on a return basis, they are, in effect, on consignment anyway. Some publishers have put the large wholesalers on a CWO (Cash With Order) basis. Even Baker and Taylor will pay up front if requested.

—Distributors. Each distributor will cut his own deal with you. Many agree to pay 90 days after they ship the books. Most will send a monthly printout of sales so you will know what size checks to expect.

Just list your terms in your dealer bulletin. Whatever you decide to do, publicize it so that everyone will know what you expect.

If a bookstore or wholesaler is slow or fails to pay, tighten up or cut them off. Many publishers follow this system: Any dealers over 60 days are put on a CWO (Cash With Order) basis forever. In other words, they get credit until they abuse it, and then they pay in advance regardless of their better credit history. Some publishers extend credit only to major wholesalers with whom they have contracts and college (tax supported) bookstores. Everyone else pays in advance. Some publishers deal only through wholesalers and direct any bookstore and library orders to those wholesalers.

Labeling. Most shipments are one invoice (or record), one package, one address. Occasionally, twenty or more identical packages must be sent to one address. Typing out all these labels is not fun. If you can't quickly print the labels with a computer, get a *Sten C Labl*® marking system. The hand-held marker is made by Esselt Pendaflex and is available in office supply and paper supply stores. Its 2 x 4 stencils can be cut on a typewriter and applied to the marker. Then just stamp the address on regular shipping labels. The ink will take some time to dry on slick-stock labels.

An alternative is to photocopy the shipping label/invoice the required number of times and trim off the tops to be used as a label. Apply to the cartons with clear tape. This way the carton bears the address, return address, date, purchase order number, sales order number, everything. Be sure to label the cartons: *1 of 6, 2 of 6,* etc.

Back orders are those that cannot be completely filled when the order is received. Usually most of the order can be filled and is shipped, while the single out-of-stock book order is put aside until the book is received and can be shipped.

Most publishers use a common code of abbreviations to cover the most frequent backorder problems: "OS" (out of stock), "TOS" (temporarily out of stock), "OP" (out of print), "TOP" (temporarily out of print), "NOP" (not our publication), and "FP" (future publication). If you use these abbreviations, make sure they are explained elsewhere on the invoice, such as on the back. Only librarians and bookstore buyers will understand the codes.

The Federal Trade Commission (FTC) has some strict rules for CWO (Cash With Order) mail order operations. If you receive money for books:

• You must ship the order within 30 days of receiving it, unless your offer clearly stated shipping would take longer. • If it appears the order will not be shipped when promised, you must notify the customer before the promised date, giving a definite new date, if known, and offering the opportunity to cancel the order with a refund. or consent to a definite delayed shipping date or an indefinite delay.

• Your notice must contain a self-addressed, stamped card or envelope with which to indicate a preference. If there is no response to this notice, you may assume agreement to the delay, but must ship the order within 30 days of the original shipping date promised or required, or the order will be automatically cancelled. A prompt refund must be made if the order is cancelled.

• Even if the customer consented to an indefinite delay, he or she retains the right to cancel the order at any time before the item is shipped.

• If the customer cancels an order that has been paid for by check or money order, you must mail a refund within seven business days.

• If they cancel a credit card order, you must issue a credit within one billing cycle following the receipt of their request. The customer may stop payment pending settlement of the matter if the purchase is over $50 and he or she is within 100 miles, or is within the same state.

All this FTC discussion regarding credit card rules may not count, as your contract with the credit card company probably says if the customer purchased by mail or telephone (without physically handing you the card) and later contests the bill, you must issue a credit.

• Credits toward future purchases are not acceptable.

• If the book ordered is unavailable, you may not send substitute merchandise without the customer's consent.

Send to the Federal Trade Commission, Washington, DC 20580, (202) 523-3598, for the following pamphlets:

1. *Shopping by Mail? You're Protected!*
2. *FTC Buyer's Guide No. 2*

The FTC rules apply to mail orders, not to telephone orders, but that may change soon. The FTC is evaluating telephone ordering.

As long as you guarantee satisfaction by offering to send a refund for any merchandise returned for any reason, you shouldn't have any run-ins with the FTC. Just treat your customers right and keep in touch with them.

Orders should be shipped as soon as possible after receipt, usually the next day. This involves a trip to the Post Office once each day to pick up the mail and to deliver the wrapped books from orders received the previous day. The sooner the orders are processed, the sooner the money will be deposited, the best incentive for speedy fulfillment.

Customers want their book as soon as possible. A few who are not familiar with mail order will even write two days later looking for their package, but this is rare. When business is slow, Post Office runs may be made every other day, say Monday, Wednesday and Friday. And if you must be away from the business, you will find that only one or two inquiries will be received if you fail to ship for up to a month.

Unordered books. Customers receiving unordered merchandise may not be pressured to pay for it or return it. They may use it or discard it as they see fit. So be careful where you ship books. See Title 39, Postal Service, section 3009.

Quality control. One way to avoid shipping errors is to employ as few people as possible in the order entry and packaging functions. Fewer people in the loop provides accountability. The second secret is cross-training so everyone understands the system (and can fill in during absences). If an error is made punching-up an order, the packer may spot it, if he or she understands the system. Try to limit order handling to the mail opener/telephone operator who receive the orders, the order entry computer operator who punches-up the orders, and the shipper who picks, packs and posts. In very small companies, one person will perform all functions but as you hire help, be sure to cross-train. If the same person handles mail opening or order entry and accounts receivable, he or she will remember the bad debts and other problems and will flag new orders.

Complaints must be viewed as an opportunity, not a problem. Complaints can be expensive if not handled quickly, and they mean a lost sale unless you can make a substitute or convince the customer you are worthy of a future order. Some mail order companies, such as Quill, the large office supply company, enclose a return form with every order to emphasize how easy it is to do business with them.

Complaints should be answered promptly. Even if the book has probably arrived by the time you get the complaint, you should answer. You must maintain credibility.

> The fewer people touching the orders, the faster, less expensively and more accurately the job will be completed.

Written complaints should be handled with a call, unless a lot of photocopied documentation is required. Customers can be cooled down easier over the telephone.

When someone calls in a complaint, you have an opportunity to wrap up the problem on the telephone at their expense, so do not offer to get back to them. Remind the caller or writer that you guarantee satisfaction. You will try to work out the problem but if you can't, you will refund the money. Most customers want the book, and the problem worked out.

A few questions about the customer will identify their needs. Then suggest some products to fill those needs.

A checklist form-letter may be used to handle common small problems, but impersonal forms should not be used for major complaints.

Inventory and Storage. Book storage cannot be taken lightly because books are not light. If your floor will not support a water bed, do not haul in a ton of books. The people downstairs will not like your books any better than the water. The best place to store your new product is in the garage, alongside the shipping table. This way, the books may be off-loaded in the driveway and stacked in the garage, wrapped as needed and placed back in the car for the Post Office run. All these operations will be with a minimum of carrying. Hauling books down steep steps into a cellar, only to be wrapped and hauled back up, gets very old very soon and makes no sense at all. This is heavy work.

Tell the printer you want the finished books shrink wrapped in stacks or packed in plastic bag-lined cardboard cartons. Just line each carton with a large garbage-type bag before inserting the books. The plastic wrap will keep the books clean, dry, dust-free, and the books will not rub on the carton. Small publishers need plastic bags and/or shrink wrapping and tightly-packed cartons because they often store the books in places without climate control, such as in an unheated garage. If the cartons are not tightly packed (filled to the top), they will crush and tip, rather than stack well.

Do not stack cartons one on top of the other. Stack them alternately like bricks. The alternating stack will be solid and will not tip over. Very little shelving is required, as books should be stored in their original cartons.

If your state has an inventory tax, you can avoid most of the bite by careful ordering, or by having your printing done in another state. Then, keeping an eye on the tax date, have the printer ship in a pallet of books as needed.

As noted above, the books should be bagged, boxed and sealed. Then the cartons should be palletized, banded three ways and trucked to you as a unit. This keeps the books from shifting in the cartons, which scratches the covers. Palletized and banded (with straps or plastic wrap) cartons are less likely to be broken open in-route but always expect at least one carton to be torn, so that the spine of some books can be read. Books delivered to home addresses, as opposed to normal places of business, are often porno books. Of course, if you are publishing pornography, expect some books to be missing from the shipment.

New titles may be drop shipped direct from the printer to your wholesale accounts. There is no reason to expend the time and money to route them, for example, from Michigan to the publisher in California and then back to Quality Books in Illinois.

Books must be kept in a cool, dry, dust-free place. Dampness may ripple or curl the pages, make them stick together and rust wire stitches (staples) in saddle stitched books. Depending upon your location, moisture and type of flooring, it may be wise to stack the cartons on pallets so air can circulate under the stack. Sunlight will fade and yellow paper. Dust will scratch the covers and dirty the edges.

Fire is always a problem, and insuring the inventory in a non-commercial (hence non-fire-rated) area may be impossible. Ask your insurance agent.

If your books are damaged, slowly or quickly, you are out of business. Your inventory must be protected and this means starting by leaving the books in their protective cartons and bags and opening only one carton at a time as needed. Unbelievably, some publishers unpack their books and place them on shelves, exposed to sun and dust.

If the pages of the books ripple due to dampness, they may straighten out when the humidity returns to normal.

Inventory control is simpler if all the books are stored in a single place. If you have cartons of books scattered around your garage, office, at the printer's, with friends, and in a mini storage warehouse, some will disappear and you will never know how many you have. If you do not have a garage or spare room, try renting warehouse space. Mini warehouses are quite common now;, check the *Yellow Pages*. Then try to store books in one place, or no more than two: bulk in the warehouse and a few cartons in the shipping area.

Visual physical inspection is the easiest way to get stock information; it is faster than going through the invoices. If you quickly count the books on hand monthly, you will be able to plot a good inventory chart. These figures will be a great help in your planning next year. Reorders must be scheduled so the reprints will arrive just before exhausting the previous supply. Having to report a delay in filling an order costs in paperwork, and time is money. Decisions to reprint will be determined by rate of sale, stock level, seasonal sales expectations (outdoor books sell better in the spring), the time required to print and, in some states, the date of the inventory tax.

Dun & Bradstreet reports that 9.5% of all business failures are due to excessive inventory. Keep the inventory low and order more often.

The shipping area is where you do the picking, packing and posting. It should be arranged so as to require as little motion as possible; books, bags, cartons, and other materials must all be within easy reach. Store hardcover and paperback editions of the same titles next to each other to make them easier to locate. Position the faster selling books closer to the shipping table.

Packing involves the placing of the books in a protective wrapper so that your customer receives the clean, unmutilated goods he or she is paying for. Books must be packaged well enough to arrive in good condition the first time. It costs too much to ship them twice.

—Saddle-stitched booklets. Small wire stitched (stapled) paperbacks may be safely shipped in a heavy kraft envelope;

make sure the size is correct. If the envelope is too large, the book will slide around inside and the cover will be scuffed.

**Shipping
bag**

—**Hardcover and perfectbound (square-back) paper-backs up to 6 x 9 require a padded bag**. Standard padded bags are heavy, dirty and can only be stapled closed. The plastic-bubble Mail-Lite® bag, on the other hand, is clean, light and waterproof when heat sealed. Compared to other plastic-lined bags, the Mail-Lite is not as smooth inside, making it difficult to stuff large books, but they offer the best protection. We have Postal tested every type of plain and padded bag, light-weight and heavy-weight, and have found the Mail Lite bag to be the best.

Mail Lite bags cost more than fiber-filled Jiffy bags but you will save on postage. A standard 6 x 9 hardcover book measures a half inch wider and longer and is a quarter inch thicker than its paperback edition. Both fit the #1 Mail-Lite bag when they have less than 200 pages.

—**Heat sealers.** The shipping bags may be stapled closed (get the heavy hand grip type stapler) or heat sealed. The sealing machines come in several sizes and provide a moisture-tight closure. Sealed Air runs heat sealer promotions from time to time. In 1986, they leased the sealers for $1/year. In 1988, they offered a 50% discount on the machines if you bought five cartons of bags. The cost was $165 for a table model capable of sealing 8 to 10 bags per minute and $195 for a foot-operated floor model capable of sealing 15 to 20 bags per minute. If your Sealed Air distributor is not running a promotion on heat sealers, contact the sealer manufacturer directly: Heat Sealing Equipment in Cleveland, Ohio, (216) 341-2022. Call for the number of the dealer nearest you.

Call Sealed Air for the name of the local paper dealer who handles their Mail-Lite bags. Sealed Air Corporation, Park 80 Plaza East, Saddle Brook, NJ 07662, (201) 791-7600.

Also contact Quill for a catalog and compare bag prices [P.O. Box 4700, Lincolnshire, IL 60197-4700, (708) 634-4800/East or (714) 988-3200/West]. Remember to add in shipping charges when comparing prices.

Multiple book orders, up to three books, may be shipped in larger shipping bags, if immobilized against rubbing by plastic bagging and taping. Greater quantities of books should be boxed.

—**8.5 x 11 softcover books** require Vari-depth mailers due to their longer spine. Vari-depth mailers are die-cut, flat shippers that can be folded around one or more books. The mailers cost more than shipping bags but offer excellent protection when the books are first placed in a plastic bag.

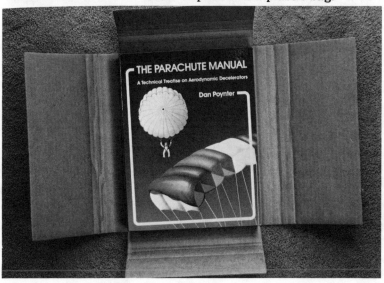

Vari-depth mailer

Cartons. Check the *Yellow Pages* for nearby paper goods dealers, and purchase standard 5.5 x 8.5 or 6 x 9 cartons (as applicable) of various depths, which ordinarily come 25 to the bundle.

If you will standardize the trim size of all your books, you will minimize the carton and bag sizes required for shipping. The best measurements for books are 5.5 x 8.5 and 8.5 x 11, as they will stack together.

Incidentally, some states do not charge sales tax on shipping supplies, probably to encourage exports. Check on this with your office supply store or state taxing authority.

① Mark desired height of box (A). Determine size of top flaps and make second line (B). Split corners to (A).

② Cut along line (B).

③ Fold along lines (A).

(Discard)

How to cut down a box

Sealing a carton with non-reinforced paper tape

To seal the cartons, the least expensive way is with 3" non-reinforced brown paper tape. The reinforced tape is strong, but it is also dirty and hard to cut with inexpensive tape dispensers.

Tape dispensers. Fancy paper tape machines cost several hundred dollars—quite a shock—so look around for a used one. Check *used* office equipment stores and swap meets. Also compare the prices at Quill. Call for a catalog (708) 634-4800. They offer an electric model for about $265 which may be good. Also call Arrow Star for a catalog (800) 645-2982.

The water will flow into the paper tape more easily if you add a little vinegar to the reservoir in the tape machine. You may, alternatively, use a couple of drops of detergent, but detergent gums up the machine more quickly than vinegar.

Tape. Plastic sealing tape costs more than paper and is harder to use but the hand-held dispensers are less expensive. The lightest weight plastic tape is sufficient; buy the cheapest, lowest mil thickness available. Be very careful of the special sales on rolls of plastic sealing tape. The *rolls* vary in length and some offers are no bargain.

You will need half-inch reinforced glass strapping tape for large cartons, so you should also use it on the small ones. Do not waste money buying wider tape.

Do not use twine; UPS does not allow it anymore. String takes too long to put on and it catches in mail handling machinery.

You will also need some cellophane tape to seal the packing list/address label envelope.

The machinery you will need includes tape dispensers, knife, stapler or heat sealer, and a scale.

Plastic bags. Take a carton and twenty books to your paper goods store. Pick up some large garbage can liner bags to line large cartons. Measure the bags against the carton. Then stack some books in one pile to fit the smaller cartons you are buying, and get some smaller plastic bag can liners to match. You have to run these packaging tests each time you buy, because the bag manufacturers are continually changing the measurements, mil thickness and gussets.

Knife. Get a common razor knife for opening cartons and keep it sharp. A sharpening stone will prolong the life of the blades. Be very careful when cutting open cartons. It is common to score the covers of the top books by cutting too deep.

AIR MAIL first class
SPECIAL
HANDLING

PRINTED MATTER - BOOKS
SPECIAL FOURTH CLASS
BOOK RATE OR LIBRARY RATE
Forwarding & Return Postage Guaranteed

Rubber stamps. The common rubber stamps you will need are here. Order them from your local office supply store.

With the Book Rate notice printed on your mailing labels and invoices, you will need this rubber stamp just for occasional packages.

When shipping a package by AIR, stamp the notice near the address on the package so that it will be more noticeable to the mail sorters. A red AIR MAIL stamp over in one corner of the carton may be missed, resulting in a high priced, slow delivery.

Turn your stamp pad over each night to make the ink flow to the top of the pad.

Ladder. Get a short, sturdy ladder or step stool so you will be able to stack cartons higher and retrieve them easily.

Scales fall into two categories and three general ranges. The categories are spring and electronic. The electronic scales should be more accurate. The three categories are 0-2 lb. letter scale, 0-5 lb. (some go to 25 lbs.) small parcel scale, and the

0-50 lbs. (or more) large parcel scale. The larger scale need only read from 0-50 lbs. Packages heavier than 50 lbs. do not protect their contents well and should not be shipped.

Book publishers do not need fancy zone/rate computing scales since books shipped at Book Rate are not zoned. A simple scale and a rate chart are all that are needed. Most small publishers will get by just fine with a 0-2 lb. letter scale and a 0-50 lb. large package scale.

The best deal for weighing heavier packages is a bathroom scale with a remote digital readout that can be placed at eye level. These scales run about $75 at many department stores.

The scale should be accurate, but do not be obsessed about its being perfect. The Postal Service rarely checks the postage on a package.

Packing. There are two important steps in successful book packaging: Keep the books clean and immobilize them. Start with cartons that are close to the size needed. If you have 5.5 x 8.5 books and can get 5.5 x 8.5 cartons in several depths, the fit will be perfect and there will not be any sliding and scuffing between books. Slip the books into a plastic bag and slide them into the carton. For the best fit, cut down the carton rather than fill it with dunnage. The books will be kept clean by the plastic bag and are immobilized by the perfect-fitting carton.

Plastic styrofoam peanuts and discs are greasy, carry grit and will work their way between the pages of a book if not separated by a plastic bag. Re-use any peanuts sent to you but do not buy them. The best shipping carton is a perfect fit or one that has been cut down to fit. The next best choice is to stuff with newspaper. But remember that newspaper is dirty, another reason to place the books in a plastic bag first.

Single orders may be prepackaged and stacked to wait for a label. Done in front of the TV set, the time passes quickly.

Labeling. Once the bag is stuffed or the carton is wrapped, it is time to apply the commercial yellow packing list/shipping label. This copy of the invoice is simply folded and inserted into a large, pressure sensitive adhesive-backed clear envelope and placed on the bag or carton. The 4.5 x 9 clear plastic packing list envelopes are available from some office supply catalog houses. See the Appendix.

Originally, the clear envelopes were made to accept the old IBM-type punch cards. If any other special insert is required, it should come with the packing slip and be included with it now. Now the person receiving the shipment will have exactly the same information as the person receiving the bill.

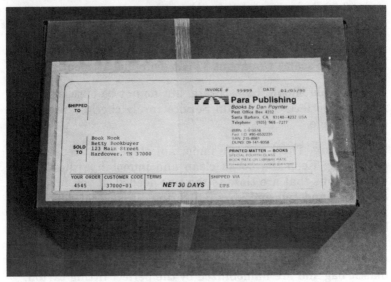

The wrapped and addressed carton

Occasionally, the person receiving the bill will not want the person receiving the books to know the prices and terms (such as in a drop shipment). In this case, simply use scissors to clip off the pricing information on the yellow copy. When the *ship to* address is not the same as the invoiced address, cross out the latter and circle the former with a felt tip pen. Or, use leftover one-across labels to cover the *sold to address*.

Place the packing slip envelope over the carton closure so the recipient will have to remove the envelope to open the carton. Do not place the packing slip on the side of the carton where it may be overlooked. The sooner the accounting department receives notice the books have been received, the sooner you will be paid and the fewer collection problems you will have.

Taping. Using non-reinforced paper tape, seal the ends of the carton as well as the long flaps. Sealing the ends will make the carton far more sturdy. Place the address label/packing slip on top in its clear envelope and seal it with transparent tape. Then reinforce the carton by banding in at least two directions with reinforcing tape. Run the tape over the clear packing slip envelope to secure it to the carton. Then if another heavy package is skidded across this one, the label will not be spindled off. When using plain shipping labels, band the carton with 2" clear plastic tape, *over* the label to protect it.

Overseas shipments should be double-boxed. Wrap a carton in the normal manner and then place it inside a second carton. Xerox copier paper cartons are slightly larger than the cartons holding four stacks of 5.5 x 8.5 books, and work very well. Seal the carton and band with reinforcing tape in all three directions to strengthen the package, as well as to guard against splitting.

When assembling cartons with paper tape, cut the tape long enough to hang over the carton by two to three inches on each end. Since folding down the four flaps and taping is a three-hand job, try this: Place the tape on the far long flap, close the carton by pulling the far side toward you and seal the near flap. Then push in the ends and seal the tape to them.

Shipping rates. Obtain both the domestic and international rate booklets from the Post Office, and make up postal charts for both the invoicing and wrapping areas. Inflate the figures on the chart for the invoicing area to allow for the price of the shipping bag, invoice, tape, envelope, the first class postage of the invoice and self-insurance (because you will replace any books which are lost or damaged in transit). It is cheaper to replace a lost book than to pay for Postal insurance.

—Book rate. Most books are shipped with the Post Office at the special fourth class *book rate*. To qualify, books must have at least eight pages, contain no advertising and be permanently bound. Book rate is much cheaper than regular parcel post and there are no Postal zones to compute. The same low rate applies to any destination with a Zip Code from Guam to the Virgin Islands, including APO's and FPO's. If, however, you are shipping a heavy parcel in the first few zones, compare the Postal Service's book rate and their regular parcel post rate along with UPS. The parcel post rate may be lowest.

Postal Rates - February 3, 1991
Surface Book Rate & Library Rate

Lbs.	U.S.	Canada	Foreign	Libraries
1	1.05	1.20	1.36	.65
2	1.48	2.08	2.32	.89
3	1.91	2.88	3.22	1.13
4	2.34	3.68	4.12	1.37
5	2.77	4.48	5.02	1.61
6	3.20	5.28	5.92	1.85
7	3.63	6.08	6.82	2.09
8	3.88	6.88	7.72	2.21
9	4.13	7.68	8.62	2.33
10	4.38	8.48	9.52	2.45
11	4.63	9.28	10.42	+.12/lb.
12	4.88	12 lbs. and over: Use		
13	5.13	"Direct Sack of Prints."		
14	5.38			
15	5.63	Canada:	Rest:	
16	5.88	.64/lb.	.72/lb.	
17	6.13	(9.60	(10.80	
18	6.38	min.)	min.)	
19	6.63			
20	6.88			Use Library Rate
				when shipping to
				libraries, schools,
21	7.13			museums, non-profit
22	7.38			organizations,
23	7.63			or bookstores
24	7.88			owned by schools.
25	8.13			
26	8.38			
27	8.63	First Class		
28	8.88	Oz.	Rate	
29	9.13	1	.29	
30	9.38	2	.52	
		3	.75	Priority Mail
				Lbs. Rate
31	9.63	4	.98	2 2.90
32	9.88	5	1.21	3 4.10
33	10.13	6	1.44	4 4.65
34	10.38	7	1.67	5 5.45
35	10.63	8	1.90	
36	10.88	9	2.13	
37	11.13	10	2.36	
38	11.38	11	2.59	
39	11.63			
40	11.88			

Rate chart

—**Library Rate.** Those packages going to public libraries, school libraries, museums, schools, colleges, universities, and even bookstores associated with academic institutions enjoy the even lower *library rate*. If the addressee has a school address, you may use the lower rate.

—**United Parcel Service** (UPS) provides excellent service including daily pickup, but their prices for single books are not competitive with the Post Office and they require more paperwork. Daily pickup service costs only $5.00 per week. Contact your local UPS office for prices and details in the form of a *UPS Customer Materials Kit.*

By way of comparison, a one pound parcel shipped coast to coast in the U.S. in 1989 would cost the following:

Postal Service
Book rate (surface): 1.05
Library rate (surface): .65
Parcel post (surface): $2.90
Priority mail (air): $2.90
Express Mail (air): $9.70

United Parcel Service
Surface: $2.21
Second Day Air: $5.25
Next Day Air: $13.50

Federal Express
Second Day: $10.50
Overnight: $20.00

Both the Postal Service and UPS will accept parcels up to 70 lbs. Over 50 lbs., however, cartons become unmanageable and are more subject to damage.

—**Overnight delivery companies.** Some customers will want your books right away, so it is wise to offer overnight delivery. Federal Express is the largest of the overnight companies, followed by Airborne, Purolator and Emery. United Parcel Service, the U.S. Postal Service and Federal Express are the three largest second-day delivery services. Most offer pickup service, but charges are lower if you drop off the package at their office or drop box. Check the *Yellow Pages* and call all the overnight services listed for supply kits of envelopes, cartons and bills of lading.

Overnight and fast deliveries to foreign countries vary greatly in price. Always call for prices before selecting a carrier. DHL is the oldest and largest international carrier.

—**International parcels** of printed matter are limited to five kilograms (11 lbs.). Larger shipments must be broken down into 5 kg. increments or wrapped in a larger carton weighing over 15 lbs., inserted into a mail sack and shipped as *direct sack of prints* in *M bags.* Visit your Post Office for some

No. 2 sacks and PS 158 tags. Also take some time to read section 225.953 of the *International Mail Manual.*

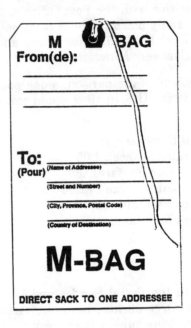

PS 158 tag

To ship in *Direct Sacks of Prints,* line a carton with a heavy plastic bag and insert the books. Make sure the books are tightly packed; that they fit the cartons perfectly. Seal and reinforce the carton in all directions. Then double box by inserting the package into another carton and seal with paper tape. Affix the shipping label with the added words: *Postage paid—Direct Sack of Prints.* Then band with reinforcing tape in all three directions. Weigh the package at this point and affix postage to a PS 158 tag (postage is paid on the contents, not the weight of the bag). Turn the carton on end and slip a No. 2 mail sack down over it. Attach a shipping label to the PS 158 tag and attach the tag to the cinch clip on the mail sack. The Postal Service will pull the package out of the sack at the border, keep the sack and let the package continue by itself.

Customs duty. As long as the carton is plainly marked *Printed Matter—Books,* and it is obvious the contents are books, no customs forms are necessary. But it never hurts to attach the small green tag, PS Form 2976. Few countries charge duty on books.

```
CUSTOMS–DOUANE C 1
May be Officially Opened
(Peut être ouvert d'office)

SEE INSTRUCTIONS ON BACK
Contents in detail:
Désignation détaillée
du contenu: _____

_____
_____
_____

Mark X here if a gift . . . . . . ( )
Il s'agit d'un cadeau

or a sample of merchandise . . . ( )
d'un énchantillon de marchandises

Value: _____ Weight: _____
Valeur          Poids
PS Form 2976, Jan. 1986
```

POD Form 2976

Posting. Weighed and stamped, you can drop the packages off at the loading dock at the rear of the Post Office. Just drop them into a wheeled bin. Do not wait in line at the counter. Most Postal employees do not know much about classes and rates (just quiz one about library rate or direct sacks), so they aren't much help after a long wait in line.

Mail is usually sent from each Post Office to a centralized facility before shipping it out of town. If you drop the packages at this central mail handling facility, they will move out faster and will be subjected to less handling. For these Postal addresses, consult your telephone directory under *U.S. Government*.

Some years ago, the author dropped off a load of packaged books at the branch Post Office where he has his Postal box. Six days later he was dropping off another load at the central mail handling facility and discovered the previous shipment. It had taken the books six days to travel ten miles.

If you like the large 1/4" x 3" rubber bands used by the Postal Service, you can get a box free. Just stop by the bulk mail office and tell them you are planning a large mailing. While there, pick up some mail trays, mail bins and some number 2 mail bags. The trays are useful when processing and carrying large direct mailings of envelopes. The bins can be used to carry many small parcels to the Post Office, and the sacks will be used for Direct Sack shipments. Do not be bashful about asking for bins, sacks and trays. The Postal Service wants to lend them to you, as they make it easier for them to handle the mail.

Once you reach the point of shipping more than 200 packages per week, investigate batching them and shipping at less expensive Bulk Rate.

Postage meters. Metered mail travels faster and is handled less while the possible loss of stamps due to theft is eliminated. Stamped parcels are taken out of the bins at the Post Office, cancelled and thrown back in. A heavy carton may come down on some of your single book packets. Whereas the Postal clerks compare stamps with weight, they rarely return metered mail for more postage. Once your firm has grown and you are afraid some employees might be walking off with stamps, you might consider a meter. You can never stop employees from running a few personal letters through the machine, but this is better than pinching a couple of one dollar stamps every day. A meter imprint makes your publishing company appear more established, by eliminating that postage-stamped *loving hands at home* look. The meter also allows you to print an advertising message on the outgoing mail.

On the other hand, postage meters cost time and money. It takes time to have them reloaded at the Post Office, there is no discount on postage, and they must be rented from the meter company.

Most postage meters come in two parts: the meter and the base unit. The base unit may be purchased outright but the meter (the part holding the postage) can only be rented. Shop for a base unit that handles both envelopes and tapes for packages. Look for bases on the used market: at used business machine stores, swap meets and in the classified ads in local newspapers. Once you have purchased the base, contact the meter dealer for a matching meter. If you contract for your meter first, you will limit yourself in your choice of base units.

Pitney Bowes used to have a lock on the market, but now there are some other companies competing with them. Meters usually rent by the month on a yearly contract. Check prices for each model and make; they vary widely.

Start out with stamps. If you have a lot of stamps to put on and don't like the taste, try an ice cube. Ice cubes never dry out and do not get gummed-up.

First class mail can be handled with a stamper machine filled with rolled stamps. Use the 100 stamp rolls; the rolls of 500 are too heavy to feed well. Stamper machines are less than $20 at most office supply stores.

Meter supplies. Buy regular gummed paper meter tape, the pressure sensitive labels are too expensive. Some rolls of meter tape have the gum on the outside, and some have it on the inside. Get the right one. Tape from sources other than the meter company is often less expensive, but is sometimes a bit too narrow. Shop around. Do not use just any ink in the meter. The red ink supplied by the meter companies is fluorescent and is recognized by postal machinery to turn the envelopes face-up. Do not use substitute ink.

Processing returns is not the best part of the book business. Anytime you are feeling depressed over a return, remember that some large New York publishers get one-third of their books back. In fact, *Publishers Weekly* reported in March of 1987 that many (larger) publishers considered a return rate of 36% to be quite acceptable. Smaller publishers rarely suffer such a high return rate.

When a book comes back, make out a receiving slip. This does not have to be a fancy form, a note on a scratch pad or your notation on their packing slip will do, but you will need some written record. Note the date received, the sender and the condition of the books. Determine whether any damage was caused in mailing, or before shipping, by the condition of the package.

Bookstore shipments almost always arrive damaged because they just will not pack the books correctly. Bookstores will dump the books in a carton without a protective plastic bag or cushioning material, so they rattle around and become scuffed and bent. Or they will place three books in an over-size Jiffy bag to rub against each other as they journey across the country.

On receipt, the good books should be returned to the storage area and the bad ones set aside in their box, pending settling-up with the dealer. Return the damaged books to the dealer with an invoice for the shipping and an explanation regarding the condition. Be sure to mark the books so they will be easy to spot if returned to you again. One publisher places a small black dot with a fine tip felt marker on the bottom edge of the book near the spine.

One well-known eastern book wholesaler frequently orders books, and returns them from different departments on the same day.

The object is to get your books into the stores. If the store has tried your book on the shelf and it hasn't sold, they should not be penalized. If, on the other hand, the book is not shelf worn, but was obviously damaged in return transit due to poor packaging, the store should eat the book.

Books returned by the customer because they were received damaged should be replaced at once. This is a cost of doing business.

Damaged books may be used as review copies, offered to acquaintances as *selected seconds*, and donated to institutions. Some publishers offer them to the walk-in traffic at a 50% discount with the explanation that *all books look like this after a week.*

When an individual retail order is returned by the Post Office marked *undeliverable*, check the original order to verify the address. If the address is wrong, slip the whole book *and* bag into another larger bag so the addressee will see what happened and what took so long. If the address is correct, date the package and put the order and book aside and wait for his or her anxious letter or call.

Some publishers have different order addresses and shipping addresses. It is expensive and disruptive when cartons of books are delivered to the editorial offices. To avoid this problem, require that returns be made on your shipping labels. Add this requirement to your *Returns Policy*.

Alternatives. There are many ways to fulfill your orders besides filling them yourself. The alternatives are listed below.

Remember, however, that you will still need a small shipping facility for review copies and other mailings. Keeping your fulfillment in-house will provide better inventory control, faster shipping of orders, fewer shipping errors, fewer damaged books, and lower fulfillment costs.

—**Joint representation** is where a large publisher accepts a smaller one with like titles. Commonly, the big firm takes over all the marketing, distribution and billing functions as well. But the cost can be high: 20% or more of the net sale. Like the commission sales reps, the firm gets credit for all the sales no matter who generates them. Not only does the arrangement cost more than doing it yourself, you never learn the ropes. You become more dependent than ever. Unless you simply do not have the time or the will to do your own marketing and fulfillment, joint representation should not be considered until you have operated long enough to make an educated decision.

—**Fulfillment warehouses**. If you are unable to spend the time picking, packing and posting, lack the necessary space, or would rather concentrate on writing and marketing, there are commercial fulfillment firms which will do the job. Typically, they may charge per order for packaging, plus postage and packing materials. Expect to pay between $1.50 and $2.50, plus postage, for large orders and fifty cents to $1.00 for single books shipped. Additionally, they may charge per month per skid of books for storage. Figure roughly one cent per book per month for warehousing. You may send your invoices to the these fulfillment warehouses or they will cut the invoices for you.

Fulfillment firms advertise in the classifieds in *Publishers Weekly* and a large listing can be found in *Literary Market Place* under *Shipping Services*; consult your library. For more information on fulfillment, see the Special Report Book Fulfillment. See the Appendix.

Remember that fulfillment houses only store and ship, they do not *sell*. They will not get your books into bookstores or sell subsidiary rights. Moving books from your garage to someone's warehouse does not mean your books have been turned into cash.

You have all the ingredients for being a successful publisher. This book is your recipe.

Chapter Eleven

Computers For Book Publishing

The computer is making self-publishing a more attractive, affordable and competitive option in today's market. This one invention is prompting an explosion in the number of authors deciding to accept the risks and rewards of publishing their own work.

This book has outlined manual methods of writing and publishing, to provide an understanding of the systems. Now, since so many people have access to computers, we will describe their use in writing and publishing.

A personal computer with a word processing program is an expensive typewriter, but a very smart one. It is a typing system which allows instantaneous editing and it has an electronic memory capable of storing everything you keyboard into it. For the writer, the word processor saves time by eliminating both the retyping of previously approved text, and redundant proofreading. The machine removes the possibility of human error inherent in retyping. For the publisher, the computer can be used to set the type and keep the books. For the smaller and newer publisher, the computer makes book publishing possible.

The author has been using a computer since 1980 and he feels it has increased his production 300 to 400%. Book writing is faster and easier with the mechanical cut and paste. News releases are not only easier to write, they can be individually tailored to each magazine. He maintains a list of over 3,000 magazines, sorted by type, to which he sends news releases and review copies. Order fulfillment and accounting are also handled by machine. Contracts, policies and over 80 special letters are all stored in the machine, requiring only minor editing for use. Setting type with a computer and then using a laser printer saves a couple of months and a few thousand dollars on each book. This book is a good example of the results.

Now we will review each step of the writing, editing, typesetting, production, fulfillment, promotion, market research and financial management processes.

Research. With a modem connected to your computer, you can save a lot of time and travel in your research. You may use your computer to search the card file at the local library, make a patent search, and find all sorts of other information. This long distance, electronic research can save you a lot of money, in time and travel away from home.

Writing. There is a lot of "electronic authoring" going on. Because of the computer, more people than ever before are writing.

Computers improve writing. There is a big difference between a manuscript written, edited and typed by hand, and one that has been worked over as many times as necessary to pull every last bit of creativity out of the prose and to wring out every redundant phrase or unnecessary word. People who type original material on a computer usually find that their style improves. They can edit while they type, catch extra words, break up long sentences, and reword for clarity.

Many magazine editors agree that authors who use computers submit articles which are generally free of typos, misspellings and awkward constructions, while being ahead of deadline. These writers can handle assignments on short notice and do not complain about revisions. What is good for magazine writers is good for book writers.

Word processing reduces procrastination. Getting started on a big project is easier. Now random thoughts may be entered, and there is no need to be completely organized. Editing is easier than creating. What is tough is getting thoughts, anything, down on paper in the first place. The machine allows you to get something down on paper to be cleaned-up later.

Books are much easier to write on a word processor. Researched material and raw ideas may be typed into the computer almost randomly. The search feature may be used to locate the right place in the text for the filing of each note. As material is added to the middle of the manuscript, the text grows, not from the end, but in both directions from the center. Then the book may be written from these notes, mostly by filling in the blanks and tying the ideas together. During the editing phase, sentences, whole paragraphs, and even entire chapters will be moved as the text is organized and refined.

Editing may be done on the computer screen before the manuscript is committed to paper. There are never any erasures or correction fluid blemishes. If even the smallest error is found, it is easy to make the change. Only when the document is ready does the computer's printer put it on paper.

With a conventional typewriter, your manuscript is exposed to new errors every time it is retyped. With a word processor, errors are caught and corrected during editing; and the machine keeps those phrases, paragraphs or pages error-free thereafter. Only corrections or additions need be proofed. Some word processors will even mark the revised portions of a document in the margin to indicate which sections need to be proofed. Then on the final printout, the revision marks are deleted. This is especially useful in lengthy manuscripts. With a computer, every iteration of the manuscript is better than the last.

Production. Computerized typesetting has arrived and, ironically, the newer publishers with fewer titles are taking more effective advantage of the new technology than the big New York publishers. The savings in both time and money are enormous.

There are two ways to set type with a computer. The first is to draft and edit the text on a computer and then to communicate it to a typesetter over telephone lines, or drop by the typesetter with your disk. The result is regular photo-composition type. Typically, this saves 30% to 40% in costs and cuts down the time to set a 150-page book from several weeks to a couple of days. Call typesetters in your area and ask if they can set type from your disk. Most can.

The other way is the most exciting: Buy your own computer, word processing software, page makeup software and a laser printer. If you are not able to purchase the printer, use the one at a nearby copy center. For a book, the savings may amount to five weeks of typesetting time, a lot of potentially frustrating and redundant proofreading, and some $2,000 to $6,000 in typesetting charges. With this saving of time and money, not to mention depreciation it is easy to see how an author/publisher can pay for a personal computer in a short time.

The 300 dpi (*dots per inch*) laser printers do a fine job of typesetting. Some people say the slightly ragged edges (under magnification) of the characters reminds them of those produced with (benchmark) wet ink and hot type. Book printers are learning to work with laser typesetting, and are able to reduce the ragged edges in the darkroom. The only people who seem to dislike this new technology are those who stand to lose the most—typesetters.

This book was set in 300 dpi laser type on an Apple Laser-Writer II NT. Look closely at the type and decide whether the quality is high enough for you. Do not let a typesetter talk you into higher resolution if 300 will do the job.

Setting your own type will save you time, save you money, and give you complete control over the project. The cost savings for one or two books will pay for all the equipment—and you will have the computer to write and edit the book, too.

Some writers have sent their work to magazine and book publishers on a disk, so that editing could be done on a screen rather than on paper. This author was the first to send a book to New York reviewers over telephone lines.

Fulfillment. Most personal computers will also run common business accounting programs. With the simple typing of an invoice, the computer will automatically subtract the items from inventory, issue packing slips and labels, then post the figures to accounts receivable and the general ledger. There is no need to re-post the information, no need to enter it twice. Accounting programs save time and avoid human error.

In the beginning, you may use the typewriter and the 33-part label system described. Sooner or later you will want to computerize. Simple programs in dBASE will capture much needed information, but eventually you will want to graduate to an order entry program for publishers. There are a lot of order entry programs, but only a few are tailored to book publishing. Book publishers must track commissions, royalties, differing discounts, and an inventory consisting of large numbers of very few items (titles). Compare that with a hardware store that stocks just a few of each of a great many items.

Most small publishers begin by keeping their books on a cash (as opposed to accrual) system. You will have a hard time trying to find a computer accounting program for cash basis accounting.

For a list of order entry software written for the book publishing industry, see the Appendix.

Promotion. Perfectly phrased form letters incorporating all the key information can be stored in the machine. Correspondence is handled quickly, easily and precisely by calling a form letter to the screen and then adding the date, address block and any customizing changes. Correspondence that used to take hours to compose and produce can be completed in a minute or two—including final typing. While the machine is printing out the letter, you can be stuffing the envelope with the enclosures. Computers speed up your book promotion work, too.

Business Letters for Publishers is a collection of form letters useful in the book trade. It is available on disk, ready to be inserted into your computer. See the Appendix.

Correspondence always fits the letterhead when printed with a computer. If the letter is not perfectly balanced, the margins may be moved or the line spacing may be changed. The retyping is done by the machine.

Word processing programs are well known for producing repetitive "personalized" letters. The operator first types the letter, leaving blanks for certain variables, and then types the mailing list with the variables, such as the amount owed and the date of the sale. The machine "merges" the two lists and the result is a letter to many addressees which incorporates a lot of personal information. This feature is especially useful when querying magazines or doing research.

Computers are very useful in maintaining frequently-revised documents. For example, many businesses must have current price lists; and during periods of high inflation the prices change quite often. As a result, the small changes are written in by hand. Soon the sheet is a mess and has to be retyped. This is no simple task, given all the numbers and columnar work. No wonder the job is continually postponed. With a computer, it is not necessary to retype and reproof the whole page. The typist simply makes the individual changes, proofs only the corrections, and the machine types out the new, clean, error-free document. In just a few minutes, everyone can have a current copy.

The computer may be asked to review the invoices for a list of all those people who have purchased a certain type of book from you. Then when you publish a second book on the same subject, it is a simple matter to send a brochure to all. Before computers, you would have spent days going through your records and typing labels. With your computer, the search can be accomplished in a matter of minutes and the labels or personal letters can be generated while you eat dinner or walk to the mail box.

Mailing lists. There are several ways to keep your list, and the most important consideration is its size. If you have just a handful of highly qualified names, you could use a card file or Rolodex.

But the best way to handle a larger list is with a personal computer and a mailing list or data base program. A computer will allow you to code, sort and print out the names in any order. If you are using a computer to write your book, you should also use it to maintain your list. The computer has made list maintenance practicable: Now all of us can set up, maintain and sell lists. You may use a mailing list program to maintain your lists, but a database program such as dBASE IV is more flexible.

Sort and maintain your lists in Zip Code order so that duplicates will be easier to find, and so they are ready to print out for the mailing house. Use the nine-digit Zip whenever possible, so that duplicate names will be next to each other.

Set up a field for the *list code* so you can separate the list according to the type of book ordered. For example, here at Para Publishing, we have two major lines of books: parachuting and publishing. Since there are very few publishers engaged in parachuting, we do not want to send information on parachute books to them. All buyers are on the same list but the list can be sorted into those interested in one subject or the other.

To print labels, get a high speed dot matrix printer (300 cps) such as the Epson EX-1000. Printing a list of 5,000 can take a long time and your computer is being tied up while the printer is working. The Epson can be purchased, discounted, for less than $600.

If you are maintaining lists of just a few hundred, you may wish to print them out on one-across pressure sensitive labels. If you have larger lists, print out four-across on the wide computer paper for mail house application. Mail houses have Cheshire label cutting/affixing machinery.

Market research. By entering address codes and buyer categories from incoming mail, it is easy to find out where your business is coming from. Once you know who is buying your books and through which promotion/advertising medium, you may plan on how to reach them cheaper and easier. See *Address Codes* in Chapter Seven.

Financial management. In addition to typing and filing, computers will automate many other routine jobs. As you grow, you may consider purchasing a financial package to automate all your accounting procedures: general ledger, accounts receivable, accounts payable, inventory control and payroll. This takes a much larger commitment to automation. For most small publishers a good data base management program will be enough to make the month-end accounting functions easy and correct.

How and what to buy. The computer must be from a company that is stable, with a growing user base so that most updates and peripherals will be available from it and other companies in the future. Your best choice is the Apple Macintosh or the IBM (or its workalike clones).

For the smaller and newer publisher, IBM and Mac are about even now. If you have either system, stick with it; there is no need to change systems. If you have never used a computer, you may be happier with the easier-to-learn Mac. The IBM with the MS-DOS/Windows operating system is an industry standard. If you select IBM, or a workalike, you can always add to it, and it will retain its resale value longer. If you buy the Macintosh, the hardware and software will work together. If you decide on the IBM (or workalike), make sure what you buy will work together.

IBM workalikes are acceptable, if from a stable, growing company with a large installed user base and local repair service. The machine must be **100%** IBM compatible so that it will run all programs. One example is Compaq.

A mouse makes the word processing software easier to learn, and is required for page layout programs.

Monitor. If most of your typesetting will be for 5.5 x 8.5 books, an EGA (Enhanced Graphics Adapter) monitor will be fine, but a VGA monitor will be sharper. If most of your books are 8.5 x 11, you will want a larger (full-page) color screen such as the NEC 5D monitor.

Software. You need a powerful, versatile word processing program, and a page layout program.

If you have an Apple Macintosh, your choices of word processing programs will be *MacWrite* or Microsoft *Word*. MS-*Word* is the newer and more sophisticated program. If you are using an IBM computer or workalike, the three most popular word processing programs are *WordPerfect*, Microsoft *Word* and *Wordstar*, in that order. *Wordstar* is old technology and it ranks third because it has been around so long. *WordPerfect* is very popular in offices, while MS-*Word* is better suited for typesetting. MS-*Word* can be used with a mouse, if desired, making it easier to learn. MS-*Word* was used to write, edit and typeset this book. *Word For Windows* is highly recommended.

When you buy a word processing program, you are marrying the company. Select a popular program so that you will be assured of periodic updates. You want a program that will gain features and functions every year. When buying software, go with the most popular program.

Editing will begin with the features of your word processing software: spelling and thesaurus. Then you may use a grammar checker such as *RightWriter* or *Grammatik III*. Grammar checkers catch double words, noun-verb agreements, punctuation problems, spilt infinitives, lack of capitalization and many other mistakes in grammar, punctuation and style. *Grammatik III* was used on this manuscript before it was turned over to a copy editor for a final look.

XTREE helps to organize the IBM hard disk and provides a more visual directory. It is available from your computer dealer.

dBASE IV is an incredibly useful data base management program. It may be used for mailing list maintenance and ac-counting/inventory control.

Page layout software selection depends on the type of computer you choose. If you are building a system around the Mac, your choices are *PageMaker* or *Ready-Set-Go*. Many people feel *Ready-Set-Go* is better suited for long documents, while *PageMaker* is best for short ones. You must consider whether most of your typesetting will be for books, brochures, newsletters or ads.

If you are building a system around the older IBM XT (or workalike), the only page layout software available is Xerox *Ventura Publisher*. If you have an IBM AT (286, 386 or worka-like), you have a choice of V*entura Publisher* or *Pagemaker*. *Ventura* is generally accepted to be better for longer documents, such as books due to its paragraph tagging feature, while *PageMaker* is better suited to ads and brochures, due to its individual page flexibility. *Ventura* provides typesetting ca-pability with " and " instead of ", •bullets, £, © and — (real em dashes). The vast majority of book publishers today use *Ventura*.

Printers. The Apple LaserWriter is the Cadillac of the in-dustry. It has more memory, the Postscript page description language, and more available fonts. The basic Hewlett-Packard LaserJet Series II is much cheaper and will do the job well, as long as you don't need several different type sizes on the same page. Extra-memory boards are now available for both to smooth out their 300 dpi type.

The next move. Computers take time to learn, but even if you only use them for word processing, they pay off quickly. For the best deal on hardware, visit local computer stores. If you buy hardware through the mail, you may get a better price but you give up local support. Almost everyone needs some help with setup, and it is nice to have someone to call when the computer stops working. Software, on the other hand, is also less expensive by mail, but the support comes from the manuals, tutorials and telephone help line, and local support is not so important.

This book was researched, written, edited, typeset and laid-out on a Compaq 386-20 with a full-page MDS Genius monitor, using Microsoft *Word, Grammatik III, dBASE IV* and *Ventura Publisher*, with output to an Apple LaserWriter II NT. It was later revised on an Everex 486-33 with a 20" NEC 5D color monitor using *Word For Windows* and *Ventura Publisher*. Output was to the same AppleWriter II NT.

For more information on buying and using computers for book publishing, see the Special Report *Computers for Publishers* as well as *Publishing Short-Run Books* by Dan Poynter. See the Appendix.

In-house laser typesetting saves money. But even more important, it provides the publisher with timeliness and control.

Chapter Twelve

Coping With Being Published

or, What Do I Do Now??

Once you become a published author, your life will change. Being in the limelight may not always be as much fun as you used to dream about. This chapter discusses some of the interesting problems you will encounter, and will provide some suggestions on how to deal with them.

Your new status. Your status will change from that private person, the "writer," to a public person, the "expert." Your friends will treat you differently once you are published. Some will be very happy for you and some will be jealous—jealous because they did not write the book. People new in your field will treat you like an idol, while those who have been around for years may be rather unkind.

To autograph your book to a stranger is easy, to autograph for a friend is difficult.—Rex Alan Smith

---

Many new authors do not foresee their new popularity, their celebrity status. There is little you can do about your new treatment except to be prepared for it. Be nice, and in a few years your reputation will be so strong that no one will take swipes at you any more.

Gary Glenn spent 27 years working as a fire investigator. When he and his wife Peggy wrote *Don't Get Burned! A Family Fire-Safety Guide*, life at work changed. The new fire fighters put him on a pedestal, while his contemporaries in the very status-conscious fire fighting community were very cool. This was not the only change. Peggy was known as a successful author-publisher, and Gary was not pleased at being referred to as "Mr. Peggy Glenn" at publishing functions. Now they are colleagues. The book project brought Gary and Peggy closer together, while Gary's in-laws suddenly saw him in a new light.

Bob Johnson wrote a book on the Triathlon. While some of the other ironman athletes were jealous and shunned him, he couldn't get rid of the groupies.

Autographing books is something you will be asked to do both in person and by mail. It is surprising how many prolific authors have never given much thought to how they might autograph a book. Confronted with an admiring fan, they are suddenly at a loss for words. Most authors simply sign: "To Kathy with best wishes," add their signature and sometimes the date. At times you want to be more personal, such as thanking a contributor for his or her help and support on the book. If there is something special about the buyer, include it in your autograph. Often, there is a question of time. On a mail order book, you can dream up something special, while at a well-attended autograph party it is difficult to think about a few well-chosen words while trying to give witty answers. And, by the way, especially when rushed, make sure you spell your buyer's name correctly. In all the hustle, it is easy to draw a blank and misspell the simplest name or word, ruining a book.

Articles. Once your book is published and you become better known, editors will contact you for material. Usually they will ask you to write an article on your subject—something you probably will not have time to do. Additionally, once your book is in print, you will find new, pertinent information and will devise new, unique ways of explaining your program and methods. Your solution to these two problems is the "interview article."

As you think of a point you want to make, draft it in the form of a question and answer. Let these questions and answers build until you have several pages of them entered into your computer. Then when an editor calls, say you are too busy to generate a specific piece, but that you have this Q&A article with all the very latest information. Say they may select the Q&A's most likely to be of interest to their readers, and to call if they need any more. Editors love this system and rarely can think of any more questions. Some editors run the Q&A's as is, while some reporters use them to generate an original article. What is important is that you have supplied an interview with written, well thought-out answers. This system gets editors off your back, saves you a lot of time, fulfills your obligation to the media and generates a lot of publicity for your book.

Spin-off is an important concept. Re-packaging the same information for various markets will bring in more money, while promoting the book. Magazine articles may be extracted from the book, book chapters may be used as a basis for conference workshops, a series of magazine articles may be combined into a book, or the book may be rewritten and directed toward a new audience. With a computer, it is easy to pull out part of the book, and add an introduction and a conclusion.

Always end your article with an "Editor's note" mentioning that the article was extracted from your book, and then give ordering information. Do not simply ask the editor to do this for you; place the words at the end of the article yourself.

Consulting. Many authors consult on their area of expertise. This author consults as a technical expert in parachute and skydiving legal cases. If you decide to sell your time, set your fee schedule early, so you will be ready with figures when you receive a call. Be advised that most beginning consultants price themselves too low. For more information on consulting see *How to Become a Successful Consultant in Your Own Field* by Hubert Bermont. For guidance on legal consulting, see *The Expert Witness Handbook* by Dan Poynter. See the Appendix.

Speaking. As a published author, you will be asked to address all sorts of groups. Make sure the gathering will be large enough to make the trip worth your while. Unless they can guarantee a large group where you may sell a number of books, you should require an honorarium. Insist on some quiet time before your speech so you can gather your thoughts.

Make sure your book can be sold in the back of the room. Do not try to handle the money yourself; you will be too busy handling questions. Try to get the organization sponsoring the event to sell the books and give them a 40% commission on each one they sell. That way, you will gain their support and an implied endorsement for your books. If they do not wish to sell the books, take an assistant to sell them for you.

Place photographic blow-ups of your books at the front of the room when you speak. They will act as *continuous communicators* because your audience will look at them all through the speech.

Provide handouts. The top sheet should have an outline of the speech and the back may contain a list of important contact addresses and a listing of your other products. The outline will help the audience follow your presentation and will suppress questions during your speech. Staple this cover sheet to any supplementary materials and your brochures. Place your handouts near the door so they may be picked up as the audience enters. This system assures that everyone will pick up and keep your promotional materials.

Promotion. Once your book is out, you will have to switch gears and put on your promotion hat. Your creativity will be redirected to brochures, sales letters and advertising copy. When sales slow down, you will have time to write another book. Remember that writing the book is just the tip of the publishing iceberg. The real work begins after you send the boards off to the printer.

Your will. Your book is a valuable asset. Draw up a will or have your current will amended. You will die, but you want your work to live on. Name an executor who understands publishing so that your books and papers will continue. The cost of a will is very little compared to the expenses of taxes and litigation, not to mention the time and the heartache a will could save your family and friends.

Stay in your field. It is nice to have your eggs in more than one basket, but you may spread your talents too thin.

You are an expert in one field—that one in which you are a *participant*. You can stay in that field and become a super expert, or you can branch out into another field and run the risk of being unable to keep up with both of them adequately. Spin off your message into speeches, articles and more books. Do more of what you do best.

The only problem you may encounter by staying in one field is that it may change and leave you without a vocation. For example, if you were an expert (and published books) on brewing beer and Prohibition were passed, you might have difficulty finding work.

Publish more than one book. Wholesalers will be more interested in your publishing company if you have a line of books. Mailing and brochure printing will be more cost effective if you can spread the costs over several titles—there is an economy of scale. With more books, you can pursue repeat business. It is much easier to sell an existing customer than to find a new one. Spin off your information into several products.

Maintain consistent and appropriate packaging. If all your books look alike, you will have a recognizable product line. They will look as though they are members of the same family. Standardize your measurements to facilitate shipping. You want to stock as few shipping cartons and bags as possible.

Ship by the carton. It takes the same amount of time to process an order for a carton of books as it does for one book. Pursue wholesale sales, rather than retail, and you will save valuable time. Pursue non-traditional sales rather than bookstores and you will ship in larger quantities, get paid sooner and will not receive returns.

Place your books in local stores. Then, when fans call up asking where they can purchase your book, you can send them to the store. This approach avoids the awkward situation where fans try to talk you into a free book, and it limits their late-hour visits. A one-hour visit for a one-book sale is not very cost efficient. The store is a more objective sales rep. You don't have to try to talk the customer out of his or her money, while they don't have to decide against the purchase with you standing there.

Do not spend money on advertising until you have exhausted all the free publicity that is available to you. Use book reviews, news releases and, if appropriate to your book, a limited amount of direct mail advertising.

Researching for revisions can bring a few surprises. Other books are likely to come out on the same subject after yours has been published. In reading them, you will find many interesting, though familiar, ideas. Many will be copied from your own work. Remember when you are writing that you are *committing history*—you will be quoted, or at least copied.

Your second book. Your big day arrives when someone calls to order a book and you get to ask "which one?".

Afterword

We *learn by doing*, and your first book will be your hardest. We *learn from our mistakes* and, hopefully, through the use of this book, your mistakes will be small ones. Learn the entire business by doing everything yourself before you begin to "farm out" some of the work. Doing it all yourself will provide you with a better understanding of publishing. I hope it introduces and guides you to a richer, more rewarding life.

The first step, the next one, is up to you. I hope you will take it. As you write, publish and market, refer to this manual. As you learn the business, make notes in it. Tell me your experiences. Let me know where this book may be improved. When you do get that first book into print, please send me a copy—autographed, of course.

Appendix

Your Book's Calendar

One of the biggest pitfalls in small publishing is the lack of sufficient planning, especially the first time around. You don't want to tie up funds by purchasing materials too soon and you don't want to miss some important publicity because you missed a filing date.

This checklist will help to keep you on track. Follow this schedule for your first book. On your second, you will want to move some items up, while skipping some others.

Now

1. Send for five copyright forms. See Chapter Five.

2. Subscribe to *Writer's Digest* and *Publishers Weekly* (or read them at your library). See the Appendix.

3. Join the Publishers Marketing Association. See the Appendix.

4. Review the Appendix. Send for the books, magazines, brochures and catalogs which interest you. Join those associations which can help you.

5. Choose a company name. File a fictitious name statement, if required.

6. Order some office supplies, such as letterhead stationery and envelopes. See Chapter Three and the Appendix.

7. Write to Bowker for ABI information and forms. See Chapter Five.

8. Apply for a Post Office box. See Chapter Three.

9. Read this book completely and highlight important areas.

10. Visit the library and study *Literary Market Place*. Order a copy now or wait until you are finished with your manuscript.

11. Contact the Small Business Administration for its publications. Write SBA, Washington, DC 20416 and request a *Directory of Business Development Publications*.

12. Apply for any local business licenses. Check with the Chamber of Commerce for advice.

13. Send to Para Publishing for a copy of *Publishing Forms, Is There a Book Inside You?, Building a Profitable Business by Chickadel and Straughn* and *The Business Planning Guide* by David H. Bangs. See the Appendix.

While writing your book

1. Review Chapter Two.

2. Write the CIP Office of the Library of Congress for "*Information for Participating Publishers*" and some "Publisher Response" forms. Fill out a form and send it to CIP 30 days before you deliver the manuscript to the printer. See Chapter Five.

3. Send to Bowker for ISBN/SAN information. See Chapter Five.

4. Send to Para Publishing for *Write Right!* by Jan Venolia *and A Business Guide to Copyright Law* by Woody Young.

When your manuscript is nearly complete

1. Send *Requests For Quotations* to 35 printers. See Chapter Four.

2. Send to Bowker for an ISBN log book sheet. See Chapter Five.

3. Design the book covers. Hire a cover designer.

4. Fill out the ABI form. See Chapter Five.

5. Write the Library of Congress for your LCCC number. See Chapter Five.

6. Send a photocopy of your ABI form to Baker & Taylor Co., Academic Library Services Selection Dept., P. O. Box 6920, Bridgewater, NJ 08807.

7. Send to Bowker for your own copy of *Literary Market Place*.

8. Research your title to make sure it is not being used.

9. Get any needed permissions.

10. Send manuscript out for peer review and copy edit.

11. Send to Para Publishing for *Book Production, Publishing Short-Run Books,* and *The Complete Guide to Pasteup* by Walter B. Graham.

When the manuscript is ready to be delivered to the typesetter.

1. Set the publication date. It will be at least five months in the future. See Chapter Seven.

2. Assign the ISBN(s). See Chapter Five.

3. Prepare a news release. See Chapter Seven.

4. Contact book clubs. See Chapter Eight.

5. Apply for a resale permit. See Chapter Three.

6. Send to Para Publishing for a copy of *Pocket Pal* by International Paper.

While the book is being typeset.

1. Set up storage and shipping areas. See Chapter Ten. Send for Para Publishing's Special Report *Book Fulfillment, Order Entry, Picking, Packing and Shipping*.

2. Maintain a good proofreading schedule. Don't hold up your typesetter.

3. Write *Contemporary Authors* for information. See Chapter Five.

4. Prepare mailing lists. See Chapter Nine.

5. Order shipping supplies and the rest of your office supplies. See Chapter Ten and the Appendix.

6. Send photocopies of the boards to certain review magazines. See "pre-publication reviews" in Chapter Seven.

7. Prepare ads for specialty magazines. See Chapter Nine.

8. Send a book announcement to all distributors.

9. Prepare brochure. See Chapter Nine.

10. Send inquiries to reviewers. See Chapter Seven.

11. Mail pre-publication offer. See Chapter Eight.

12. Print book review slips and order rubber stamps. See Chapter Seven.

13. Pursue subsidiary rights. See Chapter Eight.

14. Order reply post cards. See Chapter Seven.

15. Write to *Book Publishers of the United States and Canada* for an application form. See Chapter Five.

16. Write to *Publisher's International Directory* for an application form. See Chapter Five.

17. Write to the *International Directory of Little Magazines and Small Presses* for an application form. See Chapter Five.

18. Send to Para Publishing for Special Reports titled *Book Marketing, A New Approach, Book Reviews, News Releases and Book Publicity, Direct Mail for Publishers, Export/Foreign Rights* and *Buying Book Printing*.

19. Develop your marketing plan using the *Book Marketing* Special Report.

While the books are being printed

1. Proof the bluelines carefully.

2. Prepare review copy materials. Stuff and label the bags, then put aside until books arrive.

3. Mail your pre-publication offer to individuals.

When Book Arrive. (3+ months prior to the official publication date)

1. Check the quality of the books. Make a count for your inventory.

2. Fill orders.

3. Make promotional mailing. See "Copyrights, listings and early reviews" in Chapter Seven.

4. Photograph book and order prints.

5. Print brochure. See Chapter Nine.

6. Pursue dealer sales. You want the books to be in the stores when all the promotion hits on the publication date.

7. Draft magazine articles. See Chapter Seven.

8. File Copyright. See Chapter Five.

9. Pursue book reviews. See "Book reviews" in Chapter Seven.

10. Pursue promotional possibilities per Chapter Eight.

11 Send copy to CIP Office. See Chapter Seven.

12. Send to Para Publishing for the Special Report *Brochures for Book Publishers*.

13. Visit bookstores in your area.

Publication Date

Ninety percent of your initial promotional effort will be done before your official publication date. Your consumer advertising/promotion should be concentrated in the first few weeks after the publication date.

1. Pursue consumer-oriented promotion such as autograph parties, talk shows, author tours, etc. See Chapter Seven.

2. Outline your continuing promotional program.

Ongoing promotion

Never give up. You have given birth to your book, now you have an obligation to raise it. Review what has worked and do more of it. Review what has not worked and cut your losses.

1. Send to Para Publishing for the promotion and marketing books that will be most useful to you. If radio and TV are working for you, get *Publicity for Books and Authors* by Peggy Glenn, *On The Air* by Al Parinello, and *Book Publicity for Authors and Publishers*. If direct mail brings you a good return, get *Successful Direct Marketing Methods* by Bob Stone.

2. Work on non-traditional or special sales.

3. Implement your continuing review program.

4. Consider radio and TV interviews.

5. Consider more direct mail solicitations.

6. Look for spin-off ideas. Repackage your information. Consider consulting in your area of expertise.

7. Make up a review/testimonial sheet. Paste up good reviews and reproduce them.

Resources

Books/Bibliography

Most of these reference books may be found in your local library. In addition, there are many good books on writing, publishing, printing, marketing, distribution and other aspects of book publishing. The best are listed here. As noted, some are available from Para Publishing. Use the order blank. For the rest, you should check the card file in your library, ask the Reference Librarian and visit a nearby bookstore. Then write to the publishers for latest price and delivery information.

Be advised the R.R. Bowker Co. is a large firm with numerous functions, products and services. While they have several offices, most of them are at the same New York and New Jersey addresses. Each office should be treated separately.

Brochures on books of interest to publishers are available from the following.

Publisher's Bookshelf, P. O. Box 4232-890, Santa Barbara, CA 93140-4232.

R.R. Bowker catalog, 249 West 17th Street, New York, NY 10011.

Direct Marketing Association, 6 East 43rd Street, New York, NY 10017

Dustbooks, P.O. Box 100, Paradise, CA 95967

Gale Research Co., Book Tower, Detroit, MI 48226

Towers Book Store, P.O. Box 2038-P, Vancouver, WA 98661.

Writer's Digest Books, 1507 Dana Avenue, Cincinnati, OH 45207.

The Writer, Inc., 120 Boylston Street, Boston, MA 02116

J. Whitaker & Sons, Ltd., 12 Dyott Street, London WC1A 1DF, Great Britain.

Reference books and directories may be used and previewed at the reference desk in your public library. Write to the publishers for ordering details.

—From R.R Bowker, 121 Chanlon Road, New Providence, NJ 07974.

Literary Market Place. Very important. Lists agents, artists, associations, book clubs, reviewers, exporters, magazines, newspapers, news services, radio and TV, and many other services. Annual.

International Literary Market Place. Lists sources outside the U.S. and Canada.

Publishers' Trade List Annual. A compilation of 1,500 publishers' catalogs.

Publishers of the United States. A directory.

Ulrich's International Periodicals Directory. Lists magazines.

Irregular Serials and Annuals.

Translation and Translators: An International Directory and Guide.

International Book Trade Directory. Lists 30,000 booksellers in 170 countries that handle U.S. publications.

American Book Trade Directory. Lists 24,000 booksellers, wholesalers, etc.

American Library Directory. Lists 30,000 U.S. and Canadian libraries.

International Publishers Imprints, Agents and Distributors Directory.

Books in Print. Lists all books currently available by subject, title and author. Annual.

Forthcoming Books. Books that will appear in the next edition of *Books in Print.*

—From K.G. Saur Publishing, Inc., 121 Chanlon Road, New Providence, NJ 07974.

American Publishers Directory
International Books in Print
International Directory of Booksellers
World Guide to Libraries
Publishers International Directory

—From B. Klein Publications, P.O. Box 8503, Coral Springs, FL 33065.

Guide to American Directories.

Mail Order Business Directory. Over 10,000 mail order and catalog houses.

Directory of Mailing List Houses

—From Dustbooks, P.O. Box 100, Paradise, CA 95967

International Directory of Magazines and Small Presses. A comprehensive listing of smaller publishers.

Small Press Record of Books in Print.

Directory of Small Magazine/Press Editors and *Publishers International Yearbook*

—From Editor and Publisher, 11 West 19th Street, New York, NY 10011

Market Guide
International Yearbook
Directory of Syndicated Features

—From Gale Research Co., Book Tower, Detroit, MI 48277-0748. Send for catalog.

Encyclopedia of Associations
Directory of Publications (Formerly Ayer Directory of Publications)
Newsletters in Print
International Directories in Print
Directories in Print
Association Periodicals
Publishers Directory
Business, organizations, Agencies, and Publications Directory
Standard Periodical Directory (Oxbridge)
Directory of Special Libraries
Contemporary Authors

—From Writer's Digest Books, 1507 Dana Avenue, Cincinnati, OH 45207

Writer's Market
Writers Yearbook
Writer's Digest Books also publishes many specific publishing books such as how to publish cookbooks, children's books, etc.

—From Oxbridge Communications, Inc., 150 Fifth Avenue, New York, NY 10011

Oxbridge Directory of Newsletters
College Media Directory

—Books from publishers with one reference

Selling Books in the Bay Area
Karen Misuraca
Lagoon Publications
P.O. Box 309
Mill Valley, CA 94942

Book Buyers Handbook
American Booksellers Association
137 West 25th Street
New York, NY 10001

Broadcasting/Cable Yearbook
1705 DeSales Street, NW
Washington, DC 20036

Dewey Decimal Classification and Relative Index
Forest Press, Inc.
85 Watervliet Avenue
Albany, NY 12206-2082

Direct Mail List Rate & Data
Standard Rates and Data Service, Inc.
3004 Glenview Road
Wilmette, IL 60091

Larimi Media Guides
5 West 37th Street
New York, NY 10018

Membership Directory
Marketing to Libraries Through Library Associations
American Library Association
50 East Huron Street
Chicago, IL 60611

National Trade and Professional Associations of the U.S. and Canada
Columbia Books, Inc.
1350 New York Avenue NW #207
Washington, DC 20005

National Union Catalog
Library of Congress
Available in your local library

Working Press of the Nation. Lists newspapers, magazines, radio, TV, feature writers and internal publications.
National Research Bureau
310 South Michigan Avenue, #1150
Chicago, IL 60604

Buy Books Where-Sell Books Where?
Ruth E. Robinson Books
Rt #7, Box 162-AA
Morgantown, WV 26505

Directory of Specialized American Bookdealers
The Moretus Press
P.O. Box 1080
Ossining, NY 10562-1080

Directory of Specialist Bookdealers in the U.K. Handling Mainly New Books
Peter Marcan Publications
31, Rowliff Road
High Wycombe, Bucks., HP12 3LD
Great Britain

Proofreading Manual and Reference Guide
Directory of Editorial Resources
Peggy Smith
Editorial Experts
66 Canal Center Plaza, #200
Alexandria, VA 22314-1538

Self-Publish Your Own Picture Book
Howard Gregory
640 The Village #209
Redondo Beach, CA 90277

Yearbook of Experts, Authorities & Spokespersons
Mitchell P. Davis
2233 Wisconsin Avenue NW #406-P
Washington, DC 20007-4104

The (British) *Post Office Direct Mail Handbook*
Les Andrews.
Exley Publications
16 Chalk Hill
Watford, Herts, WD1 4BN
Great Britain

Books on writing, printing, publishing, promotion, marketing and distribution.

Publisher addresses can be found in *Books in Print*. Books may also be ordered from Publisher's Bookshelf, P.O. Box 4232-890, Santa Barbara, CA 93140-4232. (805) 968-7277. Shipping is $2.00 for the first book and .75 for each additional book. The sales tax for books shipped to California addresses is 7.75%. Use the order blank on the last page.

Radio/TV Interviews

Book Publicity for Authors and Publishers by Larry J. Rochester. You will learn how to gain maximum publicity for your book and author through radio and TV interviews. Rochester is a media producer and talk show host who tells you the inside secrets of interviews.

ISBN 0-881447-00-6 Softcover, 5.5 x 8.5, 168 pages $16.95

On The Air, How to Get on Radio and TV Talk Shows and What to do When You Get There by Al Parinello. The subtitle says it all! Parinello takes you step-by-step through the whole process so there won't be any surprises. Complete with station names and addresses.

ISBN 0-934829-85-3 Softcover, 6 x 9, 190 pages $12.95

Publicity for Books and Authors by Peggy Glenn shows authors and publishers how to get free and effective publicity for their books. The author shares her own experiences on television talk shows, radio, with magazines and newspapers—what worked and what did not. Author/publisher Glenn knows the theory of promotion, practices it with success and teaches it well. Examples and ideas.

ISBN 0-936930-91-8 Softcover, 8.5 x 11 182 pages $12.95

Print Promotion

The Copy Writer's Handbook by Robert Bly. You will learn how to write stimulating, wallet-grabbing copy that makes readers respond with book orders. Bly reveals the copy writing techniques that will help you draft brochures, ads, commercials and direct mail pieces--that get more attention and sell more books.

ISBN 0-8050-1194-3 Softcover, 5.5 x 8.25, 352 pages $12.95

Words That Sell by Richard Bayan is a thesaurus designed to be used to promote products, services and ideas. This unusual *advertising copy stimulator* provides a *short course* in writing advertisements and lists synonyms for the words you want to use. Useful and unique; worth every penny—ad copy writers cost a lot more. New lower price. One of our top sellers.

ISBN 0-87280-150-0 Softcover, 8.5 x 8.75 128 pages $12.95

Book Publishing Resource Guide is a directory by Marie Kiefer that will help you find the many resources you need for book production and promotion. It also lists the top wholesalers, book fairs, mailing list sources, books on publishing, fulfillment houses, marketing directories and much more. Essential reference.

ISBN 0-912411-28-7 Softcover, 8.5 x 11 320 pages $24.95

The Publicity Manual by Kate Kelly is all about promotion. She tells you how to increase the visibility of your books through free publicity in newspapers, magazines, newsletters, trade journals, radio and television. A complete and inexpensive course in publicity. Examples.

ISBN 0-9603740-1-9 Softcover, 8.5 x 11 243 pages $19.95

Book Fairs, An Exhibiting Guide for Publishers by Dan Poynter, contains everything you need to successfully select, arrange and operate a booth at a book fair. It contains inside tips on how to work a fair to your maximum advantage whether you are staffing a booth or working the floor. Required reading for first time exhibitors and a valuable reminder/checklist for the seasoned veteran. Don't leave for an exhibit without it.

ISBN 0-915516-43-8 Softcover 5.5 x 8.5 96 pages $7.95

Marketing

Successful Direct Marketing Methods by Bob Stone. This is the *Bible* for marketing your book via direct mail, magazines, newspapers and broadcasting direct to your reader. "Direct Marketing" is where smaller publishers of narrow-market books have the advantage over the big New York publishers. Learn how to select mailing lists and media to go direct to your customers at the least possible cost. A well-known book by a master in the field. *New, expanded edition.* Highly recommended. Glossary.

ISBN 0-87251-040-9 Hardcover, 7.5 x 9.5 575 pages $34.95

Book Marketing Made Easier, a Do-it-Yourself Marketing Kit for Book Publishers by John Kremer. How to work with wholesalers/distributors, get into bookstores, sell to catalogs, and approach all the non-traditional book markets. This is a goldmine of step-by-step book marketing procedures and ideas. Examples, resources and more.

ISBN 0-912411-34-1 Softcover 6 x 9, 384 pages $19.95

Mail Order Selling Made Easier, A Step-By-Step Guide to Organizing and Carrying Out a Successful Direct Marketing Program by John Kremer. A hands-on working guide with worksheets, sample letters, charts, checklists and the procedures you need to use direct marketing in your business. Kremer shows you how to design your direct mail package, select mailing lists, design and place ads in magazines, newspapers, radio & TV, while he discusses telemarketing, card decks, response formulas, and catalogs. Large resource section. **New**.

ISBN 0-912411-29-5 Hardcover, 6.25 x 9.25 288 pages $19.95

Selling to Catalog Houses by Ron Playle tells you how to sell books to mail order catalog houses. Contains sample letters, pricing guidelines and many addresses. This brief book is the very best on the subject.

Softcover, 8.5 x 11 48 pages $8.95

1001 Ways to Market Your Books by John Kremer is simply a most creative, informational and useful manual on book marketing. Kremer writes from detailed research and hard-earned experience. He covers advertising, promotion, distributors, bookstores, book design, libraries, spinoffs, and much more. In fact, there is little he does not cover and cover well. This is not a *basic* book.

ISBN 0-912411-19-8 Softcover, 6 x 9 384 pages $14.95

Pasteup and Layout

Book Design & Production for the Small Publisher by Malcolm E. Barker shows you how to *design* your book to achieve total harmony: Working with type, laying out the pages, photographs/halftones, and cover design. Part Two deals with production: Finding help, dealing with typesetters & printers, and materials. If you are responsible for book design, you need the only book on the subject. Outstanding and **New**.

ISBN 0-930235-08-8 Softcover, 8.5 x 11 233 pages $24.95

Complete Guide to Pasteup by Walter B. Graham is a definitive course in preparing camera-ready copy for printing. Graham reveals numerous time-saving and money-saving pasteup secrets and shortcuts. Clear step-by-step procedures for books and brochures; generously illustrated. If you perform pasteup functions or supervise pasteup, you need this book. Illustrated glossary.

ISBN 0-912920-40-8 Softcover, 8.5 x 11 216 pages $19.95

Publishing Short–Run Books, How-to Paste up and Reproduce Books Instantly Using Your Quick Print Shop by Dan Poynter, is a revolutionary concept in *short–run book manufacture*. This is the ideal production system for educators needing just a few copies for a class, business managers needing a special look for a presentation, authors who are trying to get the attention of a publisher (it is easier to sell a book than a manuscript), poets who desire a small private printing, and anyone who is in a hurry to break into print. Full of inside pasteup tips and techniques.

ISBN 0-915516-61-6 Softcover, 5.5 x 8.5 144 pages $5.95

Contracts

Business & Legal Forms for Authors & Self-Publishers by Tad Crawford provides *actual tear-out forms and contracts*, explains each one and offers negotiation check-off lists. Some of the contracts are: Author-agent, author-publisher, collaboration, licensing of audio rights, lecture contract, privacy release, permission form, nondisclosure agreement, publisher-book designer, publisher-printer, sales representative, book distributor, copyright transfer, invoice and confirmation of assignment. Essential.

ISBN 0-927629-03-8 Softcover, 8.5 x 11 176 pages $15.95

Publishing Agreements by Charles Clark provides several sample book contracts with explanations of each paragraph. Contracts range from those for general books to academic books, to paperback rights, translator's agreements, a book club contract and much more. Out of print for eight months, we now have a stock of the **new** revised third edition.

ISBN 0-941533-56-5 Hardcover, 6 x 9 238 pages $29.95

Business

Building a Profitable Business by Charles Chickadel & Greg Straughn is a proven step-by-step guide for starting and running your own business. This workbook will teach you all about business development, marketing, operations, administration and finance. Don't start a business unprepared. You need a solid foundation before you build. NEW!

ISBN 0-929586-02-6 Wirebound, 9 x 11, 324 pages $26.95

The Business Planning Guide, Creating a Plan for Success in Your Own Business by David H. Bangs. How to set up a business, organize, get your paperwork together, register in the proper places and borrow money. Strongly recommended.

ISBN 0-936894-10-5 Softcover, 8.5 x 11 149 pages $19.95

Financial Feasibility in Book Publishing by Robert Follett presents a step-by-step method for evaluating the financial future of new book projects. Worksheets, guidelines, projection methods, rules of thumb and estimating methods with explanations help you decide whether your book will make money. Highly recommended.

ISBN 0-931712-07-6 Softcover, 8.5 x 11 64 pages $12.95

How to Become a Successful Consultant in Your Own Field by Hubert Bermont tells you how to capitalize on your years of experience by opening a new profit center. How to get started, how to find clients, what to charge, proposal and report writing, how to handle clients and more. The best book on the subject.

ISBN 0-930686-22-5 Softcover, 7 x 10, 147 pages $14.95

Small Time Operator, How to Start Your Own Small Business, Keep the Books, Pay Your Taxes & Stay Out of Trouble! by Bernard Kamoroff, C.P.A. Kamoroff covers licenses, permits, business setup, bookkeeping, accounting, business expansion, taxes, deductions, and more. This is *the* book on accounting written and published by a small publisher. 35th printing, over 330,000 in print!

ISBN 0-917510-10-0 Softcover, 8.5 x 11 192 pages $14.95

Small Business: The Tax Advantage by Gena Ceci Hester and James McCornack tells you all about deductions and taxes. Operating your own business allows to you write off your lifestyle. Suddenly many of your trips, electronic toys and dining out are deductable. Full of interesting details and easy to read.

ISBN 0-879592-03-7 Softcover, 5.25 x 8.25, 112 pages $12.95

Product Development and Editing

Is There a Book Inside You?, A Step-By-Step Plan for Writing Your Book by Dan Poynter and Mindy Bingham is a step-by-step plan for writing your book. Now available in a completely revised third edition. You will learn: How to pick your topic, how to break it down into easy-to-attack projects, how and where to do research, a process that makes writing (almost) easy, how to improve your material, how to manage writing partnerships, how to evaluate your publishing options, as well as how to develop an individualized and workable plan. They will show you how to write your book, get the help you need and publish or get it published. With self-paced quizzes and resources. A Writer's Digest Book Club main selection.

ISBN 0-915516-68-3 Softcover, 236 pages. $14.95

Is There a Book Inside You? (audio tapes & book) by Dan Poynter and Mindy Bingham is a step-by-step plan for writing your book. Complete and unabridged, an album containing six one-hour cassettes and a copy of the new, third edition of the book. Now, you may listen while driving and have a book to refer back to.

ISBN 0-915516-73-X (Tape P-102 and book). $69.95

How to Make a Whole Lot More Than $1,000,000.00 Writing, Commissioning, Publishing and Selling "How-To" Information by Jeffrey Lant is an exhaustive, absolute last word on information creation and selling. This book says it all and is the best there is. Highly recommended to nonfiction book publishers.

ISBN 0-940374-16-1 Softcover, 6 x 9 552 pages $34.95

Self-Publishing to Tightly-Targeted Markets by Gordon Burgett describes the T-C-E approach to successful publishing. Burgett shows you how to Target your market, Customize your material for it and then Expand by spinning-off material into other formats. An eye-opener and very good advice. **New**.

ISBN 0-910167-17-6 Softcover, 6 x 9 200 pages $14.95

Write Right! by Jan Venolia. This desk drawer digest of punctuation, grammar and style is an important reference which should be next to your dictionary. Demonstrating proper usage with quotes from literature and politics, *Write Right!* makes editing reports and books easy and fun. This style manual is essential when copy editing. Over 200,000 sold.

ISBN 0-89815-061-2 Softcover, 5.5 x 7 127 pages $5.95

A Business Guide to Copyright Law by Woody Young explains the new copyright law. The authors show you how much research material you may legally use and how to protect your work from others. They cover fair use, permissions, licensing, foreign protection, registration procedures and much more. Examples of forms. Glossary.

ISBN 0-939513-51-X Softcover, 8.5 x 11 98 pages $14.95

Book Writing and Publishing (audio tape). Dan Poynter on how to write and publish books. Reasons to write a book, what to write, how to write, publishing options, how to self-publish and the secrets of successful self-publishing. One 76-minute cassette with workbook and resources.

ISBN 0-915516-75-6 (Tape P-101). $14.95

Photographer's Publishing Handbook by Harold Davis. Turn your photos into cards, posters and books and find a publisher (list of photography publishers included) or publish yourself. Resources and sample contracts. NEW!

ISBN 0-929667-07-7 Softcover, 8.5 x 11, 184 pages $19.95

Let Your Ideas Speak Out, A Guide to Preparing and Marketing Spoken Words on Audiotape and CD by Eugene Wheeler and Rennie Mau. Turn your books into audio tapes. Resources, contracts, release forms, and sample budgets. NEW!

ISBN 0-934793-33-6 Softcover, 5.5 x 8.5, 96 pages $8.95

Publishing

How to Get Happily Published by Judith Appelbaum. How to write, find a publisher, locate an agent or publish yourself by an author with years of varied experience in New York publishing. Learn how the book publishing industry works. This is a gold mine of publishing information with a lengthy resource section. All **new** third edition.

ISBN 0-06-273133-5 Softcover, 5.25 x 8, 317 pages $9.95

The Self-Publishing Manual, How to Write, Print & Sell Your Own Book by Dan Poynter is a complete course in writing, publishing, marketing, promoting and distributing books. It takes the reader step–by–step from idea, through manuscript, printing, promotion and sales. Along with an in-depth study of the book publishing industry, the book explains in detail numerous innovative book marketing techniques. *The Manual* is a *Bible* for writers and a constant reference for publishers.

ISBN 0-915516-74-8 Softcover, 5.5 x 8.5 352 pages $19.95

Your Book Publishing Choices (audio tape). Dan Poynter will give you the tools to make an educated decision between sending your manuscript to a large (New York) publisher, a medium sized specialized publisher, a vanity or subsidy publisher, a book packager or producer, an agent or self-publishing--doing it yourself. He discusses your choices, tells the four things you must do if you sell out to a big publisher and shares the seven secrets to successful self-publishing. One 60-minute cassette with workbook and resources.

ISBN 0-915516-76-4 (Tape P-103) $14.95

Printing

Pocket Pal, A Graphic Arts Production Handbook from International Paper. This is the best basic reference on pre-press and printing. It provides specifications and descriptions for paper (weight, comparisons, etc.), inks, copy preparation, film imposition, the mechanics of printing, binding and much, much more. Invaluable reference; you will always look it up in *Pocket Pal* first.

Order #91838 Softcover, 4.25 x 7.5 216 pages $9.95

Special Reports on various aspects of publishing by Dan Poynter

Book Marketing: A New Approach is a low-cost marketing plan for your book. It leads you through the three-step plan for selling direct to the buyer, the five-step plan for selling to bookstores, the seven-step plan for libraries, all the subsidiary rights and our specialty: the more lucrative non-traditional markets. This step-by-step plan will make sure you have completely covered every possible market. An absolute goldmine of book promotion references and sources. **Start your book promotion with this Special Report.**

ISBN 0-915516-58-6 71 pages $14.95

Book Reviews shows you in detail how to take advantage of the free publicity available to books from the pre-publication galleys to a continuing review program. **Book reviews are your least expensive and most effective form of book promotion.** Reviews are not hard to get if you follow the unwritten (until now) rules. This Report provides paint-by-the-numbers instructions for making galleys and describes in a detailed action plan how to set up a review program so your books will be reviewed again and again. It covers pre-publication reviews, early reviews, retail reviews and continuing reviews with examples of the packages for each. The Report even tells you what to do with the reviews after you receive them. Complete with lists of major reviewers and sources for the rest. Examples and resources.

ISBN 0-915516-56-X 53 pages $19.95

News Releases and Book Publicity shows you how to draft news releases and other publicity for your books. After book reviews, news releases are your most effective and least expensive form of book promotion and you may send one out every month. Yet, few publishers use or even know about news releases. Newspaper and magazine editors want to pass on interesting information to their readers. The trick is to draft an interesting news release (tied into your book) that the editor will want to use. Editorial matter is believed, advertising is viewed with skepticism. Do not spend money on advertising when you can use the same effort and less money to send off a news release. If you are not sending out a news release on each book every 30 days, get this Report. Step-by-step instructions, paint-by-the-numbers format outlines, many examples and resources are included.

ISBN 0-915516-52-7 4 pages $19.95

Direct Mail for Book Publishers shows how you can compete with the larger publishers by taking your message direct to the reader. Study the rules of direct mail such as repetition, timing, response formulas and profit analysis. Learn to find and evaluate lists. Follow the plan for drafting your brochure and cover letter; assemble a direct mail package that brings results. This Report also shows you how to assemble your own lists to rent to others—providing you with a new profit center. If you have a non-fiction book with an identifiable audience (and can find or assemble a mailing list for it), you may use direct mail successfully to sell books.

ISBN 0-915516-59-4 55 pages $19.95

Exports/Foreign Rights: Selling U.S. Books Abroad shows you how to expand your markets by selling direct to foreign readers, using an exporter in the U.S., contracting with a foreign distributor, and selling subsidiary rights to foreign publishers with variations such as international book packaging, co-production and format rights. Special sections cover options, taxes, shipping, agents, the Frankfurt Book Fair and more. Exports expand your market while foreign rights are frosting in your publishing cake: they bring in revenue while the sale amounts to a significant endorsement for your book. These endorsements help to sell more books at home. Complete with sample contracts, Postal rate charts, sample letters and instructions for locating compatible foreign publishers. Glossary and an Appendix full of resources.

ISBN 0-915516-57-8 57 pages $19.95

Buying Book Printing answers the question we hear most: How to find the best and least expensive printer for your particular book. Each printer is set up to manufacture certain kinds of books. Specialties vary depending on type of binding, book measurements, print-run, etc. This Report shows you how to make up a *Request for Quotation* and provides a mailing list of printers who specialize in book manufacture. A section on **color** printing describes how to contact local representatives of Hong Kong and other foreign printers. This Report tells you how to decide how many books to print, how to select the appropriate binding, what to look for when checking bluelines, should you use a printing broker, how to evaluate quotations, what kind of a printing job you can expect, how to inspect the final product, and even how to resolving disputes. This Report will save you thousands of dollars in printing, binding and trucking costs. Includes an action plan, forms, sample letters and an Appendix full of resources.

ISBN 0-915516-55-1 57 pages $14.95

Book Production: Composition, Layout, Editing, Design, Getting it Ready for Printing shows you how to prepare your manuscript for the printer. Good packaging sells breakfast food, pantyhose and hair spray; it should be used to sell books. Now that you have poured your heart and soul into the manuscript, you must package the information well to encourage people to buy it. This Report describes good book packaging and shows you how to layout the inside (the text) and well as the outside (the cover). The text should go through several drafts for content, peer review and copy edit. The front matter and back matter must be in the proper order. The Report shows you how to select a title that will not only describe but sell the book. It shows you how to lay out your back cover copy with a paint-by-the-numbers form. Tells you where to get bar codes and discusses appropriate binding methods. If you do not have the time or expertise to do the jobs yourself, this Report tells you where to get help. Complete with a production schedule, an action plan and an Appendix full of resources.

ISBN 0-915516-62-4 42 pages $19.95

Book Fulfillment: Order Entry, Picking, Packing and Shipping explains in detail how to set up and run your shipping department. The Report covers **order taking** (letter openers, credit cards, card terminals, 800 numbers, fax, order services, order forms, and discount structures); **order processing** (computer hardware and software, shipping labels, short slips, bad checks, overpayments, invoices, back orders, the Federal Trade Commission rules, complaints, book return policy, statements and collections); **inventory and storage** (shipping instructions to printer, book receiving, book returns, inventory control, stacking, and shipping room layout) and book packaging (how to wrap, where to get and how to use shipping bags and car-

tons, machinery such as tape dispensers, scales, postage meters and bag sealers with sources, using UPS, Direct Sacks and various Postal rates, foreign shipping and customs duty). Then the Report covers the alternatives to in-house fulfillment: using wholesalers, distributors, joint representation and fulfillment warehouses with a list of those to contact. Complete with forms and shipping rate charts, an action plan and an Appendix full of resources.

ISBN 0-915516-64-0 86 pages $19.95

Selling Book in the United States, a Guide for Foreign Publishers lists six ways to establish a presence in the U.S. and suggests foreign publishers promote books just as U.S. publishers do: With book reviews, news releases and, if appropriate to the title, with a limited amount of direct mail advertising. Details and resources. This Report is not for U.S.-based publishers.

ISBN 0-915516-60-8 13 pages $9.95

Publishing Contracts, Sample Agreements for Book Publishers on Disk is a collection of the 22 most needed legal documents covering every facet of the book publishing business including: An author-publisher contract for a trade book, a publisher-illustrator agreement, a foreign rights agreement and 19 more. Just slip the disk into your computer, call the appropriate contract to the screen, fill in the names and check the suggested percentages. Then print out these 12-page contracts. You do not have to draft the agreements, you do not even have to type them. Available for the IBM PC and workalikes (specify) and virtually any word processing program such as Microsoft *Word, WordPerfect, Wordstar* and many more (specify) and the Apple Macintosh with Microsoft *Word* or *MacWrite*

ISBN 0-915516-46-2 (Disk) $29.95

Business Letters for Publishers, Creative Correspondence Outlines is a collection of 75 letters drafted especially for publishers. They save time for the older firm and enable the newer publisher to establish company policy which conforms to current, sometimes peculiar, publishing industry standards. Available on disk for the IBM PC and workalikes (specify) and virtually any word processing program such as Microsoft *Word, WordPerfect, Wordstar* and many more (specify) and the Mac with *Word* or *MacWrite.* Now you not only do not have to draft the letters, you do not have to type them.

ISBN 0-915516-47-0 Computer disk $29.95

Publishing Forms, *A Collection of Applications and Information for the Beginning Publisher.* Get your new book listed in all the right directories easily and registered with appropriate agencies correctly. Included are applications for ABI, LC, copyright, and more. Important reviewer, wholesaler and other contacts are supplied.

ISBN 0-915516-38-1 71 pages $14.95

Brochures for Book Publishers shows you how to draft and print full color brochures for less than you are currently paying for black and white locally. Imagine full color brochures for less than four cents each! This Report covers everything from choosing the right photographer to money-saving tricks and even includes a sample request for quotation (RFQ) letter, a mailing list of specialized brochure printers and examples of color brochures. Complete with an action plan and an Appendix full of resources.

ISBN 0-915516-48-9 30⁺ pages $19.95

Bookshelf, a New Profit Center for Publishers shows how to establish a sideline business to offer other publishers' books to your customers. Combining complementary (non-competing) books with your books makes your brochures and mailings more economical while establishing you as a one-stop source for information on your subject. This Report tells you how to find complementary books, how to negotiate with their publisher (even the big ones will give you 50% if you approach the right department) and how to promote your new bookshelf. Includes an action plan, examples of large publisher discount schedules, forms, sample letters and resources.

ISBN 0-915516-54-3 40 pages $14.95

Computers for Publishers: Writing/Editing/Typesetting/Accounting helps publishers to make the tough decisions on computer hardware and software acquisitions. Complete with an action plan and an Appendix full of resources.

ISBN 0-915516-51-9 15 pages $4.95

Questions and Answers on Book Publishing covers the basics and a lot of new material in an interview format. There are lots of small pieces of vital and encouraging publishing information which do not fit in our other Reports. All authors should draft a series of questions and answers on their topic specialty so they may be supplied to editors for interview articles. This is a very cost-efficient way to get free publicity.

ISBN 0-915516-49-7 28 pages $7.95

Merchant Card Status. How to apply so your customers may pay by card. Most banks will not provide merchaant status to publishers engaged in telephone order or mail order as well as those operating from their home. This report will show you a system for overcoming these obstacles almost every time. Complete details on credit card terminals, printers, should you deal with Independent Sales Organizations (ISOs) and more. Resources.

ISBN 0-915516-71-3 34 Pages $14.95

Cooperative Book Promotion describes the many programs which enable publishers to join together to lower marketing costs. This Report describes the mail, exhibit and other programs run by several firms and associations and shows you how to run your own. Complete with an action plan and coop plan source addresses.

ISBN 0-915516-50-0 17 pages $5.95

Beyond Remainders describes creative inventory reduction. When sales of a book drop off, it is time to move out the balance before they get too old and to make room for new books. There are many easy ways to reduce inventory besides remaindering and they bring in more money. Forms, an action plan, sample letters, addresses and resources are included.

ISBN 0-915516-53-5 23 pages $14.95

To order these reports, see the order blank on the last page.

Professional organizations. Write for an application and inquire about benefits and dues. Many associations publish a magazine or newsletter. For a list of writers' associations, see *Writer's Market*.

Publishers Marketing Association
Jan Nathan
2401 Pacific Coast Hwy #102-A
Hermosa Beach, CA 90254
(310) 372-2732

Association of American Publishers
220 East 23rd Street
New York, NY 10010
(212) 689-8920

COSMEP
P.O. Box 703-P
San Francisco, CA 94101
(415) 922-9490

New Age Publishing & Retailing Alliance
P.O. Box 9
Eastsound, WA 98245
(206) 376-2702

Colorado Indep. Publishers Assn.
3031 Fifth Street
Boulder, CO 80304-2501
(303) 449-8474

Texas Publishers Association
2315 Briarwood Drive
San Antonio, TX 78209-4259

Publishers Association of the South
P.O. Box 43533
Birmingham, AL 35243-3533

Catholic Press Association
119 North Park Avenue
Rockville Center, NY 11570
(516) 766-3400

American Booksellers Association
560 White Plains Road
Tarrytown, NY 10591
(800) 637-0037

Christian Booksellers Association
P.O. Box 200
Colorado Springs, CO 80901.
(719) 576-7880

Direct Marketing Association
6 East 43rd Street
New York, NY 10017

Book Publicists of Southern California
Irwin Zucker
6430 Sunset Blvd #503
Hollywood, CA 90028
(213) 461-3921

Marin Small Publishers Association
P.O. Box 343-P
Ross, CA 94957

American Library Association
50 East Huron Street
Chicago, IL 60611
(312) 944-6780

Association of American University Presses
One Park Avenue
New York, NY 10016
(212) 889-6040

Society for Scholarly Publishing
P.O. Box 53421
Washington, DC 20009-3421

Association of Canadian Publishers
260 King Street East
Toronto, ON M5A 1K3
Canada

Independent Publishers Guild
147-149 Gloucester Terrace
London W2 6DX, Great Britain

Magazines for publishers. Write for a sample copy and current subscription rates.

Publishers Marketing Assn Newsletter
Jan Nathan
2401 Pacific Coast Hwy #102-A
Hermosa Beach, CA 90254
(310) 372-2732

Publishers Weekly
249 West 17th Street
New York, NY 10011
(212) 645-0067

Library Journal
249 West 17th Street
New York, NY 10011
(212) 645-0067
(212) 337-6812

School Library Journal
249 West 17th Street
New York, NY 10011
(212) 645-0067

American Bookseller Magazine
560 White Plains Road
Tarrytown, NY 10591
(800) 637-0037

Small Press Magazine
Rt #1, Colonial Hill
Mt. Kisko, NY 10549-9801

ALA Booklist
50 East Huron Street
Chicago, IL 60611
(312) 944-6780

Choice
Patricia E. Sabosik
100 Riverview Ctr.
Middletown, CT 06457
(203) 347-6933

Kirkus Reviews
Anne Larsen
200 Park Avenue South
New York, NY 10003
(212) 777-4554

Horn Book Magazine
(children's books)
Anita Silvey
14 Beacon Street
Boston, MA 02108
(800) 325-1170
(617) 227-1555

Canadian Author & Bookman
P.O. Box 120
Niagara-On-The-Lake, ON L0S 1J0
Canada

Newsletters

Author's Newsletter
P.O. Box 32008
Phoenix, AZ 85064

Editorial Eye
66 Canal Center Plaza, #200
Alexandria, VA 22314-4915

Huenefeld Report
P.O. Box UP
Bedford, MA 01730

Direct Response Specialist
Galen Stilson
P.O. Box 1075
Tarpon Springs, FL 34688

Memo to Mailers (free)
U.S. Postal Service
P.O. Box 999
Springfield, VA 22150-0999

TOWERS Club Newsletter
Jerry Buchanan
P.O. Box 2038-P
Vancouver, WA 98668

Publishing Poynters (free)
Dan Poynter
P.O. Box 4232-890
Santa Barbara, CA 93140-4232

Independent Publishers Trade Report
Henry Berry
P.O. Box 176
Southport, CT 06490

Book Reviewers. Here is a short list of reviewers. For a longer list, see *Literary Market Place*. For a complete list on labels, contact ParaLists, P.O. Box 4232-890, Santa Barbara, CA 93140-4232, (805) 968-7277. See the discussion in Chapter Seven.

John Barkham Reviews
27 East 65th Street
New York, NY 10021

Frances Halpern
P.O. Box 5657-P
Montecito, CA 93150

United Features
Sidney Goldberg
200 Park Avenue
New York, NY 10166

Millicent Braverman
1517 Schuyer Road #A
Beverly Hills, CA 90210

Book Talks
Marion Benasutti
1616 Huntington Pike, #403
Meadowbrook, PA 19046-8001

Alan Caruba
P.O. Box 40
Maplewood, NJ 07040

Charles Lee
Presidential Apts #D-1203
Philadelphia, PA 19131

Jerry Mack
P.O. Box 5200
San Angelo, TX 76902

San Francisco Review of Books
555 De Haro Street
San Francisco, CA 94107

Literary Lantern
Walter Spearman
103 Carl Drive, Rt #4
Chapel Hill, NC 27516

Curtis Casewit
P.O. Box 19039
Denver, CO 80219

Bloomsbury Reviews
Tom Auer
P.O. Box 8928
Denver, CO 80201

Book Talk
Dwight Myers
8632 Horacio Place NE
Albuquerque, NM 87111

Book World
Broox Sledge
P.O. Box 112
Macon, MS 39341

King Features Syndicate
Ralph Hollenbeck
235 East 45th Street
New York, NY 10017

New York Review of Books
Robert B. Silvers
250 West 57th Street
New York, NY 10107-0001

New York Times Book Review
Rebecca Sinkler
229 West 43rd Street
New York, NY 10036

Reviewing Books
Martin Kich
709 South Irving Avenue
Scranton, PA 18505

Book Report
Sheldon Tromberg
4200 River Road NW
Washington, DC 20016

About Books
Carol Felsenthal
50 East Huron Street, ALA
Chicago, IL 60611

Forrest J. Ackerman
2495 Glendower Avenue
Los Angeles, CA 90027

Sun Features
Joyce Lain Kennedy
2382-K Camino Vida Roble
Carlsbad, CA 92009

George H. Tweney
16660 Marine View Drive SW
Seattle, WA 98166

Small Press Book Review
Henry Berry
P.O. Box 176
Southport, CT 064909

Authors & Books
Gary Baranik
1272 Prospect Avenue
Brooklyn, NY 11215

Mort Blankman
P.O. Box 558
Brooklandville, MD 21022

New Pages
Casey Hill
4426 South Belsay Road
Grand Blanc, MI 48439

DeKalb Book Review
Community Service Office
College of Continuing Ed/NIU
DeKalb, IL 60115

Rainbo Electronic Reviews
Maggie Ramirez
8 Duran Court
Pacifica, CA 94044

Bookwatch, Midwest Review of Books
Diane C. Donovan
166 Miramar Avenue
San Francisco, CA 94112

Reference and Research Book News
Jane Erskine
5606 NE Hassalo Street
Portland, OR 97213

College Store Journal
528 East Lorain Street
Oberlin, OH 44074

Small Press Review
P.O. Box 100
Paradise, CA 95967

Pamphlets and reports, and other help of interest to publishers. Write for latest prices.

Federal Trade Commission
Washington, DC 20580
Shopping By Mail? You're Protected!
FTC Buyer's Guide No. 2
Consumer Alert - The Vanity Press
News Release, dated July 19, 1959
Vanity Press Findings. Docket 7005
and 7489.

P.E.N. American Center
568 Broadway
New York, NY 10012
Grants and Awards Available to American Writers

National Endowment For The Arts
Literature Program
2401 E Street NW
Washington, DC 20506
Assistance, fellowships and residencies for writers.

Poets & Writers
72 Spring Street
New York, NY 10012
Awards List
Sponsors List
Literary Bookstores in the U.S.
Writer's Guide to Copyright

Chicago Advertising Agency
28 East Jackson Blvd.
Chicago, IL 60604.
Ad Guide (Circulation and ad prices for numerous magazines)

Popular Mechanics Classified
250 West 55th Street #SG
New York, NY 10019
Profits From Classified Ads

Copyright Office
Library of Congress
Washington, DC 20559.
Circular 1, *Copyright Basics*
Circular 2, *Publications on Copyright*

Small Business Administration,
1441 L Street NW
Washington, DC 20416
(800) 368-5855.
General business guidance and booklets for the new publisher. Send for a list of available publications. They cover many subjects and some are excellent.
Directory of Business Development Publications

Strawberry Media
2460 Lexington Drive
Owosso, MI 48867.
Selling Books to the Military Market by Michael Sedge.

Postal books and manuals. The following Postal Service publications should be consulted for more information.

Domestic Mail Manual. Complete rules, regulations and Postal rate information for all classes of mail sent and received in the U.S. $17.00 for four revisions, issued as needed. Superintendent of Documents, U.S. Government Printing Office, Washington, DC 20402-0001.

International Mail Manual. Complete rules, procedures, regulations and Postal rate information for all classes of mail sent out of the U.S. $14.00 per looseleaf edition, issued as needed. Superintendent of Documents.

Express Mail Service Handbook DM201. Policies, regulations and procedures for Express Mail Service. $1.00 subscription. U.S. Postal Service, Eastern Area Supply Center, Somerville, NJ 08877-0001.

Postal Bulletin. Weekly newsletter providing specific details on procedures, rates and regulations. $71.00 per year. Superintendent of Documents.

National Five-Digit ZIP Code and Post Office Directory (Publication 65A)—Order Form 4243. Call for prices: U.S. Postal Service (800) 238-3150.

Zip +4 State Directory—Order Form 4242. Call for prices: U.S. Postal Service (800) 238-3150.

Postal Facts. Interesting folder with Postal statistics. Free from U.S. Postal Service, News Division, Communications Department, Washington, DC 20260-3121.

The following publications are available free from your local Post Office. Many deal with direct mail (bulk rate, pre-sort, etc.) rather than parcel post, but as long as you are collecting information at the Post Office, you might as well get everything.

Basic Addressing, Notice 23A
Addressing for Automation, Notice 221
A Guide to Business Mail Preparation, Publication 25
Metered Better, Treated Better, Notice 125
On-site Meter Setting, Notice 112
Bar Code/FIM Pattern Locater Gauge, Model 005
Postage Rates, Fees and Information, Notice 59
Express Mail Rate Chart, Poster 189
International Postage Rates and Fees, Publication 51
Mailer's Guide, Publication 19
Information Guide on Presort First Class Mail, Publication 61
Computer Programming for Presort First-Class Mail, Notice 244
A Bottom Line Estimate of Your Presort Savings, Notice 243
How to Prepare Presort First-Class Mail, Poster 89
ZIP + 4 codes . . . Why They Add Up for Business Mailers, Notice 186
Directory of ZIP + 4 Coding Services, Publication 148
ZIP + 4: Helping You Help Your Business, Notice 189
Express Mail International Service Guide, Publication 273
International Surface Airlift (ISAL) Service Guide, Notice 82A
International Priority Airmail Mailer Guidelines, Publication 507
INTELPOST Service Directory and Users Guide, Notice 82A
National Change of Address, Notice 47
Preparing Business and Courtesy Reply Mail, Publication 12.

Book wholesalers. The most important are listed here. For more, see the *American Book Trade Directory* and *Literary Market Place*, available in your public library.

Academic Book Center
5600 NE Hassalo Street
Portland, OR 97213

Airlift Books
12 Market Road #5-P
London N7 9PW
Great Britain

Ambassador Book Service
42 Chasner Street
Hempstead, NY 11550

Baker & Taylor Co.
P.O. Box 6920
Bridgewater, NJ 08807-0920

Ballen Booksellers International
125 Ricefield Lane
Hauppauge, NY 11788

Blackwell North America
1001 Fries Mill Road
Blackwood, NJ 08012

Blackwell North America
6024 SW Jean Road #G
Lake Oswego, OR 97035

Book House, Inc.
208 West Chicago Street
Jonesville, MI 49250

Bookazine Co.
303 West 10th Street
New York, NY 10014

Bookpeople
7900 Edgewater Drive
Oakland, CA 94621

Bookslinger, Inc.
502 North Prior Avenue
St. Paul, MN 55104

Brodart Company
500 Arch Street
Williamsport, PA 17705

Coutts Library Service
736-738 Cayuga Street
Lewiston, NY 14092

DeVorss and Company
P.O. Box 550
Marina del Rey, CA 90294

The distributors
702 South Michigan
South Bend, IN 46618

Eastern Book Company
131 Middle Street
Portland, ME 04112

EBS Book Service
290 Broadway
Lynbrook, NY 11563

Emery-Pratt Co.
1966 West Main Street
Owosso, MI 48867

Golden-Lee Book Distributors
1000 Dean Street
Brooklyn, NY 11238

Ingram Book Company
347 Reedwood Drive
Nashville, TN 37217

Inland Book Company
P.O. Box 261
East Haven, CT 06512

International Service Company
333 Fourth Avenue
Indialantic, FL 32903

Koen Book Distributors
514 North Read Avenue
Cinnaminson, NJ 08077

Midwest Library Service
11443 Charles Rock Road
Bridgeton, MO 63044

New England Mobile Book Fair
82 Needham Street
Newton Highlands, MA 02161

New Leaf Distributing
5425 Tulane
Atlanta, GA 30323-3636

Nutri-Books
P.O. Box 5793
Denver, CO 80217

Pacific Pipeline
8030 South 228th Street
Kent, WA 98032-3898

Publishers Group West
4065 Hollis Street
Emeryville, CA 94608

Quality Books
918 Sherwood Drive
Lake Bluff, IL 60044-2204

Spring Arbor Distributors
10885 Textile Road
Belleville, MI 48111

Raincoast Book Distribution
112 Third Avenue
Vancouver, BC V5T 1C8
Canada

Arthur J. Viders Co.
7906 Hopi Place
Tampa, FL 33634

Yankee Book Peddler
Maple Street
Contoocook, NH 03229

Chain bookstore. Here are the major chains. For smaller ones, see *The American Book Trade Directory*, available at your public library. Address the fiction or nonfiction, hardcover or paperback buyer.

Walden Book Company
P.O. Box 10218
Stamford, CT 06904
(203) 356-7626

B. Dalton Bookseller
105 Fifth Avenue
New York, NY 10003
(212) 206-8800, Ext 360

Barnes & Noble Bookstores
105 Fifth Avenue
New York, NY 10003
(212) 206-8800

Crown Books
3300 75th Avenue
Landover, MD 20785
(301) 731-1200

Doubleday Bookshops
Spencer Gail
673 Fifth Avenue
New York, NY 10022-4297
(212) 223-6550

Little Professor Book Centers
John Glazer
110 North Fourth Avenue
Ann Arbor, MI 48104
(313) 994-1212, (800) 521-6232

Classic Bookshops
98 Carrier Drive
Rexdale, ON M9W 5R1
Canada
(416) 675-2962

Coles Book Stores Ltd.
Director of Marketing
90 Ronson Avenue
Rexdale, ON M9W 1C1
Canada
(416) 249-9121

W.H. Smith Ltd.
Buying Manager
113 Merton Street
Toronto, ON M4S 1A8
Canada
(416) 485-6660

U.S. Government procurement offices. See the *Selling to the Government* discussion in Chapter Eight.

Department of the Army
Attn: DAAG-MSL
2461 Eisenhower Avenue #1
Alexandria, VA 22331-0512

Naval Education and Training Program
Management Support Activity (Code 042)
Naval General Library Services
Pensacola, FL 32509-5100

Navy Resale & Services Support Office
Fort Wadsworth (CG4)
Staten Island, NY 10305-5097

Air Force Libraries Section
Acquisitions Librarian
AFPMPPB-3
USAF Military Personnel Center
Randolph AFB, TX 78148

Veteran's Administration Library
810 Vermont Avenue NW
Washington, DC 20402

U.S. Information Service
Attn: Resource Development Branch
301 Fourth Street SW #314 (E/CLD)
Washington, DC 20547

DoD Dependent Schools
(DGSC-PJ)
Education Supplies Division
Richmond, VA 23297

Army and Air Force Exchange Service
Public Affairs Div., Info Serv. Br.
P.O. Box 222305
Dallas, TX 75268-02022

Commandant (G-FRS)
U.S. Coast Guard Hqs.
2100 Second Street, SW
Washington, DC 20593

Department of the Navy
HQ, Marine Corps (LFS-1)
Washington, DC 20380-0001

Pacific Stars and Stripes
Book Department
APO San Francisco, CA 96503-0110
Operates 31 bookstores and 500 book departments in the Pacific

Stars and Stripes, Europe
Book Buyer
APO NY 09175

For the addresses of other government procurement offices, call your congressional representative's local office.

Send for the following government publications to:

Superintendent of Documents
U.S. Government Printing Office
Washington, DC 20402

U.S. Government Purchasing and Sales Directory $5.50

Selling to the Government $1.80

Selling to the Military #008-000-00479-0 $8.00

Doing Business with the Federal Government #022-003-01136-6 $2.50

Starting and Managing a Small Business of Your Own, Vol 1. 045-000-00212-8 $4.75

Starting and Managing a Business From Your Home, Vol 102. $2.00

Exporters. Here are the big ones. For more, see *Literary Market Place*. See the discussion in Chapter Eight. For detailed information on exporting see the Special Report *Exports/Foreign Rights, Selling U.S. Books Abroad*.

Baker & Taylor International
P.O. Box 6920
Bridgewater, NJ 08807-0920

Worldwide Media Services
115 East 23rd Street
New York, NY 10010

Book printers. These printers specialize in manufacturing books. For more, see *Literary Market Place*.

Murray Printing
James F. Conway, III
Westford, MA 01886
(508) 692-6321

Crane Duplicating
(short runs and galleys)
Richard Price
P.O. Box 487
Barnstable, MA 02630
(508) 362-3441

Book Press
Roger Rehbein
Putney Rd.
Brattleboro, VT 05301
(802) 257-7701

Book Mart Press
Michelle S. Gluckow
2001 Forty Second Street
North Bergen, NJ 07047
(201) 864-1887

Capital City Press
Debi Saldi
P.O. Box 546
Montpelier, VT 05602
(802) 223-5207

Maple-Vail
Sam W. Vail
2695 Willow Springs Lane
York, PA 17405

Multiprint, Inc.
Louise Merriam
80 Longhill Lane
Chatham, NJ 07928

Delmar Printing
Curt Cox
P.O. Box 1013
Charlotte, NC 28201

Rose Printing
Kim Zimmerman
P.O. Box 5078
Tallahassee, FL 32301
(904) 576-4151

BookMasters
Raymond Sevin
P.O. Box 159
Ashland, OH 44805
(419) 289-6051

Edwards Brothers
Jim Sterling
2500-P South State St.
Ann Arbor, MI 48106
(313) 769-1000

Malloy Lithographing
Will Upton
5411 Jackson Road
Ann Arbor, MI 48106
(313) 665-6113

Braun-Brumfield
Thad W. Koons
P.O. Box 1203
Ann Arbor, MI 48106
(313) 662-3291

Shear-Davis
Charlotte Ellison
713 West Ellsworth Road
Ann Arbor, MI 48108

McNaughton & Gunn, Inc.
Ronald A. Mazzola
960 Woodland Drive
Saline, MI 48176
(313) 429-5411

Cushing-Malloy
Steve Kehoe
P.O. Box 8632
Ann Arbor, MI 48107
(313) 663-8554

Bookcrafters
Jeanne Atkinson
140 Buchanan Street
Chelsea, MI 48118-0370
(313) 475-9145

Thomson-Shore, Inc.
Mark Livesay
7300-P West Joy Road
Dexter, MI 48130-0305
(313) 426-3939

Harlo Press
50-P Victor Ave.
Detroit, MI 48203
(313) 883-3600

Patterson Printing
Linda J. Seaman
1550 Territorial Road
Benton Harbor, MI 49022
(616) 925-2177

Eerdmans Printing Co.
Donald Miller
231 Jefferson Avenue SE
Grand Rapids, MI 49508

Bawden Printing
400 South 14th Avenue
Eldridge, IA 52748
(319) 285-4800

Omnipress
Robert G. Hamm
P.O. Box 7125
Madison, WI 53791-9705
(608) 257-7275
(800) 828-0305 outside Wisconsin

George Banta Company
Robert J. Cornell
Curtis Reed Plaza
Menasha, WI 54942
(414) 722-7771

Viking Press
Chip Fuhrmann
7000 Washington Avenue South
Eden Prairie, MN 55344
(800) 328-7327

Whitehall Co.
Mike Hirsch
1200 South Willis Avenue
Wheeling, IL 60090

Adams Press
Joe Goodman
25-P East Washington St.
Chicago, IL 60602
(312) 676-3426

R.R. Donnelley & Sons
2223 Martin Luther King Drive
Chicago, IL 60616
(312) 326-8000

Walsworth Publishing Co.
Barbara Hagen
306 North Kansas Avenue
Marcelline, MO 64658

Morgan Printing and Publishing
Ramsey Wiggins
900 Old Koenig Lane #135
Austin, TX 78756

Publishers Press
1900-P West 2300 South
Salt Lake City, UT 84119
(801) 972-6600

Merrill Corp.
Linda Wexler
1926 East 14th Street
Los Angeles, CA 90021

Josten's Printing
P.O. Box 991
Visalia, CA 93279

Griffin Printing and Lithograph Co.
544 West Colorado St.
Glendale, CA 91204
(213) 245-3671

Delta Lithograph
Ken Hoffmann
28210 No. Avenue Stanford
Valencia, CA 91355
(805)257-0584
(800) 223-1478 in California
(800) 32D-ELTA outside California

Graham Printing
17475 Gale Avenue
Rowland Heights, CA 91748-1515
(818) 964-7354

KNI, Inc.
Rick Krulish
1261 South State College Parkway
Anaheim, CA 92806
(714) 956-7300

Kimberly Press
Bill McNally
5390-P Overpass Rd.
Santa Barbara, CA 93111
(805) 964-6469

Griffin (Spilman) Printing
Dixie Robertson
1801 9th Street
Sacramento, CA 95814
(916) 448-3511

Canadian book printers

RBW Graphics
Ken Graves
515 Consumers Road, #200
Willowdalee, ON M2J 4Z2
(416) 495-7244

Aprinco Book Manufacturers
Benjamin Chung
2220 Midland Avenue
Toronto, ON M1P 3E6
(406) 298-3265

Ashton-Potter Ltd.
Randy Davis
9010 Keele Streett
Concord, ON L4K 2N2
(416) 736-4234

Hignell Printing Ltd.
Ray Hignell
488 Burnell Street
Winnipeg, MN, R3G 2B4
(204) 783-7237

Gagne Printing
Jean-Pierre Gagne
80, St. Martin Avenue
Louisville, PQ J5V 1B4
(819) 228-2766

John Deyell Company
J. Denis Beaudin
2235 Sheppard Avenue East, #903
Willowdale, ON M2J 5B5
(416) 491-8811

T.H. Best Printing Co.
Douglas W. Best
33 Kern Road
Don Mills, ON M3B 1S9
(416) 447-7295

Mailing list brokers. For mailing list brokers and mailing services, see the *Yellow Pages* of your local telephone directory. Also see *Direct Mail Lists, Rate & Data* and *Literary Market Place* in your public library. Write for catalogs.

Advanced Publishing Systems (college professors)
403 Grand Central Avenue
Lavallette, NJ 08735
(201) 793-5600

American Business Lists (14 million businesses compiled from *Yellow Pages*)
P.O. Box 27347
Omaha, NE 68127
(402) 331-7169

American Direct Marketing Service (compiler)
1261 Record Crossing
Dallas, TX 75235
(800) 527-5080
(214) 634-2361

American Library Association (libraries)
50 East Huron Street
Chicago, IL 60611
(312) 944-6780

American List Counsel (book buyers)
88 Orchard Road
Princeton, NJ 08540-8019
(800) 526-3973
(201) 874-4300

R.R. Bowker Lists (publishing industry)
John Panza
245 West 17th Street
New York, NY 10011
(212) 337-7164

Ed Burnett Consultants (general)
99 West Sheffield Avenue
Englewood, NJ 07631
(800) 223-7777
(201) 871-1100

CMG Information Services (academic-general)
50 Cross Street
Winchester, MA 01890
(617) 729-7865

Consolidated Mailing Service (academic)
Max Bradbard
P.O. Box 495
St. James, NY 11780
(516) 584-7283

Dunhill International (executives)
2430 West Oakland Park Blvd.
Ft Lauderdale, FL 33311

Dustbooks
Len Fulton
P.O. Box 100
Paradise, CA 95969

Educational Lists Co.
500 North Broadway
Jericho, NY 11753
(516) 931-2442
(800) 331-8102

Educational Mailings Clearing House (academic)
601 East Marshall Street
Sweet Springs, MO 65351
(816) 335-6373

Hugo Dunhill Lists (general)
630 Third Avenue
New York,NY 10017
(800) 223-6454
(212) 682-8030

Educational Directory (academic)
One Park Avenue
New York, NY 10016

Educational Lists Company (schools)
161 Glen Head Road
Glen Head, NY 11545
(516) 671-5011

Executive Services Companies (buyers by age)
Response+
901 North International Parkway
Richardson, TX 75081
(800) 527-3933
(214) 699-1271

Fleetwood Communications
(Canadian schools, libraries, hospitals, newspapers)
H.A. Bezanson
P.O. Box 2134
Blaine, WA 98230
(604) 278-2560

IBIS Information Services (foreign)
152 Madison Avenue
New York, NY 10016
(212) 779-1344
(800) 433-6226

Market Data Retrieval (libraries and schools)
16 Progress Drive
Shelton, CT 06484
(800) 435-3742 (CT)
(800) 243-5538

New Pages Lists (libraries and bookstores)
4426 South Belsay Road
Grand Blanc, MI 48439
(313) 743-8055

ParaLists
P.O. Box 4232-890
Santa Barbara, CA 93140-4232
(805) 968-7277

Patterson's Mailing LIsts (schools)
P.O. Box 199
Mount Prospect, IL 60056

PCS Mailing lists (compiler/broker)
125 Main Street
Peabody, MA 01960
(800) 532-5478
(617) 532-1600

Quality Education Data (schools)
1500 Logan Street
Denver, CO 80203
(800) 525-5811

R.L. Polk & Company (general)
6400 Monroe Blvd.
Taylor, MI 48180
(313) 292-3200

Research Projects (compilers)
50 Clinton Street
Hempstead, NY 11550
(800) 645-2980
(212) 895-1048
(718) 481-4410

Resources (alternative America)
P.O. Box 134
Cambridge, MA 02238

Edith Roman Lists (compiler/broker)
875 Avenue of the Americas
New York, NY 10001
(800) 223-2194
(212) 695-3836

School Lists Mailing (schools)
1710 Hwy. 35
Oakhurst, NJ 07755
(201) 531-2212

Southam Direct Marketing (Canadian schools, libraries, bookstores, doctors and businesses)
12 Nantucket Blvd.
Scarborough, ON M1P 4W7
Canada

SpeciaLISTS
120 East 16th Street
New York, NY 10003-2150
(212) 260-5644

Willowood Lists (schools)
P.O. Box 1846
Minot, ND 58702

Mike Wilson List Counsel
(institutional)
12120 Washington Blvd.
Los Angeles, CA 90066
(800) 445-2089
(213) 398-2754

Fred Woolf Lists (compiler/broker)
280 North Central Avenue
Hartsdale, NY 10530
(800) 431-1557
(914) 946-0336
(212) 679-4311

Woodruff-Stevens Lists (book buyers)
345 Park Avenue South
New York, NY 10010
(212) 685-4600

Worldata (general)
P.O. Box 443
Jericho, NY 11753
(516) 931-2442

Alvin B. Zeller, Inc. (general)
37 East 28th Street
New York, NY 10016
(212) 689-4900
(800) 223-0814

Zeller & Letica (book buyers)
15 East 26th Street
New York, NY 10010
(800) 221-4112
(212) 685-7512

Also see *The Encyclopedia of Associations* and other references. Most organizations rent their mailing lists.

Book Publicists. These professionals will schedule you for TV appearances, write your news releases and introduce you to other media contacts. For an expanded listing, see *Literary Market Place*.

Planned Television Arts
Rick Frishman
25 West 43rd Street
New York, NY 10036
(212) 921-5111

Promotion in Motion
Irwin Zucker
6464 Sunset Blvd.
Hollywood, CA 90028
(213) 461-3921

Sensible Solutions
Judith Appelbaum
275 Madison Avenue, #1518
New York, NY 10016
(212) 687-1761

Alice Allen
320 East 72ns Street, #3B
New York, NY 10021
(212) 744-8844

Gaughen Public Relations
Barbara Gaughen
226 East Canon Perdido
SantaBarbara, CA 93101
(805) 965-8482

Book fair exhibiting services. If you cannot attend the fair yourself, you might contract with an exhibiting service to show your books. See the discussion in Chapter Nine and read *Book Fairs*.

PMA Book Exhibits
2401 Pacific Coast Highway #102-A
Hermosa Beach, CA 90254

Conference Book Service
80 South Early Street
Alexandria, VA 22314

COSMEP Exhibit Service
P.O. Box 703-P
San Francisco, CA 94101

Publishers Book Exhibit
901 South Street
Peekskill, NY 10566

Card deck printers. Send for brochures and prices.

Preiss Printing Company
265 Bethpage-Spagnoli Road
Melville, NY 11747
(800) 645-9588
(516) 752-7100

Scoville Press
14505 27th Avenue North
Plymouth, MN 55441
(612) 553-1400

Rose Printing Co.
P.O. Box 5078
Tallahassee, FL 32314
(904) 576-4151

Solar Press
550 Fontenac Road
Naperville, IL 60566
(312) 357-0100

Office Supplies. Send for catalogs.

Chiswick Trading
31 Union Avenue
Sudbury, MA 01776-0907
(800) 225-8708

Grayarc
P.O. Box 2944
Hartford, CT 06104
(800) 243-5250

Robbins Container Corp.
222 Conover Street
Brooklyn, NY 11231
(718) 875-3204

Fidelity Products Co.
P.O. Box 155
Minneapolis, MN 55440
(800) 862-3765 U.S.
(612) 536-6500
Fax: (612) 536-6584

Paper Mart
5959 Corvette Street
Los Angeles, CA 90040
(800) 722-2204 U.S.
(800) 334-8800 Southern California
(800) 531-1778 Northern California

Drawing Board
P.O. Box 220505
Dallas, TX 75222

Quill Corporation
P.O. Box 4700
Lincolnshire, IL 60197-4700

Fulfillment warehouses. Send for prices.

Publishers Storage & Shipping
E.B. Quick
231 Industrial Park
Fitchburg, MA 01420
(617) 345-2121

Wayne Public Warehouse
Herbert A. Roundtree
150 Parish Drive
Wayne, NJ 07470
(201) 696-1600

Team Distribution Center
Herbert Roundtree
P.O. Box 2248
Wayne, NJ 07474-2248
(201) 595-1751

Hamilton Distribution Services
A. Scott Marsilio
One Chris Court
Dayton, NJ 08810
(201) 329-9150

St. Joe Distributing
Joel Savino
Brooklyn Navy Yard, #3
Brooklyn, NY 11205
(718) 834-0170

Package Fulfillment Center, Inc.
Neal Confessore
1744 Goldbach Avenue
Ronkonkoma, NY 11779
(516) 737-3000

Publishers Fulfillment Group
4721 Capital Circle SW
Tallahassee, FL 32304
(904) 878-0522

Central Distribution Services
Steve Rudminas
8361 U.S. Highway 45
Neenah, WI 54956
(414) 722-2848

APEX, Inc.
Bret Butterfield
4931 South 900 East
Salt Lake City, UT 84117
(800) 654-8000, (801) 265-3000

JV Company
Ben Rose
P.O. Box 11950
Reno, NV 89510
(702) 359-9811

Order entry software.
Write for details and prices:

Publishers Business System
rh Communications
P.O. Box 271177
Escondido, CA 92027
(619) 480-5641

PIIGS
Upper Access Books
P.O. Box 457
Hinesburg, VT 05461
(800) 356-9315
Bookmark
Morse Data
P.O. Box 1007
Exeter, NH 03833-1007
(603) 772-7474

Bookmaster
Harold G. Harvey
50 Lowery Drive
Atherton, CA 94025
(415) 321-8700

BSA Prophit
Joe Gumino
1500 Lawrence Avenue, Profit Park
Ocean, NJ 07712-3400

Cat's Pajamas
1253 North Hwy 20
Anacortes, WA 98221
(206) 293-8372

Maxway Data
225 West 34th Street
New York, NY 10001
(212) 947-6100

Publishing For Profit
Time-Share Computer Systems
6500 Barrie Road
Edina, MN 55435
(612) 929-3131

QuickBooks
Quicken
Intuit
P.O. Box 3014
Menlo Park, CA 94026

Courses, conferences and seminars. There are many educational programs of interest to publishers. Some of the most important are listed here. For more, see *Literary Market Place*.

Santa Barbara Publishing Workshops
Dan Poynter
P.O. Box 4232-890
Santa Barbara, CA 93140-4232
(805) 968-7277

Huenefeld Seminars
P.O. Box UP
Bedford, MA 01730

Publishing Institute
University of Denver
2075 South University, #D-114
Denver, CO 80210

Stanford Conf. on Book Publishing
Stanford Alumni Association
Bowman Alumni House
Stanford, CA 93405

UC Berkeley Extension
University of California
Berkeley, CA 94720

New York University's Summer Publishing Institute
School of Continuing Education
Center for Publishing
48 Cooper Square
New York, NY 10211-0152

Chicago Book Clinic
100 East Ohio Street #630
Chicago, IL 60611

Publishing Program
University of Chicago
Office of Continuing Education
5835 South Kimbark Avenue
Chicago, IL 60637

Book Clubs. There are over 200 book clubs and most are very specialized. For more see *Literary Market Place*.

Literary Guild
245 Park Avenue
New York, NY 10167

The Book-of-the-Month Club
1271 Avenue of the Americas
New York, NY 10020-2686

How-to Book Club
13311 Monterey Avenue
Blue Ridge Summit, PA 17294-0850

Newbridge Book Clubs
3000 Cindel Drive
Delran, NJ 08075

Quality Paperback Book Club
1271 Avenue of the Americas
New York, NY 10020

Glossary

AAP: Association of American Publishers

AAUP: Association of American University Presses

ABA: American Booksellers Association

ABI: Advanced Book Information. Publishers supply information on their book to Bowker for inclusion in *Forthcoming Books* and *Books in Print.*

Accounts receivable: Money owed a company by credit customers.

Acquisitions editor: The person in a publishing firm who acquires new manuscripts.

Advance: An amount paid to the author on signing the contract. An advance is normally applied against royalties.

ALA: American Library Association.

American Booksellers Association: The trade association of non-chain retail bookstores in the U.S.

American Library Association: Largest library association in the U.S.

American National Standards Committee Z39. The committee responsible for standard for libraries, information science and publishing.

Anthology: A collection of one or more authors published as a single work.

Antiquarian bookseller: One who specializes in selling old or rare books.

Artwork: Any illustrative matter other than straight text.

Association of American Publishers. The trade association of the largest book publishers in the U.S.

Association of American University Presses: The trade association of university presses.

Author's alterations: Changes made by an author after type has been set. See *printer's error.*

Back Flap: The back inner flap of a dust jacket that often contains a biography of the author.

Back list: Previously published books that are still in print and available from a publisher. Not *frontlist* books which are recently published.

Back order: An order for books which are unavailable, which is held until the books become available.

Bar code: The identification and price marking in bar format on books. The bar code for books is called Bookland EAN.

Bastard title: Half title. Found on the page in front of the title page.

Belt press: A large printing press that prints many pages in one pass.

Benday: Various density screens printed on an adhesive-backed plastic sheet which may be pasted to artwork. The screening provides tonal qualities to artwork.

Bestseller: A top-selling book. There are several best seller lists that draw sales figures from different markets.

Bibliography: That part of the back matter listing books and materials consulted by the author in preparing the book, or which the author wishes to bring to the reader's attention.

Binding: The processes following printing: folding, gathering, stitching, gluing, trimming and/or casing a book.

BISAC: Book Industry Systems Advisory Committee. A committee of the Book Industry Study Group.

Bleed: Ink printed over the edge of the paper. The edge is trimmed off. Most magazines have covers with bleed.

Blueline: A proof sheet made by exposing a negative to a photosensitive paper. A blue print.

Blurb: A promotional announcement, phrase or advertisement.

Boards: The camera-ready, pasted-up copy ready for the printer.

Body type: The majority of the type used in a book. Not a headline.

Boldface: Type which is **heavier** than the text type with which it is used.

Bond: A hard finish rag or sulphite paper used for stationery and forms.

Book fair: An event where publishers display their books.

Book packager: A person or company who contracts with publishers to deliver contracted books.

Book Post: The Postal Service's book rate.

Book: A publication of 49 or more pages which is not a serial or periodical.

Booklet: A small book, usually with less than 48 pages.

Bullets: A large black dot • used to set off items in a list.

C1S: Coated One Side. Usually refers to a book cover stock which is smooth on one side.

Camera-ready copy: A completely prepared pasteup which is ready for the camera or xerographic reproduction. No further graphic arts work is required.

Caption: The line of text accompanying an illustration.

Case binding: Hardcover.

Case bound: Hardcover or edition binding.

Cataloging in Publication: Bibliographic information supplied by the Library of Congress which is printed on the copyright page. The CIP data helps libraries to shelve the book properly.

Chapbook: a small book or pamphlet of popular tales, ballads or poems.

Character: A letter, number, punctuation mark or space in printed matter.

Check Digit: A number used to validate the other numbers in the preceding numerical field. The last number in the ISBN is a *check digit*.

Clip art: Line drawings, screened pictures and illustrations designed to be cut out and pasted up.

Clipping service: A firm that collects articles of interest to the client from periodicals.

Coated stock: Paper manufactured with a variety of surfaces, which may be smooth, glossy or matte.

COD: Cash On Delivery. Where merchandise is paid for when delivered.

Cold type: Strike-on type, such as that produced by a typewriter or IBM Composer, or photocomposition type. Not hot metal type.

Collating: Gathering of printed sheets into proper order for binding.

Colophon: A listing of production details in the backmatter.

Color separation: A camera technique using different-color lenses to draw out the three primary colors and black from a color illustration or photograph. The resulting negatives are used to make the printing plates.

Composition: Typeset material. Typeset text ready to be pasted up.

Content editing: Evaluating a manuscript for organization and style.

Continuity program: A standing order for succeeding volumes in a related program.

Contrast: The degree of difference between the lightest and darkest parts of a picture.

Co-op publishing: Where more than one person or company join to produce a book. Co-publishing.

Co-op advertising: Where the publisher and the bookstore share the cost of local book advertising. The publisher pays the larger share.

Copy editing: Technical editing of a manuscript for spelling, grammar and punctuation.

Copyright: The right to retain or sell copies of artistic works which you have produced.

Copyright notice: The word placed on the copyright page such as "Copyright © 1989, Daniel F. Poynter."

COSMEP: The Committee of Small Magazine Editors and Publishers. A trade association based in San Francisco.

Credit memo: A statement showing money due a customer for returned merchandise.

Crop marks: The lines used to define the desired limits of the area of a photograph or illustration to be reproduced. See *trim marks*.

DBA: Doing business as. A sole-proprietorship operated in another name.

Defamation: Libel (written) or slander (spoken) that injures a person.

Density: The relative darkness of an image area. In photography, the blackening or light stopping ability of a photographic image, as numerically measured by a densiometer.

Direct mail advertising: Advertising matter mailed directly to a potential customer.

Display ad: A print advertisement using graphics.

Display type: Type which is larger than the text, as in a chapter headline.

Distributor: A company that acts as your marketing (usually to one market such as bookstores), warehousing and shipping department. Not a jobber or wholesaler.

Dummy: A preliminary mock-up of a book folded to the exact size of the finished job.

Dummy folio: "Working" page numbers added for identification purposes but changed before the book is printed.

Dump: A display for books usually made of cardboard.

Dust jacket: The thin paper wrap on a hardcover book.

Editing: Changing, correcting or altering typed text into the required form.

Edition: All printings of a book from the same unaltered boards. Once changes are made, the book becomes a second edition.

Elhi: The elementary school/high school market.

Em dash: A dash—the width of an "M"

En dash: A dash–the width of an "N"

Endpapers: The heavy sheets that fasten the pages of a hardcover book to the cover.

Epilogue: The last part of the text that brings the reader up to date.

Errata: A loose sheet listing errors found in the printed book.

Exclusive: 1. A news or feature story printed by one media source substantially ahead of its competitors. 2. Sole distribution rights given to a distributor.

Fair use: The allowable and legal use of a limited amount of copyrighted material without getting permission.

First edition: The entire original printing from the same (unchanged) plates.

First serial rights: The exclusive right to serialize a book in a periodical.

Flat: A printing term describing the assembling of negatives on a heavy paper sheet for platemaking. See stripping.

Flier: A printed announcement. A flier becomes a *brochure* when folded.

Flop: To flip over a photographic negative so that the image will be reversed.

Flush: To be even with, such as in "flush right."

FOB: Free On Board. "FOB origin" means the addressee pays the shipping. "FOB destination" means the shipper pays the shipping costs. "FOB Santa Barbara" means the goods are delivered free as far as Santa Barbara; the addressee pays for transportation, if any, from there.

F&Gs: Folded and gathered pages. The unbound signatures of a book sometimes sent to reviewers.

Folio: The number on the page of a book.

Font : The complete set of type in a single typeface, including characters, numbers and punctuation marks.

Foreign rights: Subsidiary rights allowing the book to be published in other countries.

Foreword: Introductory remarks about the book and its author found in the front matter. Not "forward."

Front matter: All the pages in a book before the main text.

Frontispiece: An illustration facing the title page.

FTC: Federal Trade Commission.

Fulfillment: The process of order processing, picking, packing and shipping.

Galleys: 1. Originally, a proof sheet run on the press to check the typesetting. 2. Later, the typeset pages prior to paste-up. 3. The pre-publication copies of the book sent to some reviewers.

Gang run (ganging): Putting numerous unrelated jobs together for printing by assembling them on a single printing plate. Provides lower costs by economizing on setup charges. **Ghost writer:** A professional writer who produces work for others. Work for hire.

Glossary: A list of definitions found in the back matter.

Glossy: A photograph with a shiny surface. Not matte.

Gripper margin: The unprintable edge of the sheet of paper where the printing press or photocopier clamps the sheet to pull it through the printing machine. Often on top of the sheet and usually .25".

Gutter: The space between columns of type, such as the inner margins in two facing pages of a book.

Hairline: A very finely ruled line.

Half title: Bastard title.

Halftone: A screened photograph. A tone pattern composed of dots of uniform density but varying in size. A reproduction of a photograph whereby the various tones (highlights and shadows) are translated into numerous tiny dots for printing.

Halftone screen: A screen placed in front of the negative material in the process camera to break up a continuous tone image into dots of black and white to produce a halftone. There are two types: ruled glass screens and contact screens.

Hardcover: A book bound in boards. Casebound.

Headband: Reinforcing cloth at each end of the spine of a hardcover book.

Headline: A large bold caption at the top of an article or advertisement.

Hickey: A speck or blotch on a printed page.

Highlights: The lightest (or whitest) portions of a photograph or art work.

Hot type: An older typesetting process using cast hot metal.

Hyperbole or hype: Exaggerated claims used in selling a product or person.

Illustration: Photographs and drawings. Art work.

Image area: The printable area of a page surrounded by margins.

Imprint: The imprimata the publisher uses for a book. A publisher may have several imprints.

In print: Books that are currently available from publishers.

Index: An A to Z listing in the back matter giving the location of specific material.

Insertion order: A form used by advertising agencies to place advertising in various media.

International Standard Book Number: A unique number that identifies the binding, edition and publisher of a book. ISBNs are assigned by their publisher.

International Standard Serial Number: A number like an ISBN for serials—books published in a series. ISSNs are assigned by the Library of Congress.

Inventory: Books on hand available for sale

Invoice: A bill.

Italics: Type with a *right-hand slant*. Used for quotations, titles and emphasis.

Jobber: One who buys books in large quantities for resale to retailers and libraries.

Justification: Composing lines of running text so that the left and right margins are even. Automatically performed by computerized typesetting machines.

Kerning: Removing space between letters.

Layout: A sketch or preliminary drawing of what is to be printed. A mockup.

Layout: A paste-up or mechanical.

Leading: The amount of vertical spacing, measured in points, between lines of typeset text. Rhymes with "heading."

Leaflet: A printed piece of paper folded in the center to produce four pages.

Letterpress: Printing from raised type rather than from photographic plates.

Libel: Writen defamation.

Library Edition: A book with a reinforced binding.

Library of Congress: The national library serving the U.S. Congress.

Library of Congress Catalog Card Number: A unique title control number assigned by the Library of Congress to a given work.

Library rate: The special postal rate available for shipping books to or from libraries and educational institutions.

Line art: A black and white illustration that does not require screening.

Line shot: Any negative, print, copy or printing plate which is composed of solid image areas without halftone patterns.

Line drawing: A black and white drawing with no gray tones. Line art.

List price: The suggested retail selling price of merchandise.

Literary Market Place: The directory of the book publishing industry.

Logo: A symbol or illustration used as an identifying mark by a business. Like a trademark.

Lowercase: Small letters, not capitals.

Mail order: Fulfilling orders via the mail.

Make-ready: All the printing press set-up in preparation for a print run.

Manuscript: The book (typed or handwritten) before it is typeset, pasted up and printed.

Margin: The white space around the copy on a page.

Marketing plan: A publisher's total promotional plan for a book including reviews, subsidiary rights, advertising and other customer contact.

Mass market paperback: The smaller 4 x 7, cheaper editions usually sold next to magazines.

Matte: A non-shiny, dull surface.

Mechanical: See Pasteup.

Media: Print, broadcast and other methods for delivering your message to the market.

Microfiche cards: A flat-surface film in card size. Many wholesalers send their inventory listings on microfiche to bookstores every couple of weeks.

Monograph: A short report on a single subject.

Negative: The image obtained from the original in the conventional photographic process. The tones are the reverse of those in the original subject. Positive prints are made from negatives.

News release: An announcement sent to a periodical.

Non-photo blue: A light blue pencil or ink which will not be picked up by a plate-making camera. Light blue pens and pencils are used to mark pasted-up sheets.

Nth name: Incrementally-selected names from a mailing list, such as every 10th name. Used in testing lists.

OCR: Optical Character Recognition. A device that can recognize (read) typewritten characters and convert them to electronic impulses for translation to output media language. An OCR reader can read a printed page into a computer for editing and revised printout.

Offset lithography: Where the image is transferred from the printing plate to a rubber blanket and then to, or "offset" on, the paper. Practically all lithography is done by the offset method.

Opaque: Not admitting light. Painting out parts of negatives so they will not reproduce.

Out of print: A book is no longer available.

Overrun: The books over the ordered amount. Because there are so many parts to a book, printers are allowed overruns and underruns of up to 10%.

Packing slip: A document sent with a shipment of books itemizing the contents of the shipment.

Page proof: A layout of the pages as they will appear in the book.

Pagination: The numbering or order of pages in a book.

Paperback: A softcover book.

Paste-up: An array of reproduction quality copy arranged in proper position on a paper prepared as line copy ready for the camera. Same as a mechanical.

Peer review: Manuscript editing by an expert in the subject field.

Pen name: A pseudonym.

Perfect binding: The standard glued-on cover seen on most soft-covered books. It has a squared-off spine on which the title and name of the author may be printed.

Periodical: A periodically issued publication such as a magazine.

Photocomposition: Setting type photographically by exposing a photo-sensitive paper or film to images of typed characters, in such a sequence as to create the desired text or copy.

Photodirect: Exposing an image directly to a light sensitive offset plate material.

Photomechanical transfer, PMT, diffusion transfer: A process in which the pasteup is exposed to a sheet of sensitized paper, the paper is processed in contact with a receiver sheet, and the sheets are peeled apart to produce a usable image on the receiver.

Photostat or stat: A photographic reproduction—which can be negative or positive—made from film, artwork, other stats, etc., and used as line art for many art applications.

P.I.: Per inquiry advertising, where the media provide the space or time free and get a piece of each sale.

Pica: A printing industry unit of measure equal to approximately 1/16th of an inch. There are 12 points to the pica. Usually used to measure width.

Plagiarism: Copying the work of another and passing it off as one's own.

Plate, printing: Usually the master device bearing the image to be printed. May be paper, plastic or metal.

Plugging: A press condition whereby photographs appear muddy or characters fill in. Caused by poor plate burning, over-application of ink or incorrect ink/water balance.

PMS color: The Pantone Matching System for specifying specific shades of color.

Point: A vertical measurement used in typesetting. One point equals 1/72 of an inch.

Point of purchase display (POP): A dump or rack of books.

Positive: A photographic image in which the tones correspond to the original subject. A positive on paper is usually called a "print."

PPI: Pages per inch. Used to measure the thickness of paper.

Preface: Introductory remarks by the author in the front matter. The preface gives the reason for the book and defines its aims and scope.

Premium: A book given away as part of a promotion.

Press kit: A collection of publicity materials used to promote a book, usually presented in a cardboard folder with pockets.

Press release: See news release.

Printer's error: Mistakes made by the printer in preparing for the press. Not author's alterations.

Proof: A direct impression of type or plate showing what the printed page will look like.

Pseudonym: An assumed name used to conceal an author's identity. A pen name.

Public domain: Material not protected by copyright.

Publication date: The date on which a book's promotion is slated to peak and books are available for purchase. A *launch date* usually set three to four months after the book is printed.

Publicist: One who prepares promotional materials and/or schedules media appearances.

Publishers Marketing Association: A trade association that sponsors co-op promotions to help members sell books.

Purchase order: A request for the purchase of merchandise, describing the merchandise, shipping instructions and other conditions of sale. A PO generally represents a promise to pay. Acceptance by the supplier constitutes a contract to supply the merchandise under specified terms.

Quality paperback: A softcover or trade paper book.

Quick printing: Producing a printing plate or master directly from the original boards (pasteups) to reproduce multiple copies.

Quote: 1. An endorsement for a book. 2. A price quotation for printing.

Ragged right: An uneven right-hand margin. Not justified.

Reduction: A photographic process creating a small image.

Register: The correct positioning of print on a page.

Remaindering: The selling off of the remaining stock of books after sales fall off.

Remnant space: Random advertising space in a periodical, which has not been sold and is available at a reduced rate. Occurs usually in regional editions of national magazines.

Reprint: 1. To go back to press on the same book. 2. Printing the book in another version, such as the paperback version of a hardcover book.

Reverse: To print an image white on black, rather than black on white.

Returns: Unsold books which are returned to a publisher for credit.

Review: An evaluation of a book, sometimes critical.

Review copy: A complimentary copy of a book sent to reviewers and potential quality purchasers.

Revised edition: The printing of a book after substantial changes to the contents. The ISBN should be different.

Rights: An agreement to allow someone else to use the book usually in another form. Examples are foreign rights, first serial rights and film rights.

Royalties: Money paid to authors by publishers for the right to publish their work.

Runaround: Where text is typeset around an illustration.

Running heads. The book title or chapter title found at the top of the page in many books. See the top of this page.

Saddle stitch: See stitch.

Sales rep: An individual who presents books to stores and takes orders. A *book traveler*.

SASE: Self-Addressed, Stamped Envelope.

Scaling: Using a proportion wheel to size an illustration for printing. Scaling determines how much to enlarge or reduce a photograph.

Scoring: Creasing or pressing a line into paper so that it will fold more readily and more accurately.

Screen: See halftone screen.

Serial: A publication issued in successive parts, usually at regular intervals.

Serif: The "tails" on a character that make it easier to read. The text in this book is set in a serif type. The headers at the top of the page are set in an sans serif (without serif) type.

Sheet: Two printed pages, one on each side of a leaf of paper. If the sheet is folded to create four printed pages, it is called a "leaflet."

Sheetfed press: A printing press that prints on sheets of paper, not rolls.

Short discount: Less than 40%. Textbooks are often sold on a short discount.

Signature: A part of a book obtained by folding a large single sheet of paper into sections. A book signature may contain 8, 16, 32, or 64 pages.

Smythe sewn: Where signatures are sewn together with thread prior to installing the cover on a book. Common with hardbound books.

Spine: The part of the book that connects the front to the back.

Spine-out: Displaying books on a shelf so that the spine shows. Not "face out."

Spiral binding: Continuous wire binding.

Standard Address Number (SAN): A number assigned to all organizations involved in buying, selling and lending books. The numbers are assigned by the ISBN agency at Bowker.

Statement: A periodic (usually monthly) listing of invoices, credit memos and payments. Bookstores expect a monthly statement of account.

STOP orders: A cash with order, Single Title Order Plan used by bookstores.

Stet: A proofreading term to disregard editing notes and leave as is. From the Latin meaning "to stand."

Stitch: A staple. The staple seen in magazines and brochures are "saddle stitches."

Strike-on type: Cold type created with a typewriter, Composer or computer character printer where the typeface makes an impression on paper through a carbon ribbon.

Stripping: The assembling of photographic negatives or positives and attaching them to the flat (a large sheet of heavy paper) for plate making.

Subsidiary rights: Additional rights to publish the book in other forms. Examples are book club rights, foreign rights and serial rights.

Subsidy press: A publisher who charges the author to publish a book. Subsidy presses have a bad reputation for editing, production and promotion. A "vanity press."

Tear sheets: Ads, stories, etc. torn from the magazine they appeared in.

Terms: Time, in days, allowed a customer for payment of an invoice. For example: Net 30 days.

Text: The main body of the page. Not the headlines.

Tipping-in: The pasting-in to a book of extra sheets such as fold out maps.

Title: 1. A book or stock of the same book. 2. The name of the book.

Trade paperback: A quality paperback or softcover book.

Trade publisher: One who publishes books primarily for the book trade: bookstores and libraries.

Transfer type: Sheets of characters, numerals, borders or symbols which may be burnished onto paper and added to the pasteup.

Traveler, book: A sales rep.

Trim marks: Lines made on the edges of a camera-ready board to indicate where the page will be cut (trimmed) after it is printed.

Trim size: The size of the page once trimmed to its final dimension.

Underrun: When a printer manufactures fewer copies than were ordered. "See overrun."

Unit cost: The cost to print each book.

Vanity press: A subsidy press

Velox: A positive print of a photograph or line art ready for pasteup. Usually 65-, 85- or 100-line screen is used for photographs to produce "halftones."

Vendor: The supplier of goods or services.

Wax: An adhesive material used like rubber cement to attach elements to the pasteup board.

Web press: A fast printing press, using paper on rolls as opposed to sheets.

Wholesaler: A company that buys books in quantities for resale to stores and libraries. "Wholesalers" handle books, "distributors" represent publishers.

White-out: Removing unwanted parts of a pasteup by covering with an opaque liquid.

Window: A sheet of red, orange or black paper or acetate on a pasteup, to indicate where a photograph will be positioned. These colors photograph as black, creating a clear "window" in the black negative.

Work for hire: Writing in which the writer does not retain ownership. See "ghostwriter."

Working title: A preliminary title used during manuscript preparation before the book is named.

Whether you think you can or think you can't, you're right. - Henry Ford

Index

ABA Book Buyer's Handbook: 147,
Abbreviations, list of: 55
ABI: 122, 171, 365
Accounts receivable: 322
Acid-free paper: 101
Acknowledgement: 55
Ad copy: 265, 287
Ad participation: 302
Addendum: 57
Address codes: 167, 317
Address format: 283
Advance Book Information: See ABI
Advance dating: 149
Advances, royalty: 49
Advertising copy:
Advertising: 160, 194, 297, Chapter Nine.
After publishing: Chapter Twelve
Afterword: 57
American Library Association: 178
Answering machines: 311
Anthology rights: 254
Appendix: 57
Approval plans: 236
Articles: 210, 358
Artwork: 62, 97, 114
Associations: Appendix
Audience specialization: 217
Audio: 115
Author submissions: 46
Author tours: 209
Author's notes: 57
Autographing: 212, 358
Automation: 85
Awards: 213
Back cover: 33, 106, 170
Back matter: 57
Back orders: 324
Bad checks: 318
Bags, plastic: 333
Baker & Taylor: 177, 220, 225, 226, 240, 365
Banks: 80
Barcode: 120
Bastard title: 52, 55
Best sellers: 166

Better Business Bureau: 74
Bibliography: 57
Binder, manuscript: 51
Binder, promotion: 163
Binding: 88, 107
Bluelines: 60
Boards: 88, 97, 114
Book clubs: 175, 254, Appendix
Book fairs: 260
Book rate: 337
Book reviews: See reviews.
Book-Of-The-Month-Club: 175, Appendix
Book: 15
Booklist magazine: 175, 177
Bookpeople: 228
Books in Print: 15, 35, 53, 91, 168
Books: Appendix
Bookshelf books: 258, 272
Bookstores: 231
Bound Galleys: 175
Bowker, R.R.: 120, 131, 369
Braille: 259
Brochures: 170, 186, 207, 273, 284, 303
Bulk rate mailings: 270, 272, 273
Business reply envelopes: 294
Business: Chapter Three
Calendar, book: 363
Cameras: 63
Card decks: 296
Carton: 332
Catalogs: 303
Chain stores: 230
Chapter titles: 56
Choice magazine: 177
CIP: 125, 179, 364
Clip art: 62, 96, Appendix
Clipping services: 194
Co-authorship: 47
Co-op advertising: 301
Co-op Mailing: 296
Co-op Publishing: 21, 257
Collections: 151
College market: 143, 233, 243
Colophon: 57

Color separations: 62
Commission sales reps: 304
Commissioned writing: 46
Complaints: 326
Computer: 41, 73, 186, 314, Chapter Eleven
Condensations: 253
Consignment: 146
Consulting: 359
Contemporary Authors: 132, 177
Contracts: 48, 113
Copyright page: 54
Copyright: 37, 54, 97, 127, 176, 179
Corporation: 68
COSMEP: 132
Costs: 83, 164
Cover letter: 290
Cover price: 138
Cover, book: 33, 104, 365
Credit cards: 271, 311, 313, 322
Credit: 149, 322
Crown Books: 230
Cumulative Book Index: 129
Customs: 340
Dalton, B.: 230
Dealer bulletin: 144
Dedication page: 54
Defamation: 76
Delayed billing: 146
Deposits: 154
Design: 89, 361
Direct mail advertising: 13, 216, 266
Direct response: 265
Direct Sacks: 340
Directories: 130
Disclaimer: 56
Discounts: 141, 142, 143
Disks, computer: 115
Distribution: Chapter Eight
distributors, The: 228
Distributors: 222, 225, 323
Donations: 308
Drawings: 58
Dumps: 302
Dustbooks: 300
Echo effect: 274
Editing: 58, 349
Educational campaigns: 250
800 numbers: 271
End papers: 52
Endorsements: 169, 170
Epigraph: 54,
Errata: 57
Examination copies: 243

Exchange title promotion: 258
Exclusives: 230
F&G's: 175
Fax: 312
Federal Trade Commission: 143, 146, 301, 324
Fiction: 10, 30,
Financial management: 353
Flat: 88
Flier, media: 207
Folio: 90
Footnotes: 57
Foreign sales: 259, 269, 337, 339
Foreword: 55
Front matter: 52
Four color: 97
Frontispiece: 53
Fulfillment houses: 345
Fulfillment: Chapter ten, 350
Glossary: 57
Golden-Lee: 228
Gordon's Books: 229
Grain, paper: 101
Grants: 82
Graphics: Appendix
Guarantee card: 295
Halftones: 62, 97,
Hardcover: 102, 136, 216, 330
Headlines: 95
Help in writing: 45
Horn Book Magazine: 177
Hotline: 281
Illegal reproduction: 77
Illustrations: 55, 58, 95
Index: 58
Information packaging: 87
Ingram: 225
Ink: 102
Inland Book Company: 228
Insertion order, ad: 298
Insurance: 318, 328
International Standard Book Number: See ISBN
Introduction: 55
Inventory: 112, 115, 140, 327, 329
Invoice: 151, 153, 319
ISBN: 54, 105, 118, 365
ISSN: 120
Joint representation: 345
Key contacts: 166
Keying ads: 167, 317
Kirkus Reviews: 174, 177
Labels, address: 314, 315, 323, 335
Laser printing: 350, 355

Leading: 94
Legal requirements: 74,
Letterhead: 292
Letterpress: 88
Lettershops: 271
Libel: 76
Libraries, special: 241
Libraries: 36, 143, 234
Library Journal: 174, 176
Library of Congress: 54, 123, 177, 179, 364
Library rate: 338
License, business: 74
Line drawings: 62, 95, 96
List brokers: 280
List price: 136
Literary agents: 23,
Literary Market Place: 132, 157, 167, 208, 225, 364
Logo: 71
Los Angeles Times: 175, 180
Machinery: 85
Magazines: 183, 242, 297, Appendix
Mail order distribution: 13, 310
Mailing lists: 186, 276, 352
Mailing: 65
Manuscripts: 32
Market research: 162, 353
Markets: Chapter Eight
Markup: 137, 146
Mass market paperbacks: 106, 136, 221, 252
Measurements: 91
Media package: 207
Merchandising rights: 256
Microfiche: 220
Military market: 247
Monographs: 32
Name, company: 70
New Leaf: 229
New York Times: 175, 177
News conference: 210
News release: 197
Newsletters: Appendix
Non-fiction: 31
Nonprofit organizations: 250
Nutri-Books: 229
Offer: 289
Office in the home: 71
Offset printing: Chapter Four
Opinion molders: 175
Options, publishing: Chapter One
Order form: 58, 270
Order processing: 310, 311, 314

Out of print books: 48
Overpayments: 318
Pacific Pipeline: 229
Packing: 327, 329, 335
Page count: 91
Pamphlets: Appendix
Paper: 98
Partnership: 68
Parts of a book: 52
Per inquiry advertising: 299
Performing rights: 255
Periodical rights: 252
Periodicals: 183
Permissions: 38
Photo sources: 64
Photographs: 58, 62, 63, 97, 190
Piggyback: 272, 299
Pilot system: 39
Place of business: 71
PMA: 132, 234, 241
Poetry: 10, 30, 92
Point of purchase sales aids: 302
Point size: 94
Post card: 189, 190, 204
Post Office Box: 72
Postage meters: 342
Postage: 338, 339
Pre-publication reviews: 173
Pre-publication sales: 82, 244, 291
Preface: 55
Premiums: 248
Press kit: 205
Price: 135, 272
Print run: 138, ,
Printers: 27, 83, 111
Printing: 84, 273, Chapter Four
Profit analysis: 274
Promotion services: 169
Promotion: 163, 166, 351, 360, Chapter Seven
Proofreader's marks: 61
Proofreading: 59
Publication date: 171, 367
Publications: Appendix.
Publicity: 161
Publish: 14
Publisher: 14
Publishers Group West: 220, 227
Publishers Weekly: 174, 176, 204
Quality Books, Inc.: 238
Quotes: 195, 197
Radio: 205, 207
Raising money: 79
Record keeping: 78

Recordings: 259
Refunds: 319
Regional Guides: 32
Remainders: 306
Repetition, ad: 219, 268
Reprints: 141, 223
Republishing articles: 47
Request for quotation: 109, 110
Resale number: 75
Research: 34, 348, 362
Resources: 69, Appendix
Response formulas: 273
Retailers: 142
Returned books: 154, 343,
Review copies: 185
Review slip: 187
Review/testimonial sheet: 191
Reviewers: 196
Reviews, bad: 195
Reviews, book: 164, 171, 172, 176, 185, 240
Revisions, book: 164
Right of privacy: 77
Rights: 251
Royalties: 18, 49
Rubber stamps: 190, 334
Running heads: 90
S.C.O.P.: See S.T.O.P.
S.C.O.R.E.: 69
S.T.O.P.: 147
Sales estimating: 141, 165
Sales taxes: 74, 75, 273, 322
SAN: 121
Scales: 334
Schedule, book: See Calendar
School market: 242
Seasons, selling: 219
Self-Publishing: 24
Selling out: 27
Selling stock: 82
Seminars: 212
Separations, color: 62, 112
Shipping charges: 147
Shipping: 65, 197, 328, 329
Short payments: 317
Slander: 76
Small Business Administration: 69, 80, 364
Small Press Review: 177
Small Press: 20,
Softcover: 102, 136, 330
Software: 354
Sole proprietorship: 68
Space advertising: 161

Speaking: 211, 359
Specialty outlets: 245, 361
Specialty shows: 260
Spine, book: 105
Sponsored books: 260
Standard Address Number: See SAN
Starting a company: Chapter Three.
Statements: 150
Stationery: 72
Statistics: 15, 80, 193, 216, 231, 235, 247, 259
Storage: 115, 327
Style, writing: 43
Subheads: 56
Subject: 29
Subsidiary rights: 251
Subsidy press: 21,
Table of contents: 55
Tape: 333, 337
Taxes: 77, 112
Team writing:
Teaser copy: 53
Telemarketing: 305
Telephone: 73, 150, 152, 196, 271
Television/Radio: 205, 210
Telex: 312
Terminology: 44
Terms: 84, 148
Test, advertising: 281
Testimonials: 52, 169, 170, 191, 294
Text of book: 56
Textbooks: 106, 243
Time: 33, 89
Timing, direct mail: 268,
Title page: 53
Title: 53
Translations: 48, 256
Type: 92
Typesetting: 59, 109, 349
Typewriter: 73
U.S. Government, selling to: 247
United Parcel Service: 339
Vanity presses: 21,
Vari-depth mailer: 331
Video: 115
W-4 form: 81
Waldenbooks: 230
Weight limits: 272
White mail: 274
Wholesalers: 142, 222, 225, 229, 323
Will: 360
Wilson, H.W.: 176
Writers' colonies: 82
Writing: Chapter Two, 348

A book is the only immortality. - Rufus Choate

Order Form

☎ **Telephone orders:** Call Toll Free: 1(800) PARAPUB. Have your AMEX, Optima, Discover, Visa or MasterCard ready.

✳ **Fax orders:** (805) 968-1379

✉ **Postal Orders:** Para Publishing, Dan Poynter, P.O. Box 4232-890, Santa Barbara, CA 93140-4232. USA. (805) 968-7277

Please send the following books. I understand that I may return any books for a full refund—for any reason, no questions asked.

_____

_____

_____

_____

❑ Please send the *Publishing Poynters* newsletter to me FREE

❑ Please add my name to the *Publishers' Grapevine* so that I may receive more information on book publishing

Company name:_____

Name:_____

Address:_____

City: _____State: _____Zip: _____-_____

Sales tax:
Please add 7.75% for books shipped to California addresses

Shipping:
Book Rate: $2.00 for the first book and 75 cents for each additional book
(Surface shipping may take three to four weeks)
Air Mail: $3.50 per book

Payment:
❑ Check
❑ Credit card: ❑ Visa, ❑ MasterCard, ❑ Optima, ❑ AMEX, ❑ Discover

Card number: _____

Name on card: _____Exp. date: ____/____

Call *toll free* and order now